THIRD CANADIAN EDITION

Political Ideologies and the Democratic Ideal

Terence Ball Arizona State University

Richard Dagger Arizona State University

William Christian University of Guelph

Colin Campbell University of Western Ontario

Toronto

Vice-President, Editorial Director: Gary Bennett
Editor-in-Chief: Michelle Sartor
Acquisitions Editor: Deana Sigut
Marketing Manager: Loula March
Supervising Developmental Editor: Madhu Ranadive
Developmental Editor: Allison McDonald
Project Manager: Ashley Patterson
Production Editor: Rashmi Tickyani/Aptara®, Inc.
Copy Editor: Sally Glover
Proofreader: Julie Fletcher
Compositor: Aptara®, Inc.
Photo and Permissions Researcher: Lynn McIntyre
Art Director: Julia Hall
Cover Designer: Miguel Acevedo
Cover Image: © Pasmal/amanaimages/Corbis

Library and Archives Canada Cataloguing in Publication
    Political ideologies and the democratic ideal / Terence Ball ... [et al.].
Includes index.
ISBN 978-0-321-73929-2
    1. Political science—History—Textbooks. 2. Ideology—Textbooks.
3. Democracy—Textbooks. I. Ball, Terence.

JA81.P639 2013   320.509   C2012-903506-8

ISBN 978-0-321-73929-2

To Andrew and Alexandra Ball.

T.B.

To Emily and Elizabeth Dagger.

R.D.

To Matthew, mi hijo y mi major amigo.

W.C.

To Beatrice and Adrien.

C.C.

Brief Contents

Contents

Preface to the Third Canadian Edition

'Take what you want, said God—take it and pay for it.' This obviously applies not only to individuals but to civilizations.

—George Grant

We are not now in a period of political revolution or civil war, for which we should surely be grateful. But those of us living in the English-speaking parts of the world have not escaped challenges of other kinds. We *are* living in an era of environmental degradation, of global terror, of genocide, of hot wars fought with weapons, and culture wars fought with competing ideas, and of economic turmoil on a scale unknown since the Great Depression. The economic crisis that began in 2008 has bankrupted countries and driven experienced political leaders from office. And because our world keeps changing and hurling new challenges at us, our ideas—and especially those systems of ideas called "ideologies"—change accordingly.

In this, the third Canadian edition of *Political Ideologies and the Democratic Ideal*, we have tried to take account of changes in our world and of how people interpret those changes with the aid of ideology. This is no easy task, and we sometimes fear that any account must fall short of the mark. Nevertheless, we have done our best to offer an account of the ideologies that have shaped and continue to reshape our world. As before, we have described in some detail the deeper historical background out of which these ideologies emerged and developed. The chapter on nationalism has been joined with the chapters on fascism and populism, so that it is easier to see the connections between these ideologies. Two chapters replace the previous chapter on liberalism, and two also replace the chapter on conservatism. In both cases the aim is to have one chapter on the historical background of the ideology and another on its contemporary relevance. We have made other changes in order to update and clarify the text and to update the bibliographies. "Useful Websites" in the "For Further Reading" sections at the end of most chapters have been expanded to include social media.

As in the first and second Canadian editions, we have tried to improve the Canadian edition of *Political Ideologies and the Democratic Ideal* without sacrificing the qualities that have made the book attractive to many students and teachers in both its Canadian and American versions. Its principal aims are twofold: first, to supply an informed and accessible overview of the major ideologies that shaped the political landscape of the twentieth century and now begin to give shape to that of the twenty-first; and second, to show how these ideologies originated and how and why they have changed over time. In addition to examining the major modern "isms"—liberalism, conservatism, socialism, and fascism—the book provides the reader with a sense of the history, structure, supporting arguments, and internal complexities of these and other recently emerging ideologies.

We have also significantly strengthened the pedagogical structure in a way that will help both instructors and students. Each chapter now contains learning objectives and questions for further discussion. Each also acknowledges the increasing importance of social media. Students are guided to reliable websites, Twitter feeds, and Facebook pages. The suggested further reading for each chapter is updated, and the pictures have been thoroughly revised to make them both lively and relevant.

The basic structure of the text remains the same as in previous editions: a fourfold framework—a definition of *ideology* in terms of the four functions that all ideologies perform—within which to compare, contrast, and analyze the various ideologies. It also illustrates how each ideology interprets *democracy* and *freedom* in its own way. Democracy is not, in our view, simply one ideology among others; it is an *ideal* that different ideologies interpret in different ways. Each ideology also has its own particular conception of and its own program for promoting freedom. A simple three-part model illustrates this, comparing and contrasting each ideology's view of freedom in terms of agent, obstacle, and goal. In every chapter devoted to a particular ideology, we explain its basic conception of freedom in terms of this model, discuss the origin and development of the ideology, examine its interpretation of the democratic ideal, and conclude by showing how it performs the four functions of political ideologies. We do this not only with liberalism, conservatism, socialism, nationalism, and fascism but also with the more recent ideologies that often present themselves in the form of the politics of entitlement. For example, environmentalism in one form or another has also become a major force in political life.

Barbara Christian, former manager of Writing Services at the University of Guelph, lent her expertise and her time to the creation of the learning objectives. Jessica Spence of the Osgoode Hall Law School was a valuable research assistant for us with both the second and third Canadian editions, where she was largely responsible for social media and the research of images. Hon. Michael Chong, MP, PC, helped with a photo of Prime Minister Stephen Harper. Matthew Christian provided valuable guidance and advice.

William Christian
Colin Campbell

To the Reader

We want to call three features of this book to your attention. First, many of the primary works quoted or cited in the text are also reprinted, in whole or in part, in a companion volume, *Ideals and Ideologies: A Reader*, Eighth Edition. When we cite one of these primary works in this text, we include in a box at the end of the chapter a reference to the corresponding selection in *Ideals and Ideologies*.

Second, the study of political ideologies is in many ways the study of words. For this reason we frequently call attention to the use political thinkers and leaders make of such terms as *democracy* and *freedom*. These terms appear in italics.

Third, a number of key words and phrases in the text are set in boldface type. Definitions of these words and phrases appear in the Glossary at the back of the book, just before the Photo Credits.

Supplements

MySearchLab with eText (ISBN 978-0-321-85799-6)
MySearchLab with eText provides access to an online interactive version of the text and contains writing, grammar, and research tools, and access to a variety of academic journals, Associated Press news feeds, and discipline-specific readings to help you hone your writing and research skills. Just as in the printed text, you can highlight and add notes to the eText online. You can also access the eText on your iPad or tablet by downloading the free Pearson eText app. For more information and to redeem or purchase an access code, please visit www.mysearchlab.com.

CourseSmart for Instructors (ISBN 978-0-321-73935-3)
CourseSmart goes beyond traditional expectations—providing instant, online access to the textbooks and course materials you need at a lower cost for students. And even as students save money, you can save time and hassle with a digital eTextbook that allows you to search for the most relevant content at the very moment you need it. Whether it's evaluating textbooks or creating lecture notes to help students with difficult concepts, CourseSmart can make life a little easier. See how when you visit www.coursesmart.com/instructors.

CourseSmart for Students (ISBN 978-0-321-73935-3)
CourseSmart goes beyond traditional expectations—providing instant, online access to the textbooks and course materials you need at an average savings of 60 percent. With

instant access from any computer and the ability to search your text, you'll find the content you need quickly, no matter where you are. And with online tools like highlighting and note-taking, you can save time and study efficiently. See all the benefits at www.coursesmart.com/students.

Technology Specialists

Pearson's technology specialists work with faculty and campus course designers to ensure that Pearson technology products, assessment tools, and online course materials are tailored to meet your specific needs. This highly qualified team is dedicated to helping schools take full advantage of a wide range of educational resources by assisting in the integration of a variety of instructional materials and media formats. Your local Pearson Canada sales representative can provide you with more details on this service.

Pearson Custom Library

For enrollments of at least twenty-five students, you can create your own textbook by choosing the chapters that best suit your own course needs. To begin building your custom text, visit www.pearsoncustomlibrary.com. You may also work with a dedicated Pearson Custom editor to create your ideal text—publishing your own original content or mixing and matching Pearson content. Contact your local Pearson representative to get started.

CHAPTER 1

Ideology and Ideologies

It is what men think that determines how they act.

John Stuart Mill, *Representative Government*

After completing this chapter you should be able to

1. Define the word "ideology."
2. Analyze the four functions of an ideology.
3. Explain the triadic model of freedom.
4. Describe what agents, goals, and obstacles are.
5. Understand ideologies as a modern phenomenon.

After the 9/11 terrorist attacks on the World Trade Center and the Pentagon, Canada showed its solidarity with the United States by allowing hundreds of American planes to land at its airports. In 2004 it joined with multinational forces, many of them its NATO allies, to fight against al-Qaeda forces and their Taliban allies in Afghanistan. In 2011 it contributed airplanes to the NATO-led mission to oust Libyan dictator Muammar Gaddafi.

Why were Canadian troops in Afghanistan? Why was it involved in military action in support of the Libyan rebels? Questions such as these can be answered at many levels. Certainly some have to do with our economic, political, and strategic relations with our American neighbour. But the most important reason, if you ask anyone from the prime minister to the private who served in Kandahar until the mission ended in July 2011 or who flew sorties over Libya, is that Canadians want to bring to Afghanistan some of the benefits of democracy they so proudly enjoy at home. Pollster Michael Adams reports in his book *Unlikely Utopia: The Surprising Triumph of Canadian Pluralism* (2007) that 94 percent of Canadians believe that the rest of the world admires their country, and 27 percent cite its freedom and democracy as the thing about Canada that gives them the greatest pride.

It takes two sides to fight a war. Canada is fighting to help build a liberal democracy in Afghanistan. Its Taliban enemies have a different vision. When the Taliban was in power previously, it repressed women and denied them education. The Canadian government's policy is to provide access to education and training, especially for girls and women. How do such different visions of how states should be run and how their citizens should be treated arise?

These are dramatic examples of the power of ideas—specifically, of those systems of ideas called *ideologies*. As these examples of radical Islamic and nationalist terrorism indicate, ideologies are sets of ideas that shape people's thinking and actions with regard to race, nationality, the role and function of government, the relations between men and women, human responsibility for the natural environment, and many other matters. So powerful are these ideologies that Sir Isaiah Berlin (1909–1997), a distinguished philosopher and historian, concluded that there are two factors that, above all others, shaped human history in the twentieth century. One is the development of the natural sciences and technology. The other, without doubt, stems from the great ideological storms that altered the lives of virtually all humankind: the Russian Revolution and its aftermath—totalitarian tyrannies of both right and left; and the explosion of nationalism, racism, and, in places, religious bigotry, which, interestingly, not one of the most perceptive social thinkers of the nineteenth century predicted.

> When our descendants, in two or three centuries' time come to look at our age, it is these two phenomena that will, we think, be held to be the outstanding characteristics of our century, the most demanding of explanation and analysis. But it is as well to realise that these great movements began with ideas in people's heads: ideas about what relations between men have been, are, might be, and should be; and to realise how they came to be transformed in the name of a vision of some supreme goal in the minds of the leaders, above all of the prophets with armies at their backs.[1]
>
> Acting upon various visions, armed prophets—Vladimir Lenin, Adolf Hitler, Mao Zedong, Pol Pot, and many others—left the landscape of the twentieth century littered with tens of millions of corpses of those they regarded as inferior or dispensable, or both. As the Russian revolutionary leader Leon Trotsky said with some understatement, "Anyone desiring a quiet life has done badly to be born in the twentieth century."[2]

Nor do events, such as the attacks of September 11, 2001, suggest that political ideologies will fade away and leave people to lead quiet lives in the twenty-first century. We may hope that it will prove less murderous, but so far it appears that this century will be even more complicated politically than the preceding one was. For most of the twentieth century, the clash of three political ideologies—liberalism, communism, and fascism—dominated world politics. In the Second World War, the communist regime of the Soviet Union joined forces with the liberal democracies of the West to defeat the fascist alliance of Germany, Italy, and Japan. Following their triumph over fascism, the communist and liberal allies soon became implacable enemies in a Cold War that lasted more than forty years. The Cold War ended with the collapse of communism and the disintegration of the Soviet Union, and the terrifying but easy-to-understand clash of ideologies appears to be over. The "communist menace" had largely vanished, the "evil empire" vanquished. Liberal democracy had won—or so many people naively believed, and peace and prosperity would spread around the globe.

In his novel *Absolute Friends* (2004), British novelist John Le Carré, who wrote many great spy novels about the Cold War, tried to articulate how politics has changed since the collapse of the Soviet Union and the rise of the United States as the world's only remaining superpower.[3] According to Le Carré, politics goes on, but every event happens in relation to the United States. The need for its friendship in the early twenty-first century is, as Le Carré put it, absolute. Quebec nationalists have to worry about whether Washington would recognize an independent Quebec. The Conservative Party increased military spending to support Canada's closest ally. Elections in the United Kingdom, Spain, or Taiwan can hinge on the parties' attitude toward the United States. This is the fate of modern ideologies.

---

[1] Isaiah Berlin, *The Crooked Timber of Humanity: Chapters in the History of Ideas* (New York: Vintage, 1992)

[2] As quoted in Isaiah Berlin, *Liberty* (Oxford: Oxford UP, 2002) 55.

[3] John Le Carré, *Absolute Friends* (New York: Norton, 2004).

In the late 1950s, American writer Daniel Bell wrote *The End of Ideology.*[4] How wrong his theory turned out to be! The fifty years that followed produced a bewildering number of new ideologies—feminism, gay rights, animal liberation, environmentalism, neo-Nazism, and others. Ideologies continually evolve. Consequently, we think it best to present them historically, because every ideology and every political movement has its origins in the ideas of some earlier thinker or thinkers. As British economist John Maynard Keynes observed in the 1930s, when the fascist Benito Mussolini, the Nazi Adolf Hitler, and the communist Joseph Stalin all held power,

> The ideas of economists and political philosophers, both when they are right and when they are wrong, are more powerful than is commonly understood. Indeed the world is ruled by little else. Practical men, who are quite exempt from any intellectual influences, are usually the slaves of some defunct economist. Madmen in authority, who hear voices in the air, are distilling their frenzy from some academic scribbler of a few years back.[5]

In this book we look not only at those "madmen in authority," but also at the "academic scribblers" whose ideas they borrowed and used, sometimes with bloody and deadly results, and sometimes to the benefit of humanity.

Ideologies and political movements have their roots in the past. As philosopher George Santayana remarked: those who forget the past may be doomed to repeat its mistakes. Moreover, those who forget the past can hardly hope to understand themselves or the world in which they live. Our minds, our thoughts, and our beliefs and attitudes have all been forged in the fires and shaped on the anvil of earlier ideological conflicts. If we wish to act effectively and to live peacefully, we need to know something about the political ideologies that had such a profound influence on our own and other people's political attitudes and actions.

Our aim in this book is to lay a foundation for this understanding. In this introductory chapter, we will clarify the concept of ideology. In subsequent chapters, we will examine the various ideologies that have played an important part in shaping and sometimes radically reshaping the political landscape in which we live. We will discuss liberalism, conservatism, socialism, communism, nationalism, fascism, populism, and other ideologies in turn, and in each case we will relate the birth and the growth of the ideology to its historical context. We will proceed in this way because political ideologies do not appear out of nowhere. Arising in particular historical circumstances, ideologies take shape and change in response to changes in those circumstances. This process sometimes leads to perplexing results. For instance, today's conservatives sometimes seem to have more in common with early liberals than do today's liberals. Political ideologies, far from being fixed or frozen in place, respond to changes in the world around them.

This is not to say that political ideologies react passively, like weather vanes, to every shift in the political winds. On the contrary, ideologies try to shape and direct social change. The men and women who follow and promote political ideologies—and most of us who are politically active do this in one way or another—try to make sense of the world, try to understand society and politics and economics, either to change it for the better or to resist changes that they think will make it worse. But in order to act upon the

---

[4]Daniel Bell, *The End of Ideology: On the Exhaustion of Political Ideas in the Fifties* (Glencoe, IL: Free P, 1960).

[5]John Maynard Keynes, *The General Theory of Employment, Interest, and Money* (New York: Harcourt, 1936) 383.

world in this way, they must react to the changes that are always taking place, including the changes brought about by rival ideologies.

Political ideologies, then, are dynamic. They do not stand still because they cannot do what they are meant to do—shape the world—if they fail to adjust to changing conditions. This dynamic character of ideologies can be frustrating for anyone who wishes, for example, to understand *exactly* what a liberal or a conservative is, for it makes it impossible to define liberalism or conservatism or any other ideology with mathematical precision. But once we recognize that political ideologies are rooted in, change with, and help change historical circumstances, we are on the way to grasping what any particular ideology is about.

A WORKING DEFINITION OF *IDEOLOGY*

There is at first sight something strange about the word *ideology*. Other terms ending in *ology* name fields of scientific study. So, for example, *biology*—the prefix coming from the Greek *bios,* or "life"—is the scientific study of life. *Psychology* is the study of psyche, or personality. And *anthropology* is the study of *anthropos*, or human beings. It seems only logical, to them, that *ideology* would be the scientific study of ideas. We even know when the word was created and by whom. A French philosopher, Antoine-Louis-Claude Destutt de Tracy, was trying to figure out how moral and political ideas arose so that he could create a secure basis for economic and political freedom, and in 1796 he coined the word *idéologie* for his new science.[6]

Over the past two centuries, the meaning of the word *ideology* has evolved and has been used in considerably different ways. To Karl Marx (1818–1883), *ideology* meant a distorted system of beliefs shaped by the condition of belonging to a particular social class. He considered his own theory to be science, not *ideology*. According to German sociologist Karl Mannheim (1893–1947), individuals have a *total ideology*, which leads them to believe that they see things as they really are; they call other people's beliefs an *ideology*. Thus, for Mannheim, Marx's belief that his theory was scientific and that it was simply true was an example of a *total ideology*. Russian Communist leader Vladimir Lenin (1870–1924) had yet another definition for *ideology*. His was relatively simple. The Communist Party adopted an official *ideology,* and every member of the party was supposed to accept it. What all of these approaches to *ideology* have in common is that they refer to ideas that shape how people think—and therefore how they act. The most famous statement of this change was in Marx's eleventh thesis on Ludwig Feuerbach, which he wrote in 1845: "Previously philosophers have only interpreted the world in various ways; the point is to change it."[7]

For the purposes of this book, an ideology is a fairly coherent and comprehensive set of ideas that explains and evaluates social conditions, helps people understand their place

---

[6]For accounts of the origin and history of *ideology,* see Terrell Carver, "Ideology," *Ideals and Ideologies: A Reader,* 8th ed., ed. Terence Ball and Richard Dagger (New York: Longman, 2011) selection 1; Mark Goldie, "Ideology," *Political Innovation and Conceptual Change,* ed. Terence Ball, James Farr, and Russell L. Hanson (Cambridge: Cambridge UP, 1989) 266–91; and George Lichtheim, *The Concept of Ideology, and Other Essays* (New York: Random, 1967).

[7]Karl Marx, "Theses on Feuerbach, XI," *The Marx-Engels Reader*, 2nd ed., ed. Robert Tucker (New York: Norton, 1972, 1978) 145.

in society, and provides a program for social and political action. An ideology, more precisely, performs four functions for people who hold it: these are the (1) explanatory, (2) evaluative, (3) orientative, and (4) programmatic functions. Let us look more closely at these four functions.

In ordinary speech, people often refer to various positions or ways of thinking as ideological. In this book, we talk exclusively about political ideologies, as the title suggests, and every time you read the word *ideology* here, bear in mind that it refers to something political in the sense we are about to define.

Explanatory Function. The first function of an ideology is to offer an explanation of why social, political, and economic conditions are as they are, particularly in times of crisis. At such times people will search, sometimes frantically, for some explanation of what is happening. Why are there wars? Why do economic depressions occur? What causes unemployment? Why are some people rich and others poor? What is the right balance between growth and a sustainable environment? Different ideologies supply different answers to these and many other questions. But in one way or another, every ideology tries to answer these questions and to make sense of the complicated world in which we live. A Marxist might explain wars as an outgrowth of capitalists' competition for foreign markets, for instance, while a nationalist is apt to explain them as the consequence of the need for self-determination of peoples. A social democratic will defend the need to retain universal health care, whereas a neoconservative will defend a two-tiered system as the best way to maintain quality and expand the range of health services. Their explanations are quite different, but all ideologies offer a way of looking at complex events and conditions that tries to make sense of them. Moreover, **ideologues**—people who try to persuade others to accept their ideology—typically want to reach as many people as possible, and this desire leads them to offer simple, and sometimes simplistic, explanations of puzzling events and circumstances.

Evaluative Function. The second function of an ideology is to supply standards for evaluating social conditions. There is a difference, after all, between explaining why certain things are happening and deciding whether those things are good or bad. Are all wars evils to be avoided, or are some morally justifiable? Are economic depressions a normal part of the business cycle or a symptom of a chronically sick economic system? Is full employment a reasonable ideal or a naive pipe dream? Are vast disparities of wealth between rich and poor desirable or undesirable? Can justice be achieved for Aboriginal peoples, or are they destined to be marginalized and live in poverty? Again, an ideology supplies its followers with the criteria required for answering these and other questions. If you are a libertarian, for example, you are likely to evaluate a proposed policy by asking if it increases or decreases the role of government in the lives of individuals. If it increases government's role, it is undesirable. If you are a feminist, you will probably ask whether a proposed policy will work for or against the interests of women, and then either approve or disapprove of it on that basis. If you are a Quebec nationalist, you will probably ask whether a proposed policy will work for or against your primary goal of creating a sovereign state. Those who follow one ideology may evaluate favourably something that the followers of a different ideology greatly dislike—welfare liberals approve of an activist state, while business liberals want to restrain the range of government involvement in society and in the economy. Whatever the position may be, however, it is clear that all ideologies provide standards or cues that help people assess, judge, and appraise social policies and conditions so that they can decide whether those social policies and conditions are good, bad, or indifferent.

Orientative Function. The third function of an ideology is to supply its holder with an orientation and a sense of identity—of whom he or she is, of the group (race, nation, gender, and so on) to which he or she belongs, and of how he or she is related to the rest of the world. Just as hikers and travellers use maps, compasses, and landmarks to find their way in unfamiliar territory, so people need something to find their social identity and location. Like a compass, an ideology helps people to orient themselves—to gain a sense of where they are, who they are, and how they fit into a complicated world. For example, if you are a communist, you most likely think of yourself as a member of the working class who belongs to a party dedicated to freeing workers from capitalist exploitation and oppression and are therefore implacably opposed to the ruling capitalist class. If you are a Nazi, you probably think of yourself as a white person and a member of a party dedicated to preserving racial purity and enslaving or even eliminating "inferior" races. If you are a feminist, you are apt to think of yourself as first and foremost a woman (or a man sympathetic to women's problems) who belongs to a movement that aims to end sexual oppression and exploitation. Other ideologies enable their adherents to orient themselves—to see their situation or position in society—in still other ways, but all perform the function of orientation.

Programmatic Function. The fourth function of an ideology is to tell its followers what to do and how to do it. It performs a programmatic or prescriptive function by setting out a general program of social and political action. Just as doctors prescribe medicine for their patients and trainers provide a program of exercise for their clients, so ideologies prescribe remedies for sick societies and treatments designed to keep the healthy ones in good health. If an ideology provides a diagnosis of social conditions that leads you to believe those conditions are bad and growing worse, it will not be likely to win your support unless it can also supply a prescription or program for action that seems likely to improve matters. And this is exactly what ideologies try to do. If you are a populist, you believe it is necessary to destroy the forces that stand in the way of the unity of the common people. Nazis thought it important for the "superior" white race to isolate, separate, subordinate—and perhaps exterminate—Jews, blacks, and other "inferior" peoples. If you are a libertarian, your political program will include proposals for reducing or eliminating government interference in people's lives. But if you are a traditional conservative, you may want the state or government to intervene in order to promote morality or traditional values. Different ideologies recommend very different programs of action, as these examples demonstrate, but all recommend a program of some sort.

Ideologies perform the above four functions because they try to link thought—ideas and beliefs—to action. Every ideology provides a vision of the social and political world as it is and as it should be, in hopes of inspiring people to act either to change or to preserve their way of life. If it does not perform all four functions, it is not an ideology. In this way, our functional definition helps to sharpen our picture of what an ideology is by showing us what it is—and what it is not.

One thing an ideology is *not* is a scientific theory. To be sure, the distinction between an ideology and a scientific theory is sometimes difficult to draw. One reason for this is that the proponents of ideologies often claim that their views are truly scientific. Another reason is that scientists, particularly social scientists, sometimes fail to see how their ideological biases shape their theories. And ideologies frequently borrow from scientific theories to help explain why the world is as it is. For example, some anarchists and some liberals have used Darwin's theory of evolution for their own purposes, as have Nazis and some communists.

Difficult as it may sometimes be to separate the two, there is a difference between a scientific theory, such as Darwin's, and an ideology that draws on—and often distorts—that theory. Scientific theories are **empirical** in nature, which means that they are concerned with *describing* and explaining some feature or features of the world, not with *prescribing* what people ought to do. To the extent that these theories carry implications for how people *can* live, of course, they also carry implications for the **normative** problem of how people *should* live. This is especially true of theories of society, where empirical and normative concerns are remarkably difficult—some say impossible—to separate. But to say that scientific theories have implications for action is not to accept that they are ideologies. The scientist is not directly concerned *as a scientist* with implications for action, but the ideologue certainly is.

We can also use our functional definition to distinguish ideologies from some of the other *isms,* such as terrorism, that are occasionally mistaken for ideologies. Because the names of the most prominent ideologies end with the suffix *ism,* some people conclude that all *isms* must be ideologies. This is clearly a mistake. Whatever else they are, alcoholism, magnetism, and hypnotism are not ideologies. Nor is terrorism. Terrorism may offer a program for social and political action, thus performing the programmatic function, but it does not itself explain and evaluate conditions or provide people with an orientation. Terrorism is a strategy that some ideologues use to try to advance their causes, but it is not itself an ideology. Our functional definition also helps distinguish democracy from ideologies. Unlike socialism, conservatism, and the other ideologies, democracy offers no explanation of why things are the way they are, and it is only in a loose sense that we can say that democracy serves the evaluative, orientative, or programmatic functions. Furthermore, almost all ideologies claim to be democratic, which is something they could hardly do if democracy were an ideology itself. One can easily claim to be a conservative democrat, a liberal democrat, or a social(ist) democrat, for instance—much more easily than one can claim to be a socialist conservative, say, or a liberal fascist. This suggests that democracy, or rule by the people, is an *ideal* rather than an ideology—a topic to be pursued further in Chapter 2.

In all these cases, our functional definition helps clarify what an ideology is by eliminating possibilities that do not perform all four functions. There are other cases, however, where our functional definition is not so helpful. The task of distinguishing a political theory or philosophy from an ideology is one of them. In this case our functional definition offers no help, for political theories typically perform the same four functions. The chief difference is that they do so at a higher, more abstract, more principled, and perhaps more dispassionate level. The great works of political philosophy, such as Plato's *Republic* and Rousseau's *Social Contract*, certainly attempt to explain and evaluate social conditions, just as they try to provide the reader with a sense of his or her place in the world. They even prescribe programs for action of a very general sort. But these works and the other masterpieces of political philosophy tend to be highly abstract and complex—and not, therefore, the kind of writing that stirs great numbers of people into action. Ideologies draw on the works of the great political philosophers, much as they draw on scientific theories, to promote their causes. Because their concern to link thought to action is so immediate, ideologies tend to simplify the ideas of political philosophers in order to make them accessible—and inspiring—to masses of people. The difference between a political philosophy and an ideology, then, is largely a difference of degree. They do the same things, but an ideology does them in simpler, less abstract ways because its focus is more tightly fixed on the importance of action.[8]

Similar problems arise in the task of distinguishing an ideology from religion. Most religions—perhaps all—perform the explanatory, evaluative, orientative, and programmatic functions for their followers. Does this mean they are ideologies? It does if we define *ideology* as simply "a belief system," as some scholars propose.[9] Many scholars and quite a few ideologues have noted, moreover, the ways in which ideologies take on the characteristics of a religion for their followers; one account of communism by disillusioned ex-communists, for instance, is called *The God That Failed.*[10] There is no denying that religious concerns have played, and continue to play, a major role in ideological conflicts, as we shall see in subsequent chapters. Still, there is an important difference between religion and ideology.

To understand the difference between religion and ideology better, consider the following two examples. Islamists have taken political steps to create religiously based states in places such as Pakistan, which they believe are fundamentally secular. In Canada, the Christian Right supported first the Reform Party, then the Canadian Alliance, and then the Conservative Party because it believed that those were the best political vehicles to fight such liberalizing social measures as a woman's right to abortion and gays' rights to marry, which the Christian Right believes are contrary to its religious beliefs. The goal of a religion is to provide guidance to its followers as to how they should live in this world and, for some faiths, to prepare themselves for the next. Religion addresses itself to believers and potential believers. Politics is a matter for citizens who may hold any faith or none.

HUMAN NATURE AND FREEDOM

For an ideology to perform four functions—explanatory, evaluative, orientative, and programmatic—it must draw on some deeper conception of human potential, of what human beings are capable of achieving. This means that implicit in every ideology are two further features: (1) a set of basic beliefs about *human nature* and (2) a conception of *freedom*.

Human Nature

Some conception of human nature—some notion of basic human drives, motivations, limitations, and possibilities—is present, at least implicitly, in every ideology. Some ideologies assume that it is the nature of human beings to compete with one another in

---

[8]For further discussion of the relationship between political philosophies and political ideologies, see Michael Freeden, *Ideologies and Political Theory: A Conceptual Approach* (Oxford: Clarendon, 1996) 27–46.

[9]Philip Converse, "The Nature of Belief Systems in Mass Publics," *Ideology and Discontent,* ed. David Apter (New York: Free P, 1964).

[10]Arthur Koestler, et al., *The God That Failed*, ed. R. H. S. Crossman (Freeport, NY: Books for Libraries, 1972).

hopes of acquiring the greatest possible share of scarce resources; others hold that people are naturally inclined to cooperate with one another and to share what they have with others. So, for example, a classical liberal or a contemporary libertarian is likely to believe that human beings are naturally competitive and acquisitive. A nationalist believes that a common language, culture, and heritage bind its members together into a community regardless of their other differences. Still other ideologies take it for granted that human beings have a natural or innate racial consciousness that compels them to associate with their own kind and to avoid associating or even sympathizing with members of other races. Thus, Nazis maintain that it is natural for races to struggle for dominance and unnatural to seek interracial peace and harmony.

These conceptions of human nature are important to the understanding of ideologies because they play a large part in determining how each ideology performs the four functions. They are especially important because each ideology's notion of human nature sets limits on what it considers to be politically possible. When a communist says that you ought to work to bring about a classless society, for instance, this implies that he or she believes that a classless society is something human beings are capable of achieving, and something, therefore, that human nature does not rule out. When a conservative urges you to cherish and defend traditional social arrangements, on the other hand, this implies that he or she believes that human beings are weak and fallible creatures whose schemes are more likely to damage society than to improve it. Other ideologies take other views of human nature, but in every case the program an ideology prescribes is directly related to its core conception of human nature—to its notion of what human beings are truly like and what they can achieve.

Freedom

Strange as it may seem, every ideology claims to defend and extend freedom (or its synonym, liberty). Freedom figures in the performance of both the evaluative and programmatic functions, with all ideologies condemning societies that do not promote freedom and promising to take steps to promote it themselves. But different ideologies define freedom in different ways. For instance, a classical conservative's understanding of freedom differs from that of a classical liberal or a contemporary libertarian; both, in turn, disagree with a communist's view of freedom, and all three diverge radically from a Nazi's notion of freedom. This is because freedom is an **essentially contested concept**. In other words, what counts as being free is a matter of controversy because there is no one indisputably correct definition of *freedom*.

Because every ideology claims to promote freedom, that concept provides a convenient basis for comparing and contrasting different ideologies. In later chapters, therefore, we will examine each ideology's conception of freedom by fitting it within the triadic, or three-cornered, model proposed by Gerald MacCallum.[11] According to MacCallum, every conception of freedom includes three features: (A) an agent, (B) a barrier or obstacle blocking the agent, and (C) a goal at which the agent aims. And every statement about freedom can take the following form: "A is (or is not) free from B to achieve, be, or become C."

---

[11]Gerald MacCallum, Jr., "Negative and Positive Freedom," *Philosophical Review* 76 (1967): 312–334.

To say that someone is free, in other words, is to say that he or she is *free from* something and therefore *free to do* something. The *agent* is the person or group that is or should be free. But an agent is not simply free; to be free, an agent must be *free to* pursue a *goal,* whether it is speaking one's mind, practising one's religion, or merely going for a stroll in the park. No one can be free to pursue a goal, however, unless he or she is also *free from* particular *obstacles,* barriers, or restraints. These may take a wide variety of forms—walls, chains, prejudices, and poverty, to name a few—but the point is that no one can be free when there are obstacles that prevent him or her from doing what he or she wants to do. So *freedom* refers to a relationship involving an agent who is both free from some obstacle and free to achieve some goal. See Figure 1.1 for a diagram of this relationship.

Consider how the three features of freedom are present even in so ordinary a question as "Are you free tonight?" The agent in this case is "you," the person being asked the question. There are no obvious obstacles or goals specified in the question, but that is because the point of the question is to learn whether some obstacle keeps the agent from pursuing a particular goal. That is, when we ask someone whether he or she is free tonight, we are trying to determine whether anything—such as the need to study for a test, to go to work, or to keep a promise to someone else—prevents that person from doing something. If not, then the agent in this instance is free.

But what of *political* freedom? According to MacCallum, people have different views of what counts as freedom in politics because they identify A, B, and C in different ways. Let us examine each of the features, beginning with the agent, proceeding to a consideration of the agent's goals, and returning to examine the barriers or obstacles facing the agent in pursuing those goals.

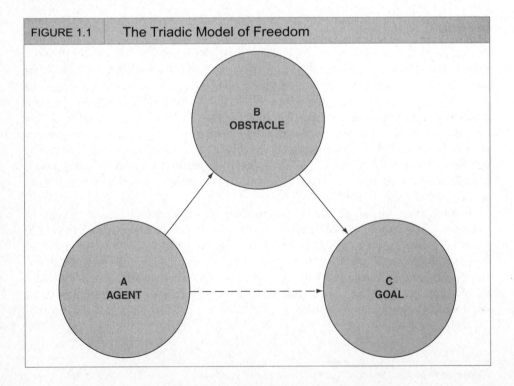

| FIGURE 1.1 | The Triadic Model of Freedom |

The Agent. The agent can be an individual, a class, a group, a nation, a gender, a race, or even a species. As we shall see in Chapter 3, liberals typically speak of freedom as the freedom of the individual. Marx and the Marxists, by contrast, focus their attention on the freedom of a particular class—the working class. Mussolini and the Italian fascists identified the agent as a nation-state, and German fascists (Nazis) identified it as a race. For feminists, the gender identity of the agent is all-important.

Goals. Agents have goals. Different kinds of agents have different kinds of goals. A Nazi's goal is the "purity" and supremacy of the white race. A communist's goal is the achievement of a classless communist society. A liberal's goal is to live in his or her own way, without undue interference from others. A feminist's goal is to live in a society that recognizes and rewards the capacities and worth of women—and so on for all other ideologies.

Obstacles. In pursuing their goals, agents often encounter obstacles. These obstacles can take a variety of forms—material or physical conditions (poverty or physical disabilities, for instance), crime, social and political and economic ideas, ideologies, institutions, practices, traditions, and beliefs. Feminists confront sexism and sexual discrimination. Populists confront the powerful vested interests that divide the common people. Nazis confront Jews, blacks, and other "inferior" races. Ideologies also frequently see other ideologies as obstacles or barriers to be removed. Fascists, for instance, see the liberal emphasis on the individual and the socialist emphasis on equality as obstacles in the way of a united, disciplined, and well-ordered society. Whatever form the obstacles take, they must be overcome or removed. The more obstacles these agents can remove, the freer they will be. To the degree that they are unable to overcome the barriers, they are "unfree." And when the individuals, class, race, or gender that an ideology defines as its agent are not free to realize their goals, then the ideology will call for action to remove the obstacles to their freedom. Throughout the history of ideologies, that action has often taken the form of revolution.

IDEOLOGY AND REVOLUTION

In its original political use, the word **revolution** referred to a return to an earlier condition. Like the revolution of the earth around the sun, a political revolution was a revolving back to a starting point. But after the American and French revolutions of the eighteenth century, *revolution* took on a more radical meaning. The American Revolution may have begun as an attempt to *restore* the colonists' rights as Englishmen, but it ended with the creation of a new country with a new system of government. Then, while that new system was still taking shape, the French Revolution began with the intention not of returning to the old ways but of introducing a radically new social and political order. As we shall see in Chapter 3, this revolution went further than the people who launched it intended, and it ended in a way that none of them wanted. But it did bring about sweeping changes in the social, economic, and political life of France. Indeed, the French Revolution sent shock waves through all of Europe and much of the rest of the world, waves so strong that their effects are still felt today. One sign of this is the way political positions are now commonly described as **left**, **right**, or **centre**. These terms come from the seating arrangements in the National Assembly of the revolutionary period. Moderates sat in the centre, those who favoured radical change congregated on the left side or "wing" of the chamber, and those who argued against change gathered in the right wing. That is why, even today, we talk of the right wing, the left wing, and centrists in politics.

Modern revolutionaries do not simply want to replace one set of rulers or leaders with another or to make minor changes or reforms in the political structure. Their aim is to overthrow the old order, which they believe to be fundamentally rotten or corrupt. Changes or reforms are not enough, in their view, if the government and society are diseased at the roots. When this is the case, they say, the only solution is to uproot the whole social order and replace it with something better. This is literally a radical approach, for the word "radical" comes from the Latin *radix,* meaning "root."

Of course, people will not undertake anything so radical as a revolution unless they believe that it is indeed possible to bring about a fundamental change for the better in society. This is why conservatives tend to be suspicious of revolutions; their low estimate of human nature generally leads them to believe that sweeping improvements in society are practically impossible. Conservatism is very different from the other ideologies in this respect, however. All of the others hold that human reason and action can bring about great advances in society, politics, and quality of life. Each ideology has its own idea of what counts as an advance or improvement, to be sure, but all except conservatism have been generally optimistic about the possibility of dramatic progress and significant improvement in the quality of human life.

In this respect, ideologies are products of the modern world. In earlier times, most people had every reason to believe that their lives would be much the same as their parents' and grandparents' lives. Most people made their living from the soil or the sea, and changes in their ways of life were so slow in coming that they usually had little reason to believe that their children's or grandchildren's lives would be significantly different from their own. In the modern world, however, the pace of change has become so rapid that we now have futurists (or futurologists) who make careers of anticipating the changes to come; others, meanwhile, fear that they will not be able to adjust or keep up with change as their jobs, and perhaps even their attitudes, become obsolete. For better or worse, we live in an age of innovation. And ours, for better or worse, is also an age of ideology.

Ideologies and innovation are connected in an important way. The scientific, technical, and even artistic advances that marked the beginnings of the modern world in Europe instilled in many people a faith in progress, a belief that life on earth could become far more rewarding for many more people than it had ever been. Before people could enjoy the fruits of progress, however, society itself would have to be reordered. The old ways of life retarded progress, especially when they prevented creative and vigorous individuals from using their energies and initiative to improve life for themselves and for others. So the institutions that upheld the old ways of life—notably the Roman Catholic Church and the economic order of feudalism—came under attack from those who sought to free individuals to make the most of themselves in a new world of opportunity, progress, and reason. This attack took a number of forms, including the philosophical movement known as the **Enlightenment**, which saw the world as something to be comprehended by human reason and perfected by human action.

Even before the Enlightenment, the attack on the old ways of life also took the form of liberalism, the first of the ideologies. How liberalism arose as a protest against religious conformity and feudalism in the name of tolerance and opportunity is a story told in Chapter 3. For now, the important point is that first liberalism and later all the other ideologies except conservatism grew out of a conviction that human life and society can and should be dramatically changed. It is this conviction that inspires people to lead or join movements to reshape and even revolutionize their societies. It is this conviction, in short, that gives rise to ideologies.

Conclusion

We began by noting how important ideologies are in the conflicts that characterize modern political life. We then defined *ideology* as a more or less coherent and comprehensive set of ideas that performs four functions for those who accept it: (1) it *explains* why social conditions are the way they are; (2) it *evaluates* those social conditions; (3) it *orients* people so they can understand their place in society; and (4) it *provides a program* for social and political action. In every ideology, moreover, there are core assumptions about *human nature* and *freedom*—assumptions that have led most ideologies, at one time or another, to call for revolution.

In later chapters we will examine the history and structure of different ideologies. Before doing that, however, we need to look more closely at the concept of democracy. As we explain in Chapter 2, democracy is not itself an ideology but an ideal that different ideologies either reject outright or, more often, pursue in different ways.

For Further Reading

Arendt, Hannah. *On Revolution.* New York: Viking, 1963.

Baradat, Leon. *Political Ideologies.* Pearson, 2011.

Berlin, Isaiah. *Liberty.* Oxford: Oxford UP, 2002.

————. "Nationalism: Past Neglect and Present Power." *Against the Current: Essays in the History of Ideas.* Ed. Isaiah Berlin. Harmondsworth, UK: Penguin, 1982.

Campbell, Colin, and William Christian. *Parties, Leaders and Ideologies in Canada.* Toronto: McGraw-Hill, 1996.

Christian, William, and Colin Campbell. *Political Parties and Ideologies in Canada.* 3rd ed. Toronto: McGraw-Hill, 1990.

Cranston, Maurice. *Freedom: A New Analysis.* London: Longmans, 1967.

Dunn, John. "Revolution." *Political Innovation and Conceptual Change.* Ed. Terence Ball, James Farr, and Russell L. Hanson. Cambridge: Cambridge UP, 1989.

Ignatieff, Michael. *Human Rights as Politics and Idolatry.* Princeton: Princeton UP, 2001.

————. *The Lesser Evil: Political Ethics in an Age of Terror.* Edinburgh: Edinburgh UP, 2004.

Journal of Political Ideologies. Oxford: Carfax, 1996–.

Kaligian, Dikran. *Armenian Organization and Ideology under Ottoman Rule: 1908–1914.* Piscataway, NJ: Transaction Publishers, 2009.

Kohn, Hans. *Nationalism: Its Meaning and History.* Princeton, NJ: Van Nostrand, 1955.

Lichtheim, George. *The Concept of Ideology, and Other Essays.* New York: Random, 1967.

Minogue, K. R. *Alien Powers: The Pure Theory of Ideology*. London: Weidenfeld, 1985.

Pfaff, William. *The Wrath of Nations: Civilization and the Furies of Nationalism*. New York: Simon, 1993.

Yack, Bernard. *The Longing for Total Revolution*. Princeton, NJ: Princeton UP, 1986.

Useful Websites and Social Media

http://pewresearch.org PEW Research Center

www.transparency.org Transparency International

www.transparency.ca Transparency International Canada

From the Ball and Dagger Reader *Ideals and Ideologies,* US Eighth Edition

Part One: The Concept of Ideology

Discussion Questions

1. Religion has an impact on politics. The United States has the Christian Right, and Islamicism exists in the Middle East. Is religion just a form of ideology?

2. Is it theoretically possible for societies to function without ideology?

3. Can the 99 percent that the Occupy Wall Street movement talked about be as free as the 1 percent?

4. Marx suggested that the role of ideologies is to change the world. Can conservatism be an ideology?

MySearchLab   MySearchLab with eText offers you access to an online interactive version of the text, additional quizzes and assessment, extensive help with your writing and research projects, and provides round-the-clock access to credible and reliable source material. Go to **www.mysearchlab.com** to access these resources.

CHAPTER 2

The Democratic Ideal

No one pretends that democracy is perfect or all-wise. Indeed, it has been said that democracy is the worst form of government except all those other forms that have been tried from time to time.

Sir Winston Churchill

LEARNING OBJECTIVES

After completing this chapter you should be able to

1. Understand why the term *democracy* is such a contested concept.
2. Describe the shifts in attitude toward democracy from Greek to modern times.
3. Assess the differences between the development of democratic ideas in the United States and in Canada.
4. Explain the Hartz/Horowitz Thesis.
5. Describe the three principal visions of democratic thinking in the modern world.

INTRODUCTION—A WORD FOR ALL SEASONS

One of the most striking features of contemporary politics is the widespread popularity of democracy. There are few people nowadays, whether major political leaders or ordinary citizens, who do not praise democracy and claim to be democrats. Some might argue that the Qur'an and popular rule are fundamentally incompatible or protest that, although they would like to have a democracy, their people are not ready or the time is not ripe. Most people agree that democracy of some sort is desirable, but this agreement comes in the midst of vigorous, sometimes violent, ideological conflict. How can men and women of almost all ideological persuasions—liberal and socialist, communist and conservative— share a belief in the value of democracy?

One possible explanation is that many people use the word *democracy* in a hypocritical or deceptive way. Democracy is so popular that everyone tries to link his or her ideology, whatever it may be, to it. The formal title of East Germany before the collapse of its communist regime in 1989–1990 was the German Democratic Republic, for instance. Yet the government of this "democracy" strictly limited freedom of speech and effectively outlawed competition for political office. Many East Germans believed that their country was far more democratic than Canada because East Germany was not run by large corporations and because it had such a comprehensive social safety net. With this and other examples in mind, some critics have complained that the word *democracy* has been so broadly used as to rob it of any clear meaning.

A second explanation is that followers of different ideologies simply have different ideas about how to achieve democracy. Almost all agree that democracy is a good thing, but they disagree about how best to bring it about. Most people in Canada regard a dictatorship as an obviously undemocratic regime, but Mao Zedong (1893–1976), the leader of the Chinese Communist Party for more than forty years, maintained that his government was a "people's democratic dictatorship." Mao apparently saw no contradiction in this because he believed that China needed a period of dictatorship to prepare the way for democracy. Perhaps, then, there is a genuine and widespread agreement that democracy is the true end or goal of ideological activity, with disagreement arising only over the proper means for achieving that end.

Although there may be merit in both of these positions, we think a third explanation provides a deeper insight into the problem: different people quite simply mean different things by *democracy*. They may all want to achieve or promote democracy, but they disagree about how to do this because they disagree about what democracy truly is. With respect to ideologies, we may say that democracy is an ideal that most ideologies espouse; but because people have very different understandings of what democracy is, they pursue it in very different ways. They may even come into conflict with one another in their attempts to achieve or promote democracy as they understand it.

Democracy, then, like freedom, is an **essentially contested concept**. The democratic ideal is itself deeply involved in the ideological conflict of the modern world. To understand this conflict, we need to know more about democracy and the democratic ideal. In particular, we need to know what *democracy* originally meant and why it is only in the past two centuries or so that democracy has been widely regarded as a desirable form of government.

THE ORIGINS OF DEMOCRACY IN ANCIENT GREECE

Democracy the word and democracy the form of political life both began in ancient Greece. The word comes from a combination of the Greek noun *demos,* meaning "people" or "common people," and the verb *kratein,* meaning "to rule." For the Greeks, *demokratia* meant specifically "rule or government by the common people"—that is, rule by those who were uneducated, unsophisticated, and poor. Because these people made up the majority of the citizenry, democracy was identified, as it often is today, with majority rule. But it is important to note that this majority consisted mainly of a single class: the *demos.* Many Greeks thus understood democracy to be a form of class rule—government by and for the benefit of the lower or working class. As such, it stood in contrast to aristocracy, rule by the *aristoi*—the "best"—those supposedly most qualified to govern.

The centre of political activity in ancient Greece, which was not united under a single government, was the self-governing *polis,* or city-state. Athens, the largest *polis,* provides the best example of a democratic city-state. Throughout most of the second half of the fifth century BC, the period renowned as the Golden Age of Athens, Athenians called their *polis* a democracy. Not everyone willingly accepted this state of affairs, but those who did seemed to embrace democracy enthusiastically. This is evident in the words attributed to Pericles, the most famous leader of the Athenian democracy, in his Funeral Oration:

> Our form of government does not enter into rivalry with the institutions of others. We do not copy our neighbors but are an example to them. It is true that we are called a democracy, for the administration is in the hands of the many and not of the few. But while the law secures equal justice to all alike in their private disputes, the claim of excellence is also recognized; and when a citizen is in any way distinguished, he is preferred for the public service, not as a matter

of privilege but as the reward of merit. Neither is poverty a bar, but a man may benefit his country [*polis*] whatever be the obscurity of his condition.[1]

Pericles's words hint at the tension between aristocrats and democrats in ancient Athens. The aristocrats generally believed that only the well-established citizens, those with substantial property and ties to the noble families, were wise enough to govern. Pericles and the democrats, however, believed that most citizens were capable of governing if only they could afford to take the time away from their farms and work. To this end, the Athenian democracy paid citizens an average day's wages to enable poor as well as rich to go to the assembly and decide policy by direct vote. Citizens also were paid to serve on juries, sometimes for as much as a year at a time. As further testimony to their faith in the *demos,* the Athenians filled a number of their political offices not by election but by randomly selecting citizens through a lottery.

Pericles's Funeral Oration also suggests another distinction of great significance to the Athenians—between the public-spirited citizen (*polites*) and the self-interested individual who preferred a private life (*idiotes*). In Athens, Pericles said,

> an Athenian citizen does not neglect the state [*polis*] because he takes care of his own household; and even those of us who are engaged in business have a very fair idea of politics. We alone regard a man who takes no interest in public affairs, not as harmless, but as a useless character; and if few of us are originators, we are all sound judges of a policy.[2]

Even more significant to Athenian democracy was another aspect of citizenship as Athenians understood it. To be a citizen, one had to be an adult, free, male Athenian. Women, resident foreigners, and slaves (who may have made up the majority of the population) were all excluded. In fact, only about one out of ten inhabitants of Athens was considered a citizen. From the vantage point of the twenty-first century, then, it appears that Athenian democracy was hardly democratic at all.

This judgment becomes even more striking when we consider that Athenian democracy provided little if any protection for minority rights. Although citizens were equal in the eyes of the law, this did not mean that any citizen was free to express his opinions, regardless of how unpopular those opinions might be. The Athenian assembly sometimes banished citizens temporarily from Athens without trial and even without legal charges being brought against them simply because the majority of the assembly thought these citizens posed a danger to the *polis.*This was the practice of ostracism, so called because of the shell or piece of pottery (*ostrakon*) on which Athenian citizens wrote the names of those they wished to banish.

Sometimes the punishment for voicing unpopular opinions was even harsher. We know this especially from the case of Socrates (470–399 BC), the philosopher whose mission it was to sting the citizens of Athens out of complacency by raising questions about their most basic beliefs. "I never cease to rouse each and every one of you," he said, "to persuade and reproach you all day long and everywhere I find myself in your company."[3] In 399 BC, when the democratic faction was in control, some citizens

---

[1]Pericles's Funeral Oration, in Thucydides, *History of the Peloponnesian War,* vol. I, 2nd. ed., trans. Benjamin Jowett (Oxford: Clarendon, 1900) 127–128. Also in Terence Ball and Richard Dagger, eds., *Ideals and Ideologies: A Reader,* 8th ed. (New York: Longman, 2011) selection 2.3.
[2]Pericles's Funeral Oration 129.
[3]Plato, "Apology," trans. G. M. A. Grube, *The Trial and Death of Socrates* (Indianapolis: Hackett, 1983) 33.

stung back, falsely accusing Socrates of impiety and corrupting the morals of the youth of Athens. Socrates was tried, convicted, and condemned to death by poison. Thus Athens, the first democracy, created the first martyr to the cause of free thought and free speech.

In the fifth and fourth centuries BC, however, those who favoured democracy found themselves facing a different criticism—that democracy is a dangerously unstable form of government. Foremost among those who made this complaint was Socrates's student and friend, Plato (427–347 BC).

Plato believed that democracy is dangerous because it puts political power into the hands of ignorant and envious people. Because they are ignorant, he argued, the people will not know how to use political power for the common good. Because they are envious they will be concerned only with their own good, which they will seek to advance by plundering those who are better off. Because they are both ignorant and envious they will be easily swayed by demagogues—literally, leaders of the *demos*—who will flatter them, appeal to their envy, and turn citizen against citizen. From democracy, in short, comes civil war and anarchy, the destruction of the city-state. When democracy has left the *polis* in this wretched condition, according to Plato's analysis, the people will cry out for law and order. They will then rally around anyone strong enough to bring an end to anarchy. But such a person will be a despot, Plato said, a tyrant who cares nothing about the *polis* or the people because he cares only for power. From democracy—rule by the people—it is but a series of short steps to tyranny.[4]

Aristotle's Classification of Governments

This argument against democracy found favour with a number of political thinkers, including Plato's student Aristotle (384–322 BC). Aristotle maintained that democracy is one of six basic kinds of political regimes or constitutions. He proposed in his *Politics* that governing power may be in the hands of one person, a few people, or many, and this power may be exercised either for the good of the whole community—in which case it is good or true—or solely for the good of the rulers—in which case it is bad or perverted. By combining these features, Aristotle arrived at the six-cell classification of governments illustrated in Figure 2.1

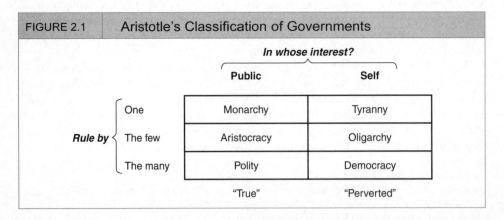

FIGURE 2.1	Aristotle's Classification of Governments	
	In whose interest?	
	Public	**Self**
Rule by — One	Monarchy	Tyranny
Rule by — The few	Aristocracy	Oligarchy
Rule by — The many	Polity	Democracy
	"True"	"Perverted"

---

[4]For Plato's account of democracy, see Book VIII of his *Republic*.

Two features of Aristotle's classification are especially noteworthy. The first, of course, is that he followed Plato in considering democracy to be bad or undesirable. For Aristotle, democracy was a corrupt form of rule because the *demos* tends to be short-sighted and selfish. The common people will recklessly pursue their own interests by taking property, wealth, and power from the few with no regard for the peace and stability of the *polis* as a whole. But this serves their interests only in the short run, and in the end they will bring chaos and ultimately despotism to the whole *polis*.

In Book V of *Politics*, Aristotle analyzes the close connection between democracy and tyranny by showing how the former can and often does turn into the latter. First, a demagogue persuades the common people that their democracy is in grave danger from some real or imagined enemy, whether foreign or domestic. Next, he endears himself to the people by presenting himself as their friend and their saviour from this foe. He then starts a war against this real or imagined enemy based on bogus reasons that the gullible people accept (fear having made them even more gullible), leaving them "always in need of a leader." This war serves to distract the people, preventing them from paying attention to what the demagogue-turned-tyrant is doing domestically, including undermining the constitution, making his cronies and hangers-on wealthy at public expense, and expanding his powers into areas that were previously constitutionally off-limits. The tyrant maintains and increases his power by distrusting anyone outside his inner circle; he tells lies that the people believe; he plants spies in their midst to ferret out critics and dissidents; he withholds information and practices censorship. He divides the people among themselves by "sowing dissensions" and "creating quarrels" over real or imaginary issues of little or no importance, thereby turning the people against each other so that they wrongly see their fellow citizens as enemies and don't pay attention to what the tyrant is doing. The tyrant also implicates as many people as possible in his crimes so that they too are guilty. He subverts the administration of justice by "altering the constitution" and putting innocent people on trial, letting guilty men go unpunished if they are willing to serve him. He uses the courts and other agencies of government to help his friends and harm his enemies; he distracts the people with spectacles and entertainments; he makes some people beholden and loyal to him by enriching them at public expense. And, above all, the tyrant maintains the *appearance* of being a good man and a just ruler: he *pretends* to be a "guardian of the public treasury" even as he plunders it by spending recklessly. He will *seem* to be a "steward of the public rather than a tyrant", and—not least—he will "*appear* to be particularly devout in his worship of the gods." By these means, Aristotle notes, the tyrant lulls the people into a deep civic sleep. If and when they wake up, it's likely to be too late to retrieve their rights and to restore their liberties.

Another noteworthy feature of Aristotle's classification is the inclusion of **polity**, a good form of rule by the many. For Aristotle, polity differs from democracy because it mixes elements of rule by the few with elements of rule by the many. The virtue of this **mixed constitution (or government)** is that each group can keep an eye on the other— the well-to-do few on the many, and the many on the well-to-do few—so that neither class can pursue its interest at the expense of the common good. Aristotle also suggested that polity may differ from democracy in its distribution of wealth and property; that is, in a democracy, the many will be poor. According to Aristotle, this is simply the way things usually are, and there is little one can do about it. However, in those rare but fortunate circumstances where most of the people are neither rich nor poor but

Aristotle (384–322 BC)

"have a moderate and sufficient property," one can expect the many to rule in a prudent manner.[5] This is because the many, when they have some property, will avoid the excesses of the envious poor and the arrogant rich. Seeing the good of the *polis* as their own good, the many of moderate means will work to maintain peace and stability in the city-state.

In the final analysis, Aristotle believed polity to be good—he even suggested that it is the best of the six regimes—while democracy is bad. But he also argued that democracy is better than tyranny and oligarchy. This is largely because many heads are better judges than one or a few. Even if none of the common people is an especially good judge of what is right and wrong or good and bad, their collective judgment is still better than that of any individual or small group, including a group of experts. This is true in the same way that "a feast to which many contribute is better than a dinner provided out of a single purse,"[6] Aristotle said. Besides, democracy gives more men the chance to participate in the active life of the citizen—to rule and be ruled in turn, as he put it.

Yet even as Aristotle was celebrating the citizen and the *polis,* this way of life was falling victim to a much larger political unit—**empire**. First under the leadership of Philip of Macedonia (r. 359–336 BC), then under his son (and Aristotle's student) Alexander the Great (r. 336–323 BC), the Hellenic Empire spread across Greece, throughout the Middle East, and all the way to India and Egypt. As the empire concentrated power in the hands of the emperor, the self-governing city-state died, and rule by the many, whether in the form of democracy or polity, perished with it.

---

[5] *The Politics of Aristotle,* ed. and trans. Benjamin Jowett (New York: Modern Library, 1943) 192; also Ball and Dagger, selection 4.
[6] *The Politics of Aristotle* 146; also Ball and Dagger, selection 4.

REPUBLICAN ROME

Popular government survived in the ancient world, but in the form of **republican** rather than democratic government. *Republic* derives from the Latin *res publica,* which literally means "the public thing," or "public business." It took on a more specific meaning, however, in the hands of the Greek historian Polybius (c. 200–c. 118 BC).

Republican Mixed Government

Polybius spent some seventeen years in Rome as a hostage. This experience inspired his interest in the growth of Roman power, which Polybius saw as part of a cycle of the rise and fall of great powers. Every powerful empire or country is doomed to decline, Polybius said, for both history and nature tell us that no human creation lasts forever. Still, some hold their power far longer than others, and Polybius thought the example of Rome helped to explain why this is so.

The key to Rome's success, Polybius argued in his *Histories,* was its mixed government. This was not an entirely new idea—Plato had hinted at it, as had Aristotle in his discussion of the polity—but Polybius developed it more clearly than his predecessors. He said that the Roman Republic was a mixed government because neither one person, nor the few, nor the many held all the power. Instead, the republic mixed or balanced these three regimes in a way that provided the benefits of each form while avoiding its defects. In other words, rather than give all power to one person, to a few people, or to the common people, the Roman Republic divided power among the three. Thus, the people as a whole exercised some control over policy-making through their assemblies—at least the free, adult males did—but so, too, did the aristocrats, who controlled the senate. Then, in place of a monarch, the republic relied on consuls to put the policies into effect. In this way, no group was able to pursue its own interest at the expense of the common good. Each kept watch over the others and the result was a form of government that was free, stable, and long lasting. Like an alloy that is stronger than any one of the metals that make it up, a mixed government, Polybius believed, will prove more durable than any "pure" or unmixed form of rule.

A republic, then, was a form of popular government, but its defenders insisted that it not be confused with a democracy. Democracy promoted vice—the self-interested rule of the common people—while a republic promoted virtue. Republican virtue was the ability of an individual to rise above personal or class interest to place the good of the whole community above one's own. Only active citizens could achieve and exercise this virtue, the republicans argued. Such citizens would be eager to participate in the political process yet wary of any person or group who might try to seize power. Mixed government served both these purposes by encouraging some degree of popular participation in government while making it difficult for anyone to acquire enough power to threaten liberty and the common good.

Within one hundred years of Polybius's death, however, the Roman Republic had given way to the Roman Empire. Beginning with Julius Caesar, a series of emperors drained the power from Rome's republican institutions and concentrated it in their own hands. Almost 1500 years would pass before the republican ideal was fully revived in the city-states of northern Italy during the **Renaissance**, and it was longer before the democratic ideal was itself revived.

Christianity and Democracy

There were many important developments in the intervening years, perhaps the most significant being the rise of Christianity. In some respects, Christianity seems a natural ally of democracy, for it proclaims that every person, regardless of gender, nationality, or status, is a child of God. Certainly by the standards of the ancient world, Christianity stood for radical equality. Rich or poor; slave or free; citizen or alien; Greek, Jew, or Roman; woman or man—Christians preached that none of these differences really mattered because all are one in Christ and equal in the eyes of God.

We might expect, then, that the early Christians would argue that everyone should have an equal voice in government. But they did not. This was not because the very early Christians were antidemocratic but because they were apolitical. Early Christians believed that life on earth is a preparation for, and an often painful pilgrimage to, the Christian's true home in heaven; by themselves the affairs of this world had no true value or lasting significance. Many early Christians also believed that the end of the world was near. These beliefs led some to take a lawless attitude. The common or orthodox position with regard to the law, however, was that Christians are obligated to obey human laws and earthly rulers. As St. Paul stated, "Let every person be subject to the governing authorities. For there is no authority except from God, and those that exist have been instituted by God. Therefore, he who resists the authorities resists what God has appointed, and those who resist will incur judgment."[7] In other words, where politics was concerned, the Christian message was simply to obey those in power and seek no power yourself.

Matters could not remain so simple, however, particularly when various Roman emperors sought to destroy this new and (to their eyes) dangerous religion. Matters became even more complicated when, in the fourth century AD, Christianity survived the persecutions to become the official religion of the Roman Empire. Then, following the collapse of the Roman Empire around AD 500, the Christian church became the dominant institution in Europe. It remained so throughout the period we know as the Middle Ages—roughly from AD 500 to 1400. With the disintegration of the Roman Empire, the church itself gradually divided into two wings: the Eastern Orthodox Church led by the Byzantine emperor, who ruled from Constantinople (now Istanbul); and the Roman Catholic Church headed by the bishop of Rome, who came to be known as the pope. The rise and rapid spread of the Islamic faith throughout the Middle East, across northern Africa, and into Spain in the seventh and eighth centuries also meant that much of the Mediterranean world was lost to Christianity. Yet the Roman Catholic Church saw itself as the one true church—*catholic* means "universal"—and it preached its message and enforced its doctrines wherever possible.

The Roman Catholic Church provided the spiritual bond that united most of Western and Central Europe throughout the Middle Ages. There was no comparable political bond. The collapse of the Roman Empire brought a return to localism, although not of the Greek city-state variety. There were some independent city-states in the Middle Ages—Rome, for instance, where the pope ruled—but more common varieties of local rule developed around tribal loyalties or the old military regions of the fallen empire. In the latter case, some regional commanders of the Roman army managed to keep their forces together and their regions secure even as the Roman Empire crumbled. From these *duces*

---

[7]The New Testament, Romans 13: 1–2.

and *comites,* who found themselves governing their territories as best they could, came the dukes and counts of the Middle Ages.

There were occasional attempts to revive a more nearly universal political bond in the form of a new empire, the most notable beginning on Christmas Day in the year 800, when Pope Leo III placed a crown on the head of Charlemagne, King of the Franks, and proclaimed him emperor. Despite repeated efforts over the centuries, however, the new Holy Roman Empire never achieved the power and stature of the old; as the historian Edward Gibbon later quipped, it was neither holy, nor Roman, nor an empire. Local ties and loyalties simply proved stronger than the desire for a politically united Christendom.

These local ties and loyalties also encouraged **feudalism**. This form of social organization, rooted in the need for protection from marauding Vikings and Magyars, led to a great emphasis on status and hierarchy—that is, one's station or position in society relative to that of others. A few people were aristocrats or nobles, some were free, and a great many more were serfs—peasants who lived and worked in bondage to an aristocrat in exchange for protection. According to the feudal ideal, every person occupied a rank or station in society and was expected to perform the duties and enjoy the privileges of that rank or station. In this way everyone supposedly contributed to the common good, just as every bee in a hive does what is best for all by performing its own strictly defined duties.

In such a society, there was little room for the democratic ideal. The outlook began to shift with the Renaissance, however, as a renewed concern for human achievement led to a revival of republicanism.

The Renaissance and Republicanism

In the late Middle Ages, particularly in the thirteenth century, several developments prepared the way for the Renaissance (or "rebirth"). One of these was Western civilization's renewed contact with the East. This came about partly through the Crusades—the attempts to recapture the Christian holy land of Palestine from the "infidel" Muslims— and partly through dealings with Islamic Spain, which Muslims had conquered in the early 700s. As so often happens, the contact with strange people and different cultures stimulated many in the West to examine their own customs and beliefs. The discovery that other people live quite satisfactorily in ways very different from what one has always assumed to be the natural and only reasonable way to live is often unsettling and disturbing. But it can also encourage creativity as people begin to see that it is possible to live in different, and perhaps better, ways. This happened most directly as Christian scholars rediscovered, through Spain, many works of ancient scholarship that had been lost to the West since the collapse of the Roman Empire. The most significant of these in political terms was Aristotle's *Politics,* which was translated into Latin in 1260—but only after the church convened a committee of scholars to determine whether the "pagan" philosopher's ideas were compatible with Christianity.

A second development preparing the way for the Renaissance was the revival of the city-state in Italy.[8] Many Italian cities enjoyed a measure of independence before the

---

[8]See Quentin Skinner, "The Italian City-Republics," *Democracy: The Unfinished Journey,* ed. John Dunn (Oxford: Oxford UP, 1992) 57–69.

thirteenth century, but they remained subject to the Germanic head of the Holy Roman Empire. After years of struggle, they seized the opportunity presented by the death of Emperor Frederick II in 1250 to become self-governing city-states. Even as empire and monarchy were the predominant forms of rule, the citizens of these city-states looked for a way to justify their "new" form of government. They found this justification in the ancient theorists of republicanism.

These and other developments led to the flowering of Western culture in the fourteenth through sixteenth centuries that scholars of that time took to be a renaissance—a rebirth or revival that began in the Italian city-states. Under the inspiration of the classical philosophers and of Christian theologians such as Thomas Aquinas, who stressed the coherence between classical philosophers such as Aristotle and Christianity, scholars of that time concluded that life on earth is not simply a wearisome journey on the way to the kingdom of God in heaven. On the contrary, life on earth, so rich and diverse, is not only worth living but also worth living freely and fully. Human beings are capable of many wondrous things—not the least of which is self-government.

Drawing on the writings of Aristotle and Polybius and the examples of the ancient republics of Rome and Sparta, the Renaissance republicans argued for a revival of civic life in which public-spirited citizens could take an active part in the governance of their independent city or country. The key concepts in this republican discourse were liberty, virtue, and corruption. Nowhere were these concepts deployed more sharply and effectively than in the writings of Niccolò Machiavelli (1469–1527).

Machiavelli was a prominent official in the republic of Florence in 1512 when the Medici family overthrew the republican government and installed themselves as rulers

Niccolò Machiavelli (1469–1527)

of the city-state. Implicated in a plot to overthrow the Medici and restore the republic, Machiavelli was arrested, tortured, and banished to his family estate in the countryside. While in exile, he wrote two books. The better known of the two is *The Prince,* a small text in which Machiavelli apparently instructs princes and petty tyrants to put conscience aside and do whatever it takes—lie, steal, even murder—to stay in power. Indeed, Machiavelli became so notorious that Shakespeare later referred to him as "the murderous Machiavel"; even today we sometimes call a cunning and unscrupulous person "machiavellian."[9]

Whether this is a fair reading of Machiavelli's purposes in *The Prince* is something scholars continue to debate,[10] but it definitely does not capture his purposes in his second, longer book, *The Discourses.* In this book Machiavelli makes clear his distrust of princes as he analyzes the factors that promote the longevity of a vital, virtuous, and free form of government—the republic.

For Machiavelli, a republic is a mixed government in which no single class rules. Instead, all classes share power as each checks the potential excesses of the others. It is a system of government in which vigilant citizens jealously guard their liberties against encroachment by would-be tyrants in their midst. For liberty, as Machiavelli understands it, is self-government; it is something found not in private life but in public action. But why must citizens be vigilant? Because as soon as they become complacent and indifferent to public affairs, they will find a tyrant waiting to relieve them of the burden of self-government and deprive them of their liberty. Thus Machiavelli insists that the greatest enemies of free government are complacent and self-interested citizens.

Such citizens care more for money and luxury than they care for the commonwealth. The love of wealth, luxury, and ease, together with a corresponding indifference to public affairs, is what Machiavelli calls "corruption." To keep corruption at bay, citizens must have "virtue." They must be attentive and alert to public affairs, always striving to do what is best not for themselves as private persons but for the commonwealth. If citizens are to be "virtuous," then, they must be free—free to assemble, to argue among themselves, to expose corruption, and to criticize their leaders and one another. If citizens neither enjoy nor exercise these essential liberties, their republic is doomed to an early death.

According to Machiavelli, the greatest danger a republic faces is that it will be destroyed from within by corruption. But because foreign enemies are also likely to threaten republics, a genuinely free republic must require all able-bodied males—and only males could be citizens—to be members of a citizen militia, prepared to take up arms against any external threat to their liberty.

Above all, Machiavelli maintained that a free government must be ruled not by the whim or caprice of any person or persons, or even of the majority of citizens, but by law. A free government is a government of laws, not of men. A government of laws is more consistent, more concerned with fairness, than a government of men. More important, laws are impersonal. We can depend upon the laws without losing our independence. When we depend upon individuals or even a majority, we are subject to their

---

[9]William Shakespeare, *King Henry the Sixth,* Third Part, Act III, Scene 2.
[10]See, for example, Mary Dietz, "Trapping the Prince: Machiavelli and the Politics of Deception," *American Political Science Review* 80 (September 1986): 777–799, along with the response by John Langton and rejoinder by Dietz in *American Political Science Review* 81 (December 1987): 1277–1288.

will—and this can hardly be called liberty. This is why Machiavelli, like Aristotle, considered pure democracy to be a bad form of government and a mixed constitutional republic to be the best.

A mixed government, a virtuous citizenry, the rule of law—these were the republican ideals of Machiavelli's *The Discourses*, a way of thinking about politics that spread from Italy to England in the seventeenth century, and from there to Britain's American colonies in the eighteenth.[11]

The English Civil War

In England, the turmoil of the 1600s sparked interest in both republicanism and democracy. Civil war broke out in 1642 as King Charles I and the English Parliament each claimed to be the sovereign of, or highest authority in, the land. The war ended with the parliamentary forces victorious under the leadership of Oliver Cromwell, and in January 1649 Charles I was beheaded. An attempt to establish a republic followed, but it failed as Cromwell assumed the powers, if not quite the title, of monarch (his official title was Lord Protector). After Cromwell's death in 1658, another attempt to establish a republic also failed and the monarchy was restored in 1660 when Charles II, son of Charles I, returned to the throne.

In these turbulent times, many Englishmen turned their thoughts to public matters. Among them was James Harrington (1611–1677), who published his *Oceana* (1656), apparently in hopes of persuading Cromwell to create a republic with a mixed or balanced system of government. More than a mixture of rule by one, the few, and the many, Harrington's balance included an effort to distribute land in a more nearly equal fashion so that no citizen would be dependent upon another for his livelihood. This balance would help ensure liberty under a government of laws, not of men. Harrington also advocated regular and frequent elections and a system of representation in which representatives would be rotated in and out of office. Like term limits in American politics, this "rota" would presumably protect liberty by preventing anyone from acquiring too much power by winning re-election to office term after term. It would also promote virtue by enabling more citizens to take an active and responsible part in the government of the Commonwealth.

During the English Civil War, other supporters of the parliamentary cause took the radical position of advocating democracy. They reached this position in part because of their religious convictions. Like most of northern Europe, England had legally forsaken Catholicism in the sixteenth century as the Protestant Reformation shattered the religious unity of Christendom. The new Protestant forms of Christianity emphasized a direct, immediate relationship between the individual and God. For Protestants such as John Calvin (1509–1564), this direct and solitary individual relationship with God overruled the authority of collective institutions such as the church.

Although Calvin and other Protestant leaders such as Martin Luther did not conclude that an emphasis on individual conscience and faith made democracy desirable, others did. In the 1640s, an English group called the Levellers claimed that political authority could be founded only on the consent of the people. For the Levellers, this meant that the

---

[11]See J. G. A. Pocock, *The Machiavellian Moment: Florentine Political Thought and the Atlantic Republican Tradition* (Princeton NJ: Princeton UP, 1975).

franchise—the right to vote—had to be extended to all adult males except those who had surrendered this right either by committing crimes or by putting themselves, like servants and recipients of public charity, into dependence upon others. Such was the birthright of all men, the Levellers claimed, regardless of how much—or how little—property they owned. The most famous statement of this position came from Colonel Thomas Rainsborough, an officer in Oliver Cromwell's New Model Army:

> For really I think that the poorest he that is in England hath a life to live as the greatest he; and therefore truly, sir, I think it's clear, that every man that is to live under a government ought first by his own consent to put himself under that government; and I do think that the poorest man in England is not at all bound in a strict sense to that government that he hath not had a voice to put himself under. . . .[12]

The radically democratic doctrine of that day became the conventional view of later times. But the Levellers failed to convince Cromwell and others in power of the wisdom of their arguments. For the most part, those engaged in political activity and debates continued to regard democracy as a dangerously unstable form of government. Still, the efforts of the Levellers mark the beginning of a remarkable, although gradual, shift in attitude toward democracy.

The English Civil War was also in part a clash between two rival ideologies that would produce differing conceptions of democracy and the use of democratic power in the modern era. The Royalist party in the English Civil War primarily held feudal (or, to use the more common British-Canadian term, *tory*) ideas about the nature of society. In the tory view, society was an organic unity in which different classes or groups had distinct but harmonious functions. The aristocracy, through tradition, wealth, and education, was best suited to govern, and all of society, including the poorest, would benefit from its rule. As a natural result of the privilege to govern, rulers bore the responsibility for the welfare of the ruled. In this view, the nation (or collective group) rather than the individual, and hierarchy (or social stratification) rather than equality, were the leading principles of political life. On the other hand, the parliamentary party held *bourgeois* (or, to use the more common British-Canadian term, *liberal*) ideas about the nature of society. The liberal view is characterized by an emphasis on the importance of the individual and the value and benefit of individual freedom. This view was closely connected with the development of Protestantism and with the emergence of market-based capitalism, which encouraged individual effort and initiative and rejected a collectivist approach that limited individual economic freedom. This view opposed tory restrictions and regulations—frequent religious holidays, minimum wages, maintenance of community property or "commons"—which at times had the effect of protecting the poor from the rising capitalist class. Neither of these ideologies was initially democratic—tories viewed democracy as inconsistent with the notion of hierarchy, and liberals viewed democracy as a threat to individual freedom, particularly the freedom of the industrious and successful capitalist to own and amass property.

---

[12]Rainsborough's remarks are from Andrew Sharp, ed., *The English Levellers* (Cambridge: Cambridge UP, 1998) 103.

DIFFERENT CONCEPTIONS OF DEMOCRACY IN CANADA AND THE UNITED STATES

Events during the English Civil War proved critical to the development of democracy in Canada and the United States and to the ideological differences that continue to exist between the two countries. American political scientist Louis Hartz pointed out that the political development of colonial societies such as Canada and the United States was powerfully influenced by the degree to which they reflected the political makeup of their parent society (Britain for the United States, and Britain and France for Canada) in their formative stages.[13] Canadian political scientist Gad Horowitz applied this conceptual analysis to Canada in what is often referred to as the Hartz-Horowitz Thesis.

The first English settlers in the colonies that were to become the United States disproportionately reflected the liberal and Protestant views of the parliamentary party in the English Civil War, and these views came to dominate the political life and ideas of the American colonial societies. The dominance of these views was clear during the American Revolution, when the minority of settlers who held more tory views were driven out (many settled in Canada as United Empire Loyalists). As a result, the United States represented only a fragment—a liberal, or bourgeois, fragment—of the political and social ideas of its parent society. Meanwhile, Britain exhibited both the feudal, or tory, ideas of the medieval era and the liberal ideas that had become influential during the seventeenth century.

Canada, on the other hand, was settled first by people from seventeenth-century France, a society that, in the terms we have been using, was completely feudal, or tory, in its views. Later British settlers brought with them both liberal and tory views. The absence of any desire for the revolutionary disruption of the British connection ensured that both kinds of views endured in Canada. This last point, as we will also note later, has given Canada and the United States somewhat different political orientations and values, including different views about the proper use of state power in a democratic society.

In Canada, one of the most important legacies of having both liberal and tory views has been the development of an enduring socialist or social democratic political tradition; in contrast, this tradition is almost absent in the United States. Socialism can be seen as a synthesis of the idea of individual freedom, which is at the root of liberalism, and the ideas of the importance of the collective element in society and the use of collective power to protect the weak, which came from the feudal, or tory, tradition. In this process of ideological development, sometimes described as **dialectic**, two conflicting sets of ideas eventually produce—in something like a chemical reaction—an entirely new set of ideas.

Because the feudal, or tory, tradition was entirely lacking in the political society of the United States (or had been driven out in the American Revolution), the dialectical process of ideological development, or synthesis, did not occur. In Canada, by contrast, an indigenous socialist movement developed and has persisted. In this respect (as in others), Canada has proven to be less a fragment of its European parent societies than a reflection of them. On the other hand, the United States has tended to be less tolerant of deviation

---

[13]See Louis Hartz, *The Founding of New Societies* (New York: Harcourt, 1964); Gad Horowitz, *Canadian Labour in Politics* (Toronto: U of Toronto P, 1968) chapter 1.

from the liberal ideas that dominated it. Liberal values came to be identified with the American identity itself, and those who rejected liberal values were seen as "unAmerican." Canada has generally exhibited a greater tolerance for ideological diversity and dissent because of its more complex ideological makeup.

The American Revolution

Democratic ideas and arguments played a part in the American War of Independence against Britain, but there were few favourable references to democracy either then or during the drafting of the Constitution of the United States in 1787. In general, *democracy* continued to stand for a form of class or even mob rule. It was, as Aristotle observed long ago, the bad form of popular government; the good form was the republic.

Throughout the quarrel with Britain that led to the Declaration of Independence in 1776, the American colonists typically couched their arguments in liberal and republican, not democratic, terms. They had an idealized view of the British Constitution as "republican," with the Crown, the House of Lords, and the House of Commons sharing the powers of government in a mixture or balance of rule by one, the few, and the many. The problem with the system of government, as the colonists saw it, was corruption. Corrupt British officials were working to upset the balanced British Constitution so that they could concentrate all power in their own hands. Spurred by ambition and avarice, these officials aimed to replace a government of laws with a government of men, and their first target in this corrupt enterprise was the individual rights of Britain's American colonists.[14]

When the thirteen American colonies achieved independence, the favoured form of government in the United States was not democratic but liberal and republican. Indeed, Americans were intolerant of the tory elements they had defeated, and the United Empire Loyalists fled, mostly to the British North American colonies. The Constitution of the United States makes no mention of democracy, but it does guarantee to each state "a Republican Form of Government."

The separation of the government's powers into three branches—legislative, executive, and judicial—puts each branch in a position to "check and balance" the other two. This is a modification of the old idea of mixed or balanced government. The executive branch corresponds to the monarchical element, rule by one; the judicial to the aristocratic, rule by the few; and the legislative to the popular, rule by the many.

This system of checks and balances also reflects the republican fear of corruption. James Madison (1751–1836) observed in his defence of the new Constitution that checks and balances are necessary because men are not angels. On the contrary, they are ambitious and competitive, and the key to good government is to keep ambitious men from destroying the liberty of the rest. The consistent emphasis is on limiting and restricting power of government in order to protect individual rights. According to Madison,

> Ambition must be made to counteract ambition. . . . It may be a reflection on human nature, that such devices should be necessary to control the abuses of government. But what is government

---

[14]For an elaboration of this analysis, see Bernard Bailyn, *The Ideological Origins of the American Revolution* (Cambridge, MA: Harvard UP, 1967).

itself, but the greatest of all reflections upon human nature? If men were angels, no government would be necessary. If angels were to govern men, neither external nor internal controls on government would be necessary. In framing a government which is to be administered by men over men, the great difficulty lies in this: you must first enable the government to control the governed; and in the next place oblige it to control itself.[15]

Other republican features of the U.S. Constitution appear in the Bill of Rights (1791)—the first ten amendments to the Constitution. The First Amendment, for instance, guarantees that Congress shall make no law depriving people of freedom of speech and assembly—two freedoms that republican writers saw as absolutely essential to the preservation of free government. In the Second Amendment, the republican emphasis on a civil militia also appears: "A well-regulated militia being necessary to the security of a free state, the right of the people to keep and bear arms shall not be infringed."

During the nineteenth century, the U.S. Constitution was effectively democratized, particularly after the election of Andrew Jackson as president in 1828 and the advent of so-called Jacksonian Democracy. The franchise was extended widely, and by 1913, when senators became directly elected, both the legislative and executive branches of the U.S. government were democratically elected (although the vestiges of indirect presidential election, in the form of the Electoral College, remain). Notwithstanding the democratization of the U.S. Constitution, it remained liberal in the sense that it checked, defused, and restricted the power of government and maximized individual liberty, including economic liberty.

Canada as a Parliamentary Democracy

After the thirteen southern British colonies in North America became the United States, the remaining colonies in British North America continued to have similar governments to those of the pre-revolutionary American colonies. These governments had an elected legislature and a British-appointed executive, with the potential (as had happened in the southern British colonies) for conflict between executive and legislature. As the British North American colonies matured and grew, that potential for conflict was realized, most seriously in the Rebellions of 1837 in Upper and Lower Canada. The Canadian solution to this problem, however, was not to replace British control of the executive branch with a Canadian-controlled executive separated from and checked and balanced by the legislature. Instead, the solution was to adopt the system of parliamentary, or "responsible," government, which was emerging at the same time in the United Kingdom. The conflict between legislature and executive was resolved by making the executive responsible to the legislature and ultimately controlled by the legislature, thus coordinating rather than separating the two branches.

The British North American colonies achieved responsible government in the 1840s, so that prior to Confederation in 1867, each colony was internally self-governing, with the executive chosen from the majority group in the elected legislature. By uniting the executive and legislative branches in the system of responsible parliamentary government, the United Kingdom and Canada showed an absence of the fear of government power and the desire to check that power that existed in the United States. In a more positive sense, it also reflected the greater acceptance in Canada and the United Kingdom of

[15]Terence Ball, ed. *The Federalist* (Cambridge: Cambridge UP, 2003), No. 51; 252.

the use of government power to achieve the purposes of society as a whole, even where that involved some restriction of individual rights (and, in particular, individual economic rights). Acceptance of the legitimacy of the use of governmental power in turn reflects the feudal, or tory, view that has persisted in one form or another in all West European societies. This view has become a part of Canadian political culture, while it is largely missing in that of the United States. Thus, Canada enjoys a system of constitutional or parliamentary democracy that differs in important respects from the system of republican democracy in the United States.

THE GROWTH OF DEMOCRACY

Democracy became ever more popular after the seventeenth century because of a number of social and economic developments during the Industrial Revolution of the late eighteenth and nineteenth centuries. The most important of these were the growth of cities, the spread of public education, and improvements in communication and transportation such as the telegraph and railroad. Each of these developments helped spread literacy, information, and interest in political matters among the populations of Europe and North America, thereby contributing to the growing faith in the common people's ability to participate knowledgeably in public affairs.

In nineteenth-century Britain, arguments for democracy tended to centre on two concerns: self-protection and self-development. According to the "philosophical radicals," or **Utilitarians**, the duty of government was to promote the greatest happiness of the greatest number. The best way to do this, they concluded, was through representative democracy, which enables every man to vote for representatives who will protect his interests. One Utilitarian, John Stuart Mill (1806–1973), went on to argue in *The Subjection of Women* (1869) that this chance at self-protection through voting ought to extend to women as well.

Mill also maintained that political participation is valuable because of the opportunity it provides for self-development. Mill believed that democracy strengthens civic virtue among the common people through "the invigorating effect of freedom upon the character." Political participation—not merely voting for representatives, but direct participation at the local level—educates and improves people by teaching them discipline, sharpening their intelligence, and even shaping their morality. Thus Mill drew attention to

> . . . the moral part of the instruction afforded by the participation of the private citizen, if even rarely, in public functions. He is called upon, while so engaged, to weigh interests not his own; to be guided, in case of conflicting claims, by another rule than his private partialities; to apply, at every turn, principles and maxims which have for their reason of existence the common good: and he usually finds associated with him in the same work minds more familiarized than his own with these ideas and operations. . . . He is made to feel himself one of the public, and whatever is for their benefit will be for his benefit.[16]

---

[16]Both quotations are from Mill's "Considerations on Representative Government," in Mill, *Utilitarianism, Liberty, and Representative Government* (New York: Dutton, 1951) 196, 197; also in Ball and Dagger, selection 9.

Such arguments helped bring about a gradual extension of the franchise over the past 150 years. The right to vote was first extended to all adult males—although this was not fully accomplished in Canada until the 1870s and in the United Kingdom until 1885. Canadian women first voted in 1917 in a federal election, but Quebec women did not cast their first ballot until 1944. These extensions did not come easily or swiftly. Switzerland, sometimes called the world's oldest continuous democracy, did not grant full voting rights to women until 1971, and women are still not allowed to vote in national elections in Saudi Arabia.[17] Often these changes came only after heated debate, protests, and violence.

Populism

Another variant of liberal and democratic thinking that developed in the eighteenth century and later had considerable influence in Canada and the United States was what is often called *populism*. This ideology drew its initial inspiration from Jean-Jacques Rousseau and the writings of Thomas Jefferson, the author of the American Declaration of Independence who later became president of the United States.[18] Populist theory argued that the majority of individuals in a society, provided their judgment was not distorted or corrupted by self-interest and by being a member of a vested interest, could act together as the "people" in a unity of will and purpose. Acting in this way, such a majority not only expressed the **general will** of the community but directed it to the common good of all, rising above individual self-interest or the self-interest of special interest groups. Populism was particularly hostile to economic, social, and religious groups claiming special privileges, and it sought to put its principles into effect by making popular government an active principle of politics. Thus, populists developed mechanisms to exert popular control over government and elected officials to prevent them from being dominated or corrupted by special interests and corrupt political practices. These mechanisms included political party organizations outside the legislature and devices such as the **recall**, the **initiative**, and the **referendum**, which ensured that elected officials truly reflected the will of those who had elected them rather than special interests. At various times in the nineteenth and twentieth centuries, populist movements have been a significant, if sometimes temporary, force in both Canada and the United States, from the Progressive and United Farmer movements in early twentieth-century Canada to the Progressives in late nineteenth- and early twentieth-century United States and the Reform/Alliance movement in Canada in the 1990s. The Tea Party movement or faction within the Republican Party in the United States also has strong populist tendencies.

Democracy as an Ideal

As we noted at the beginning of this chapter, democracy is now so popular that most ideologies and most countries claim to favour it. Yet these supposedly democratic ideologies are in constant competition and occasional conflict with one another. The best

---

[17]For a discussion of democracy and liberty in Switzerland, see Benjamin Barber, *The Death of Communal Liberty* (Princeton: Princeton UP, 1974).

[18]See particularly, Jean-Jacques Rousseau, *The Social Contract* (London, 1762).

explanation for this oddity is to say that different ideologies do indeed pursue and promote democracy, but they do so in different ways because they disagree about what democracy is. They can disagree because democracy is not a single thing, as our brief history of democracy makes clear. Rather than a specific kind of government that must take a definite form, democracy is instead an ideal.

To say that democracy is an ideal means that it is something toward which people aim or aspire. In this respect it is like true love, inner peace, or a perfect performance. Each is an ideal that inspires people to search or strive for it, but none is easy to find or even to define. What one person takes to be true love, for instance, is likely to be quite different from another person's idea of it. So it is with democracy. Everyone agrees that democracy is government, or rule, by the people, but exactly what that means is subject to sharp disagreement. Who are the "people" who are supposed to rule? Only the "common" people? Only those who own substantial property? Only adult males? Or should everyone who lives in a country—including resident foreigners, children, and convicted felons—have a formal voice in its government?

Moreover, how are the "people" to rule? Should every citizen vote directly on proposed policies, as the Athenians did, or should citizens vote for representatives, who will then make policy? If they elect representatives, do the people then cease to govern themselves? With or without representatives, should we follow majority rule? If we do, how can we protect the rights and interests of individuals or minorities, especially those who say and do things that anger or offend the majority? But if we take steps to limit the power of the majority—as a constitutionally entrenched charter of rights or a system of constitutional checks and balances does, for instance—are we not restricting or even retreating from democracy? The current debate in Canada about the role of the courts, particularly the Supreme Court of Canada, in striking down laws enacted by democratically elected legislatures through the application of restrictions on government action set out in the Canadian Charter of Rights and Freedoms reflects this dilemma. Are the courts improperly frustrating the democratic will of the majority, or are they protecting individual or minority rights that are more important than democratic majority rights?[19]

These are difficult questions that, as our brief history of democracy suggests, have been answered in very different ways over the centuries. Such questions have also led a number of political thinkers to worry about the instability of democracy, with a particular concern for its supposed tendency to degenerate into anarchy and despotism. Despite the difficulties of defining it, however, the democratic ideal of rule by the people remains attractive. This is due in part to its connection with freedom and equality, since democracy implies that in some sense every citizen will be both free and equal to every other citizen. But exactly what freedom and equality are, or what form they should take and how the two relate to each other, is open to interpretation.

This is where ideologies enter the picture. Whether they accept or reject it, all ideologies must come to terms with the democratic ideal. Coming to terms in this case means that ideologies have to provide more definite notions of what democracy involves. They do this by drawing on their underlying conceptions of human nature and

---

[19]For different views on this issue, see F. L. Morton and Rainer Knopff, *The Charter Revolution and the Court Party* (Peterborough, ON: Broadview, 2000); and Kent Roach, *The Supreme Court on Trial. Judicial Activism or Democratic Dialogue* (Toronto: Irwin Law, 2001).

freedom to determine whether democracy is possible and desirable and, if so, what form it should take.

To put the point in terms of our functional definition of ideology, we can say that an ideology's explanation of why things are the way they are largely shapes its attitude toward democracy. If an ideology holds, as fascism does, that society is often in turmoil because most people are incapable of governing themselves, it is hardly likely to advocate democracy. But if an ideology holds, as liberalism and socialism do, that most people have the capacity for freedom and self-government, then the ideology will embrace the democratic ideal—as most of them have done. The ideology that does so will then evaluate existing social arrangements and provide a sense of orientation for individuals based largely on how democratic it takes these arrangements to be. If the individual seems to be an equal partner in a society where the people rule in some suitable sense, then all is well; but if he or she seems to be merely the pawn of those who hold the real power, then the ideology will encourage people to take action to reform or perhaps to overthrow the social and political order.

Every ideology, then, offers its own interpretation of the democratic ideal and interprets or defines it according to its particular vision. In turn, the men and women who promote ideologies will use their vision of democracy to try to inspire others to join their cause.

Three Conceptions of Democracy

To clarify the connection between ideologies and the democratic ideal, let us examine briefly the three principal versions of democracy in the modern world. Although all three share several features, their differences are sharp enough to make them distinctive and competing conceptions of democracy.

Liberal Democracy. As the name suggests, **liberal democracy** emerged from liberalism—the ideology examined in Chapters 3 and 4. As with liberalism in general, liberal democracy stresses the rights and liberty of the individual. For liberals, democracy is certainly rule by the people, but an essential part of this rule includes the protection of individual rights and liberties. This means that majority rule must be limited. In this view, democracy is rule by the majority of the people, but only as long as those in the majority do not try to deprive individuals or minorities of their basic civil rights, including property rights. The right to speak and worship freely, the right to run for public office, and the right to own property are among the civil rights and liberties that liberals have generally taken to be necessary to realize the democratic ideal as they interpret it. Consequently, liberal democracy embraces equality of opportunity, which flows from the assumption that all individuals possess the same rights, but it rejects the proposition that society should seek equality of condition—that is, that all individuals should have equality of property and social and economic power. Equality of condition is seen as incompatible with individual rights to property and freedom of enterprise.

Social Democracy. Within the Western democracies, especially in Europe and Canada, the chief challenger to the liberal conception is **social democracy**. This view is linked to the ideology of socialism. From a social democratic or democratic socialist perspective, the key to democracy is equality, especially equal social and economic power in society and government. Social democrats argue that liberal democracy puts poor and working-class people at the mercy of the rich. In the modern world, they say, money is a major source of power, and those who have wealth have power over those who do not. Wealth makes it possible to run for office and to influence government policies (through large campaign donations, for example), so the rich exercise much greater influence when public policies are made. Yet this advantage is hardly democratic, social democrats insist. Democracy is rule by the people, and such rule requires that every person have a roughly equal influence over the government. This is in keeping with the slogan "one person, one vote." But we will not really have this equal influence, social democrats say, unless we take steps to distribute power—including economic power—in a more nearly equal fashion. This is why the program of social democrats typically calls for the redistribution of wealth to promote equality, public financing of campaigns and elections, public rather than private control of natural resources and major industries, and workers' control of the workplace. Like liberals, then, social democrats want to preserve civil liberties and promote fair competition for political office. Unlike liberals, however, they deny that most people can be truly free or political competition fair when great inequalities of wealth and power prevail.

Even in societies such as Canada, where liberal democracy has been stronger and more popular than social democracy, social democratic ideals and policies have often had a significant effect on public policy and have influenced the development of liberal democracy. In Canada, for example, the New Democratic Party (NDP) and its predecessor, the Cooperative Commonwealth Federation (CCF) (which was described by Prime Minister Mackenzie King [PM 1921–1925; 1926–1930; 1935–1948] as "Liberals in a hurry"), exerted pressure for social democratic reform that influenced other parties, including the Liberals, to adjust certain of their policies.

People's Democracy. Historically, in communist countries, the prevailing version of the democratic ideal was **people's democracy**. In some ways people's democracy is closer to the original Greek idea of democracy—rule by and in the interests of the *demos,* the common people—than liberal or social democracy. From a communist perspective, the common people are the **proletariat**, or the working class, and democracy cannot be achieved until government rules in their interest. This does not necessarily mean that the proletariat must itself directly control the government. As we shall see in Chapter 7, communists once called for the **revolutionary dictatorship of the proletariat**, a form of dictatorship that Karl Marx described as ruling in the interests of the working class. The immediate purpose of this dictatorship is to suppress the capitalists, or **bourgeoisie**, who have previously used their power and wealth to exploit the working class. By suppressing them, the dictatorship of the proletariat supposedly prepares the common people for the classless society of the communist future, when the state itself will wither away. In the meantime, people's democracy consists of rule by the communist party for the benefit of the working majority. This is the sense in which Mao Zedong spoke of a "people's democratic dictatorship" in the People's Republic of China.

When the Soviet Union and its communist regime disintegrated in the early 1990s, the idea of people's democracy suffered a serious blow. But in China, the leaders of the Chinese Communist Party continued to insist on the need for a "people's democratic dictatorship." The alternative, they said, was "bourgeois liberalization"—otherwise known as liberal democracy—and this they found completely unacceptable. Yet today, they share this view only with the communist leaders of Vietnam, Cuba, and North Korea. The Chinese embrace of a free market capitalist economy with significant inequality of wealth suggests that the language of people's democracy is used only to mask a purely authoritarian regime in an attempt to avoid the conclusion that liberal economic ideas (a free market and individual property rights) must lead to individual civil rights, which would undermine the powers of the ruling elite. It is perhaps more accurate to characterize the government in China today as oligarchic.

Conclusion

Liberal democracy, social democracy, and people's democracy are the main visions of the democratic ideal in the modern world. In this democratic age, it is important to understand these visions and how they relate to various ideologies. With this in mind we shall explore in the succeeding chapters the major ideologies of the modern world—liberalism, conservatism, socialism, and nationalism—and some of their recently emerging rivals. Each discussion will conclude with an assessment of the connection between the particular ideology and its interpretation of the democratic ideal.

For Further Reading

Dagger, Richard. *Civic Virtues: Rights, Citizenship, and Republican Liberalism.* New York: Oxford UP, 1997.

———. "Republican Citizenship," in E.F. Isin and B.S. Turner, eds., *Handbook of Citizenship Studies.* London: Sage, 2002.

Dahl, Robert. *Democracy and Its Critics.* New Haven, CT: Yale UP, 1989.

———. *On Democracy.* New Haven, CT: Yale UP, 1998.

Dunn, John, ed. *Democracy: The Unfinished Journey.* Oxford: Oxford UP, 1992.

Farrar, Cynthia. *The Origins of Democratic Thinking.* Cambridge: Cambridge UP, 1988.

Gooch, G. P. *English Democratic Ideas in the Seventeenth Century,* 2nd ed. New York: Harper and Brothers, 1959.

Gould, Carol C. *Rethinking Democracy.* Cambridge: Cambridge UP, 1988.

Hanson, Russell L. *The Democratic Imagination in America: Conversations with Our Past.* Princeton, NJ: Princeton UP, 1985.

Held, David. *Models of Democracy.* Stanford, CA: Stanford UP, 1986.

Honohan, Iseult. *Civic Republicanism.* London: Routledge, 2002.

Lipset, Seymour M. *Continental Divide: The Values and Institutions of the United States and Canada.* New York: Routledge, 1990.

Macpherson, C.B. *The Life and Times of Liberal Democracy.* Oxford: Oxford UP, 1977.

———. *The Real World of Democracy.* Oxford: Oxford UP, 1966.

Mansbridge, Jane. *Beyond Adversary Democracy.* Chicago: U of Chicago P, 1983.

Pateman, Carole. *Participation and Democratic Theory*. Cambridge: Cambridge UP, 1970.

Pettit, Philip. *Republicanism: A Theory of Freedom and Government*. Oxford: Clarendon P, 1997.

Pocock, J. G. A. *The Machiavellian Moment: Florentine Political Thought and the Atlantic Republican Tradition*. Princeton, NJ: Princeton UP, 1975.

Rahe, Paul. *Republics Ancient and Modern: Classical Republicanism and the American Revolution*. Chapel Hill: U of North Carolina P, 1992.

Sandel, Michael. *Democracy's Discontent: America in Search of a Public Philosophy*. New York: Basic Books, 1996.

Skinner, Quentin. *The Foundations of Modern Political Thought,* 2 vols. Cambridge: Cambridge UP, 1978.

Walzer, Michael. *Radical Principles*. New York: Basic Books, 1980.

Wood, Gordon. *The Creation of the American Republic. 1776–1787*. Chapel Hill: U of North Carolina P, 1969.

Useful Websites and Social Media

www.dominion.ca The Dominion Institute

www.elections.ca Elections Canada

www.parl.gc.ca Parliament of Canada

www.un.org/en/globalissues/democracy/index.shtml United Nations Global Issues: Democracy

www.thecanadianencyclopedia.com/articles/social-democracy The Canadian Encyclopedia "Social Democracy"

www.thecanadianencyclopedia.com/articles/populism The Canadian Encyclopedia "Populism"

From the Ball and Dagger Reader *Ideals and Ideologies*, US Eighth Edition

Part Two: The Democratic Ideal

Discussion Questions

1. Why did the leading Greek philosophers, Plato and Aristotle, not favour democracy?
2. How do Canadian and American conceptions of democracy differ?
3. What ideas did Macchiavelli and the U.S. Founding Fathers have in common?
4. Is the meaning of *democracy* so broad that it no longer has any real meaning?

MySearchLab

MySearchLab with eText offers you access to an online interactive version of the text, additional quizzes and assessment, extensive help with your writing and research projects, and provides round-the-clock access to credible and reliable source material. Go to **www.mysearchlab.com** to access these resources.

CHAPTER 3

The Origins of Liberalism

Over himself, over his own body and mind, the individual is sovereign.

John Stuart Mill, *On Liberty*

LEARNING OBJECTIVES

After completing this chapter you should be able to

1. Explain the basic tenets of liberalism.

2. Describe the historical developments that contributed to the rise of liberalism.

3. Demonstrate how the ideas of Hobbes, Locke, Paine, Smith, Bentham, and Mill articulate liberal premises.

4. Discuss the development of liberalism in Canada.

For more than three centuries, the hallmark of liberalism has been the promotion of individual liberty. But this very broad goal leaves room for liberals to disagree among themselves as to what exactly liberty is and how best to promote it. Indeed, this disagreement is now so sharp that modern liberalism is split into two rival camps of neoclassical (or business) and welfare liberals. In the following chapter we shall see how this split occurred. But first we need to look at the origin of liberalism in that broad area of common ground on which all liberals meet—the desire to promote individual liberty.

The words *liberal* and *liberty* both derive from the Latin *liber,* meaning "free." *Liberal* did not enter the vocabulary of politics until early in the nineteenth century, however, long after *liberty* was widely used as a political term—and at least a century after ideas now regarded as liberal were in the air. Before the nineteenth century, *liberal* was commonly used to mean "generous" or "tolerant"—an attitude that supposedly befit a gentleman, just as a "liberal education" was meant to prepare a gentleman for life. *Liberal* still means generous or tolerant, of course, as when someone says that a teacher follows a liberal grading policy or a child has liberal parents. But nowadays, through an extension of this common use, *liberal* more often refers to a political position or point of view.

The first clear sign of the political use of *liberal* occurred in the early nineteenth century, when a faction of the Spanish legislature adopted the name *Liberales.* From there the term travelled to France and the United Kingdom, where the party known as the Whigs evolved by the 1840s into the Liberal Party. These early liberals shared a desire for a more open and tolerant society—one in which people would be free to pursue their own ideas and interests with as little interference as possible. A liberal society was to be, in short, a free society.

But what makes a society free? What is freedom, and how can we best promote it? These questions have occupied liberals for more than three centuries, providing the grounds not only for arguments among liberals but also for disputes between liberalism and other ideologies.

LIBERALISM AND HUMAN NATURE

In Chapter 1, we noted that a conception of human nature provides the underpinnings for every ideology. In the case of liberalism, the emphasis on individual liberty rests on a conception of human beings as fundamentally rational individuals. There are significant differences among liberals on this point. But in general liberals stress individual liberty largely because they believe that most people are capable of living freely. This sets them apart from those who believe that human beings are at the mercy of uncontrollable passions and desires, first pushing in one direction, then pulling in another. Liberals acknowledge that people do have passions and desires, but they maintain that people also have the ability to control and direct their desires through reason. Most women and men, they insist, are rational beings who know what is in their own interests and, given the opportunity, are capable of acting to promote those interests.

Liberals generally agree that self-interest is the primary motive for most people's actions. Some argue that self-interest should be given free rein, while others respond that it should be carefully directed to promote the good of all; but most hold that it is wisest to think of people as beings who are more interested in their own good than in the well-being of others. This implies in turn that all these rational, self-interested men and women will find themselves competing with one another in their attempts to promote their personal interests. This is healthy, liberals say, as long as the competition remains fair and stays within proper bounds. Exactly what is fair and where these proper bounds lie is a subject of sharp disagreement among liberals, as is the question of how best to promote competition. For the most part, though, liberals are inclined to regard competition as a natural part of the human condition.

When individuals are viewed as naturally competitive rather than cooperative, the importance of the collective—society or nation—becomes downgraded in favour of the individual. Liberals tend to see the collective as a possible threat to individual liberty, a source of restriction and regulation. Competition implies the pursuit of self-interest; cooperation implies the pursuit of a common interest that may conflict with the self-interests of a minority of the population who do not feel represented by the common interest. Few liberals deny the existence of entities beyond the individual level, or the need for certain things in society to be done at the collective, or group, level. However, they tend to minimize the collective aspect of political life or to rationalize it as the product of individuals pursuing their own self-interests.

LIBERALISM AND FREEDOM

In the liberal view, then, human beings are typically rational, self-interested, and competitive. This implies that they are capable of living freely. But what does it mean to live freely? In other words, how do liberals conceive of freedom?

To answer this question, let us use the model introduced in Chapter 1 depicting freedom as a triadic relationship involving an *agent* who is free from some *obstacle* to pursue some *goal*. (See Figure 3.1.) In the case of liberalism, the agent is the individual. Liberals want to promote the freedom not of a particular group or class of people, but of each and every person as an individual. To do this, they have sought to free people from a variety of restrictions or obstacles. In the beginning, liberals were most concerned with removing social and legal barriers to individual liberty, especially social customs,

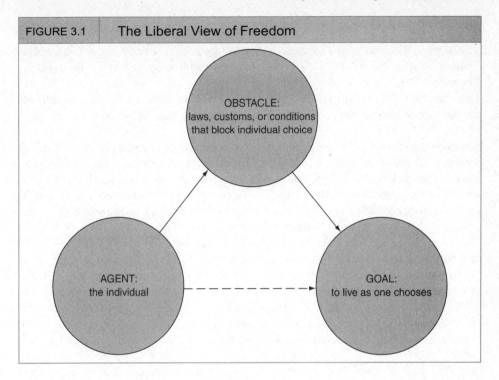

FIGURE 3.1	The Liberal View of Freedom

OBSTACLE:
laws, customs, or conditions
that block individual choice

AGENT:
the individual

GOAL:
to live as one chooses

ties of feudal dependence, and **religious conformity**. Since then other liberals have claimed that poverty, racial and sexual prejudice, ignorance, and illness are also obstacles to individual liberty.

But in spite of these differences, liberals agree that the individual must be free to decide for himself—and, more recently, herself—what goals to pursue in life. Most liberals have believed that the individual is the best judge of what is in his or her interest, so each person ought to be free to live as he or she sees fit—as long as the person does not choose to interfere with others' freedom to live as they see fit.

For this reason, equality is an important element in the liberal conception of freedom. In the liberal view, each person should have an equal opportunity to enjoy liberty. No person's liberty is more important or valuable than any other's. This does not mean that everyone must be equally successful or have an equal share of the good things of life, whatever they may be. Liberals do not believe that everyone can or should be equally successful, but that everyone should have an *equal opportunity to succeed*—that is, **equality of status**, not **equality of condition**. Anything that prevents a person from having an equal opportunity—whether it be privileges for the aristocracy, monopolies that block economic competition, or discrimination based on race, religion, or gender—can be an obstacle to a person's freedom that ought to be removed.

In short, liberalism promotes individual liberty by trying to guarantee equality of status and opportunity within a tolerant society. In the English-speaking world, liberal ideas are so much a part of our lives and our thinking that they seem natural. However, these ideas were not always taken for granted, not even in England and Europe. To appreciate their full significance, we need to see how liberalism began as a reaction against European society in the Middle Ages.

Medieval Origins of Liberalism

The origins of liberalism can be traced back to a reaction against two of the characteristic features of medieval society in Europe: **religious conformity** and **ascribed status** (or hierarchy). This reaction, which developed over the course of centuries, took different forms in different times and places. By the time *liberal* entered the political vocabulary in the early nineteenth century, a distinct political viewpoint had clearly emerged.

Religious Conformity. Liberals called for freedom of religion and separation of church and state. These ideas ran counter to the dominant ways of thinking in the Middle Ages, when church and state were supposed to be partners. Indeed, there was no clear distinction between church and state in medieval Europe. For its part, the Christian church saw its mission as saving souls—something that could best be done by teaching and upholding orthodoxy, or "correct belief." Those who took an unorthodox view of Christianity or rejected it altogether thus threatened the church's attempts to do what it saw as the work and will of God. In response to these threats, the church used its powers, and called on the kings and other secular authorities to use theirs, to enforce conformity to church doctrine. For their part, the secular rulers were usually willing—either out of religious conviction or a desire to maintain order in their domains—to suppress those whom the church considered heretics or infidels. Throughout medieval Europe, then, religious and political authorities joined forces to ensure conformity to the doctrines of the church.

Ascribed Status. Early liberals also objected to *ascribed status*—that is, power and social standing that is determined at birth. In a society based on hierarchy and ascribed status, a person's social standing is fixed, or ascribed, at birth, and there is little that people can do to change their status. This stands in contrast to a society based on **achieved status**, in which everyone is supposed to have an equal opportunity to achieve their own status based on their own efforts and choices. To be sure, Christians in the Middle Ages professed that all people are born equal in the eyes of God, but this kind of equality was compatible in their eyes with great inequalities in life here on earth. What counted was the state of one's soul, not one's status in society.

Feudalism. Status mattered very much in earthly life, for one's position and prospects were fixed by his or her social *rank*, *order*, or *estate*. This was especially true under **feudalism**, which became the main form of social and economic organization in Europe after the disintegration of Charlemagne's empire in the ninth century. Under feudalism, an intricate web of relationships developed in which one knight (the lord) would give the use of land to a lesser knight (the vassal) in return for military service. The vassal might then divide the land into parcels to be offered to others, who then, in exchange for various services, became his vassals. In the beginning the original lord retained ownership of the land, with the vassal receiving only the right to use it and enjoy its fruits. These relationships gradually became hereditary, however, leading to a complicated hierarchy of rank, status, and loyalty.

In one respect, feudalism simplified matters by reinforcing the existing tendency of society to divide into two broad classes of people: nobles and commoners. But as feudal relationships were passed down the generations, a distinct class of land-owning nobles, or aristocrats, took shape. These nobles thought themselves naturally superior to the commoners, who were the great majority of the people. They also believed that their noble birth entitled them to exercise authority over the commoners and to enjoy privileges and liberties unavailable to common men and women.

This emphasis on social rank or estate was reflected in the parliaments or estates general that began to appear in the late Middle Ages. These political bodies, usually summoned by kings, spoke for the different orders of society. The Estates General of France, for instance, which first convened in 1302, comprised representatives of the clergy (the First Estate), the nobility (the Second Estate), and the commoners (the Third Estate). Because the members of this last group lived mostly in cities and towns—*bourgs* in French—they were called the **bourgeoisie**.

There were no representatives for those who were not free, such as the serfs. Serfs (from the Latin *servus,* meaning "slave") were commoners, but they were not free. They were peasants, or agricultural labourers. But unlike free peasants, serfs owned no land. Instead, they farmed small plots of land owned by the lord of the manor; and from their plots they had to provide for their families and pay rent to the lord, typically in the form of crops.

The most distinctive feature of serfdom, however, was the serfs' lack of freedom to choose where to live and what work to do. Serfs were often legally *attached* to the land or the person of the lord. By custom and law they were bound—hence the term *bondsman*—either to remain on and work the land where they were born or, if attached to a person, to serve the lord wherever required. In exchange, serfs received protection from the lord. If they thought this a poor bargain, there was nothing they could do, as a rule, to earn release from serfdom. Some tried to win their freedom by force of arms; others ran away to the towns and cities; and still others accepted their condition as part of the natural course of life, although perhaps cherishing a hope that their lord might one day free them.

Thus, in medieval Europe, everyone—whether serf, noble, or free commoner—was born into a certain rank or estate and could do little to change it. The church was the only exception to this rule, for people from all ranks of society always had the option of becoming a nun, monk, or priest. In other respects, though, medieval society was firmly rooted in ascribed status. For the most part, nobles were those born into the nobility, while the children of free commoners and serfs were virtually locked into the social position of their parents. No amount of effort or ability could significantly improve their stations in life. Even freedom was a matter of social position, with different liberties attached to different levels of status in society. For example, in the Magna Carta, the Great Charter of rights that the feudal barons of England forced King John to accept in 1215, the king agreed that "No free man shall be taken, or imprisoned, . . . or outlawed, or exiled, or in any way destroyed . . . except by lawful judgment of his peers or by the laws of the land."[1] But the term "free man" (*liber homo*) referred only to the barons and other nobles. Those of lesser rank could still be taken, imprisoned, or killed without the lawful judgment of their peers—without a trial by a jury.

Against this society rooted in ascribed status and religious conformity, liberalism emerged as the first distinctive ideology. But this reaction did not take definite shape until a number of social, economic, and cultural changes disturbed the medieval order. Many of these were directly related to the outburst of creativity in the fourteenth and

[1]A translation of Magna Carta as confirmed by Edward I with his seal in 1297, section 29; see http://www.archives.gov/exhibits/featured_documents/magna_carta/translation.html.

fifteenth centuries known as the **Renaissance**. There was also the Black Death, an epidemic that devastated Europe from 1347 to 1351, killing about one of every three people. This epidemic opened new opportunities for survivors from the lower ranks of society and loosened the rigid medieval social structure. The expansion of trade and commerce in the late Middle Ages also played a part in the breakdown of the medieval order, as did the wave of exploration set in motion by this expansion. The attempts of explorers such as Christopher Columbus, John Cabot, and Jacques Cartier to find new trade opportunities led to the discovery of what was, for Europeans, an entirely New World that became a symbol of great possibilities. But of all the historical developments that contributed to the decline of the medieval order and the rise of liberalism, the most important was the **Protestant Reformation**.

The Protestant Reformation

The Protestant Reformation can be dated from 1521, the year the Roman Catholic Church excommunicated Martin Luther (1483–1546). Luther was a priest and professor of theology at the University of Wittenberg in Germany when he posted his famous Ninety-five Theses on the door of Castle Church in Wittenberg in 1517. By themselves, the Ninety-five Theses were not a direct threat to the authority of the church. Their immediate purpose was to call for a debate on the sale of *indulgences*, which were issued on the authority of the pope to raise money for church projects. In 1517, the project was the rebuilding of St. Peter's Basilica in Rome. Although the purchase of an indulgence was supposed only to release a sinner from some acts of penance, eager salesmen sometimes led people to believe that an indulgence could secure a place in heaven. This practice provoked Luther to issue his challenge to a debate.

With the aid of the printing press, a relatively new invention, Luther's theses circulated quickly through the German principalities and found a receptive audience among Christians disturbed by the corruption of the church. They also caught the attention of the German nobles, many of whom regarded the church as their main rival for earthly power. The resulting furor led Luther's superiors in the church to command him to admit that he was mistaken and to submit to the authority of the pope. But Luther refused, saying, as legend has it, "Here I stand. I can do no other." Thus began the Reformation.

In Luther's view, the church had vested too much authority in priests and too little in the Bible. In place of the church's emphasis on tradition, rituals, and sacraments, Luther favoured strict attention to the Scriptures, the Word of God. And in place of the church's emphasis on the authority of priests, bishops, and the pope, Luther favoured the "priesthood of all believers." All that matters is faith, he declared, and the only way to nurture faith is to read the Bible and to do as God there commands us to do. With that in mind, Luther and his colleagues translated the Bible into German to make it accessible to those who could not read Latin.

Despite some early remarks defending freedom of conscience, Luther never meant to encourage people to believe and worship in whatever way they chose. Apparently he expected that everyone who read the Scriptures could not help but understand them as he did. But this did not happen. To the contrary, Luther's proclamation of the "priesthood of all believers," with its stress on individual conscience, opened the floodgates for a variety of interpretations of the Bible and a profusion of Protestant sects. Luther neither foresaw nor welcomed this development.

Nor did Luther intend to separate church from state. Indeed, one reason that Luther's challenge to the supremacy of the church succeeded where earlier challenges had failed is that Luther was able to win the protection of the German princes, many of whom saw in the controversy a welcome opportunity to gain wealth and power at the church's expense. In any case, in Germany and elsewhere the immediate effect of the Reformation was to forge an alliance between a king or prince, on the one hand, and the leaders of a reformed or Protestant church, on the other. In this way, various local or national churches began to challenge the authority of the universal church.

England soon provided the clearest example of a national church. King Henry VIII (r. 1509–1547), angered by the pope's refusal to grant him permission to divorce his first wife, declared the Church of England separate from Rome and, with the approval of the English Parliament, made himself its head. A church of a different sort emerged in Geneva. Now part of Switzerland, Geneva was an independent city-state when Jean Calvin (1509–1564), a French Protestant, became its leader in political as well as in religious matters. Like most of the other Protestants or reformers, Calvin was no more inclined to distinguish politics from religion, or church from state, than were his Roman Catholic opponents. The point of the Reformation was not to enable people to believe as they saw fit, but literally to *reform* the church so that people could believe as reformers thought they should. Under Calvin's leadership, Geneva became a **theocracy**. The law of the city was to be a direct reflection of God's will, to the extent that a pastor could enter a house at any hour of the day or night to make sure that no one was violating God's commandments.

Where the political authorities remained loyal to the Roman Catholic Church, they often tried to suppress the Protestants. In such cases Luther and Calvin usually counselled their followers not to resist their rulers, since God gave rulers their power to do His will. Later, however, some of Calvin's followers concluded not only that resistance is sometimes justified but also that the people have a right to overthrow any ruler who denies them the free exercise of their religion. By this, they meant the exercise of their form of Calvinism, to be sure, because few of them wanted to allow the free exercise of other religions. Yet their arguments for freedom of conscience, which rested in part on the claim that government receives its authority from the consent of the people, planted the seeds of the argument in favour of religious toleration.

Before the seeds of religious toleration could sprout, however, people had to be convinced that it was either wrong or simply impossible to replace enforced conformity to the Roman Catholic Church with enforced conformity to one or another of the Protestant churches. This belief did not begin to take hold until the seventeenth century, and then only after a series of bloody religious wars persuaded some, such as John Locke, that it was better to tolerate some differences of religion than to try to win converts at the point of a sword.

Quite unintentionally, then, the Protestant reformers helped to prepare the way for liberalism. By teaching that salvation comes through faith alone, Luther and the other reformers encouraged people to value individual conscience more than the preservation of unity and orthodoxy. Moving from individual conscience to individual liberty was still a radical step for the time, but it was a step that the early liberals took.

The Emergence of Capitalism

The individualism inherent in Protestant religious belief was also connected with the emergence of capitalism in Western Europe. The system of economic organization generally referred to as capitalism is characterized by free markets; that is, economic activity with minimum restrictions that leaves individuals to acquire as much wealth and property as their talents, enterprise, and good fortune allow. An emphasis on individual contact with and responsibility to God made Protestants inner-directed and self-disciplined. Protestant theology sometimes led its followers to believe that material success was a sign of God's favour and was in fact something to be striven for. Roman Catholic religious holidays were viewed as invitations to laziness and sinful self-indulgence by the peasants; the property of the church was viewed as something to be taken and turned to greater profit. Although some capitalist attitudes and procedures, such as banking, started in the Northern Italian Renaissance city-states, capitalism reached its full flowering in the Protestant north—England, Holland, and Scotland.

Liberalism began as an attempt to free individuals from the constraints of religious conformity and ascribed status. It also began, as most ideologies have begun, as an attempt to bring about a fundamental transformation of society. It was, in short, revolutionary. To see this more clearly, we need to look at the great revolutions of the seventeenth and eighteenth centuries.

LIBERALISM AND REVOLUTION

The English Revolution of 1688

In 1588, under the leadership of Queen Elizabeth I, England defeated the Spanish Armada and entered the seventeenth century more secure and powerful than it had ever been. Culture and learning flourished, with contributions to literature by William Shakespeare, John Donne, and John Milton; to philosophy by Thomas Hobbes and John Locke; and to science by Isaac Newton and William Harvey, the physician who discovered the circulation of blood. Commerce and exploration also flourished and English colonies sprang up in North America.

But the seventeenth century was also a time of turmoil for England. Elizabeth was succeeded in 1603 by a distant cousin, James Stuart, King of Scotland. The new king soon found himself engaged in a power struggle with Parliament, a struggle that grew more heated during the reign of his son, Charles I. Money was often at the root of the conflict, with Charles insisting that he had a right, as king, to gather revenue through taxes, while Parliament insisted that this was its right as the body representing the people of England. In 1642 the conflict erupted into civil war.

The war between Crown and Parliament was further fuelled by religious, social, and economic conflicts. For many people the war was primarily a religious conflict. As king, Charles I was the official head of the Church of England, and all the English were expected to conform to the beliefs and practices of that church. Those loyal to the Church of England tended to support the king, while the dissenting Puritans took the side of Parliament. Puritans often disagreed with one another—some were Presbyterians, some Independents or Separatists (eventually called Congregationalists)—but all wanted to "purify" the Church of England of the traces of Roman Catholicism they thought it had retained. Their hope, in general, was to enforce conformity to their religion, just as those who supported the established church sought to enforce conformity to theirs.

The social and economic divisions are less clear, but generally the land-owning aristocracy supported the king while the smaller landowners and the merchants supported Parliament.

In the English Civil War, pen and ink played as great a part as bullets and swords. From every side came a vast outpouring of pamphlets, treatises, sermons, and even major works of political theory. In Chapter 2, we noted the efforts of James Harrington, who argued for a republican form of government, and of the Levellers, who pressed the case for a more democratic form. The first major works of political philosophy to bear the distinctive stamp of liberalism were Thomas Hobbes's *Leviathan* and John Locke's *Two Treatises of Government* and *Letter concerning Toleration*.

Thomas Hobbes. Thomas Hobbes (1588–1679) wrote *Leviathan* in France, where he had fled to avoid the war, and published it in 1651, two years after the beheading of Charles I brought the war to an end. There was nothing new in the conclusion he reached in *Leviathan*. Like St. Paul and many others, Hobbes maintained that the people of a country should obey those who have power over them. But he refused to base this conclusion on the simple claim that this was God's will. Even though Hobbes cited the Scriptures, his argument was fundamentally secular—and, he thought, "scientific"—as it was based on self-interest rather than divine commands.

According to Hobbes, the individual should obey whoever is in power, as long as the person or persons in power protects him or her. The only reason for government in the first place is to provide protection or security. To prove his point, Hobbes asked his readers

Thomas Hobbes (1588–1679)

to imagine that they were in a **state of nature**, a condition of perfect freedom in which no one had any authority over them. In such a state, he said, all individuals are equal—no one is born to hold a higher rank or status than anyone else—and have a **natural right** to do as they wish. The problem is human nature: "I put for a general inclination of all mankind, a perpetuall and restlesse desire of Power after power, that ceaseth onely in Death."[2] This "restlesse desire" for power leads individuals into conflict with one another and turns the state of nature into a "warre of every man against every man" where life can be nothing but "solitary, poore, nasty, brutish, and short."[3]

Hobbes's state of nature thus became a state of war. In Hobbes's view, nothing could be worse than this. So the fearful, self-interested, and rational individuals in the state of nature enter into a **social contract** to establish political authority. To provide for their security, they surrender all but one of their natural rights—the right to defend themselves—to those to whom they grant authority. On Hobbes's argument, then, government is founded on the consent of the people. But by their consent, the people authorize the sovereign—the person or persons in power—to do anything necessary to maintain order and peace. The sovereign's authority includes the power to force everyone to worship as he or she requires, for Hobbes saw religious differences as one of the leading sources of conflict. For the sake of security, the people grant the sovereign absolute, unlimited power, retaining only the right to defend themselves when the sovereign directly threatens them.

Given this conclusion, the claim that *Leviathan* bears the distinctive stamp of liberalism may seem odd. Liberals certainly have not made a habit of supporting absolute rulers or enforcing religious conformity. What gives Hobbes's theory a distinctly liberal tinge is not his conclusion, but his premises. Individuals are competitive and self-interested, on Hobbes's account, and everyone equally has a natural right to be free. They create government through their consent in order to protect their interests. In these respects, Hobbes's position is very much that of a liberal or, as some prefer to say, a "protoliberal"—that is, one who articulated the main premises of an emerging liberal ideology. It remained for John Locke to use these premises to reach conclusions that were definitely liberal.

John Locke. John Locke (1632–1704) was sixteen years old when Charles I was beheaded and Parliament abolished the monarchy. Yet only eleven years later, Parliament invited the son of the late king to return from his exile in France—where Hobbes had been one of his tutors—to restore the monarchy. This Restoration brought relief from political turmoil, but it proved to be only temporary. As Charles II grew older, it became clear that he would leave no legitimate heir to the throne, which placed his brother, James, next in succession. Suspicion arose that James, a Roman Catholic, would try to take England back into the Roman Catholic camp—and would become, like his cousin Louis XIV of France, an absolute ruler. To prevent this, an effort was mounted to exclude James from the throne. During the Exclusion Crisis of 1680–1683, Charles II suspended Parliament and his opponents responded with plots and uprisings against him. The effort failed—James became King James II upon Charles's death in 1685—but it did lead John Locke to begin writing his *Two Treatises of Government*.

---

[2]Thomas Hobbes, *Leviathan*, chapter 11; see Terence Ball and Richard Dagger, eds., *Ideals and Ideologies: A Reader*, 8th ed. (New York: Longman, 2011) selection 3.10.
[3]Hobbes, chapter 13.

John Locke (1632–1704)

Locke completed the *Two Treatises* while in exile in Holland, where he had fled for safety in 1683. In Holland, then the most tolerant country in Europe, Locke also wrote his *Letter Concerning Toleration.* Both works were published in England after the Glorious Revolution of 1688 forced James II to flee to France. James's daughter Mary and her husband, William, Prince of Orange (in the Netherlands), became England's new monarchs. In assuming the throne, however, William and Mary accepted the Bill of Rights, which recognized the "true, ancient, and indubitable rights of the people of this realm"[4] and the supremacy of Parliament. From this time forward, England would become a **constitutional monarchy**, with the king or queen clearly subject to the law of the land. Furthermore, in the *Toleration Act* (1689), Parliament granted freedom of worship to dissenters—those Protestants who refused to join the established Church of England. (The act did not apply to Roman Catholics.)

These developments were very much to Locke's liking. In the *Letter Concerning Toleration,* he argued that it is wrong for governments to force their subjects to conform to a particular religion. Drawing a distinction between private and public matters, Locke said that religious belief is normally a private concern and not a proper subject for government interference. Governments should tolerate diverse religious beliefs unless the practice of those beliefs directly threatens the public order. But Roman Catholicism should *not* be tolerated for exactly this reason: Roman Catholics owe their first loyalty to

---

[4]Quoted in Herbert Muller, *Freedom in the Western World: From the Dark Ages to the Rise of Democracy* (New York: Harper, 1963) 307. The English Bill of Rights should not be confused with the U.S. Bill of Rights, which comprises the first ten amendments to the U.S. Constitution.

a foreign monarch, the pope, so they cannot be trustworthy members of a commonwealth. Locke also denied toleration to atheists for a similar reason, claiming that anyone who denied the existence of God, salvation, and damnation could not be trusted at all. If these seem severe restrictions by our standards, they were nonetheless quite liberal, even radical, by the standards of Locke's time.

As important as his argument for toleration was, Locke's theory of political authority in the second of his *Two Treatises of Government* (1690) marked an even more important milestone in the development of liberalism. Locke's purpose in the *Second Treatise* was much the same as Hobbes's in *Leviathan*—to establish the true basis for political author- ity or government—and in several crucial respects his premises resemble Hobbes's. He began his argument, as Hobbes did, with the state of nature, where everyone is free and equal. There is no ascribed status in this state of nature, "there being nothing more evi- dent, than that Creatures of the same species and rank promiscuously born to all the same advantages of Nature, and the use of the same faculties, should also be equal one amongst another without Subordination or Subjection."[5] There are natural rights, though, which Locke usually referred to as "life, liberty, and property." A person may surrender or forfeit these rights—by attacking others, for instance, a person may forfeit his right to life or liberty—but no one can simply take them away.

Unlike Hobbes's state of nature, Locke's is *not* a state of war. It is "inconvenient," however, largely because many people are unwilling to respect the rights of others. Recog- nizing this difficulty, people in the state of nature enter into a social contract to establish a political society with laws and a government to make, interpret, and enforce those laws. But we should remember, Locke said, that people create government to do a job—to pro- tect their natural rights. The government has authority only insofar as it does what it needs to do to preserve the lives, liberty, and property of its subjects. If the government begins to violate these rights by depriving its subjects of life, liberty, and property, then the people have the right to overthrow the government and establish a new one in its place.

Although he began with premises very similar to Hobbes's, Locke reached a very different conclusion. Both denied that social status is somehow fixed or ascribed by nature, and both believed that government is founded on the consent of the people, but Locke believed that people can consent to create and obey only a limited or constitutional government. To give anyone total and absolute power over people's lives would be both irrational and contrary to the will of God. Both also believed that people have natural rights, but for Locke these included a right to worship as one chose, within limits, and *a right of* **revolution**—a right that would later be invoked in the American Declaration of Independence.

The American Revolution

Neither the American nor the French Revolution was the direct result of Locke's writ- ings. In both cases a variety of social, economic, and religious factors combined with philosophical and political issues to lead to revolution.

The thirteen English colonies that eventually became the United States were settled during England's turbulent seventeenth century. Perhaps because it was preoccupied with

---

[5]John Locke, *Second Treatise of Government,* paragraph 4; see Ball and Dagger, selection 3.11.

problems at home, the government in London generally left the colonists to look after their own affairs during the 1600s. This continued throughout the first half of the eighteenth century, a relatively stable period in British politics. The colonies had governors appointed by the Crown, but they also had their own legislatures and raised their own taxes. The colonists consequently took it for granted that they enjoyed all the rights of Englishmen, including the right to constitutional self-government through elected representatives.

But in 1763, at the end of the Seven Years' War, the British government began to levy taxes on the colonists in order to pay for the war and the defence of the colonies. The colonists objected that this violated their rights as Englishmen. Parliament had no right to tax the American colonists, they argued, as long as the colonists elected no representatives to Parliament. For Parliament to tax them when they had no voice in the matter was tantamount to taking their property without their consent. Indeed, the colonists' position was quite simple: "No taxation without representation!"

Parliament's response was to point out that the colonists were in exactly the same situation as most of the people of England, where only a small minority enjoyed the right to vote at this time. Because of corruption and an archaic electoral system, whole cities were without representatives; yet all British subjects were virtually represented by the members of Parliament who looked after the interests of the entire Commonwealth. The colonists replied to this argument by saying, in effect, that if the people of England were foolish enough to settle for virtual representation, so much the worse for them. As the colonists saw it, if representation is not actual, it is not representation at all.

This quarrel was what led to armed revolt in 1775. In the beginning the colonists maintained that they were loyal subjects of the Crown who fought only to restore their rights—rights that the British government was supposed to protect but had instead violated. Yet in little more than a year they abandoned this position to take the radical step of declaring themselves independent of the United Kingdom.

The colonists took steps toward independence in part because of the arguments set out in *Common Sense,* a pamphlet written and published in February 1776 by Thomas Paine (1737–1809). The arguments of *Common Sense* are quite similar to Locke's in the *Second Treatise,* but Paine expressed them in a vivid and memorable way. Society is always a blessing, Paine said, but government, even the best government, is a "necessary evil."[6] It is evil because it coerces us and controls our lives, but it is necessary because most of us, fallen creatures that we are, cannot be trusted to respect the natural rights of others. To protect our natural rights, we create government. If the government does its job, it deserves our obedience. But if it fails to protect our natural rights—if it turns against us and violates our rights—the government ceases to be a necessary evil and becomes an intolerable one. When this happens, Paine concluded, the people have every right to overthrow their government and replace it with one that will respect their rights.

Paine believed the American colonies should sever their ties with Britain and establish themselves as an independent, self-governing state. If it is to be truly self-governing, though, the new state must be a republic. Paine took this to mean that there must be no king, for he believed monarchy to be absolutely incompatible with individual liberty. In this respect, he went beyond Locke, who may have preferred to abolish monarchy but did not say so in the *Second Treatise.*

---

[6]Thomas Paine, *Common Sense* (Philadelphia, 1776); see www.bartleby.com/133/1.html.

The argument of the American Declaration of Independence of 1776, as well as some of its striking phrases, closely resembles Locke's.[7] Certain "truths" are "self-evident":

> that all men are created equal, that they are endowed by their Creator with certain unalienable Rights, that among these are Life, Liberty, and the pursuit of Happiness.—That to secure these rights, Governments are instituted among Men, deriving their just powers from the consent of the governed.—That whenever any Form of Government becomes destructive of these ends, it is the Right of the People to alter or to abolish it, and to institute new Government, laying its foundation on such principles, and organizing its powers in such form, as to them shall seem most likely to effect their Safety and Happiness.[8]

The claim that "all men are created equal" caused some embarrassment when the declaration was issued. A number of colonists, American patriots as well as pro-British tories, pointed out that it was hypocritical for a slave-holding country to proclaim the equality of all humankind. This embarrassment reveals a more general problem in the position of the early liberals. They spoke a democratic language when they proclaimed that all men are naturally free and equal and that government rests on the consent of the people, yet they never explained whom they counted as "men" or "the people." For instance, Locke's references to men and the people make him seem to be a democrat. But Locke did not clearly advocate an extension of voting rights beyond the property holders who were allowed to vote in his day; he also held shares in a company engaged in the slave trade.[9] Locke and other early liberals simply took it for granted, moreover, that natural equality and the right to self-government did not include women.[10] By making these claims, however, early liberals provided an opening for those who could say, "If all men are created equal, why isn't this or that group of men or women being treated as equals?" By speaking the language of equality, in other words, they contributed, perhaps unwittingly, to the growth of democracy and the expansion of the franchise.

The defence of the rights and liberties of individuals against government is also typical of early liberals, who saw government as a continuing threat to individual liberty. This attitude shows the influence of classical republicanism, with its constant warnings about the danger of corruption. Indeed, the republican and liberal traditions were so closely entwined at this point that it is difficult to separate them. But there were differences of emphasis. The republicans worried about the corruption of the people as much as the corruption of the government, while early liberals were concerned almost exclusively with the abuse of power by government. As republicans saw it, freedom was largely a matter of governing oneself through political participation, and therefore closely connected with civic virtue; in the liberal view, freedom was more a matter of being free from interference by the government, and virtue something to be learned and practised in private life.

---

[7]For a systematic comparison of the Declaration of Independence and Locke's arguments, see Garrett Ward Sheldon, *The Political Philosophy of Thomas Jefferson* (Baltimore: Johns Hopkins UP, 1991) 42–49.

[8]See Ball and Dagger, selection 3.13.

[9]See James Farr, "'So Vile and Miserable an Estate': The Problem of Slavery in Locke's Political Thought," *Political Theory* 14 (1986): 263–289.

[10]For a debate on Locke's feminism, see Melissa Butler, "Early Liberal Roots of Feminism: John Locke and the Attack on Patriarchy," *American Political Science Review* 72 (1978): 135–150; and Terence Ball, "Comment on Butler," *American Political Science Review* 73 (1979): 549–550, followed by Butler's "Reply," ibid., 550–551.

The French Revolution

To understand the French Revolution and liberalism's role in it, we need to know something about the *ancien régime*—the old order of French society in the years before the Revolution. Three features of this old order are particularly important: its religious conformity, its aristocratic privilege, and its **political absolutism**.

In the years following the Reformation, France suffered a series of bloody civil wars between Huguenots (French Protestants) and Roman Catholics. Most of the violence ended in 1598 with the Edict of Nantes, a compromise that granted freedom of worship to the Huguenots while acknowledging Roman Catholicism as the official religion. This lasted until 1685, when Louis XIV, the so-called Sun King, revoked the edict and required all his subjects to conform to Roman Catholic doctrine. From then until the eve of the Revolution, religious conformity remained government policy. This favoured status, together with its wealth from its extensive landholdings, made the Roman Catholic Church a bulwark of the *ancien régime*—and a major obstacle for those who desired a more open society. Chief among these were the thinkers of the **Enlightenment**, such as Voltaire (1694–1778), who believed that the light of reason would lead to a better understanding of the world and a freer, more rational society. For this to happen, however, reason would first have to overcome the forces of superstition—forces led, as they saw it, by the Roman Catholic Church.

Aristocratic privilege, the second leading feature of the old order, was a vestige of feudalism. In France, the roots of the aristocracy were very deep indeed. Most aristocrats, or nobles, were anxious to preserve the special rights they enjoyed, including exemption from most taxes. This exemption was greatly resented by those who bore the burden of taxation—the middle class (bourgeoisie) and the peasants. Another important privilege the nobles enjoyed was their almost exclusive right to high positions in the government, military, and church. Louis XVI, who was king when the Revolution began, chose almost all his advisers and administrators from the nobility and required all candidates for officer's rank in the army to have at least four generations of noble blood.[11] Aristocratic privilege meant that in the *ancien régime*, ascribed status counted far more than ability or effort—something else the bourgeoisie greatly resented.

Finally, political absolutism placed the king above the law and concentrated political power in the throne. This was the legacy of Louis XIV, whose long reign (r. 1643–1715) set the pattern for absolute monarchy. According to tradition, the king of France was responsible to the Estates General, which consisted of representatives of the three orders or estates of the country: the clergy, the nobility, and the bourgeoisie. But Louis XIV never convened the Estates General—it had last met in 1614—and found ways of appeasing and weakening the three estates. He secured the church's support by suppressing the Huguenots; he drew the nobility to his extravagant court at Versailles, where they became dependent upon his favour; and he flattered the bourgeoisie by choosing some of his government ministers from their ranks. With no effective opposition to limit his power, Louis XIV was able to govern as he saw fit. As he supposedly said, "*L'état, c'est moi*" ("I am the state").

Neither of his successors—Louis XV (r. 1715–1774) and Louis XVI (r. 1774–1792)—was as adept as the Sun King at exercising absolute authority, but both followed his

---

[11]Muller 382.

example. Neither summoned the Estates General, for instance, until a financial crisis in 1788 finally forced Louis XVI to do so. This event sparked the Revolution.

When Louis XVI called for elections to the Estates General in the winter of 1788–1789, he and the nobles expected the representatives of the First and Second Estates—the clergy and the nobility—to prevent any drastic action by the Third Estate, or the people. But the Third Estate insisted on double representation, and public pressure forced the king to concede. Then, with the support of some liberal nobles and parish priests, the deputies of the Third Estate declared themselves the National Assembly and began to draft a constitution for France. The French Revolution had begun.

Although the Revolution ended ten bloody years later with a new form of absolutism, the revolutionaries' original aim was to establish a limited government that would protect the natural rights of French citizens—rights that the French kings had refused to acknowledge. The revolutionaries wanted to overthrow the *ancien régime* and to replace religious conformity with tolerance, aristocratic privilege with equality of opportunity, and absolute monarchy with constitutional government. These aims are evident in their Declaration of the Rights of Man and of the Citizen of 1789. In the first of the declaration's seventeen articles, the National Assembly attacked aristocratic privilege and ascribed status:

> I. Men are born, and always continue, free and equal in respect of their rights. Civil distinctions [i.e., ranks or estates], therefore, can be founded only on public utility.

The second and third articles attacked political absolutism, proclaiming that government rests on the consent of the governed:

> II. The end [i.e., goal] of all political associations is the preservation of the natural and impre-scriptible rights of man; and these rights are liberty, property, security, and resistance of oppression.

> III. The nation is essentially the source of all sovereignty; nor can any individual, or any body of men, be entitled to any authority which is not expressly derived from it.

Nor did the National Assembly overlook religious conformity. In the tenth article of the declaration it declared,

> X. No man ought to be molested on account of his opinions, not even on account of his *religious* opinions, provided his avowal of them does not disturb the public order established by the law.[12]

Liberalism was not the only current of thought in the French Revolution; republicanism, with its emphasis on civic virtue, also played a part. "Liberty, Equality, Fraternity"—the famous slogan of the Revolution—suggests how liberalism and republicanism were entwined, as they had been in the American Revolution. Every man has a right to be free, the argument went, because all are born equal, and each should have an equal opportunity to succeed. Yet liberty and equality were also prized in republican terms as the chief ingredients in an active public life directed toward virtue. The cry for **fraternity** also evoked republican themes, suggesting that the divisive civil distinctions be replaced with a sense of common citizenship. With this in mind, the revolutionaries abandoned the

---

[12]As translated in Thomas Paine, *The Rights of Man* (1792); emphasis in original. For the full text of the Decla-ration of Rights, see Ball and Dagger, selection 16.

traditional titles or salutations of *monsieur* and *madame* and began to address everyone as *citoyen* or *citoyenne* ("citizen"). *Fraternity* implied that there is more to life than being free to pursue one's private interests; indeed, a citizen has a responsibility to participate actively in public life.[13] *Fraternity* also implied an interest in solidarity, in putting the common good ahead of one's private desires. The term took on nationalistic overtones as the French thought of themselves less as subjects of a monarch than as citizens of a single nation.

As the Revolution continued, church lands were secularized and sold, and in 1791, the National Assembly drafted a constitution that limited the powers of the king, abolished the three estates, and granted the right to vote to more than half the adult males. France thus became, in theory, a constitutional monarchy, with a government more limited and a franchise more democratic than the monarchy in Britain.

Once begun, the Revolution could not be stopped. The more radical revolutionaries demanded greater democracy, help for the poor, and less concern for the protection of property. War broke out when Prussia and Austria sent armies to the French borders to check the spread of revolution and restore the *ancien régime*. One economic crisis followed another. Under the pressure of these circumstances, the revolutionaries abolished the monarchy and established the Republic of France on September 22, 1792; later revolutionaries proclaimed this the first day of the first month of the Year I, the beginning of a new era of history that required a new calendar. The events of the next year were no less dramatic. The execution of Louis XVI in January was followed by a new constitution granting universal suffrage to men. Then came the Reign of Terror, from June 1793 until July 1794. During this period the guillotine became the chief symbol of the Revolution. Some 300 000 people were arrested on suspicion of betraying the Republic, and more than 17 000 were executed before cheering crowds. The Terror ended when its principal leader, Maximilien Robespierre, was himself beheaded; in 1795 a measure of calm was restored under another constitution. Less democratic than its predecessor, the Constitution of 1795 restricted the vote to the property-owning bourgeoisie and created a five-member Directory to head the government. This arrangement survived until 1799, when Napoleon Bonaparte seized power and turned France into a military dictatorship. He later proclaimed himself emperor with almost absolute powers.

LIBERALISM AND ECONOMIC LIBERTY

In both the Old World and the New, then, liberalism was a vigorous revolutionary force. In the name of natural rights and the rights of man, liberals struggled for individual liberty against the social, political, and religious arrangements inherited from the Middle Ages. A central aspect of this struggle was the quest for *economic liberty*.

By opposing ascribed status, early liberals sought wider opportunities for more people beyond the privileged few born into the nobility. Economic opportunity was particularly important to the merchants, bankers, and lawyers who made up the middle class, or bourgeoisie. For them, acquiring wealth was the main avenue of social advancement. But in early modern Europe, this avenue was blocked by numerous restrictions on manufacturing and commerce. These restrictions included the traditional Christian limits on

---

[13]Michael Walzer, "Citizenship," *Political Innovation and Conceptual Change,* eds. Terence Ball, James Farr, and Russell L. Hanson (Cambridge: Cambridge UP, 1989) 211–219, provides an insightful account of the notion of citizenship in the French Revolution.

usury—the practice of charging interest on loans—and various local regulations concerning working conditions and the production, distribution, and sale of goods. In the seventeenth and eighteenth centuries, still other restrictions stemmed from the economic theory of **mercantilism**.

Mercantilism

According to mercantilist theory, one country could improve its economic strength only at the expense of others. Acting on this theory, European nation-states engaged in economic warfare that frequently led to real combat. One tactic was to establish colonies, extract their resources, and forbid the colonists to buy from or sell to anyone but the mother country. Another was to set high tariffs, or taxes on imported goods, to discourage the sale of foreign goods and encourage the growth of domestic industries. A third tactic involved **monopoly**, the practice of granting exclusive control over a market to a single firm on the grounds that this was the most efficient way to handle the risks of trade between the far-flung colonies and the European homeland. Two leading examples of monopolies were the Dutch East India and the British East India Companies, each of which had the exclusive right to govern as well as to trade with vast colonial territories.

Mercantilism attempted to promote the national interest directly through the use of restraints and monopolistic privileges. These attempts worked to the advantage of some—especially those who were able to secure the privileges—and to the disadvantage of others. The middle class, which generally fell into this second camp, pressed for a wider and more nearly equal opportunity to compete for profits. They believed that anything less was an unjust obstacle in the way of individual liberty. This liberal belief found expression in the economic theory of **capitalism**.

Capitalism

Under capitalism, economic exchanges take place in a free market as a private matter between persons pursuing profits. This emphasis on private profit ran against the grain of much of the Roman Catholic and republican traditions, neither of which assigned great value to either the private realm or to profits. However, as we have noted, the emphasis on private profit was more consistent with Protestant attitudes. The 1700s produced some forceful statements of the argument that people ought to be free to pursue their private interests, including their economic interests. One of the first was *The Fable of the Bees,* published in 1714 by Bernard de Mandeville (1670–1733). Mandeville's fable is the story of a hive in which the bees, shocked by their own selfishness, decide to reform and act with the good of others in mind. But reform proves disastrous. Soldier, servant, merchant, and most of the other bees are thrown out of work because there is no demand for their services. The richness and variety of life are gone. Indeed, Mandeville suggests, the hive was much better off in the old, selfish days when the bees acted out of vanity and greed—a time when

every Part was full of Vice,

Yet the whole Mass a Paradise;

. . .

Such were the Blessings of that state;

Their Crimes conspir'd to make them Great.

The moral of the story, captured in the subtitle of the *Fable,* is *Private Vices, Publick Benefits.*

This idea—that the best way to promote the good of society as a whole is to let people pursue their private interests—became the cornerstone of liberal economic thought in the eighteenth century. In the middle of the century a group of French thinkers, the **Physiocrats**, developed this idea into an economic theory. Arguing against mercantilism, the Physiocrats maintained that the true basis of wealth is neither trade nor manufacturing but agriculture. Furthermore, they claimed, the best way to cultivate wealth is not through regulations and restrictions but through unrestrained or free enterprise. Their advice to governments—remove regulations and leave people alone to compete in the market-place—was captured in the phrase *laissez faire, laissez passer* ("let it be, leave it alone").

Adam Smith. The most thorough and influential defence of *laissez-faire* approach was Adam Smith's *An Inquiry into the Nature and Causes of the Wealth of Nations* (1776). Smith (1723–1790), a Scottish philosopher and economist, agreed with the Physiocrats' attack on mercantilism and monopoly. Far from serving the public interest, Smith said, restraints on economic competition serve only the interests of those few people who are able to take advantage of them. For most people, lack of competition simply means higher prices and scarcer goods.

As a remedy, Smith recommended an economic policy that would allow individuals to compete freely in the marketplace. This is not only the fairest policy, since it gives

Adam Smith (1723–1790)

everyone an equal opportunity, but also the most efficient. There is nothing like self-interest—in this case, the desire for profits—to motivate people to provide the goods and services that others want. As Smith put it, "It is not from the benevolence of the butcher, the brewer, or the baker that we expect our dinner, but from their regard to their own interest. We address ourselves, not to their humanity but to their self-love, and never talk to them of our own necessities but of their advantage."[14] Smith reasoned that removing economic restrictions and privileges will encourage people to produce and sell goods for a profit. In order to turn a profit, producers have to produce either a better or a cheaper good than their competitors; otherwise, people will not buy their products. Private interest, set free, will thus indirectly promote the public good by making available more and better and cheaper goods. It is, Smith said, as if an invisible hand were directing all of these self-interested competitors to serve the common interest of the whole society.

Smith also argued against the mercantilists for free trade between countries. If people in some foreign land can sell us something we want for less than it costs to produce it ourselves, then let them do it. Smith said that high taxes on foreign imports may encourage industry at home, but it does so at great cost to the consumer, who has fewer and more expensive goods available. In the long run, peaceful and unrestricted trade between countries benefits everyone.

From Smith's point of view, government should have as little as possible to do with economic exchanges. Government has only three proper functions, he said. First, it must defend the country against invasion. Second, it must promote justice—mostly by protecting property rights—and maintain order. Finally, it must provide certain "public works" and institutions that private enterprise will not provide, such as roads, bridges, canals, and harbours (what economists now term the infrastructure necessary to the conduct of business), as well as public education. All other matters are best left to the private business of self-interested individuals, who should be free to make their way in the world as they see fit. In this respect, Smith and other advocates of capitalism took a liberal position.

Britain was not only the principal source of the theory of classical **laissez-faire** liberal capitalism, but also the place where a market-based capitalist economy first came fully into existence in the late eighteenth and early nineteenth centuries.

LIBERALISM IN NINETEENTH-CENTURY BRITAIN

At the beginning of the nineteenth century, the British Empire continued to expand. The thirteen American colonies had gained their independence, but Britain continued to control India, the various colonies in British North America (Canada), and Australia, and it was soon to acquire vast territories in Africa as well. The Industrial Revolution was also making Britain the world's first great industrial power. Beginning in about 1750, the invention of new machinery, the discovery of steam power, and the development of assembly lines and other mass production techniques brought about a remarkable increase in productive power. British merchants were able to import raw materials such as cotton and to manufacture goods to be sold at home and abroad for handsome profits. With its

---

[14]Adam Smith, *The Wealth of Nations*, book I, chapter 2; see Ball and Dagger, selection 3.15.

combination of empire and industry, Britain became "the workshop of the world"—and the world's greatest imperial power—in the nineteenth century.

But power comes at a price, and in Britain the price was a society more sharply divided along class lines. Although the landed aristocracy was still the dominant force in the early 1800s, middle-class merchants and professionals made enormous political and economic gains during the first half of the century. The same cannot be said of the men, women, and children of the working class. Poor and numerous, they toiled in the mines, mills, and factories that sprang up during the Industrial Revolution, and their situation was bleak indeed. Without unemployment compensation, regulation of working hours or safety conditions, or the legal right to form trade or labour unions, they worked under extremely harsh and insecure conditions. Just how harsh conditions were is suggested by a bill proposed in Parliament early in the century to *improve* the workers' position. The bill forbade factories from employing children under the age of ten, putting anyone under eighteen on night work (i.e., from 9:00 p.m. to 5:00 a.m.), and requiring anyone under eighteen to work more than ten and a half hours a day. This bill did not even pass until, after years of debate, it had been so weakened as to be ineffective.[15]

In economic status and in political power, too, the working class fell far behind the middle class in the first half of the nineteenth century. The Reform Bill of 1832 lowered property qualifications enough to give middle-class males the right to vote, but most adult males and all women were still denied suffrage. This was a matter of some concern to the leading liberal writers of the day, a group known then as the Philosophic Radicals and later as the **Utilitarians**.

Utilitarianism

Jeremy Bentham. The original leader of the Utilitarians was the English philosopher Jeremy Bentham (1748–1832). Society must be made more rational, he insisted, and the first step in this direction is to recognize that people act out of self-interest. Moreover, everyone has an interest in experiencing pleasure and avoiding pain. As Bentham put it, "Nature has placed mankind under the governance of two sovereign masters, *pain* and *pleasure.* It is for them alone to point out what we ought to do, as well as to determine what we shall do."[16] This is simply a fact of human nature, he thought, and there is nothing we can do to change it. But once we understand that all people seek pleasure and avoid pain in everything they do, we can take steps to be more efficient pleasure-seekers and pain-avoiders.

Bentham did not mean that we should seek pleasure in immediate gratification—in getting drunk, for example—because the pain we or others suffer later will probably outweigh the short-term pleasure. He meant that we should seek **utility**. Something has utility—a hammer for a carpenter, for instance, or money for almost everyone—if it helps someone do what he or she wants. Since people want to be happy, utility promotes happiness.

---

[15]J. Bronowski and Bruce Mazlish, *The Western Intellectual Tradition: Leonardo to Hegel* (New York: Harper, 1960) 455.

[16]Jeremy Bentham, *Introduction to the Principles of Morals and Legislation* (New York: Hafner, 1948) 1.

Jeremy Bentham (1748–1832)

Bentham recognized that people will sometimes fail to see what does and does not have utility for them—for example, someone who drops out of school may not appreciate the utility of education. He also admitted that in pursuing our own pleasures, we may bring pain to others. But the purpose of government is to solve these problems. In Bentham's words, "The business of government is to promote the happiness of society, by punishing and rewarding."[17] By punishing those who cause pain to others and by rewarding those who give pleasure, government can and should act to promote the greatest happiness of the greatest number.

Bentham drew two general conclusions about government. The first was that government could promote the greatest happiness of the greatest number simply by leaving people alone. Individuals are usually the best judges of their own interests, so government should usually let people act as they see fit. For this reason Bentham accepted the *laissez-faire* arguments of Adam Smith. His second conclusion was that government is not likely to promote the greatest happiness of the greatest number if it is controlled by a small segment of society. In the pursuit of utility, everyone has to count equally, Bentham declared. Government must weigh everyone's interests, and this requires that almost everyone be allowed to vote. Although Bentham's views on voting are not altogether clear, he did support universal male suffrage and, with certain reservations, the vote for women.[18]

---

[17]Bentham 70.
[18]For Bentham's views on voting, see Terence Ball, "Utilitarianism, Feminism and the Franchise," *History of Political Thought* 1 (1980): 91–115.

John Stuart Mill (1806–1873)

John Stuart Mill. The views of John Stuart Mill (1806–1873) on the vote for women are not in doubt, for Mill was an ardent advocate of women's rights. An influential Utilitarian, Mill was the leading liberal philosopher of the nineteenth century. Whether supporting women's rights or arguing that government should set minimum educational standards for all, Mill's greatest concern was to defend and extend individual liberty. This concern is most evident in his essay *On Liberty.*

When Mill published *On Liberty* in 1859, liberalism seemed to have triumphed, at least in England and the United States. The old enemies—ascribed status, religious conformity, and absolute government—were no longer the obstacles to individual liberty they once had been. Yet Mill was alarmed by what he took to be a new threat to liberty in the growing power of public opinion. In the old days, Mill said, the chief enemy of freedom was the government, but now that we elect representatives, the government is more responsive to the desires of the people. However, government is responsive to the majority of the people, or at least to the majority of those who vote, allowing them to use government to restrict or take away the liberty of those who do not share the majority's views. Moreover, the majority can bring social pressure to bear on those who do not conform to the ordinary, conventional ways of life. Without going through the government or the law, the moral coercion of public opinion can stifle freedom of thought and action by making social outcasts of individuals who do not conform to social customs and conventional beliefs. Mill was worried about the **"tyranny of the majority."**

On Liberty was Mill's attempt to deal with this new form of tyranny. There he advanced "one very simple principle": "The only purpose for which power can be rightfully exercised over any member of a civilized community, against his will, is to prevent harm to others. His own good, either physical or moral, is not a sufficient warrant."[19] According to this principle—sometimes called the **harm principle**—every sane adult should be free to do

---

[19]John Stuart Mill, *On Liberty*, chapter 1; see Ball and Dagger, selection 3.17.

whatever he or she wants so long as his or her actions do not harm or threaten to harm others. Government and society should not interfere with an individual's activities unless that individual is somehow harming or threatening to harm others. Government has no business prohibiting the sale of alcohol, for instance, on the grounds that drinking harms the drinker; but government should certainly prohibit drunken driving on the grounds that it poses a serious threat of harm to others.

Mill defended his principle by appealing not to natural rights, as most of the early liberals had done, but to utility. He argued that freedom is a good thing because it promotes "the permanent interests of man as a progressive being." By this he meant that both individuals and society as a whole will benefit if people are encouraged to think and act freely. For the individual, freedom is vital to personal development. Our mental and moral faculties are like muscles, Mill said. Without regular and rigorous exercise, they will weaken and shrivel. But people cannot exercise their minds and their powers of judgment when they are constantly told what they can and cannot do. To be fully human, individuals must be free to think and speak for themselves—as long as they neither harm nor threaten harm to others.

It is possible that people who speak and act freely will make others, perhaps even the majority of society, uncomfortable and unhappy. But in the long run, Mill argued, the ideas of nonconformists such as Socrates, Jesus, and Galileo work to the benefit of society. Progress is possible only when there is open competition between different ideas, opinions, and beliefs. As in economics, a free marketplace of ideas yields a greater variety to choose from and allows people to distinguish good ideas from bad. Without freedom of thought and action, society will remain stuck in the rut of conformity and will never progress.

Mill's desire to promote individual liberty also led him to recommend representative democracy as the best possible form of government. In *Considerations on Representative Government* (1861), he maintained that political participation was one of the best forms of exercise for the mental and moral faculties. And only in a democracy is this kind of exercise available to all citizens. Even so, Mill's fear of "the tyranny of the majority" kept him from embracing democracy wholeheartedly. Among other things, he favoured a form of plural voting in which every literate man and woman would have a vote, but some—those with higher levels of education, for instance—would have two, three, or more. Plural voting would enable everyone to enjoy the benefits of political participation, yet allow more enlightened and better informed citizens to protect individual liberty. Such a system was necessary at least until the overall level of education was high enough to remove the threat of majority tyranny, Mill believed.

As for economic matters, Mill began his career as a staunch defender of *laissez-faire* capitalism. Toward the end of his life, however, he called himself a socialist. This shift in his thinking was one of the first signs of an even greater shift on the part of many liberals in the latter part of the nineteenth century—a shift that divided liberalism into rival camps. Before we examine the division among liberals in the following chapter, we will examine the development of liberalism in Canada.

Liberalism in Nineteenth-Century Canada

We have defined liberalism as the ideology that seeks to maximize individual liberty and opportunity. In nineteenth-century Canada, liberalism expressed itself as a struggle against restrictions in three areas: (1) the limiting power of local oligarchies and Britain's control of the colonial executive; (2) attempts to maintain or establish state assistance for certain religious groups; and (3) government intervention that inhibited economic liberty and freedom of enterprise.

The struggle for a greater degree of self-government made unlikely allies of two groups: liberal reformers in Upper Canada (now Ontario), and French Canadians in Lower Canada (Quebec). Liberal reformers in Upper Canada sought responsible government—that is, an executive controlled by a locally elected legislature—in order to remove the local oligarchy, called the Family Compact, and to frustrate attempts to make the Anglican Church the official church of Canada. In Lower Canada, most French Canadians held deeply conservative views and sought political reform to defeat their local oligarchy, called the *Château Clique,* in order to use government power to continue the effective establishment of the Roman Catholic Church in Quebec and to prevent public funds from being spent on economic development projects.

In Upper Canada, a small minority held radical liberal ideas. The most prominent was William Lyon Mackenzie, who wanted not responsible government but American-style direct election of the executive and of judges. In 1837, continued resistance by the Family Compact and *Château Clique,* as well as Britain's insensitivity to the colonies' needs, prompted the radicals to rebel openly. The Lower Canada Rebellion, led by Louis Joseph Papineau, was more serious because it had linguistic and racial overtones. But both rebellions soon collapsed or were put down because the majority of both French- and English-speaking Canadians showed little enthusiasm for revolution. In Lower Canada, English-speaking liberals faced a particular dilemma, for they supported responsible government in general but did not want the French-speaking majority to use government power for non-liberal purposes.

The Rebellions of 1837 prompted the British government to send Lord Durham (1792–1840) to Canada to investigate. His report, issued in 1839, highlighted the ideological conflict between French and English colonists, contrasting the "enterprising" English speakers, who saw the purpose of government as being "to promote, by all possible use of its legislative and administrative powers, the increase of population and the accumulation of property," with the "uninstructed, inactive, unprogressive" French Canadians, who saw the role of government as "to guard the interests and feelings of the present race of inhabitants."[20] Durham's solution was to grant responsible government on the British model to the colonies and to unite Upper and Lower Canada (which occurred in 1841) in an attempt to assimilate the French speakers into an English-speaking majority.

Durham's recommendations were eventually adopted by Britain, and responsible government took effect in 1848–1849 in all British North American colonies. But the French Canadians refused to be assimilated. They skilfully used their political leverage within the united Canadian legislature, in alliance with English-speaking conservatives such as John A. Macdonald, to achieve their fundamental goals: protection of French Canadian culture and of the position of the Roman Catholic Church. The resulting frustration among English-speaking liberal reformers, now led by George Brown, was a significant factor in bringing about Confederation, which offered English-speaking liberals the opportunity to free themselves from the often non-liberal policies sought by French

---

[20]John George Lampton, First Earl of Durham, *The Report and Dispatches of the Earl of Durham* (1839; London: Methuen, 1902).

Canadians. Thus Confederation was partly driven by the desire of Ontario liberals to separate themselves from Quebec conservatives.

By the mid-nineteenth century, responsible government had been achieved in Canada, and attempts to establish Anglicanism in Ontario had been defeated. While Ontario liberals deeply resented the establishment of Roman Catholic separate schools in Ontario (imposed by the vote of French-speaking Catholics in the pre-Confederation legislature of Canada and entrenched at Confederation in the *British North America Act*), with the separation of Ontario and Quebec, the religious issue retreated into the background.

In the later nineteenth century, Canadian liberals became increasingly focused on economic liberty and freedom of enterprise—the belief of classical liberal economists like Adam Smith that the free market should rule and government intervention should be minimized. Although in the early nineteenth century there was general support for some government action in promoting infrastructure developments such as canals and railways (as aids to economic development and free enterprise), liberals turned against government action in the extended controversies surrounding the railway-building policies of the Macdonald government. Liberals led by Edward Blake and Alexander Mackenzie opposed government assistance for the Canadian Pacific Railway and the imposition of the tariffs that were required to finance it, and they encouraged the development of manufacturing in central Canada. They preferred a *laissez-faire* policy of reliance on American transportation connections, low tariffs, and generally closer economic relations with the United States. In 1891 and 1911, Canadian liberals (in 1911 led by Wilfrid Laurier) fought and lost elections on the issue of free trade with the United States. Their opposition to the nation-building policies of the federal government made the liberals champions of provincial rights in the nineteenth century, which allowed the Liberal Party to gain support in conservative Quebec. Ironically, conservative Quebec voters often sought to use provincial power to promote policies or principles liberals would have rejected.

Finally, although liberals in nineteenth-century Canada supported the British connection, they tended to be distrustful and skeptical about Canadian involvement in imperial and world affairs. To a Canadian liberal, Europe was a dangerous maelstrom of largely non-liberal governments ranging from absolutist conservatism to socialism in its more extreme forms. Canada was best to avoid involvement and contamination, and liberal governments resisted efforts to give Canada a greater role in imperial and world affairs. The United States was different. Here was a purely liberal society, which exerted a strong attachment for Canadian liberals, and the isolationist attitude of Canadian liberals was similar to that in the United States.

For Further Reading

Ashcraft, Richard. *Revolutionary Politics and Locke's Two Treatises of Government*. Princeton, NJ: Princeton UP, 1986.

Berlin, Isaiah. *Liberty.* Oxford: Oxford UP, 2002.

de Ruggiero, Guido. *The History of European Liberalism*. trans. R. G. Collingwood. Boston: Beacon, 1959.

Elton, G. R. *Reformation Europe, 1517–1559*. New York: Harper, 1963.

Gray, John. *Liberalism*. Milton Keynes, UK: Open UP, 1986.

Halévy, Elie. *The Growth of Philosophic Radicalism*. London: Faber, 1928.

Macpherson, C. B. *The Political Theory of Possessive Individualism*. Oxford: Oxford UP, 1962.

Manning, D. J. *Liberalism*. New York: St. Martin's, 1976.

Useful Websites and Social Media

http://plato.stanford.edu/entries/liberalism Stanford Encyclopedia of Philosophy "Liberalism"

http://plato.stanford.edu/entries/mill Stanford Encyclopedia of Philosophy "John Stuart Mill"

www.tyndale.ca/seminary/mtsmodular/reading-rooms/history/16th-century Tyndale Seminary 16th Century Reformation Reading Room

http://plato.stanford.edu/entries/utilitarianism-history Stanford Encyclopedia of Philosophy "History of Utilitarianism"

www.econlib.org/library/Enc/bios/Smith.html Library of Economics and Liberty "Adam Smith"

From the Ball and Dagger Reader *Ideals and Ideologies*, US Eighth Edition

Part Three: Liberalism

Discussion Questions

1. Compare the ideas of Thomas Hobbes and John Locke.

2. "Liberalism and capitalism are inseparable—one cannot exist without the other." Discuss.

3. What was more important to the development of liberalism: the English Revolution of 1688, the American Revolution, or the French Revolution?

4. Discuss the origins of liberalism in Canada.

MySearchLab   MySearchLab with eText offers you access to an online interactive version of the text, additional quizzes and assessment, extensive help with your writing and research projects, and provides round-the-clock access to credible and reliable source material. Go to **www.mysearchlab.com** to access these resources.

CHAPTER 4

Modern Liberalism

Man is bound neither to his language nor to his race; he is bound only to himself because he is a free agent, or, in other words, a moral being.

Ernest Renan

LEARNING OBJECTIVES

After completing this chapter you should be able to

1. Differentiate between the two different streams of modern liberalism, and describe their origins.

2. Describe modern Canadian liberalism and its relationship to federalism and nationalism.

3. Analyze why modern liberals disagree about the role of government in relationship to individuals and groups in society.

4. Explain how liberalism fulfils the four functions of an ideology.

In the later nineteenth century, liberals experienced differing reactions to the social effects of the Industrial Revolution and liberalism, and liberal thought divided into two different streams. The main features of each stream continue to define modern liberalism. The misery of much of the English working class became increasingly obvious, in part through the depiction of their plight in the popular novels of Charles Dickens. Reform movements were underway and socialism was gaining support, especially on the European continent. Some liberals began to argue that government should rescue people from poverty, ignorance, and illness. Because of their concern for the well-being, or "well-faring," of the individual, this group came to be called **welfare liberals**. Other liberals maintained that any steps of this sort would invest too much power in government, which they continued to regard as a necessary evil and one of the main obstacles to individual liberty. Because their position was so close to that of early liberalism, it is often called **neoclassical liberalism**. Because it stresses property rights rather than, for example, personal human rights, we sometimes refer to this position as **business liberalism**.

NEOCLASSICAL OR BUSINESS LIBERALISM

Since the second half of the nineteenth century, neoclassical liberals have consistently argued that government should be as small as possible in order to leave room for the exercise of individual freedom. The state or government should be nothing more than a night watchman whose only legitimate business is to protect the person and property of individuals against force and fraud. Some neoclassical liberals have based this argument on an appeal to natural rights, others on an appeal to utility. In the late 1800s, however, the most influential among them based their arguments on Darwin's theory of evolution.

In his book *Origin of Species* (1859), Charles Darwin used the idea of natural selection to account for the evolution of life forms. Darwin held that individual creatures within every species experience random changes in their biological makeup. Some changes enhance a creature's ability to find food and survive, while others do not. Those lucky enough to have beneficial changes are more likely to survive—and to pass these biological changes along to their offspring—than less fortunate members of the species. Thus nature "selected" certain creatures with certain mutations and thereby directed the path of evolution. But all this was accidental and unintentional. This biological good fortune also puts the members of some species at an advantage over others in competition for food—for instance, giraffes are able to eat the leaves on the higher branches of trees, which is a distinct advantage when food is scarce. Such changes thus account not only for the evolution of species, but also for their survival or extinction.

Although Darwin did not derive any social and political implications from his theory, others were quick to do so. Many who had stressed the importance of economic competition seized upon Darwin's theory of natural selection as proof that the struggle for survival was natural to human life and that government should not interfere in that struggle. One of the most important of these **Social Darwinists** was Herbert Spencer.

Social Darwinism. Herbert Spencer (1820–1903), an English philosopher, had begun to think in evolutionary terms even before Darwin's *Origin of Species* appeared, and he took Darwin's work to confirm the main lines of his own thought. In particular, Spencer claimed that there is a natural struggle for survival within the human species. Nature means for individuals to be free to compete with one another. Those who are strongest, smartest, and most fit for this competition will succeed and prosper; those who are unfit will fail and suffer. This is simply nature's way, Spencer said. Helping the poor and the weak impedes individual freedom and retards social progress by holding back the strong. Indeed, it was Spencer who coined the phrase "survival of the fittest." Such views made Spencer a leading advocate of the minimal or night watchman state.

Most neoclassical liberals have not been as extreme in their views as the Social Darwinists; few neoclassical liberals today base their arguments on evolutionary premises. But in the latter part of the nineteenth century, Social Darwinists were quite influential in England and the United States, especially among businessmen who sought scientific support for *laissez-faire* capitalism.

Welfare Liberalism

Like early and neoclassical liberals, welfare liberals believe in the value of individual liberty. But welfare liberals maintain that government is not just a necessary evil. On the contrary, when properly directed, government can be a positive force for promoting individual liberty by ensuring that everyone enjoys an equal opportunity in life.

T. H. Green. One of the first scholars to make the case for **welfare liberalism** was T. H. Green (1836–1882), a professor of philosophy at Oxford University. Green said that the heart of liberalism has always been the desire to remove obstacles that block the free growth and development of individuals. In the past that meant limiting the powers of government so that people could be free to live, worship, and compete in the marketplace as they saw fit. By the mid-1800s these aims had largely been accomplished in countries like England, and it was time to recognize and overcome still other obstacles to freedom and opportunity—such as poverty, illness, prejudice, and ignorance. To overcome *these* obstacles, Green argued that it was necessary to enlist the power of the state.

Green based his argument on a distinction between two different ways of thinking about freedom, ways that he called **negative freedom** and **positive freedom**. The early liberals regarded freedom as a *negative* thing, he said, for they thought of freedom as the *absence* of restraint. Someone who was restrained—tied up and locked in jail, for instance—was not free, while someone who was unrestrained was. But Green believed that there is more to freedom than lack of restraint. Freedom is not merely a matter of being left alone; it is the positive power or ability to *do* something. Thus we may say that a child born into poverty, with no real opportunity to escape, is not truly free to grow and develop to the full extent of his or her abilities. Even if no one is intentionally restraining that child by keeping him or her in poverty, the child is still not free. But if we admit this, Green argued, anyone who values individual liberty will want to take steps to overcome those circumstances that are such formidable obstacles to freedom.[1]

Green and other welfare liberals believed that a society should act through government to establish public schools and hospitals, to aid the needy, and to regulate working conditions to promote workers' health and well-being. Only through such public support would the poor and powerless members of society become truly free. Neoclassical liberals complained that these policies simply robbed some individuals of their freedom by forcing them to transfer their property, through taxes, to others. Green responded that everyone gains freedom when he or she serves the common good. *Positive* freedom is the ability to realize or achieve our ideal or higher selves in cooperation with others. Human beings are not merely pleasure-seekers and pain-avoiders. They have higher ideals, including ideals of what they can and ought to be as persons. Laws and programs that help the unfortunate, smooth social relations, and restrict all-out competition are positive *aids* to liberty, not restraints that limit freedom. They may restrict our selfish or lower selves, but laws and programs of this sort encourage our higher selves to realize nobler and more generous ideals through social cooperation.[2]

In the late nineteenth and early twentieth centuries, many scholars and political figures adopted views similar to Green's. These other welfare liberals saw an active government as a useful, even necessary tool in the campaign to expand individual liberty. Like Green, they also insisted that human beings are social creatures, not isolated individuals who owe nothing to anyone else. Gradually their ideas and arguments prevailed among liberals. By the middle of the twentieth century, in fact, welfare liberals were usually known simply as "liberals," while their neoclassical rivals were often called "conservatives"—a piece of terminological confusion that we shall try to clarify in Chapter 5.

The Welfare State. As we shall see in later chapters, socialists also advanced schemes for social reform, but it is important to distinguish welfare liberalism from *socialism*. Socialists want to do more than tame or reform capitalism; they want to replace it with a system of publicly owned and democratically controlled enterprises. Welfare liberals, by contrast, prefer private ownership and generally take a competitive capitalist system for granted. From the perspective of the welfare liberal, the role of government is to regulate

---

[1]See the essay by T. H. Green, "Liberal Legislation and Freedom of Contract," part of which appears in Ball and Dagger, selection 3.19.

[2]For an important and influential critique of positive liberty, see Isaiah Berlin, "Two Concepts of Liberty," in Isaiah Berlin, *Liberty* (Oxford: Oxford UP, 2002). For a critique of Berlin and a defence of positive freedom, see Charles Taylor, "What's Wrong with Negative Liberty?" *The Idea of Freedom*, ed. Alan Ryan (Oxford: Oxford UP, 1979).

economic competition in order to cure the social ills and redress individual injuries wrought by capitalist competition. In short, unlike socialists, welfare liberals regard economic competition as a good thing—but not if it comes at the expense of individual welfare and true equality of opportunity.

It is also important to note that the grandfather of the modern welfare state was neither a socialist nor a liberal of any sort. Otto von Bismarck (1815–1898), the ardently antisocialist "Iron Chancellor" who united Germany in the latter part of the nineteenth century, believed that the welfare state was the best way to oppose socialism. Through a state-sponsored system of taxing employers and employees to support ill, injured, and unemployed workers, the German state stole the thunder of the socialists, who had played upon the anxieties of workers subject to the up-and-down cycles of a capitalist economy.

The birth of the welfare state also coincided roughly with the expansion of voting rights throughout much of Europe. In England, reforms in 1867 and 1885 brought the franchise to most adult males and thus made the working class a more powerful political force. The political representatives of this class contributed not only to the growth of the welfare state but also to the prominence of welfare liberalism in the twentieth century.[3]

LIBERALISM AFTER 1900—THE DOMINANCE OF WELFARE LIBERALISM

Another factor also contributed to the dominance of welfare over business liberalism. By the beginning of the 1900s, capitalist competition looked quite different from what it had been a century before. In the industrialized world, the lone entrepreneur who ran his or her own business had largely given way to the corporation, the trust, the syndicate, and the conglomerate. Business was now "big business," and many people began to call for government intervention in the marketplace, not to restrict competition, but to keep the large corporations from stifling it.

In one form or another, however, the neoclassical liberals' faith in individual competition and achievement survived into the twentieth century, most notably in the United States. This faith was severely tested by the Depression of the 1930s. Individuals, no matter how rugged, seemed no match for this devastating economic collapse. The political and economic effects were felt throughout the world as ideologues of every stripe sought to explain and exploit the situation. Many blamed the Depression on capitalism and turned either to socialism or communism, on the one hand, or to fascism, on the other. In the English-speaking countries, by contrast, the main response was to turn to the welfare state.

The liberal case for active government gained further support from the theory advanced by English economist John Maynard Keynes (1883–1946). In *The General Theory of Employment, Interest and Money* (1936) Keynes argued that governments should use their taxing and spending powers to prevent depressions and maintain a healthy economy. Put simply, Keynes's theory holds that governments should try to manage or fine-tune the economy. When output is growing rapidly, the government should run a budget surplus to take spending power out of the economy and prevent it from overheating. If the economy appears headed into a recession, it should go into deficit. Spending on social programs to

---

[3]For an overview, see Michael Freeden, "The Coming of the Welfare State," *The Cambridge History of Twentieth-Century Political Thought*, ed. Terence Ball and Richard Bellamy (Cambridge: Cambridge UP, 2003).

stimulate the economy and maintain high levels of employment went hand in hand with this theory. Whatever the strategy at any particular time, Keynes's approach calls for active government management of economic matters—an approach welcomed by welfare liberals. Between the end of the Second World War and the early 1980s, Keynes's theory was put into practice by all advanced capitalist countries, including Canada.

The Depression had largely come to an end before the end of the Second World War, but the war gave central government enormous taxing and spending powers they were reluctant to give up. Even classical liberal states became activist. Welfare liberalism became the dominant ideology of the Western world. Welfare liberals usually reached some sort of accommodation with their socialist and conservative rivals, as most parties accepted the desirability of the welfare state. Indeed, this consensus seemed so broad and firm that some political observers, such as Daniel Bell, began to speak in the late 1950s of the end of ideology. However, the welfare liberal consensus soon faced new challenges.

In the 1960s the New Left, vaguely socialist in orientation, rejected both the obsolete communism of the Soviet Union and the consumer capitalism of the liberal countries. Most New Leftists accepted the liberal emphasis on individual rights and liberties, and most also supported government programs to promote equality of opportunity. But they complained that liberal governments worked first and foremost to protect the economic interests of capitalist corporations. Although they agreed that these governments did take steps to improve the material circumstances of their people, the New Leftists charged that most people were reduced to mere consumers, when they ought to be encouraged to be active citizens. This led to the call for participatory democracy, a society in which average people would be able to exercise greater control over the decisions that most closely affected their lives. The emergence of the New Left was also closely connected with opposition to the Vietnam War and the view that the war was a product of an alliance of business and the military in the United States—a military-industrial complex driven by profits from arms manufacturing.

A stronger challenge, in the form of a mixture of neoclassical liberalism and conservatism, appeared in the 1970s and 1980s, as first Margaret Thatcher in the United Kingdom and then Ronald Reagan in the United States became heads of government. Neither leader dismantled the welfare state, although both moved in that direction. But dismantle it we must, the neoclassical liberals continue to insist. So the contest within liberalism continues, with neoclassical, or business, and welfare liberals engaging in ongoing disputes at the philosophical as well as the political levels. In the United States, this discourse takes its most acute form in the struggle between the more extreme wing of the Republican Party, the so-called Tea Party, and the welfare liberalism of Barack Obama. This contest is equally apparent in twentieth- and twenty-first-century liberalism in Canada.

Modern Canadian Liberalism

Canadian liberalism in the twentieth and twenty-first centuries reflects the same divisions in liberalism between positive and negative, or business and welfare, liberalism that developed in other Western democracies. William Lyon Mackenzie King (Liberal Party leader 1919–1948 and PM 1921–1925; 1926–1930; 1935–1948) led the Liberal Party in 1919 to commit itself to the gradual establishment of a welfare state in Canada, including unemployment insurance, universal health care, and a universal pension scheme. At the same time, the traditional liberal hostility to trade unions, with their emphasis on a group-based, collectivist approach to industrial relations, was significantly modified by the acceptance of the legitimacy of the role of unions in industrial relations and the economy. Actual implementation of the welfare state in Canada took fifty years, culminating in the establishment of the public health care system in 1970. The welfare state was promoted not only by welfare liberals but also by socialists and the Red Tory conservatives discussed in Chapter 5.

Welfare liberalism remains a strong force in the Canadian Liberal Party, which, under the leadership of Paul Martin (PM 2004–2006), Stéphane Dion (leader 2006–2008) and Michael Ignatieff (leader 2008–2011), has been a defender of the health care system (and an advocate of extensions such as universal medication care) in the face of neoconservative or neoliberal arguments for private funding and individual responsibility. The openness of welfare liberals to government regulation has also made federal and provincial Liberals strong advocates of government intervention to deal with climate change and other environmental issues.

Welfare liberalism also provided the bridge that enabled Bob Rae, the former NDP premier of Ontario, to leave the NDP (itself one of the bearers of welfare liberalism in Canada) and become a candidate for the Liberal leadership in 2006 and a prominent front-bench Liberal MP and interim leader of the party in 2011.

Business, or neoclassical, liberalism also persisted in Canada, resisting the establishment or extension of the welfare state, seeking to limit or reduce government expenditures and the size of government in general, and promoting the classical liberal policies of free trade and deregulation. This strain of liberal thinking became particularly strong with the resurgence of neoclassical liberal ideas inspired in the 1970s and 1980s by the Thatcher government in the United Kingdom and in the 1980s by the Reagan government in the

William Lyon Mackenzie King (1874–1950)

United States. It has had a significant impact within the Canadian Liberal Party at both the federal and provincial levels and an even stronger influence on the Reform/Alliance Party and the reconstituted Conservative Party after 2003.

Different variants of liberalism have had an effect on Canadian **federalism**. As we noted, in the nineteenth century liberals tended to support greater provincial rights as a means of restraining economic intervention by the federal government. To some extent this approach has continued in the twentieth and twenty-first centuries. For example, the development of the welfare state and the management of the economy along Keynesian principles were considered to be best done by the federal government, and the financing of the welfare state and the management of disparities of wealth among the provinces required significant federal intervention. Although welfare liberals have recognized that provincial governments had a significant role to play in achieving the welfare state, they clearly favour a stronger federal government. By contrast, business or neoclassical liberals have tended to be more sympathetic to provincial rights. This is reflected in the Harper government's willingness to restrict federal spending and programs in deference to provincial wishes, particularly in Quebec.

Canadian Liberalism and Nationalism

Canada's most distinctive contribution to modern liberal thinking was its response to nationalism—particularly Quebec nationalism directed to separating Quebec from Canada as an independent nation. The liberal response was articulated and defended by Prime Minister Pierre Elliott Trudeau (PM 1968–1979; 1980–1984). Trudeau's opposition to Quebec nationalism was explicitly based on his liberal individualism. He quoted approvingly the statement of the French Catholic philosopher Ernest Renan: "Man is bound neither to his language nor to his race; he is bound only to himself because he is a free agent, or, in other words, a moral being."[4] Trudeau argued on this basis that French-speaking Canadians were not primarily members of a group or collectivity, but individuals who had the rights to use their language. In this view, the solution to the problem of language rights was to safeguard individual language rights in the same manner as liberals in the past had sought to protect other individual rights—not to create or protect the rights of a linguistic group or collectivity by giving enhanced power to the province of Quebec. Trudeau rejected the notion that the state or the collectivity had rights (for example, the right to independence) because the state existed primarily to serve individual ends: "Men do not exist for states; states are created to make it easier for men to attain some of their common objectives."[5]

Trudeau also connected nationalism with the emotional and the irrational and looked for its replacement by the liberal ideal of individual reason:

> Thus there is some hope that in advanced societies, the glue of nationalism will become as obsolete as the divine right of kings; the title of the state to govern and the extent of its authority will be conditional upon rational justification; a people's consensus based on reason will supply the cohesive force that societies require; and politics both within and without the state will follow a much more functional approach to the problem of government.[6]

---

[4] Pierre Elliott Trudeau, *Federalism and the French Canadians* (Toronto: MacMillan, 1968) 159.
[5] Trudeau 8.
[6] Trudeau 26.

On this basis, Trudeau rejected the use of nationalism as the basis for government:

No doubt, the level of individual action, emotions and dreams will still play a part; even in modern man, superstition remains a powerful motivation. But magic, no less than totems and taboos, has long since ceased to play an important role in the normal governing of states. And likewise, nationalism will eventually have to be rejected as a principle of sound government.[7]

Trudeau's solution to the problem posed by nationalism was federalism. By dividing sovereignty in a federal state between different levels of government, different national or ethnic groups could be accommodated within a single political framework. This allowed nationalist feeling an outlet but at a level where the harm it could do was minimized, and in the long run promoted toleration and worked toward the eventual elimination of nationalist feeling. Trudeau therefore was a bitter opponent of Quebec separatists and effectively polarized political debate in Canada, particularly in Quebec, for the past thirty years.

Trudeau completely rejected any ethnic-based nationalism and was responsible for many of the policies that created a uniquely multicultural society in Canada. However, Canadian welfare liberalism under Trudeau's influence came to be viewed as a proponent of **pan-Canadian nationalism**. This paradox can be explained by three factors:

1. Pan-Canadian nationalism is not ethnic-based and does not promote the kind of ethnic divisiveness and related potential violence that concerned Trudeau.

Pierre Elliot Trudeau (1919–2000)

---

[7]Trudeau 34.

2. Much of the focus of pan-Canadian nationalism has been directed at liberalism in the United States. As the United States became more heavily influenced by business, or neoclassical, liberalism in the late twentieth century, it became less attractive to Canadian welfare liberals. The election of Barack Obama as the U.S. president in 2008 might alter this perception.

3. Pan-Canadian nationalism was seen as a means of preserving a greater degree of freedom of action for individual Canadians in the face of growing American cultural influence.

The opposition of liberalism to ethnic-based Quebec nationalism and the tension between welfare and neoclassical liberals, including welfare liberalism's nationalist undertones, continue to mark Canadian liberalism in the twenty-first century.

LIBERALISM TODAY

Now that we have traced liberalism from its beginnings to the present, what can we say about its current condition? Three points deserve special mention here. The first is that liberalism is no longer the revolutionary force it once was—at least not in the West. But in other parts of the world the liberal attack on ascribed status, religious conformity, or political absolutism still strikes at the foundations of society. This is most evident in Iran, Afghanistan, and other countries of the Middle East and Northern Africa, where liberalism has provoked a radical response from Islamic fundamentalists. Elsewhere, champions of change in communist and formerly communist countries have often claimed liberalization as their goal. In the Western world, however, the aims of early liberals are now deeply entrenched in public policy and public opinion. Here liberalism is no longer a revolutionary ideology but an ideology defending a revolution already won.

The second point is that liberals remain divided among themselves. Despite their agreement on fundamental ends, especially the importance of individual liberty, liberals disagree sharply over means—over how best to define and promote these ends. Welfare liberals believe that we need an active government to give everyone an equal chance to be free; neoclassical, or business, liberals believe that we need to limit government to keep it from robbing us of freedom.

The third point is that liberals are now wrestling with a set of very difficult problems that stem from their basic commitments to individual liberty and equality of opportunity. The first problem is: How far should individuals be able to go in exercising their freedom? Most liberals, welfare and neoclassical or business alike, accept something like Mill's harm principle—people should be free to do as they wish unless they harm (or violate the rights of) others. When it comes to applying this principle, however, the difficulty of defining "harm" becomes clear. Many liberals say that victimless crimes such as prostitution, gambling, and the sale of drugs and pornography should not be considered crimes at all. If one adult wants to be a prostitute and another wants to pay for his or her services, no one is harmed, except perhaps those who enter into this exchange. And if no one else is harmed, government has no business outlawing prostitution. To this argument other liberals respond that victimless crimes are not as victimless as they appear. Pimps force women into prostitution, and loan sharks take unfair advantage of people who borrow money at very high interest rates. Those who favour abolishing victimless crimes counter by arguing that the government can carefully regulate these activities if they are legal—as prostitution is in the Netherlands and parts of Nevada in the United States, for example. But the argument continues without a resolution. Despite their desire to separate the sphere of private freedom from that of public control, liberals have found the boundary between private and public difficult to draw with any precision.

Part of the reason for this boundary problem is that liberals disagree about the proper role of government in helping people lead a good or decent life. According to some, the job of government in a liberal society is to preserve justice and protect the individual's right to live as he or she sees fit. It is not the government's business to promote one way of life or conception of the good—say, the life of the devout Christian—at the expense of others—say, the life of the devout Jew or of the atheist who thinks all religions are merely forms of superstition. Government should remain neutral with respect to these and other competing conceptions of the good life, confining themselves, like a referee at a sports match, to limiting and settling conflicts without taking sides in disputes about how people ought to live. But other liberals insist that government neither can nor should be completely neutral in this way. Liberal societies depend upon citizens who are rational, tolerant, far-sighted, and committed to the common good, they argue, and a good government will necessarily encourage people to develop and display these desirable traits. As they see it, political liberalism betrays the liberal tradition by depriving liberalism of its concern for character and virtue.[8]

The second problem grows out of the liberal commitment to equal opportunity. For libertarians, this means simply that everyone ought to be free to make his or her way in the world without unfair discrimination. Only discrimination on the basis of ability and effort is justified. The liberal state should then outlaw discrimination on the basis of race, religion, gender, or any other irrelevant factor. By contrast, most welfare liberals maintain that government ought to help disadvantaged people enjoy equal opportunity. Thus they support publicly funded schools, health care, and financial assistance for those in need. But how far should this go? Should we try to distribute wealth and resources in a more nearly equal way? Will this promote true equality of opportunity? And is this fair to those who have earned their wealth without violating the rights of others?

To overcome a legacy of discrimination against women and racial minorities, many welfare liberals advocate **affirmative action** programs. Such programs give special consideration in education and employment to members of groups that have suffered from discrimination. But how is this to be done? By providing special training? By setting aside a certain number of jobs or places in colleges and professional schools for women and minorities? Aren't these ways of discriminating against some people—white males— by discriminating in favour of others? Can this be justified in the name of equality of opportunity?

Another problem arises from the liberal commitment to individual liberty and individual rights. The next chapters describe how conservatives, socialists, and fascists have often maintained that liberals give too much attention to the individual and too little to the community or society of which he or she is a part. In recent years this complaint has arisen

---

[8]See, for example, William Galston, *Liberal Purposes* (Cambridge: Cambridge UP, 1991); George Sher, *Beyond Neutrality: Perfectionism and Politics* (Cambridge: Cambridge UP, 1997); and Thomas A. Spragens, Jr., *Civic Liberalism: Reflections on Our Democratic Ideals* (Lanham, MD: Rowman, 1999).

within the ranks of liberalism as well. In this case the complaint is that liberals are so concerned with protecting individual rights and interests that they ignore the common good and the value of community. According to these critics, whose ideas are based on **communitarianism**, rights must be balanced by responsibilities. Individuals may have rights against others, such as the right to speak or to worship in ways that others do not like, but individuals must also recognize that they owe something to the community that enables them to exercise these rights. In Canada, critics of the Supreme Court's activist application of individual rights set out in the Canadian Charter of Rights and Freedoms suggest that excessively promoting individual rights frustrates the rights of the community as a whole, expressed through a democratically elected majority.[9] To counteract this overemphasis on individual rights, these critics want government to promote the good of the community.

Some attempts to strengthen community have led to disagreement among liberals, largely because they raise the fear of the tyranny of the majority. Should cities or public schools be able to sponsor Christmas pageants or display nativity scenes? Do the members of a community, or a majority of them, have the right to limit freedom of speech by outlawing or regulating the distribution of pornography? Should the police be allowed to stop cars at random in order to check for drunken drivers? Are the increased powers granted to police and other security agencies to combat terrorism a threat to individual rights? Or do these attempts to promote the public well-being amount to intolerable infringements of individual rights?

These and other questions of individual liberty and equality of opportunity are especially troublesome for liberals because their creed forces them to confront such issues head-on. And there is, as yet, no obvious or agreed-upon "liberal" answer to these questions. Some critics see this as a serious or even fatal weakness; the response of others might be that liberalism is still doing what it has always done—searching for ways to advance the cause of individual liberty and opportunity. Certainly anyone who agrees with Mill's claim that flexing our mental and moral muscles is vital to individual growth will find plenty of room for exercise in contemporary liberalism—which is just as Mill would want it.

Conclusion

Liberalism as an Ideology

What can we conclude about liberalism as an ideology? Given the rift between welfare liberals and neoclassical, or business, liberals, does it even make sense to speak of liberalism as a single ideology? We think it does, although the division between the two camps is deep and may be widening. At present, however, their differences are largely matters of emphasis and disagreement about means, not ends. A quick look at how liberalism performs the four functions that all ideologies perform should make this point clear.

Explanatory Function. First, all ideologies purport to explain why things are the way they are, with particular attention to social, economic, and political conditions. For

---

[9]For different views on this issue, see F. L. Morton and Rainer Knopff, *The Charter Revolution and the Court Party* (Peterborough: Broadview, 2000); and Kent Roach, *The Supreme Court on Trial. Judicial Activism or Democratic Dialogue* (Toronto: Irwin Law, 2001).

liberals, these explanations are typically individualistic. Social conditions are the result of individual choices and actions. Liberals recognize that the choices open to individuals are often limited and frequently have consequences that no one intended or desired. Yet despite the limits on their foresight and understanding, individuals still make choices that, taken together, explain why social conditions are as they are.

Why, for example, do economic depressions occur? Liberals generally believe that they are the wholly unintended results of decisions made by rational individuals responding to the circumstances in which they compete—or in some cases are prevented from competing—in the marketplace. Welfare liberals generally follow Keynes's economic views and argue that the job of the government is to shape these choices, perhaps by lowering or raising taxes to give people more or less disposable income, in order to prevent or lessen economic distress. The neoclassical liberal position is that the competitive marketplace will correct itself if left alone and it is wrong for government to interfere. Despite these different views of what should be done, however, both sides share the fundamental premise that individual choices ultimately explain why things are as they are.

Evaluative Function. When it comes to evaluating conditions, liberalism again turns to the individual. As a rule, conditions are good if the individual is free to do as he or she wishes without harming or violating the rights of others. The more freedom people have, liberals say, the better; the less freedom, the worse. And what freedom there is must be enjoyed as equally as possible. Thus the liberal view of freedom requires that individuals have an equal opportunity to succeed. On this point all liberals agree. But they disagree, with welfare liberals going in one direction and business liberals in another, on how best to provide equality of opportunity. For both, however, a society in which individuals enjoy an equal opportunity to choose freely is clearly better than one in which freedom is restricted and opportunity unequal.

Orientative Function. Ideologies also provide people with some sense of identity and orientation—of who they are and where and how they fit into the great scheme of things. Liberalism pictures people as rational individuals who have interests to pursue and choices to make. This is to say that liberals direct our attention to the characteristics that they believe all people share, not toward the differences that separate people from one another. Some liberals push this much further than others, and Bentham and the Social Darwinists perhaps furthest of all, but there is a tendency among liberals to believe that deep down all women and men are fundamentally the same. Differences of culture, race, religion, gender, or nationality are ultimately superficial. Our identity is an individual—not a group—identity. At the base, most people are rational, self-interested individuals who want to be free to choose how to live. Once we understand this, liberals believe we will respect the right of others to live freely, and will expect them to respect ours in return.

Programmatic Function. Liberals espouse programs for promoting individual liberty and opportunity. Historically, this has meant that liberals have opposed religious conformity, ascribed status, economic privileges, political absolutism, and the tyranny of majority opinion. With these obstacles removed, individuals are free to worship (or not) as they see fit; to rise or fall in society according to their efforts and ability; to compete on an equal footing in the marketplace; to exercise some control over government; and to think, speak, and live in unconventional ways. On these points liberals seldom disagree.

When some liberals began to say that freedom is not merely a matter of being left alone but a positive power or ability to do what one chooses, disagreements emerged. Welfare liberals insist that the government must be enlisted in the struggle against illness, ignorance, prejudice, poverty, and any other condition that threatens liberty and equality of opportunity, while neoclassical liberals complain that government meddling is itself the chief threat to liberty and equality.

The welfare and neoclassical schools of liberalism offer rival political programs, not because their goals are different but because they disagree on how best to achieve those goals. The dispute is over means, not ends. This is why we believe that liberalism, divided as it is by the internal dispute between the two camps, remains a single, albeit fragmented, ideology.

Liberalism and the Democratic Ideal

At the outset of the twenty-first century, liberals are firmly committed to democracy, but this has not always been the case. Throughout most of its history, in fact, liberalism has been more concerned with protecting people from their rulers than with establishing rule by the people. From its inception, liberalism has fought to remove obstacles that stand in the way of the individual's freedom to live as he or she sees fit, and in the beginning most of those obstacles—religious conformity, ascribed status, political absolutism, monopolies, and other restraints on economic competition—were either provided or supported by government. Rather than strive to enable people to rule themselves *through* government, the first liberals struggled to free people *from* government. In other words, they tried to reduce the areas of life that were considered public in order to expand the private sphere.

From the beginning, however, liberalism also displayed several democratic tendencies, the most notable being its premise of basic equality among human beings. Whether couched in terms of natural rights or the Utilitarians' claim that everybody is to count for one and nobody for more than one, liberals have always argued from the premise that every person's rights or interests should count as much as everyone else's. Early liberals defined "person" in such narrow terms that the only true "person" was a free adult male who owned substantial property. But as they spoke and argued in terms of natural equality, liberals opened the door for those—including later liberals—who demanded that slavery be abolished and that women and the propertyless should be extended the right to vote, to run for public office, and to be politically equal to property-owning males.

This liberal tendency did not lead in an openly democratic direction until the 1800s, when Bentham and the Utilitarians began to argue that democracy gave every citizen the chance to protect his (and later her) interests. If the business of government is to promote the greatest good of the greatest number, they reasoned, then the only way to determine the greatest good is to allow every citizen to decide what is good for him or her. Earlier liberals had proclaimed that government must rest on the consent of the people, and they had devised constitutions and bills of rights in order to limit the powers of government. But it was not until the 1800s that liberals began to regard the vote as a way to give everyone an equal chance to protect and promote his or her interests.

For the most part, liberals favour democracy because it enables citizens to hold their government accountable, thereby protecting their personal interests. Some, such as John Stuart Mill, have gone further, arguing that democracy is good because it encourages widespread political participation, which in turn enriches people's lives by developing their intellectual and moral capacities. Yet most liberals have attached no particular value to political activity, seeing it as simply one possible good among many. The state should be neutral, they say, leaving people free to pursue whatever they consider good—as long as they respect others' freedom to do the same. If people find pleasure or satisfaction in public life, well and good; but if they derive more pleasure from private pursuits, then they should be free to follow that path.

As a rule, **liberal democracy** emphasizes the importance of individual rights and liberty. In liberal democracy, democracy is defined mainly in terms of the individual's right to be free from outside interference to do as he or she thinks best. Everyone is supposed to be free to participate in public life; but the primary concern is to protect people from undue interference in their private affairs. Consequently, deciding what counts as private and how far an individual's right to privacy extends are matters of debate (as in the abortion controversy). For the liberal, democracy is good so long as it protects these rights and interests in privacy and free action. It does this primarily by making the government responsive to the needs and interests of the people, thus preventing arbitrary and tyrannical government. But if rule by the people begins to threaten individual rights and liberties, then one can expect liberals to demand that it be curbed.

For Further Reading

Boaz, David. *Libertarianism: A Primer.* New York: Free P, 1997.

Campbell, Colin, and William Christian. *Parties, Leaders and Ideologies in Canada.* Toronto: McGraw-Hill, 1996 (chapter 3).

Chrétien, Jean. *My Years as Prime Minister.* Toronto: Alfred A. Knopf Canada, 2007.

Dworkin, Ronald. *Taking Rights Seriously.* Cambridge, MA: Harvard UP, 1977.

Etzioni, Amitai, ed. *New Communitarian Thinking: Persons, Virtues, Institutions, and Communities.* Charlottesville, VA: U of Virginia P, 1995.

Friedman, Milton, and Rose Friedman. *Free to Choose.* New York: Avon, 1981.

Goodin, Robert. "The End of the Welfare State?" *The Cambridge History of Twentieth-Century Political Thought.* Ed. Terence Ball and Richard Bellamy. Cambridge: Cambridge UP, 2003.

Hayek, Friedrich. *The Road to Serfdom.* Chicago: U of Chicago P, 1976.

Miller, James. *Democracy Is in the Streets: From the Port Huron Statement to the Siege of Chicago.* New York: Simon, 1987.

Moon, J. Donald. *Constructing Community: Moral Pluralism and Tragic Conflicts.* Princeton, NJ: Princeton UP, 1993.

Raz, Joseph. *The Morality of Freedom.* Oxford: Oxford UP, 1986

Sandel, Michael. *Liberalism and the Limits of Justice.* Cambridge: Cambridge UP, 1982.

Skinner, Quentin. *The Foundations of Modern Political Thought.* 2 vols. Cambridge: Cambridge UP, 1978.

Trudeau, Pierre Elliott. *Federalism and the French Canadians.* Toronto: Macmillan, 1968.

——. *Against the Current: Selected Writings 1939–1996,* Toronto: McClelland & Stewart, 1996.

Useful Websites and Social Media

www.adaction.org Americans for Democratic Action.

www.liberal.ca Liberal Party of Canada.

Twitter:

> @liberal_party

Facebook:

> www.facebook.com/LiberalCA

www.moveon.org MoveOn.org

www.pfaw.org People for the American Way

www.prospect.org *The American Prospect*

www.cato.org The Cato Institute

www.nlc-bnc.ca/primeministers/h4-3375-e.html Library and Archives Canada "Pierre Elliott Trudeau"

www.thecanadianencyclopedia.com/articles/william-lyon-mackenzie-king The Canadian Encyclopedia "William Lyon Mackenzie King"

From the Ball and Dagger Reader *Ideals and Ideologies*, US Eighth Edition

Part Three: Liberalism

Discussion Questions

1. How do business liberalism and welfare liberalism differ?

2. Compare the contributions to Canadian liberalism of Mackenzie King and Pierre Trudeau.

3. How can affirmative action programs be justified by liberal theory?

4. Who among the following is the most true to the core principles of liberalism: Bob Rae, Stephen Harper, or Sarah Palin?

MySearchLab   MySearchLab with eText offers you access to an online interactive version of the text, additional quizzes and assessment, extensive help with your writing and research projects, and provides round-the-clock access to credible and reliable source material. Go to **www.mysearchlab.com** to access these resources.

CHAPTER 5

The Roots of Conservatism

To be attached to the subdivision, to love the little platoon we belong to in society, is the first principle (the germ as it were) of public affections. It is the first link in the series by which we proceed towards a love to our country, and to mankind. The interest of that portion of social arrangement is a trust in the hands of all those who compose it; and as none but bad men would justify it in abuse, none but traitors would barter it away for their own personal advantage.

Edmund Burke, *Reflections on the Revolution in France* (1790)

LEARNING OBJECTIVES

After completing this chapter you should be able to

1. Understand the underlying principles of conservatism and describe the historical development of conservative ideology in Great Britain, Europe, and North America.

2. Illustrate the contribution of Edmund Burke to conservative ideology.

3. Articulate and distinguish between the philosophies of Burke, de Maistre, Disraeli, and John A. Macdonald.

4. Demonstrate the differences between classical British, Canadian (including early French versus English Canadian), and American conservatism.

THE DAWN OF CONSERVATISM

In one sense conservatism is easy to define; in another, quite difficult. It is easy because all conservatives share a desire to conserve or preserve something—usually the traditional or customary way of life of their societies. But these traditions or customs are likely to vary considerably from one society to another. Even where they do not, different conservatives are likely to have different ideas about what elements or parts of their established way of life are worth preserving. Conservatives may all want to conserve something, but they do not all want to conserve the same things. And that is what makes conservatism so difficult to define.

This difficulty is evident in two ways. First, the word *conservative* is often applied to anyone who resists change. There is nothing wrong with this use of the term, except that it means that two people who bitterly oppose each other's position can both be described as conservative. For instance, as China moves toward a free-market economy, some of its leaders, who still call themselves communists, resist this change. Although they are communists, they are sometimes called conservatives. Yet these conservative communists are the old and bitter enemies of those who are known as conservatives in the English-speaking world. Indeed, *anti*communism has been one of the defining marks of conservatism in the West since at least the Russian Revolution of 1917, and most American-style conservatives advocate a free-market economy.

In Canada, the Canadian Alliance, with its tax-cutting, free-enterprise agenda, called itself conservative; the Progressive Conservative Party traditionally believed in activist government and the continuation of the welfare state; and maverick David Orchard, who twice ran for the leadership of the Progressive Conservative Party, is a strong environmentalist and anti-American. The Conservative government of Stephen Harper pursues a law-and-order agenda that is normally associated with conservatives, but it runs budgets deficits that are more common with centrist or centre-left parties. All that variety is confusing.

DIFFICULTY IN UNDERSTANDING CONSERVATISM

If conservatism is a distinct political position, as we believe it to be, it must entail more than the simple desire to resist change. There must be some underlying principles or ideals that conservatives share—some general agreement on what is worth preserving. But here we encounter the second difficulty in defining conservative. This difficulty is evident in the contrast between the early conservatives and the most prominent self-proclaimed conservatives of recent years. As we shall see, traditional conservatives were in large part trying to preserve or restore an aristocratic society under attack from liberalism in general and the French Revolution in particular. They defended the traditional social hierarchy; they insisted on the need for a government strong enough to restrain the passions of the people; and they were often skeptical of attempts to promote individual freedom and equality of opportunity in a competitive society. By contrast, the best known conservatives of the late twentieth century—British Prime Minister Margaret Thatcher, U.S. President Ronald Reagan, Canadian Prime Minister Brian Mulroney, and U.S. President George W. Bush—were conservatives who advocated reducing the size and scope of government in order to free individuals to compete for profits.[1] With its enthusiasm for **laissez-faire** capitalism, in fact, their brand of conservatism is remarkably similar to classical and **neo-classical liberalism**. What early conservatives resisted, many self-described conservatives now embrace.

Understanding conservatism is much more difficult than making sense of liberalism. Certainly the divisions run deep enough for one conservative to complain that "what popularly passes for 'conservative' in America is often only a petrified right-wing of atomistic *laisser-faire* liberalism."[2] Later in this chapter, we will explore the different varieties of conservatism. But first we need to begin with a point on which the house of conservatism was built and upon which it still stands—a shared conception of human nature.

THE POLITICS OF IMPERFECTION

Chapter 1 noted that every ideology rests on a conception of human nature, including some notion of human potential—of what men and women have in them to do and to be. In the case of conservatism, the fundamental conviction is that human beings are, and always will be, deeply flawed. This is why some scholars call conservatism "the political philosophy of imperfection."[3]

But what does it mean to say that human beings are imperfect? According to conservatives, it means that we are neither as intelligent nor as good as we like to think we are.

---

[1]Given the growth in government spending and deficits during their administrations, due largely to increased military expenditures, it is doubtful that either achieved this aim.

[2]Peter Viereck, *Conservatism: From John Adams to Churchill* (New York: Van Nostrand, 1956) 19.

[3]Anthony Quinton, *The Politics of Imperfection* (London: Faber, 1978); and N. K. O'Sullivan, *Conservatism* (New York: St. Martin's, 1976) chapter 1.

We may believe ourselves capable of governing solely by reason, but we are wrong. The light of reason does not shine far enough or brightly enough to enable us to see and avoid all the problems that beset people and societies, conservatives say, and even the smartest among us can never foresee all the consequences of our actions and policies. That is why the boldest attempts to do good often do the greatest harm.

Moreover, in the face of our passions and desires, human reason is weak, even impotent. When we want something that we know is not good for us, for instance, or when we want to do something that we know may harm others, we often find ways to rationalize our conduct—to invent reasons for following our desires. Human beings are not only intellectually imperfect, but morally imperfect, too. We tend to be selfish, to put our desires and interests above others', and to reach for more power and wealth than is good either for us or for social peace and stability. Indeed, most conservatives have believed that in some sense, either theological or psychological, human beings are marked by **original sin**. That is, they believe that the story of Adam and Eve's defiance of God in the Bible's Book of Genesis conveys a basic truth about human nature.

According to traditional conservatives, human nature is how it always has been and always will be. To hope for some radical change—to hope that our intellectual and moral imperfections can be removed—is arrogant and foolish. More, it is also dangerous. Any attempt to remake human beings by remaking their societies is likely to end in disaster. As they see it, the best we can do is to restrain the passions and instincts that lead to conflict. And we can do this through government, which imposes restraints on us, or through education—whether in schools, churches, families, or other groups—which teaches us self-restraint. As one conservative puts it,

> The function of education is conservative: not to deify the child's "glorious self-expression," but to limit his instincts and behaviour by unbreakable ethical habits. In his natural instincts, every modern baby is still born a caveman baby. What prevents today's baby from remaining a caveman is the conservative force of law and tradition, which slow accumulation of civilized habits separating us from the cave.[4]

Or, as another conservative has said, "Every new generation constitutes a wave of savages who must be civilized by their families, schools, and churches."[5]

This view of human nature leads directly to the conservative warning against bold attempts to improve society. Radical proponents of some other ideologies hold out visions of utopian societies; they call for revolutions to create perfect societies; or they promise at least to bring about great progress. Conservatives are skeptical of these ideological claims—so skeptical that conservatism has been called an "anti-ideology."[6] In their view, all these grandiose attempts to transform human life and society are doomed to end not only in failure but also in catastrophe. We do much better, conservatives argue, to proceed slowly and cautiously in our attempts to improve society, and we are much wiser to cherish a peaceful and stable society than to risk its loss in the futile quest for

---

[4]Peter Viereck, *Conservatism Revisited* (New York: Collier, 1962) 35; see also William Golding's novel, *Lord of the Flies* (New York: Putnam, 1954).

[5]Robert Bork, *Slouching Towards Gomorrah: Modern Liberalism and American Decline* (New York: Harper-Collins, 1996) 21. An excerpt from Bork's book appears in Terence Ball and Richard Dagger, eds., *Ideals and Ideologies: A Reader,* 8th ed. (New York: Longman, 2011) selection 4.28.

[6]Isaac Kramnick and Frederick Watkins, *The Age of Ideology: 1750 to the Present,* 2nd ed. (Englewood Cliffs, NJ: Prentice-Hall, 1979) 27.

perfection. This has been the fundamental conviction of conservatism from its beginning more than 200 years ago in the writings of Edmund Burke.

THE CONSERVATISM OF EDMUND BURKE

At every period in history, there have been people who had a conservative disposition, a preference for home and the familiar rather than distant horizons and the new. Our earliest ancestors would not have survived if they had wandered from their customary hunting grounds on a whim or tried to eat each new plant they found. Yet a disposition, or a mood, is not an ideology.

There is widespread agreement that the true founder of conservatism as an ideology was Edmund Burke (1729–1797), an Irishman who moved to England and served for nearly thirty years in the House of Commons of the British Parliament. Burke never called himself a conservative—neither conservatism nor liberalism entered the vocabulary of politics until the 1800s—but in his speeches and writings he expressed a distinctively conservative political position.

Burke developed and expounded his views in the heat of political controversies, particularly in reaction to the French Revolution. When the Revolution began in 1788–1789, many observers in England hailed it as a great step forward for both France and the cause of liberty. But almost from the beginning Burke saw the French Revolution as a foolhardy attempt to create a new society from the ground up. Nearly three years before the Revolution's Reign of Terror, Burke issued his condemnation and warning in *Reflections on the Revolution in France* (1790). In particular, Burke took exception to the revolutionaries'

Edmund Burke (1729–1797)

view of human nature and government, which he thought mistaken, and their conception of freedom, which he thought misguided.

Human Nature and Society

Burke's opposition to the French Revolution rests largely on the claim that the revolutionaries misunderstood human nature. By concentrating on the rights, interests, and choices of the individual, he charged, the revolutionaries had come to think of society as nothing more than a collection of individuals who happened to form a state. From Burke's perspective, this **atomistic view of society** (and humans), as later conservatives called it, is simply wrong. It loses sight of the many important ways in which individuals are connected to and depend upon one another. Political society is no mere heap of individuals, but, similar to a living and changing organism, it is a whole that is greater than the sum of its parts. In this **organic view of society**, individuals are related to one another and to the society in the same way that the heart and eyes and arms are related to the body—not as separate and isolated units but as interdependent members of a living organism. Or, to use one of Burke's favourite metaphors, society is like a fabric—the *social fabric*—and its individual members are like the interwoven threads of a richly textured tapestry. Far from being artificial institutions that individuals choose to create, society and government are outgrowths of human nature that are necessary to human life.

Based on his view of society and government, Burke rejected the claim that civil society is brought into existence—and can just as easily be dissolved—by consenting individuals who enter into a **social contract**. If civil or political society rests on a contract, he said, it is no ordinary contract between individuals, but a sacred covenant that binds whole generations together. To recognize that "society is indeed a contract" does not mean that it is nothing better than a partnership agreement in a trade of pepper and coffee, calico or tobacco, or some other such low concern to be taken up for a little temporary interest and to be dissolved by the fancy of the parties to the contract. It is a partnership in all science; a partnership in all art; a partnership in every virtue and in all perfection. As the ends of such a partnership cannot be obtained in many generations, it becomes a partnership not only between those who are living but between those who are living, those who are dead, and those who are yet to be born.[7]

To preserve this partnership, Burke believed that both government and long-standing customs and traditions are indispensable. People often act out of self-interest (a view Burke shared with the early liberals) and short-sightedness, which is precisely why they need the power of government to restrain them and to keep their passions in check. But government is not a machine that can be taken apart and reassembled whenever and however people want. It is a complex and delicate organism that must be rooted in the customs and traditions of the people, who must acquire the habit of obeying, respecting, and even revering it.

Freedom

As we mentioned, Burke also believed that the French revolutionaries' conception of freedom was misguided. From his point of view, freedom is not necessarily good. It *can* be, but it does not *have* to be. Like fire, freedom is good if it is kept under control and put

---

[7]Edmund Burke, *Reflections on the Revolution in France*, ed. Conor Cruise O'Brien (Harmondsworth, UK: Penguin, 1968) 194–95; see Ball and Dagger, selection 4.24.

to good use. Used wisely and with restraint, freedom is very valuable indeed. But the destructive power of people freed from all legal and traditional restraints is truly terrifying. In Burke's words, "The effect of liberty to individuals is that they may do what they please; we ought to see what it will please them to do, before we risk congratulations, which may be soon turned into complaints."[8]

For Burke and traditional conservatives, liberty is worthwhile only when it is properly ordered. In terms of the triadic model, the agents are individuals who are part of an interconnected social network. Their goal is to exercise their freedom in a harmonious, stable, and orderly society. Because human beings are subject to desires, the obstacles to this goal are radical ideas and innovation, which unleash destructive forces that undermine traditional institutions. (See Figure 5.1.) Unlike the early liberals, furthermore, Burke did not regard government as a major obstacle to freedom, and therefore as a necessary evil. In Burke's eyes, the very fact that government prevents people from doing just anything they happen to desire is what makes ordered liberty possible. For without government restraints, more people would do more things that endanger both themselves and social peace. Burke would surely agree with the observation of a more recent conservative:

> Freedom is comprehensible as a social goal only when subordinate to something else, to an organization or arrangement which defines the individual aim. Hence the aim of freedom is at the same time to aim at the constraint which is its precondition. . . . One major difference between conservatism and liberalism consists, therefore, in the fact that, for the conservative, the value of individual liberty is not absolute, but stands subject to another and higher value, the authority of established government.[9]

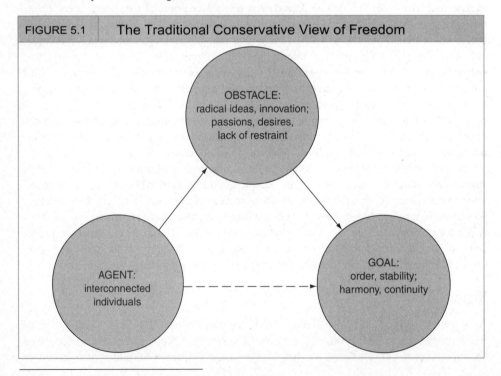

FIGURE 5.1	The Traditional Conservative View of Freedom

OBSTACLE:
radical ideas, innovation;
passions, desires,
lack of restraint

AGENT:
interconnected
individuals

GOAL:
order, stability;
harmony, continuity

---

[8] Burke 91.

[9] Roger Scruton, *The Meaning of Conservatism* (London: Macmillan, 1984) 19.

Revolution and Reform

Burke was not opposed to all revolutions. He looked back with approval to England's Glorious Revolution of 1688, and as a member of Parliament, he was sympathetic to the American colonies in their struggle with the British government. But in Burke's view these were revolutions in the old-fashioned sense. As we saw in Chapter 1, **revolution** referred originally to a return or restoration—a revolving back to a starting point. According to Burke, the English and Americans had fought to restore their rights in order to return to a condition they had previously enjoyed. But the French were engaged in a revolution of a new and much more radical sort. They sought to uproot the settled order of their society and government in order to replace it with something new and untried— and therefore certain to end in disaster, Burke believed.

Burke never claimed that *the existing state of affairs* in France was perfect, nor did he flatly oppose any and all attempts at change. On the contrary, he regarded change as a necessary feature of human life and society. But change should be brought about carefully and gradually—the kind of change that Burke called **reform**—and not through **innovation**. As he saw it, innovation is the attempt to do something entirely new or novel on the grounds that the new must be better than the old. Innovation is therefore radical change for the sake of change, based on abstract reason. It abandons the old ways, the habits that have stood the test of time, in order to launch drastic and dangerous experiments. A revolution like the French was more likely to lead to chaos than a fairer and more prosperous society.

Burke believed that the French revolutionaries were like people who lived in a house with a leaky roof and broken windows. Rather than make the necessary repairs, they decided that the house that had sheltered them all their lives must be torn down to make way for a new, glorious, rational structure. Drawing their plans with no experience of architecture or carpentry, they would soon find themselves homeless and unprotected. The revolutionaries had rejected the tried-and-true way of reform for the path of innovation and were now following it to their ruin.

So Burke preferred reform to innovation because it was safer and surer. After all, a successful reform will do some good, and an unsuccessful one will do little harm. Customs and traditions have gradually evolved over the generations, so they reflect the lessons that people and societies have learned, bit by bit, in the course of their lives. The fact that traditions have lasted so long is evidence that they have literally stood the test of time. They embody the accumulated wisdom not just of one or two people but of generations— a wisdom we seldom appreciate because we simply take our customs for granted as they become second nature.

Government

With tradition as our guide, we can reform government and preserve society without exposing them to the dangers of innovation. But what sort of government and society did Burke have in mind? What was his idea of a sound body politic? Burke believed that there is no one best form of government. Government must reflect the history, habits, and common sense of a people: a form of government that ably serves the needs of one country could fail utterly in another. Even so, Burke's speeches and writings suggest that there were certain features of government and society that he thought especially desirable, at least in countries like the United Kingdom. These features include **representative**

government; a "true **natural aristocracy**"; private property; and the distribution of power among the families, churches, and voluntary associations that form the "**little platoons**" of society.

Representative Government. It is scarcely surprising that Burke, a member of Parliament, should favour representative government. But we should not take this to mean that he also favoured democracy. In Burke's day only a small minority of the British population, principally male property owners, could vote or stand for election, and Burke saw no need to expand the electorate significantly. The interests of the people should be represented in government, but people do not have to vote to have their interests well represented. What matters more than the right to vote is having the right kind of person in office—a wise, prudent, and well-informed person to whom they can entrust their interests. In his "Speech to the Electors of Bristol" in 1774, Burke stated his case in this way:

> Certainly, Gentlemen, it ought to be the happiness and glory of a representative to live in the strictest union, the closest correspondence, and the most unreserved communication with his constituents. Their wishes ought to have great weight with him; their opinions high respect; their business unremitted attention. It is his duty to sacrifice his repose, his pleasure, his satisfactions, to theirs—and above all . . . to prefer their interest to his own. But his unbiased opinion, his mature judgment, his enlightened conscience, he ought not to sacrifice to you, to any man, or to any set of men living. . . . Your representative owes you not his industry only, but his judgment; and he betrays, instead of serving you, if he sacrifices it to your opinion.[10]

Like many conservatives, Burke thought that democracy would seriously threaten the health of representative government. If the masses of people gained the franchise, they would vote for candidates who pander to their passions and desires. They would thus elect representatives who will respond to their momentary wishes instead of promoting the society's long-term interests.

The Natural Aristocracy. But even under a restricted franchise, where are these unbiased, mature, and enlightened trustees to be found? Burke's answer is to look to what he called a "true natural aristocracy." These are the people, the rare few, who have the ability, the experience, and the inclination to govern wisely in the interest of the whole society. These are the people who are natural leaders, who learn from an early age that others look to them for direction. These are the people who had the leisure as children to study, to gain knowledge of politics and society, and to develop their abilities. These people are most likely to come from the hereditary aristocracy, Burke thought.

Burke did not say that the true natural aristocracy and the hereditary aristocracy are one and the same, but he did believe that a person could not achieve a place in the natural aristocracy without both the ability *and* the necessary opportunity to learn the art of governing wisely and well. In Burke's day the people who were most likely to have the opportunity were those who came from the hereditary aristocracy. Society was accustomed to looking to the nobility for leadership, after all, and the nobles were accustomed to providing it. Perhaps even more important was the opportunity the hereditary aristocracy enjoyed as the largest landholders in a society where wealth came primarily from the land. Because they had wealth, the sons of the aristocracy enjoyed leisure; because they

---

[10]In Hanna Pitkin, ed., *Representation* (New York: Atherton, 1969) 174–175.

enjoyed leisure, they had time for education; because they were educated, they could gain the knowledge and develop the abilities necessary to play a leading part in politics. For all these reasons, Burke thought that they were bound to form the core of the true natural aristocracy. There was room for others—non-aristocratic commoners such as himself— but a society deprived of its hereditary aristocracy was deprived of many of its best and brightest members. The French revolutionaries and others who attacked **aristocratic privilege** in the name of liberty and equality were guilty of the worst kind of folly, for the destruction of the hereditary aristocracy would surely set off a mad scramble for power among men whose only claim to leadership was their ability to rouse the rabble.

Private Property. Burke's own respect for aristocratic privilege was due in part to the connection he saw between aristocracy and property. In general, he regarded private property to be a stabilizing and conservative force in society. People who own property, especially property in land, identify their interests, and even themselves, with their property, which strengthens their attachment to the society and government that surround and protect their property. This is especially likely to happen when property is passed down generation after generation within a family, so that attachment to land, family, and country become practically indistinguishable from one another. And this is most likely to happen among the hereditary aristocracy.[11]

The "Little Platoons." Burke's notion of a good government is one that draws enlightened representatives from the natural aristocracy to defend private property and the common good. To do its job properly, the government must be strong. Yet its strength should not be concentrated in one person or in one place, lest this tempt those in power to abuse it. This is why Burke stressed the importance of the "little platoons," those secondary associations—clubs, churches, neighbourhood organizations, local governments, et cetera—that make up a society. Burke argued that power should be spread throughout society. Local concerns should be dealt with at the local level, not the national; and instead of placing all power in the government itself, the traditional authority of churches, families, and other groups should be respected. In this way government would be strong enough to protect society, but not so strong as to smother the "little platoons" that make ordered liberty possible.

Burke's Legacy

Many conservatives continue to share Burke's views on the desirable features of government. Although most conservatives have come to accept democracy, they still prefer a representative government that is not directly responsive to the will of the people. Few conservatives now defend hereditary aristocracy, but some still believe that some form of true natural aristocracy is necessary if society is to be stable, strong, and healthy. Moreover, all contemporary conservatives share Burke's faith in the value of private property and his desire to defeat the concentration of government power by maintaining the strength of society's "little platoons." Despite the differences that divide them, today's conservatives owe enough to Burke to make it clear why he is often called the father of conservatism.

---

[11]For an ironic comment by a twentieth-century conservative on this claim, see Evelyn Waugh's novel *A Handful of Dust* (London: Chapman, 1934).

CONSERVATISM IN THE NINETEENTH CENTURY

Edmund Burke died in 1797, two years before Napoleon Bonaparte seized power in France and halted the French Revolution that Burke so feared and despised. Yet in some respects the Revolution continued until Napoleon's final defeat at the Battle of Waterloo in 1815. Napoleon's regime preserved many of the changes the revolutionaries had fought for, including the abolition of **feudalism**, with its aristocratic powers and privileges.

Many aristocrats resisted these changes throughout the Revolution and the Napoleonic era that followed. Some even saw the Revolution as the enemy of all that was good and worthwhile in life. Their reaction against it was so fierce and uncompromising that they became known as *reactionaries*.

Conservatism and Reaction

To say that someone is a **reactionary** is to say that he or she not only reacts against the present but also wants to return to an earlier form of society. Unlike Burkean or traditional conservatives, whose concern is to preserve the traditional features of existing society through cautious reform, reactionaries want to turn back the clock to restore society as it used to be. Their task is to overthrow the current social and political arrangements in order to return to the ways of the past. This is precisely what the European reactionaries proposed to do.

Joseph de Maistre

Among the most important of the reactionaries was Joseph de Maistre (1753–1821). De Maistre was born in Savoy, now a part of France but then a French-speaking province of the Kingdom of Piedmont-Sardinia. De Maistre reacted vehemently against the revolutionaries' attacks on monarchy, aristocracy, and religion. As he saw it, the Revolution was primarily an assault on "throne and altar," king and church. But without these two institutions to provide the subjects with a sense of majesty and unity, no society could survive. Once throne and altar are gone and people are left with nothing to respect and nothing to rely on but their own wits and reason, chaos and catastrophe are sure to follow. That, de Maistre said, is precisely what happened during the French Revolution. How could people be surprised at the bloodshed of the Reign of Terror when the revolutionaries had uprooted the old society, the majestic work of God, to replace it with the work of mere man? Indeed, de Maistre went so far as to reject the notion that a people is capable of drafting and establishing a suitable constitution for its society. A written constitution is downright dangerous, he declared, because it exposes the weakness of government:

> The more that is written, the weaker is the institution, the reason being clear. Laws are only declarations of rights, and rights are not declared except when they are attacked, so that the multiplicity of written constitutional laws shows only the multiplicity of conflicts and the danger of destruction.[12]

De Maistre's quarrel with the French Revolution was part of his larger struggle against the spirit of the eighteenth century. The French *philosophes* had proclaimed this

---

[12]Joseph de Maistre, "Considerations on France," *The Works of Joseph de Maistre,* ed. Jack Lively (New York: Macmillan, 1965) 78; see Ball and Dagger, selection 4.25.

the time of **Enlightenment**, the period when human reason was beginning at last to rout the forces of superstition, **prejudice**, and ignorance. But de Maistre saw the Enlightenment as an age of arrogance that led to the downfall of the most sacred and necessary social institutions—throne and altar. So not only the Revolution but also the eighteenth century's rationalist mentality must be defeated in order to return society and government to their proper conditions.

De Maistre lived long enough to see the Reaction, as it was called, take effect in the years after Napoleon's defeat. The chief architect of this attempt to restore the old aristocratic order was Prince Klemens von Metternich (1773–1859). As foreign minister of the Hapsburg (or Austrian) Empire, Metternich presided over the Congress of Vienna in 1815. This Congress brought together representatives of the forces at war with Napoleonic France—chiefly Britain, Russia, and Austria—in order to find some basis for preserving peace and stability in Europe. Under Metternich's guidance, the Congress settled on hereditary monarchy as the only legitimate form of rule and aimed to restore their thrones to the European kings who had been ousted from power after 1789.

Metternich's reactionary work endured for more than thirty years. In 1848, however, a series of liberal uprisings swept through Europe, and Metternich himself was forced from office, a victim of the forces he had sought to repel.

Throughout this period and well into the second half of the nineteenth century, the leadership of the Roman Catholic Church also played a conservative, and often reactionary, role in Europe. Given the church's privileged position in the old aristocratic order— as the First Estate in France's Estates General, for instance—this is hardly surprising. When early liberals attacked the church as an enemy of reason and freedom, the church counterattacked at every opportunity. Thus in 1864, Pope Pius IX issued his *Syllabus of Errors,* in which he sharply criticized liberalism for undermining religion and the traditional order. Among the grievous errors of liberalism, Pius IX included the following mistaken beliefs:

> 3. Human reason, without any regard to God, is the sole arbiter of truth and falsehood, of good and evil; it is a law to itself, and by its natural force it suffices to secure the welfare of men and nations . . .

> 77. In the present day, it is no longer expedient that the Catholic religion shall be held as the only religion of the State, to the exclusion of all other modes of worship.[13]

But reaction was not the only form that conservatism took in the nineteenth century. There were more moderate forms too, particularly two that emerged in Britain: **cultural conservatism** and **tory democracy**.

Cultural Conservatism

When the French Revolution began, many people in England greeted it as the dawn of a glorious new age. As William Wordsworth (1770–1850) put it in his poem, "French Revolution as It Appeared to Enthusiasts at Its Commencement,"

> Bliss was it in that dawn to be alive,

> But to be young was very heaven.

---

[13]Viereck, *Conservatism* 165–166.

But Burke's *Reflections on the Revolution in France* and subsequent events—especially the execution of King Louis XVI—soon quelled this early enthusiasm for the Revolution. War between England and France began in 1793 and continued almost without interruption until 1815. Compared with the countries of the European continent, England survived the revolutionary era with relatively little social upheaval, leaving English conservatives little reason to become reactionary.

But English conservatives did oppose the French Revolution and the changes it wrought. Even Wordsworth turned against it, arguing that the revolutionaries placed too much faith in reason and too little in people's emotional or spiritual tie to nature. But for Wordsworth, his friend and fellow poet Samuel Taylor Coleridge, and other English conservatives of the early 1800s, the greatest threat to English society came not from the French Revolution but from another, very different kind of revolution—the Industrial Revolution that was reshaping English society from top to bottom. In particular, English conservatives after Burke defended the traditional agricultural society against the ravages of industry and commerce. Commerce and capitalism were the enemies of spirituality and culture, they argued. The new creed of production in pursuit of profit simply fostered crass materialism. All the old virtues, all loyalties, all ties to persons and places were vanishing in the pursuit of money—a pursuit that would end with men and women out of touch with themselves, with one another, and with nature. As Wordsworth complained in a sonnet from 1806,

> The world is too much with us; late and soon,
>
> Getting and spending, we lay waste our powers:
>
> Little we see in Nature that is ours;
>
> We have given our hearts away, a sordid boon!

With its suspicion of commerce and its abhorrence of materialism, cultural conservatism proved to be an enduring theme, not only in England but also in the United States and elsewhere. In England more than other countries, however, cultural conservatism found an ally in a political party that made conservatism an effective political force: the Tories.

Tory Democracy

Throughout the eighteenth century, the various **Tory** (conservative) and **Whig** (liberal) factions vied for power in Britain. This competition continued into the 1800s, with the Tories generally defending the interests of the landowning aristocracy, and the Whigs favouring a more commercial and competitive society. The differences between the two parties gradually focused on their attitudes toward the expansion of the electorate. Tories typically opposed any expansion of voting rights beyond the small minority who already held them. But the Whigs campaigned to win the vote for middle-class males—merchants, industrialists, and professional men, for the most part—until they succeeded in 1832 in passing the Great Reform Bill. With the influx of new voters eager to support their cause, the Whigs looked forward to a long period of political dominance.

The Tories, on the other hand, could look forward only to losing elections unless they could find some way to attract new voters to their cause. The leader who found the way was Benjamin Disraeli (1804–1881). Most historians consider Disraeli the founder of the modern British Conservative Party. Disraeli's solution was to form an alliance between the aristocratic upper class and the working class. To accomplish this, he pursued the policies of tory democracy.

Tory democracy attempted to address the needs of the working class while instilling in the workers a respect for the traditional order of English life—including a respect for the monarchy, the aristocracy, and the established Church of England. In Disraeli's words,

> Instead of falling under . . . the thralldom of capital—under those who, while they boast of their intelligence, are more proud of their wealth—if we must find a new force to maintain the ancient throne and monarchy of England, I, for one, hope that we may find that novel power in the invigorating energies of an educated and enfranchised people.[14]

So Disraeli set out both to include the workers in the electorate and to improve their condition in life. His support of the Reform Bill of 1867 helped bring the vote to the working-class males of the cities, and in his second term as British prime minister (1874–1880) he made trade unions legal and recognized the workers' right to strike against their employers. With these and other measures, Disraeli extended the cultural conservatives' dislike of the commercial middle class into a political alliance between the conservative aristocracy and the potentially revolutionary working class—hence the term *tory democracy*. This was to be the dominant form of British conservatism, under the leadership of Sir Winston Churchill and others, until Margaret Thatcher became British prime minister in 1979.

Origins of English-Canadian Conservatism

After the American colonies successfully won their independence from Britain in 1783, many of the colonists who had supported the British cause feared reprisals. Some returned to Britain and others fled north to the colonies that remained loyal in British North America. They settled in what is now Nova Scotia, New Brunswick, the Eastern Townships of Quebec, and Ontario and came to be known as United Empire Loyalists. Like Burke, they believed in a "manly, regulated liberty," but they were conservatives rather than liberals because they strongly believed in the importance of a hierarchical social system of which the monarchy was the keystone that held the whole together.

The early Canadian conservatives also shared the view of the British social conservatives that religion and spiritual values were central to society. In the English-speaking parts of British North America, the influence of the Anglican Church was central to society and politics, and John Strachan (1778–1867), bishop of Toronto, was the most important figure. Although he failed to protect the Anglican dominance in religion, he recognized the importance of education in maintaining the influence of spiritual values, and he founded Trinity College in 1851.

Origins of French-Canadian Conservatism

Quebec conservatism stemmed from different religious roots. The settlement in New France was Roman Catholic, and immigration from France came at a time before the liberal

---

[14]Viereck, *Conservatism* 44.

and rationalist ideas of the Enlightenment had penetrated the French countryside. The settlers who came to New France carried largely feudal values with them, and immigration completely ceased after the British conquest in 1763. After the French Revolution in 1789, which was strongly opposed to the Roman Catholic Church, Quebec Roman Catholics felt alienated from France. They looked directly to the pope, whom they believed was infallible, for religious strength and for social and political guidance. The doctrine they adopted, expressed in a number of papal teachings called *encyclicals,* was **Ultramontanism**. This doctrine rejected any compromise with modern liberal or economic ideas and insisted that politicians should defer to church teachings as expressed by its bishops.

Politically, Quebec conservatives were called *Bleus.* Under the leadership of Sir George-Étienne Cartier, they formed an alliance with Sir John A. Macdonald's English-Canadian Conservatives that governed Canada for most of the first twenty-five years of Confederation. They combined loyalty to the Roman Catholic Church with loyalty to the British monarchy. However, after the execution of the visionary Métis leader Louis Riel in 1885 by Macdonald's government, Quebec conservatives turned inward and, for the next seventy years, concentrated their efforts on defending Quebec's hierarchical social structure, the role of the church, and the province's autonomy against the centralizing inroads of the federal government. The most important conservative leader in Quebec during that time was Maurice Duplessis (premier 1936–1939, 1944–1959). His death in 1959 marked the collapse of conservatism in Quebec.

English-Canadian Conservatism under Sir John A. Macdonald

Sir John A. Macdonald (1815–1891) is generally credited as one of the founders of the Canadian Conservative Party, established in 1854. His conservatism was not in the reactionary style of the continental conservatives, but squarely in line with Canada's British heritage. It looked directly back to Burke.

At the time of Confederation in 1867, the United States had just finished a bloody five-year civil war that Macdonald and other Canadian conservatives attributed in part to the extreme form of democracy that prevailed there. He was determined that Canada would not make the same mistake. So when he was designing Canada's central parliamentary institutions, he ensured they reflected Burke's key principles.

First, the House of Commons was representative but not democratic. It was elected, but only men with property were allowed to vote, and members of Parliament were very much expected to use their judgment rather than jump to satisfy the wishes of their constituents.

Second, the Senate incorporated most of the principles Burke thought important in a legislature. Senators had to be at least thirty years old so that they would be mature, and their appointments were for life so they would not be looking over their shoulder at the electorate when they made their decisions. Most Burkean of all was the requirement that Senators own a substantial amount of land. In Burke's view, people who owned farms had an attachment to their country in a way that speculators in stocks and bonds did not.

Disraeli was British prime minister at the time of Confederation, and he was another influence on Macdonald's conservatism. Neither Disraeli nor Burke trusted the free market. Macdonald agreed with them. He set out on an aggressive policy of nation building. In 1869 his government bought an immense territory from the Hudson's Bay Company that consisted of Canada's north plus the provinces of Manitoba, Saskatchewan, and

Alberta. In 1878 he adopted the National Policy. It consisted of two elements: high tariffs to protect Canadian manufacturers against foreign competition, and active government involvement in the construction of a transcontinental railway. Macdonald was determined that political imperatives would prevail over economic ones.

Tory democracy remained a distinctly British form of conservatism. In Germany, Prussian Chancellor Otto von Bismarck (1815–1898) accomplished something similar by providing state-supported insurance and benefits to workers. Yet Bismarck was no democrat. Nor was he much of a conservative; he was more interested in consolidating the various provinces of Germany into a united and powerful **nation-state** than he was in preserving the traditional way of life. Elsewhere, especially in the United States, what came to be called *conservatism* was a far cry from tory democracy.

Conservatism in the United States

American conservatism followed a different course in the nineteenth century. When the U.S. Constitution was drafted in 1787, the free population of the United States comprised about 3 million people, almost all of whom were Protestants of European descent. Lacking experience of feudalism and hereditary aristocracy, and having no monarch, no aristocracy, and no established national church, American conservatives were hardly likely to follow the path of Burke or of de Maistre's reactionary appeal to throne and altar or tory democracy. In a country founded on the principles of liberalism—or perhaps more accurately, as we noted in Chapter 3, on a mixture of liberal and republican principles—American conservatives were chiefly concerned with preserving an essentially liberal society and way of life.

Two of the American foundering fathers, John Adams (1735–1826) and Alexander Hamilton (1757–1804), are sometimes taken to be conservatives in the Burkean mould. But the differences between them and Burke are more telling than the similarities. Like Burke, Adams often spoke favourably of the natural aristocracy, but Adams could not look to a hereditary nobility, as Burke did, to provide the core of this group of natural leaders, for there was no such class in the United States. The closest Adams could come was men of property, and this was a much broader group in the United States than in Burke's England. As for Hamilton, his claim to the credentials of a traditional conservative rests largely on his defence of constitutional monarchy at the time of the founding. But the plan he drafted as secretary of the treasury—a plan to make the United States a great commercial power—hardly displayed a traditional conservative's suspicion of commerce and reverence for the settled forms of social life.

In the early and middle 1800s, there were several figures in the United States whose views could be linked to cultural conservatism. Perhaps the most important of these, at least in retrospect, were two friends who became giants of American literature—Nathaniel Hawthorne (1804–1864) and Herman Melville (1819–1891). Through their literature, both authors criticized what they saw as the foolishly optimistic temper of their times. For instance, Hawthorne depicted the vanity and futility of the quest for perfection in his story "Earth's Holocaust," and then portrayed the tragic consequences of such a quest in stories like "The Birthmark." Similarly, Melville heaped scorn on those who preached the doctrine of faith in human nature in his bitterly ironic novel *The Confidence Man*; his "Bartleby the Scrivener: A Story of Wall Street" can be read as an attack on the dehumanizing consequences of capitalism.

As in England, cultural conservatism has remained an important thread in the fabric of American conservatism. More characteristic, however, was the shift in the direction of *laissez-faire* capitalism that took place in the late nineteenth century. This was the period when the name "conservative" began to be applied to the businessmen and industrialists who had previously been seen as the enemies of tradition. What was called liberalism in other countries was called conservatism in the United States. How did this happen? Two principal factors seem to have been at work.

First, businessmen and industrialists stressed the importance of private property (a point on which conservatives and liberals agree) as well as individualism. Because these ideals had a long tradition in the United States, the captains of industry could in a sense appeal to traditional values of their country when they defended *laissez-faire* capitalism. The United States had been founded on the belief in the individual's natural rights to life, liberty, and the pursuit of happiness, after all. Once American business leaders interpreted these rights to mean that every individual should be free to pursue profits in the competitive marketplace, they could then be regarded as conservatives.

The second factor was the development of **welfare liberalism** in the late nineteenth century. The rise of this new form of liberalism, with its call for government action to promote individual liberty and equality of opportunity, meant that those who clung to the views of early or classical liberalism were now in danger of being left behind. As we saw in Chapter 3, a split between welfare and neoclassical liberalism developed. Because neoclassical liberals remained true to the faith of early liberals—especially the faith in what men and women can do when they are freed from the restraints of that "necessary evil," government—neoclassical liberals came to be seen as old-fashioned. By sticking to the older form of liberalism, there was a sense in which they were surely conservatives.

For both these reasons, classical liberalism came to be called *conservatism* in the United States. Even the **Social Darwinists**, whom we described in Chapter 3 as neoclassical liberals, were included. Men like Herbert Spencer and William Graham Sumner advanced an atomistic conception of society, with every person locked in a struggle for survival with every other. No traditional or cultural conservative could accept such an atomistic and anti-organic vision. But in the United States the Social Darwinists' defence of private property and competitive individualism, coupled with their attack on government regulations, placed them squarely, if a bit uncomfortably, in the conservative camp.

Thus over the past century, conservatism in the United States has suffered from the continuing tension between traditional conservatives, on the one hand, and those who see conservatism as primarily the defence of *laissez-faire* capitalism, on the other. There are points on which the two sides agree, such as the value of private property and the folly of abstract social planning—especially in the form of **socialism** or **communism**. But there are so many points on which they disagree that the two sides seem to be enemies as often as allies. Certainly it is difficult to see how anyone with a Burkean distrust of innovation can join comfortably with someone who, in the name of competition and progress, constantly seeks new products to sell to more people in hopes of a better, and more profitable, life.

Conservatism is an ideology that constantly evolves. The next chapter examines its development over the past hundred years.

For Further Reading

Armenteros, Carolina. *French Idea of History: Joseph de Maistre and His Heirs, 1794–1854*. Ithaca: Cornell UP, 2011.

Berlin, Isaiah. "Joseph de Maistre and the Origins of Fascism," in Isaiah Berlin, ed., *The Crooked Timber of Humanity: Chapters in the History of Ideas*. New York: Vintage, 1992.

Dunn, Charles W., and J. David Woodard. *The Conservative Tradition in America*. Lanham, MD: Rowman, 1996.

Farthing, John. *Freedom Wears a Crown*. Toronto: Kingswood, 1957.

Flannagan, Tom. *Harper's Team: Behind the Scenes in the Conservative Rise to Power*. Montreal: McGill-Queen's UP, 2007.

Gwyn, Richard J. *Nation Maker: Sir John A. Macdonald: His Life, Our Times*. Toronto: Random House of Canada, 2011.

Kirk, Russell. *The Conservative Mind from Burke to Elliot*. 7th revised edition. New York: Regnery, 1986.

Hodgson, Godfrey. *The World Turned Rightside Up: A History of the Conservative Ascendancy in America*. New York: Houghton, 1996.

Lebrun, Richard. *Joseph de Maistre's Life, Thought and Influence, Selected Studies*. Montreal: McGill-Queen's University Press, 2000.

O'Brien, Conor Cruise. *The Great Melody: Thematic Biography and Commented Anthology of Edmund Burke*. Chicago: University of Chicago Press, 1994.

O'Gorman, Frank. *Edmund Burke: His Political Philosophy*. London: Allen, 1973.

Orchard, David. *The Fight for Canada*. Toronto: Stoddart, 1998.

Steinfels, Peter. *The Neoconservatives*. New York: Simon, 1979.

Useful Websites and Social Media

http://plato.stanford.edu/entries/burke Stanford Encyclopedia of Philosophy "Edmund Burke"

www.bbc.co.uk/history/historic_figures/burke_edmund.shtml BBC History "Edmund Burke

www.newadvent.org/cathen/09554a.htm New Advent "Joseph de Maistre"

www.bbc.co.uk/history/historic_figures/disraeli_benjamin.shtml BBC History "Benjamin Disraeli"

http://farnboroughhillhistorydept.wikispaces.com/file/view/disraeli+and+tory+demo cracy.pdf Farnborough Hill History Department "Tory Democracy"

http://www.thecanadianencyclopedia.com/articles/sir-john-alexander-macdonald The Canadian Encyclopedia "Sir John Alexander Macdonald"

www.biographi.ca/009004-119.01-e.php?BioId=40370 Dictionary of Canadian Biography Online "Sir John Alexander Macdonald"

From the Ball and Dagger Reader *Ideals and Ideologies*, US Eighth Edition

Part Four: Conservatism

4.24. Edmund Burke—Society, Reverence, and the "True Natural Aristocracy," page 134

4.25. Joseph de Maistre—Conservatism as Reaction, page 141

Discussion Questions

1. Human beings display many weaknesses: they lie, steal, and kill. Are these flaws inherent in human nature or can they somehow be eradicated?

2. Is society made up of individuals or of members of groups?

3. The United States wants to export liberal democracy to the Middle East. Theoretically, is this possible?

4. What would Stephen Harper's response be to the tory idea that the role of the state is to care for the poor?

MySearchLab MySearchLab with eText offers you access to an online interactive version of the text, additional quizzes and assessment, extensive help with your writing and research projects, and provides round-the-clock access to credible and reliable source material. Go to **www.mysearchlab.com** to access these resources.

CHAPTER 6

Contemporary Conservatism

To be conservative, then, is to prefer the familiar to the unknown, to prefer the tried to the untried, fact to mystery, the actual to the possible, the limited to the unbounded, the near to the distant, the sufficient to the superabundant, the convenient to the perfect, present laughter to utopian bliss. Familiar relationships and loyalties will be preferred to the allure of more profitable attachments; to acquire and to enlarge will be less important than to keep, to cultivate and to enjoy; the grief of loss will be more acute than the excitement of novelty or promise.

Michael Oakeshott, *"On Being Conservative"*

LEARNING OBJECTIVES

After completing this chapter you should be able to

1. Understand the conservative argument against mass society in the twentieth century.

2. Distinguish between and describe the four distinct and often incompatible strands of contemporary conservatism.

3. Evaluate how conservatism performs the four functions of an ideology.

TWENTIETH CENTURY DEVELOPMENTS

In recent years the tension between the two kinds of conservatism has spread beyond the United States, leading most notably to a division in the ranks of conservatives in the United Kingdom. In the early years of the twentieth century, however, conservatives in Europe and traditional conservatives in the United States were united in their attacks on what they called **mass society**.

Critique of Mass Society

The nineteenth century had been an age of increasing democracy. The franchise had been greatly extended throughout the Western world. The power of the old aristocracy had been broken, and the spread of public education meant that many of the barriers to social mobility and advancement were falling. At the beginning of the twentieth century, moreover, the rapid development of industrial mass production made it seem as if economic barriers were collapsing as well. Items that once would have been available only to the wealthy few—the automobile, for instance—were now being built for and sold to the masses.

Some people welcomed these developments, but not the traditional conservatives. From their point of view, this new mass society posed the same threat that democracy had always posed—that the masses would throw society first into chaos, then into despotism. In arguments similar to those of Plato, Aristotle, and, more recently, Alexis de Tocqueville, traditional conservatives maintained that the common people were too weak and too ignorant to take charge of government. Too weak to curb their appetites or restrain their desires, the people will want more and more—more wealth, more property, more power—like gluttons who ruin their health because they cannot stop eating. And they are too ignorant and too short-sighted to see the disaster they are bringing upon their society and themselves. Once their unchecked demands have taken society to the brink of anarchy, the masses will then cry out for a strong and decisive leader who will restore law and order—even at the expense of liberty.

Canadian conservatives in the mid-nineteenth century also viewed American democracy with distaste. They saw political corruption, elected judges, social instability, rampant capitalism, and civil war. By contrast, Canada enjoyed a stable monarchy and a society committed to moderation and fair play. Its appointed judges were impartial, and British justice was perhaps the greatest value to which a society could aspire. Democracy in itself was always going to be a threat to social order because it would be a threat to property. Only a minority owned property, and if the majority won power in an election, that property would be in danger. The democratic majority also posed a threat to property in another way. There were more debtors in society than creditors. Democracy gave politicians an incentive to adopt inflationary measures to buy the votes of the poor, because inflation lessens the real value of debt. For most of the nineteenth century, the right to vote in Canada was tightly tied to the right to hold property.

The conservative argument against mass society gained credence in the 1920s and 1930s as fascists and Nazis came to power in Italy, Spain, and Germany. To the conservative eye, these brutal movements were the logical result of the democratic excesses of mass society. All the hard-won accomplishments of European civilization, particularly representative government in parliaments, were in danger of being ground under the boot-heels of fascist "blackshirts" and Nazi "storm troopers" and their dictatorial leaders. Even defenders of **liberal democracy**, such as Spanish philosopher José Ortega y Gasset (1883–1955), adopted a conservative stance in the face of fascism. In *The Revolt of the Masses,* Ortega asserted that

> Nothing indicates more clearly the characteristics of the day than the fact that there are so few countries where an opposition exists. In almost all, a homogeneous mass weighs on public authority and crushes down, annihilates every opposing group. The mass . . . does not wish to share life with those who are not of it. It has a deadly hatred of all that is not itself.[1]

In response to this threat, conservative critics of mass society maintained that the masses need to learn, or be taught, self-restraint. As R. B. Bennett, Canada's Conservative prime minister during the Depression of the 1930s, put it:

> It is almost incomprehensible that the vital issues of life and death to nations, peace or war, bankruptcy or solvency, should be determined by the counting of heads and knowing as we do that the majority under modern conditions—happily the majority becoming smaller—are untrained and unskilled in dealing with the problems which they have to determine.[2]

---

[1] José Ortega y Gasset, *The Revolt of the Masses* (New York: Norton, 1932), 77; see Ball and Dagger, selection 28. The twin themes of mass society and mass politics have been sounded by sociologists and social theorists since the nineteenth-century studies of Gustav Le Bon (see chapter 7) and others. See, for example, William Kornhauser, *The Politics of Mass Society* (Glencoe, IL: Free P, 1959), and the historical overview and critical reassessment by Richard Bellamy, "The Advent of the Masses and the Making of the Modern Theory of Democracy," *The Cambridge History of Twentieth-Century Political Thought,* ed. Terence Ball and Richard Bellamy (Cambridge: Cambridge UP, 2003).

[2] R. B. Bennett, "Democracy on Trial," *Canadian Problems as Seen by Twenty Outstanding Men of Canada* (Toronto: Oxford UP, 1933).

This meant that the masses must learn either to curb their appetites and respect the traditional ways or, more likely, to recognize that it is better to entrust their government to the aristocracy or elite—that is, to those with superior wisdom, experience, and foresight. This view is similar to the argument Burke made on behalf of his "true natural aristocracy." The difference is that by the twentieth century, few conservatives looked to the hereditary aristocracy to form the core of this natural governing elite. Still, conservatives believed—and traditional conservatives continue to believe—that in every society there will be some small number of men and women who are suited by ability, experience, and temperament to govern, while the great majority are utterly unsuited in one or more of these respects. If we must live in mass society, conservatives say, we should at least be prudent enough to put a substantial share of power in the hands of those who rise above the mass. As Canadian Conservative leader Robert Stanfield said, "I think a successful leader has to have a streak of ruthlessness. It may not be talked about much, but it is essential."[3]

Equality

An abiding fear of mass society explains why so many conservatives, from Burke to the present, have opposed what they call **levelling**. Conservatives have typically been suspicious of attempts to achieve greater democracy or equality because they believe these will "level" society. One can presumably promote equality either by improving the condition of people at the bottom of society or by worsening the condition of those at the top. As conservatives point out, attempts to make the people at the bottom better off usually involve taking something away from the top—as in "soak the rich" tax policies. The problem with such schemes, according to the conservative argument, is that they raise the people at the bottom very little, lower the people at the top a great deal, and in the long run reduce everyone in society to the same low level. In the name of equality, conservatives claim, levelling programs simply promote economic and social stagnation.

Instead of levelling policies, conservatives often favour tax cuts. Ontario Premier Mike Harris portrayed himself as the "tax fighter" when he ran for office in 1995, and the centrepiece of his Common Sense Revolution was a 30 percent cut in personal income taxes and the introduction of a Taxpayer Protection Act that made it difficult for subsequent governments to raise taxes.

Levelling is culturally harmful, too, according to conservatives. In this age of equality, everyone is taught that his or her opinions or beliefs are just as good as anyone else's. Thus we find ourselves in an age of fads and fancies, with fashions changing constantly and the only standards of worth being novelty and popularity. Serious literature, music, and art are overwhelmed by the levelling tendencies of mass society. The quantity of sales counts for more than the quality of the work in this age of bestselling books and blockbuster movies, all produced according to formulae that appeal to a mass audience. Even in colleges and universities, students forsake philosophy, literature, and history to study advertising and marketing—two disciplines that are concerned not with truth but with increasing the sales of products of dubious value.

---

[3]"Robert Stanfield: On Politics, Polls and Leadership," interview by James G. Frank, *Canadian Business Review* 15.2 (Summer 1988).

Conservatives have often seen levelling as a threat to society in another way as well. In addition to its harmful effects in economic and cultural matters, they see levelling as the enemy of social variety and diversity. Drawing on arguments similar to Burke's praise of the "little platoons" of society, conservatives frequently defend the neighbourhood, the town, and the region as centres of local variety and diversity—centres that are always in danger of being squashed by the levelling forces of mass society. Within a society, conservatives say, it is healthy to have diverse communities. Diversity is a sign of health, for it shows that people at the local level are able to muster the resources they need to meet the challenges of life—challenges that will vary considerably from one community to another. We should especially hope to preserve communities where people are disposed to follow the customs and habits of their ancestors. Such a disposition—or prejudice, in Burke's sense—inclines people not only to follow the time-tested ways but also to remain loyal to a community that they see themselves sharing with their ancestors, their children, and generations yet to come.

This sense of tradition can be found in *I'll Take My Stand,* a collection of essays published in 1930 by a group of American writers known as the Southern Agrarians.[4] The Agrarians defended the traditional agricultural society of the southern United States against the invasion of industrialism from the northern states. They argued that an agricultural society will necessarily be traditional, for it will necessarily be concerned with property and family. Both literally and figuratively, an agricultural society is concerned with roots. Industrial society, however, is rootless, and all traditional loyalties and affections give way in face of the demands for production and consumption that characterize mass society.

From early in the twentieth century, conservatives have issued warnings against the excesses of mass society. Mass society threatens to degenerate into anarchy and despotism, or at least to level society into a rootless crowd of consumers who relentlessly seek new name-brand commodities to consume.

Anti-Communism

One of the pervasive themes of twentieth-century conservatism is its resolute opposition to communism. This is one of the few points on which most conservatives agree. Throughout the twentieth century, conservatives were consistent opponents of communism. Why were conservatives so united and so vehement in this opposition?

At bottom, the answer lies in two contrasting views of human nature and freedom. For conservatives, human beings are fundamentally imperfect creatures who are likely to abuse freedom through their selfishness and short-sightedness. But communists, as we shall see in Chapters 7 and 8, take a more optimistic view. Communists typically argue that the source of social problems is not human nature but social conditions—especially the division of society into social and economic classes based on the ownership and control of property. Once people are freed from these crippling conditions, communists say, they will grow and flourish. This belief contrasts sharply with the conservative view.

Out of this general opposition emerge three more particular respects in which conservatives are fundamentally at odds with communism: progress, perfectibility, and planning. In all three respects, conservatives reject the communist position.

---

[4]Twelve Southerners, *I'll Take My Stand* (New York: Harper, 1930).

First, following Burke, most conservatives argue that faith in progress is unwarranted. Social change is not necessarily change for the better. Every change carries with it certain risks, and the kind of revolutionary changes communists call for are far too risky—and unrealistic—to be taken by prudent persons.

Second, the communists' faith in progress rests on their utterly unjustified faith in the ultimate perfectibility of human nature and society. According to conservatives, this faith runs counter to all human experience. Indeed, some conservatives suggest that belief in perfectibility is a heresy—a view that contradicts certain religious truths. When communists claim that men and women must free themselves from oppressive social conditions in order to live rich and full lives, they deny original sin and human imperfection. The fact that many communists, including Karl Marx, have been atheists has only fuelled the hostility of conservatives of a religious orientation. And those conservatives who are not themselves religious attack the communist belief in perfectibility as a dangerous illusion, if not a heresy.

Third, most conservatives dislike the communists' emphasis on planning. Like neo-classical liberals, some conservatives believe that social planning is always inefficient; we should instead leave matters to competition on the open market. Burkean or traditional conservatives believe that some planning is necessary and desirable, but only planning on a small scale for gradual, piecemeal social change. But communists have often called for social planning of the broadest, most comprehensive sort. According to their conservative critics, they want to survey all aspects of society in order to anticipate all social needs, to estimate the resources available to meet those needs, and to take action to solve all social problems. Conservatives claim that planning on such a grand scale places entirely too much faith in human reason. It encourages grandiose social schemes that are almost certain to collapse in failure, thereby sinking people deeper in the misery from which the communists had planned to rescue them.

Moreover, planning of this sort requires that power be concentrated in the hands of a few at the centre of society. There is no room for diversity or variety—no room for freedom—at the local level. The "little platoons" of society are absorbed into the homogeneous mass as everyone in society is levelled to a similar condition—that is, everyone but the few who hold power. In short, the price of grand social planning is neither progress nor perfection but misery, brutality, and despotism. Instead of freeing people from oppressive social conditions, conservatives charge, Soviet-style central planning sacrifices freedom to the oppression of communist planners.

In view of the differences between them, it is hardly surprising that conservatives have been so bitterly opposed to communism. This opposition was particularly strong in the years following the end of the Second World War in 1945. As communist regimes came to power in Eastern Europe, Asia, and elsewhere, communism became the chief focus of conservative concern. As the principal representative of international communism, the Soviet Union appeared to many conservatives to be an "evil empire," as U.S. President Ronald Reagan called it. Since the sudden collapse of communism in Eastern Europe in 1989 and the disintegration of the Soviet Union itself two years later, however, conservatives find themselves in an odd position. They remain very much united in their opposition to communist ideology, but that ideology no longer seems to be a serious threat. Now that their common enemy apparently is vanquished, the question facing conservatives is whether they will find a new reason to make common cause with one another or, failing that, split into quarrelling factions.

CONSERVATISM TODAY

Even before the demise of Soviet communism, conservatism seemed to be giving way to a variety of incompatible and even competing conservat*isms*. There are points on which conservatives continue to agree, such as a general respect for private property and an opposition to communism, but there are so many differences of opinion and emphasis that we can now identify four distinct strands of thought in contemporary conservatism. Two of these, **traditional** (or classical) **conservatism** and **individualist conservatism**, are familiar from our discussion of the split in conservatism in the United States in the 1800s. The remaining two, **neoconservatism** and the **Religious Right**, have become prominent in the past four decades. Each of these four deserves a closer look, with special attention to the two most recent forms.

Traditional Conservatism

The heirs of Edmund Burke—those who cling closely to the positions of the traditional and cultural conservatives—are now often called traditional (or Burkean) conservatives. Like Burke, they think of society as a delicate fabric in which individual lives are woven together. In this view, a society of self-seeking individuals, each of whom is essentially independent of the others and therefore free to pursue his or her own self-interest, is deranged and disordered—a threadbare fabric that hardly deserves to be called a society. Society should promote freedom, to be sure, but traditional conservatives share Burke's conviction that this must be ordered liberty. Society does not consist of isolated or atomistic individuals but of people involved in a complex web or network of interdependent and mutual relationships. Each person has a particular status and a stake in the larger society into which he or she is born, lives, and dies. The purpose of political activity is to preserve the social fabric within which these vital human activities are carried on from generation to generation. Because this fabric is easily torn, it requires our constant care and respect.

By the middle of the twentieth century, traditional conservatives in Canada found their values increasingly under attack as liberal capitalism and popular democracy became the dominant modes of social organization. Traditional conservative John Farthing (1897–1954) launched a vigorous rearguard action against individualism and democratic government. In *Freedom Wears a Crown,* he argued, in line with Burke, that only a living historical tradition, drawing life from one age and passing it on to another, can give strength and wisdom to a society and ensure a political life in harmony with an eternal order. Canada needed to remain faithful to its British and monarchical traditions if it were to enjoy Burke's vigorous but regulated liberty. "The British tradition, rooted in and centred upon the idea of kingship," he wrote, "embraces the whole idea of a kingdom or of a freely ordered realm of life."[5]

Not all conservatives, though, even those who believe strongly in the importance of tradition, are monarchists. British philosopher Michael Oakeshott (1901–1990) denied that politics had anything to do with an eternal order or a monarchy. Atheists could be conservatives, and so could people who lived in republics. For Oakeshott, conservatism consisted of three key elements. The first was a preference for the familiar to the

---

[5]John Farthing, *Freedom Wears a Crown,* ed. Judith Robinson (Toronto: Kingswood, 1957).

unknown and for certainty over change. The second was an acceptance of change when necessary. It was not something to be sought after for its own sake. The third was the belief that change should follow what Oakeshott called "the intimation of institutions," or the inner logic of tradition. According to Oakeshott, the goal of politics is nothing more than attending to the arrangements of one's society. We don't set out as adventurers for some distant and unknown port. We are happy enough if we keep the ship of state afloat during our lifetime and pass it on in a seaworthy state to our children.[6]

Like Burke, traditional conservatives see private property as essential to social stability. They do not equate private property with unbridled capitalism, however, which they continue to regard with some suspicion. According to American conservative columnist George Will, capitalism at its worst is a "solvent" that can dissolve the web of traditional relationships.[7] Government must therefore take care to see that the economic competition of capitalism is kept within bounds—a point on which traditional conservatives sharply disagree with the individualists.

Individualist Conservatism

In the nineteenth century, as we have seen, businessmen, industrialists, and others who held to the views of the early liberals came to be called conservatives in the United States. Until recently, this use of *conservative* was unique to the United States, but in recent years especially it has spread into Canada and elsewhere. For these individualist or free-market conservatives, society is not a delicate fabric but a rough-and-tumble, competitive marketplace. Rather than talk about how individuals are inevitably situated in a web of interdependency and connected across generations with their ancestors and their unborn successors, as traditional conservatives do, individualist conservatives prefer to talk about rugged individualists pulling themselves up by their bootstraps. For the individualist, furthermore, freedom is not ordered liberty but the freedom of individuals to compete with one another, particularly in the economic arena of the free market.

Individualist conservatism is the conservatism of people like former U.S. Senator Barry Goldwater, U.S. President Ronald Reagan, and British Prime Minister Margaret Thatcher. Contrary to traditional conservatives, who stress the intricacy of society and the complexity of its problems, individualist conservatives are inclined to be the sort of rationalists that Burke condemned, those who think that they can solve society's problems with their individual reason. Brian Mulroney, Canada's prime minister during the 1980s, did not fall into the same mould as Reagan and Thatcher, to whom he was often compared. His approach to politics shared some of their goals but was much more traditional.

However, these individualist conservatives all agreed that many of society's ills stemmed mainly from too much government. American conservatives trace the problem back to Franklin Roosevelt's attempt to solve the difficulties of the Great Depression of the 1930s through his activist use of government in the New Deal. In the United Kingdom, the Labour Party took a very active role in managing the economy and even nationalized

---

[6]See the essays in Michael Oakeshott, *Rationalism in Politics* (Indianapolis: Free P, 1991), especially "Rationalism in Politics," "Political Education," and "On Being Conservative."

[7]George Will, *Statecraft as Soulcraft: What Government Does* (New York: Simon, 1983) 119–120.

key sectors such as the steel industry. The economic doctrines of John Maynard Keynes, discussed in Chapter 3, which taught that the state could avoid future depressions by active intervention in the economy, became mainstream policy doctrine in both the United Kingdom and Canada from the 1940s to the 1970s. The individualist conservative critique of this approach was that it led to too much government interference in the operations of the free market. The corresponding solution is simple: "Get government off our backs!" Reduce government spending, particularly for social welfare, and give the free market a free rein in economic if not in moral matters.

Some traditional conservatives have criticized these individualist schemes to cut spending for health services, education, and social welfare, complaining that these amount to cuts or tears in the social fabric of civility and stability. When she was prime minister of the United Kingdom, Thatcher and her followers responded by dubbing these critics "wet hanky" conservatives, or "wets" for short. Let the free market do its work, individualist conservatives say, and everyone will eventually benefit. So the tension between traditionalists and individualists continues within conservatism.

Neoconservatism

To complicate matters further, other forms of conservatism emerged from the social turmoil of the 1960s. One of these, called *neoconservatism,* occupies a position somewhere between traditional and individualist conservatism. Neoconservatism takes its bearings from a group of prominent American academics and public figures, including former U.S. Vice President Dick Cheney and others who have held important positions in recent Republican administrations, including Lynne Cheney, who chaired the National Endowment for the Humanities from 1986–1993 before her husband became vice president. Other prominent neoconservatives include the late Senator Daniel Patrick Moynihan (D-NY), author Irving Kristol (and his son, William, editor of *The Weekly Standard*), UN Ambassador Jeanne Kirkpatrick, former *Commentary* editor Norman Podhoretz, sociologist Nathan Glazer, and—until their recent disavowal of neoconservatism—authors Francis Fukuyama and Michael Lind. Neoconservatives are often described as disenchanted welfare liberals. Like most conservatives, American neoconservatives are strongly anti-communist. It is in domestic policy that they are distinctive. Once enthusiastic supporters of President Lyndon Johnson's "Great Society" programs in the 1960s, neoconservatives became disillusioned with these programs and with the general direction of welfare liberalism. Government is trying to do too much, they concluded, and it is making things worse, not better. The time has come for government to do less for people so that they may be encouraged to do more for themselves.

Like traditional conservatives, neoconservatives regard capitalism with a mixture of admiration and suspicion. They acknowledge its merits as an economic system capable of generating great wealth, but they also are aware of the social disruption and dislocations brought about by a freewheeling market economy—including labour unrest, unemployment, and an apparently permanent underclass of the uneducated and unemployed. As one neoconservative, Irving Kristol, once said, capitalism deserves two cheers but not three.[8] According to Daniel Bell, capitalism harbours a number of "cultural contradictions" through which it undermines its own moral and intellectual foundations.[9] On the

---

[8]Irving Kristol, *Two Cheers for Capitalism* (New York: Basic, 1978).
[9]Daniel Bell, *The Cultural Contradictions of Capitalism* (New York: Basic, 1976).

one hand, capitalism rests on people's willingness to defer pleasures and gratifications—to save and invest in the present in order to receive a greater return in the future. On the other hand, capitalism in the age of the credit card and installment plan creates such abundance that people tend to think there are no limits—that anything is possible—and that one can have it all, here and now. So capitalism is, in a sense, at odds with itself. It praises the virtues of thrift, saving, and hard work while its advertising agencies and marketing experts encourage people to buy now, pay later, and aspire to a life of luxury and ease.

This buy now, pay later attitude is not confined to economic matters. It spills over into other areas as well, the neoconservatives say. It is especially dangerous insofar as it shapes attitudes about government. As the neoconservatives complain, too many people now expect too much too quickly from all their institutions, including their government. They want lower taxes and at the same time increased government spending for their pet projects. They want to live on their lines of credit in politics as they do in their personal finances. These attitudes, on which contemporary capitalism relies, have potentially disastrous social and political consequences. This is particularly true in modern democracies, where every interest group clamours for an ever-larger share of the public pie. The consequences, neoconservatives say, are too obvious to miss—runaway debt, budget deficits too large to comprehend, and, worst of all, a citizenry incapable of checking its appetites and demands. And as these problems mount, demands on government increase—and government loses its capacity to govern.

Neoconservatives believe that power—military power in particular—should be used to achieve ends deemed to be in the national interest. Acting on this belief, Vice President Cheney and other "neocons" in President George W. Bush's administration led the United States to invade Iraq and overthrow Saddam Hussein's regime in 2003. The subsequent attempt to establish stability and democracy there has gone badly, however, provoking a bloody and costly civil war among religious sects and ethnic groups within Iraq, and drawing radical Islamists from other countries into Iraq—all contrary to neoconservative hopes and expectations. The result has been a widespread condemnation of neoconservatism, and some who were once happy to call themselves neoconservatives now disavow the movement.

Inspired by German-American philosopher Leo Strauss, other neoconservatives emerged in the 1960s who were concerned with cultural impoverishment. The most famous of these was Allan Bloom. His book *The Closing of the American Mind* (1987) became a bestseller in the United States. Allan Bloom argued, as did Harold Bloom in *The Western Canon: The Books and School of the Ages* (1994), that the cultural mission of American universities had decayed under the attack of political correctness.[10] Professors, they both argued, no longer taught the great classics of world literature such as Homer's *Iliad,* Plato's *Republic,* or Shakespeare's *King Lear.* Instead, they offered students works thought to be more socially relevant or culturally sensitive. As a consequence, students lacked taste and judgment. To the extent they had culture at all, it was vulgar. Their music was crude, their literature common, their theatres and movies pornographic, and they preferred posters and cartoons to art.

---

[10]Allan Bloom, *The Closing of the American Mind: How Higher Education Has Failed Democracy and Impoverished the Souls of Today's Students* (New York: Simon, 1987); see also Harold Bloom, *The Western Canon: The Books and School of the Ages* (New York: Harcourt, 1994).

Indeed, neoconservatives sometimes suggest that an adversary culture of left-leaning intellectuals, feminists, and assorted malcontents poses a greater threat to our values and way of life than do any real or imagined threats to the free market. So the political struggle that "true" conservatives wage must be, in their view, a cultural and intellectual struggle against this adversary culture. Highbrow culture and university education may initially influence the outlooks and attitudes of only a relatively small segment of society, but these attitudes and values eventually trickle down to the masses—just as the long hair and drug dabbling of college radicals in the 1960s gradually spread throughout North American society. One of the projects undertaken by neoconservatives, consequently, is the attempt to remind people of the value of work, discipline, and virtue.[11]

Like other cultural conservatives, neoconservatives see politics and culture as two sides of the same coin. Whether expressed by the intellectuals of the adversary culture or the stars of popular music, movies, and television, the attitudes of too many cultural leaders have set the tone for the rest of society—and with disastrous effects. Rock and rap music lyrics feature four-letter words that have lost their capacity to shock and disgust many people. This amounts to "defining deviancy down," according to Daniel Patrick Moynihan.[12] That is, actions once regarded as aberrant, shocking, and shameful are now accepted as normal. For example, men and women who live together without being married and have children out of wedlock are no longer viewed as shameful and abnormal but as normal and acceptable. Illegitimacy has lost its stigma. Thus it comes as no surprise, according to another leading neoconservative, that the percentage of illegitimate births has increased to a startling percentage since World War II. Girls today are far more sexually active than was formerly the case. Why this increase in sexual activity? Well, the popular culture surely encourages it. You can't expect modesty (to say nothing of chastity) from girls who worship Madonna.[13]

Neoconservatives insist that to preserve or to restore the discipline and self-restraint necessary to any decent society, we must attend to cultural changes—and strive to stem the cultural tide.

Business Liberals in Canada. In Canada, business liberals are often called conservatives. Until recently, Canada has not been home to neoconservatives. One aspect that distinguishes much of Canadian conservatism from conservatism elsewhere in the world is that anticommunism did not play a big role in Canadian politics and generally did not define differences between liberals and conservatives. In addition, both liberals and conservatives accepted the consensus that developed around the moderate welfare state that arose in Canada after the Second World War and was consolidated in the 1960s. Business liberals were discussed in Chapter 3. They agree with neoconservatives that there are many matters relating to the economy that governments do not do well and, when government restrictions stand in the way of making money, they try to remove them. Business liberals also resent what they think are excessive government regulations—what

---

[11]William Bennett, ed., *The Book of Virtues: A Treasury of Great Moral Stories* (New York: Simon, 1993); James Q. Wilson, *On Character,* 2nd ed. (Washington, DC: AEI, 1995).

[12]Daniel Patrick Moynihan, "Defining Deviancy Down," *The Essential Neoconservative Reader,* ed. Mark Gerson (New York: Addison Wesley, 1996) 356–371.

[13]Irving Kristol, "'Family Values'—Not a Political Issue," *Wall Street Journal* 7 Dec. 1992: 14, quoted in Mark Gerson, *The Neoconservative Vision: From the Cold War to the Culture Wars* (Lanham, MD: Madison, 1996) 270.

they call "the paper burden." However, all Canadian liberals have grown up within the Canadian tory tradition of activist government. Thus, Canadian businesses are accustomed to government aid in a variety of areas, whether it involves grants or tax concessions for establishing a plant in a poor area of the country or a Team Canada trade mission abroad led by the prime minister and provincial premiers.

Neoconservative Organizations in Canada. Canadian neoconservatism arose much later in Canada than in the United States and shared an antigovernment, not anticommunism, agenda with its American counterpart.

Colin Brown created the first important neoconservative organization in Canada in 1967, the National Citizens Coalition (NCC). A lobby group funded by private donations, the NCC has directed its efforts primarily against what it sees as the policies of self-serving politicians. For example, it opposes overgenerous pensions, restrictions on third-party advertising during election campaigns, and state funding for political parties. It has been remarkably successful in mounting court challenges and overturning legislation. It is also against union closed shops and the Kyoto accord.

Another successful neoconservative organization is the Fraser Institute. It was founded in 1974 as an educational institute whose mission was to inform Canadians of the role of the free market in economic well-being. The Institute has published a number of controversial academic books on subjects such as rent control, trade unions, and the underground economy. It attracted distinguished free market economists such as Friedrich Hayek and Milton Friedman and is perhaps best known to the general public for creating Tax Free Day. If you lumped all taxes together, the Institute said, when would average Canadians working from the beginning of the year start working for themselves? Not until the middle of June, according to the NCC's calculations.

Red Toryism in Canada. There are three key elements in **Red Toryism**. First, Red Tories are sympathetic to the British elements in Canada's heritage, and they are resistant to the intrusion of American politics, economics, and culture. They prefer an orientation to Europe rather than continental integration. At heart, they are anti-American. Second, they support the use of the state for nation-building purposes. For example, conservative governments created the first transcontinental railway, Ontario Hydro, the Bank of Canada, and the Canadian Broadcasting Corporation (CBC), and believed this use of the state to be entirely proper. Third, on balance, they doubt whether capitalism in an unregulated form could possibly serve Canada's best interests. In Grant's words,

> No small country can depend for its existence on the loyalty of its capitalists. International interests may require the sacrifice of the lesser loyalty of patriotism. Only in dominant nations is the loyalty of capitalists ensured. In such situations, their interests are tied to the strength and vigour of their empire.[14]

Normally, *Red Tory* was used to describe politicians who belonged to the Progressive Conservative Party, such as party leaders Robert Stanfield and Joe Clark, who promoted social policy issues. When the Progressive Conservative Party merged with the Canadian Alliance, many former Progressive Conservative members self-identified as Red Tories to distinguish themselves within the newly formed Conservative Party.

---

[14]Grant 69–70.

George Grant (1918–1988)

Under the leadership of Stephen Harper, ideological debate with the Conservative Party has languished because of the tight control the prime minister exercises on his supporters and his refusal to tolerate debate about government policies and principles. Harper was once president of the National Citizens' Coalition and his finance minister, Jim Flaherty, who held the same post in Mike Harris's Ontario provincial government, had a record of cutting taxes and pursuing broadly conservative economic policies. Harper's government puzzled fiscal conservatives who wanted lower income taxes and disappointed the religious right because it has taken no significant steps to reverse the status of gay marriage, which Harper seemed to oppose in opposition. The Conservative government's cut of 2 percent from the GST can be understood from the perspective of the party's populist heritage, although it was inconsistent with the ideological preferences of the more powerful business liberals in the party, who wanted reduced personal and corporate income taxes to encourage investment (rather than consumption), a reduction of the national debt, or a combination of both.

The 2011 general election handed Harper his first majority government, which quickly developed several policy initiatives that confirmed his conservative orientation. One was more active respect for the monarchy. He welcomed the Duke of Cambridge and his wife in an official visit, and he restored the term *royal* to the names of the Royal Canadian Navy and the Royal Canadian Airforce. He also advanced a controversial crime bill that aimed to emphasize the deterrent element in sentencing criminals, and he made a significant military contribution to the NATO force that helped drive Libyan dictator Muammar Gaddafi from office.

Stephen Harper (1959–)

The Religious Right

The Religious Right in the United States. In the years after the Second World War, a number of evangelical American Protestant ministers led campaigns against the dangers of what they called "Godless, atheistic communism." In the 1970s, these campaigns grew into a larger movement known as the Religious Right. This movement marked a reaction against the changes many saw—and deplored—in American society during the 1960s. High divorce and crime rates, urban decay and riots, growing welfare rolls, the decline of patriotism, widespread drug use, and legalized abortion—all these were signs that the United States had lost its way. The time was ripe for a movement that would restore the country to its traditional ways and, according to the Religious Right, for a return to morality in government and society.

As defined by the leaders of the Religious Right, *morality* is the moral code of Christian fundamentalism. Christian fundamentalists believe that the Bible is to be read literally, not symbolically, with every word taken to express the will of God. Since the nineteenth century, they have protested against the teaching of Darwin's theory of evolution in public schools, for instance, and they generally decry the growth of what they describe as liberal or secular humanism. In their view the United States was founded and has prospered as a Christian nation, and it must return to its roots. It comes as no surprise that the leaders of the Religious Right have often been ministers of evangelical churches—Reverends Jerry Falwell of the Moral Majority, and Pat Robertson of the Christian Coalition perhaps foremost among them. This group's power was clear in the 2004 presidential election, when they were instrumental in re-electing George W. Bush. Bush skillfully mobilized the group's support by opposing gay marriage and stem cell research (sometimes considered a code word for abortion), both of which are defining issues for the Religious Right.

The Religious Right also claims to be democratic, by which it means that society should follow the lead of a righteous or moral majority of Christians. Where will this moral majority lead? To less government intervention in the economy, as the individualist conservatives wish, but to a larger and more active government in other respects. In the past the Religious Right campaigned for a strong defence to check and turn back the threat of communism. In the Middle East, the group generally supports Israel because it believes that it is necessary for Israel to attain certain historical boundaries as a condition for Christ's return. It also wants increased government intervention in activities and areas of life that others, including many other conservatives, deem to be private. The Religious Right wants the government to ban abortions, to permit prayer in public schools, to restrict or outlaw certain sexual activities, and to purge schools and public libraries of materials that they regard as morally offensive. In these and other respects, the Religious Right would greatly expand the powers of government. In that respect their views stand in sharp contrast to the professed views of other conservatives.

In their broad vision of what they hope to accomplish, however, the conservatives of the Religious Right agree with other conservatives. According to Ralph Reed, former director of the Christian Coalition, the members of his coalition pray and work for a spiritual awakening that will lead to a political and cultural restoration. If this were to happen, he writes,

> America would look much as it did for most of the first two centuries of its existence, before the social dislocation caused by Vietnam, the sexual revolution, Watergate, and the explosion of the welfare state. Our nation would once again be ascendant, self-confident, proud, and morally strong. Government would be small, the citizenry virtuous, and mediating institutions such as churches and volunteer organizations would carry out many of the functions currently relegated to the bureaucracy. Instead of turning to Washington to solve problems, Americans would turn to each other.[15]

In their efforts to bring about the political and cultural restoration that Reed calls for, conservatives of the Religious Right sometimes take steps or give voice to opinions that definitely distinguish them from other conservatives. One way in which they do this is by calling for the legal recognition of the United States as a Christian (or Judeo-Christian) nation. In 2003, for example, Judge Roy Moore of Alabama insisted on displaying the Ten Commandments in his courtroom, which led to his suspension from his post. Judge Moore and his supporters maintain that the Ten Commandments belong in courtrooms and other public buildings because the U.S. Constitution is based on the commandments. Critics have been quick to point out that this claim is both historically and textually dubious. The Constitution says nothing at all about God, or about having no other gods before Him or coveting thy neighbour's wife or honouring one's parents—and so on for all ten of the commandments. In fact, the only mention of religion in the Constitution is a negative one, which prohibits any religious test for holding public office (Article VI).

---

[15]Ralph Reed, *Politically Incorrect: The Emerging Faith Factor in American Politics* (Dallas, TX: Word, 1994) 35–36; see Ball and Dagger, selection 32.

Furthermore, critics note, the Bill of Rights mentions religion only in the First Amendment, and it, too, is in the negative voice: "Congress shall make no law respecting an establishment of religion, or prohibiting the free exercise thereof."[16] Some Religious Right conservatives concede these points and advocate amending the Constitution to designate the United States as a Christian nation that constitutionally outlaws same-sex marriage and abortion, among other actions and activities they consider to be contrary to Christianity.

Another way the Religious Right has distinguished itself from other kinds of conservatism is in the tendency of some of its leaders to claim that disasters befalling the United States are signs of God's displeasure. In an appearance on Pat Robertson's television show, for example, Reverend Jerry Falwell once blamed the terrorist attacks of September 11, 2001, on America's toleration of "the pagans, and the abortionists, and the feminists, and the gays and the lesbians . . ., the ACLU [American Civil Liberties Union], People for the American Way, all of them who have tried to secularize America." Falwell subsequently apologized for this remark, but he did so while continuing to hold that God may have lifted "the veil of protection which has allowed no one to attack America on our soil since 1812."[17] In this interpretation of events, God was punishing the United States for its moral laxity, and the terrorists were doing God's work—which is exactly what the terrorists themselves thought they were doing. In this respect, Religious Right conservatism and radical Islamism seem to converge.

To be sure, not all Religious Right conservatives share Falwell's and Robertson's tendency to view political and natural events, such as September 11 or Hurricane Katrina, as God's judgment on a wicked people. Nor do all religious conservatives identify themselves with the Religious Right. For example, John Danforth, a three-term Republican senator from Missouri, published a book in 2006 in which he chides Religious Right conservatives for invoking God for political purposes.[18] Danforth's book is itself testimony to the significance of the Religious Right, however, for he surely would not have thought it worthwhile to write the book unless he regarded the Religious Right as a potent force in American politics—and especially within American conservatism.

The four aforementioned kinds of conservatism were cobbled together in a powerful but uneasy coalition by Ronald Reagan in the 1980s that was renewed, twenty years later, by George W. Bush's chief strategist, Karl Rove. Holding the coalition together has proved difficult, however. Religious Right conservatives emphasize "traditional" or "family" values, want prayer in public schools, and seek the prohibition of abortion, pornography, and gay marriage. Individualist conservatives want to reduce government spending, balance the budget, and generally shrink the size of the government, leaving individuals to live as they please as long as they respect the rights of others. Neoconservatives want a militant and muscular foreign policy that makes maximum use of American power—political, economic, and especially military—in Iraq, Iran, and elsewhere. Traditional conservatives, by contrast, prefer a cautious foreign policy and insist that there is nothing conservative about engaging in risky foreign adventures whose outcomes are uncertain; good intentions, they say, do not guarantee good results.

---

[16]For these and other criticisms, see Isaac Kramnick and R. Laurence Moore, *The Godless Constitution* (New York: W. W. Norton, 2005).

[17]For Falwell's remarks, see http://articles.cnn.com/2001-09-14/us/Falwell.apology_1_thomas-road-baptist-church-jerry-falwell-feminists?_s=PM, as of August 24, 2007.

[18]John C. Danforth, *Faith and Politics: How the "Moral Values" Debate Divides America and How to Move Forward Together* (New York: Viking Penguin, 2006).

In the run-up to the 2006 congressional elections, this strained coalition threatened to come apart. Religious Right conservatives—and Protestant fundamentalists in particular—complained that the Bush administration and the Republican-controlled Congress had not done nearly enough to advance Christian conservative causes, such as initiating constitutional amendments banning abortion and gay marriage or affirming that the United States is a Christian nation. As Dr. James Dobson of Focus on the Family lamented, he and other conservative Christians "have been extremely disappointed with what the Republicans have done with the power they were given."[19]

Individualist conservatives, by contrast, complained that the Bush administration had kowtowed to the Religious Right while running up record deficits even as it cut taxes, increased government spending, and launched expensive wars in Iraq and Afghanistan. Prominent conservative columnist and author Andrew Sullivan argues that "the conservative soul" has been lost, or hijacked, by the Religious Right. "The conservatism I grew up around," Sullivan says, "was a combination of lower taxes, less government spending, freer trade, freer markets, individual liberty, personal responsibility and a strong anti-Communist foreign policy."[20] The conservative Christian base of the Republican Party cares much less about these issues than about reinstating God and prayer in the classroom and outlawing abortion and gay marriage. These fundamentalist Christians, Sullivan contends, are the Christian counterpart to radical Islamists: both are absolutely certain that they are right, that God (or Allah) is on their side, and that almost any means are justifiable in attempting to achieve righteous ends.

For their part, neoconservatives complain that the Bush administration did not commit nearly enough troops to fight in Iraq and Afghanistan or to stand up to nuclear threats from Iran and North Korea. Traditional conservatives complain that neoconservatives are incautious, imprudent, and arrogant. According to David Keene, Chairman of the American Conservative Union, "The principal sin of the neoconservatives is overbearing arrogance," inasmuch as they make mistake after mistake and never admit to being wrong.[21]

Besides tensions and disagreements among several kinds of conservatism, there are emerging disagreements within each type. These disagreements are especially sharp within the Religious Right, where some say, for example, that being pro-life means not only opposing abortion but also capital punishment ("Thou shalt not kill" and "'Vengeance is mine,' sayeth the Lord"). According to some evangelical Christians, being consistently pro-life also requires "caring for creation" as stewards or caretakers of the natural environment. Increasing numbers of evangelical Christians have come to believe that being conservative requires, as the word implies, conserving life: not only the life of the unborn but also all of God's creation, including plants, animals, habitats, ecosystems—in short, the natural environment. The U.S. Conference of Catholic Bishops has called upon Catholics and their fellow Christians to be caretakers or stewards of the environment. In a similar spirit, such Protestant organizations as EarthCare and the Evangelical Environmental Network cite Genesis 2:15—"Then the Lord God put the man [Adam] in the Garden of Eden to cultivate it and take care of it"—and call upon Christians to engage in creation care.

---

[19]David D. Kirkpatrick, "Republican Woes Lead to Feuding by Conservatives," *New York Times*, Oct. 20, 2006, pp. A1, A16.

[20]Andrew Sullivan, *The Conservative Soul: How We Lost It, How to Get It Back* (New York: HarperCollins, 2006), p. 2. See also Sullivan's blog at www.andrewsullivan.com.

[21]David D. Kirkpatrick, "Republican Woes Lead to Feuding by Conservatives," *New York Times*, Oct. 20, 2006, pp. A1, A16.

This concern led eighty-six evangelical Christian leaders to sponsor the Evangelical Climate Initiative and in February 2006 to issue An Evangelical Call to Action against global warming. Such actions have led to an increasingly bitter and public split within the ranks of American evangelical Christians. Moreover, a small but growing number of evangelical Christians have come out of the closet and publicly acknowledged their same-sex orientation. They want to be accepted by and admitted into mainstream evangelical Christian churches, but such acceptance is relatively rare; most gay evangelicals worship together in their own congregations, meeting mostly in members' homes. They have also created several organizations, such as Soulforce (www.soulforce.org), founded by Reverend Jerry Falwell's former assistant, Reverend Mel White, and Evangelicals Concerned (www.ecwr.org), and they maintain such websites as gaychristian.net and christianlesbians.com.

As these rifts within the Religious Right indicate, modern conservatism—at least in the United States—is increasingly a house divided. The Reagan–Rove coalition that once proved so powerful is now under considerable strain, and the question facing American conservatives is whether the issues that divide them are stronger than those that bring them together. And, as if this were not division enough, the conservative house became even further divided in the wake of the worldwide economic meltdown that began in 2007 and the 2008 presidential and congressional elections, which installed a centre-left Democratic president, Barack Obama, and clear Democratic majorities in the Senate and House of Representatives. Invited by the new president to join a bipartisan partnership—particularly for the purpose of stimulating the ailing American economy, aiding automobile manufacturing, and reforming health care and the financial system—most conservative Republican legislators opted for an oppositional role. Many conservative Republican state governors, by contrast, eagerly embraced the president's economic stimulus package as providing a positive way forward for their states' sagging economies. To what extent these and other rifts within conservative ranks may be healed remains an open question.[22]

The Religious Right in Canada. The event that brought the Religious Right into active existence in Canada was the Supreme Court's decision *R. v. Morgentaler* in 1988, which affirmed that women have the right to an abortion. Prior to that, many evangelical Christians had become increasingly uncomfortable in Pierre Elliott Trudeau's Canada. A separated parent with a promiscuous, drug-using wife, he seemed to represent the moral decay of the country. As well, the rise of feminism and the legalization of homosexual acts between consenting adults represented the spirit of a godless age. The introduction of the Canadian Charter of Rights and Freedoms introduced a new set of ideological conflicts and became the supreme law of the land (subject only to the rarely used and unpopular parliamentary override). Conservative religious people perceived that the Supreme Court interpreted the Charter in a liberal manner that supported abortion rights and was sympathetic to same-sex marriage. They complained that the Charter was fundamentally undemocratic because it allowed the imposition of liberal values by unelected judges even over the wishes of elected legislators. This concern resulted in a new political religious movement with strong connections to the renascent populism of the Reform/Alliance movements.

The first effort of the Religious Right to organize politically occurred in 1988 when it formed the Christian Heritage Party, a pro-life, pro-family party.[23] Electorally unsuccessful,

[22]W. James Antle, III, "The Conservative Crack-up." *The American Conservative* (November 17, 2003); also in Ball and Dagger, eds., *Ideals and Ideologies,* selection 32.

[23]Ralph Reed, "Bill C-33 Awakens Christians," *Western Report* 2 Sept. 1996: 36.

most members of the Religious Right moved to the Reform Party and then to the Canadian Alliance. As in the United States, opposition to abortion and gay marriage were their two main concerns, though they were also uncomfortable with the extent to which Canada had moved toward a multicultural society in which non-Christians were increasing rapidly in number, mostly through immigration.

However, for four reasons, the Religious Right is not as powerful a force in Canada as it is in the United States. First, most Canadians tend to see the government as a source of benefit rather than as an enemy of freedom, so Canadians are unlikely to join a movement that is openly antigovernment. Second, evangelical Christians compose less than 10 percent of the Canadian population, whereas over a third of Americans are evangelicals. As well, almost half of Canadians are at least nominally Roman Catholics, who, while opposing abortion and same-sex marriage, tend to take liberal or even social democratic positions on many economic and welfare matters; they also tend to oppose capital punishment and, if not pacifist, are skeptical about the use of military power. Third, extreme Protestant sects in Canada tend to be more reclusive than in the United States. For example, many Mennonites shun political action. Fourth, the Canadian Radio-television and Telecommunications Commission (CRTC), which controls television broadcasting, has been unwilling to give licences to denominationally based applicants. Thus, unlike in the United States where Christian television stations broadcast the Religious Right's messages, Canadian religious conservatives have difficulty gaining a mass audience for their messages.

Certainly, the Christian Right and individualist conservatives managed to join with populists to form the Reform Party. And for a while, the Christian Right advanced in prominence in the Canadian Alliance. But the neoconservatives gained control of the conservative agenda when the Canadian Alliance merged with the Progressive Conservative Party in 2002. Since then, the Religious Right has remained a marginalized form of conservatism in Canada, one whose policies cannot hold the attention of any party for very long.

Conclusion

What can we say about the condition of conservatism today? The answer is that the present is like the past. There has always been a spirited debate among conservatives about who really is conservative. George W. Bush's presidency brought the Christian Right and individualist conservatives into the forefront in the United States. In the United Kingdom, individualist conservatives predominate.

In Canada, the once-powerful Red Tories and traditional conservatives have been pushed aside by neoconservatives. Traditional and social conservatives still exist, but their influence is primarily intellectual rather than political. Moreover, under the leadership of Stephen Harper, ideological debate with the Conservative Party has languished because of the tight control the prime minister exercises and his refusal to tolerate debate about government policies and principles. Many Canadians consider Harper's Conservatives to be neoconservative because of their tax-cutting policies. But like most Canadian Conservative governments, Harper's does not fall neatly into any one brand of conservatism. His policies have puzzled fiscal conservatives who want lower income taxes; and they have disappointed the Religious Right because the government has taken no significant steps to reverse the status of gay marriage, which Harper seemed to oppose while in the official opposition. The 2007 and 2008 GST tax cuts can be understood from the perspective of the party's populist heritage, but they are inconsistent with the ideological preferences of the more powerful business liberals in the party, who really wanted reduced personal and corporate income taxes. In the 2008 and 2011 election campaigns, although the Conservative party emphasized its record of fiscal responsibility, support for the military, and commitment to law-and-order policies, there was little that distinguished it ideologically from other centrist or centre-right parties, though undoubtedly many of its members held views that were more ideologically defined than the leader advanced during the campaign.

Conservatism as an Ideology

With all the division and diversity within the conservative camp, does it still make sense to speak of conservatism as a single ideology? It does, as long as it is understood that the varieties of conservatism are like members of a family: very similar in some ways and very different in others. These similarities and differences can be clarified by considering how conservatism performs the four functions that all ideologies perform.

Explanatory Function. For most conservatives, the basis for explaining social conditions is human imperfection. Conservatives do refer to other factors—historical circumstances and economic conditions, for instance, and certainly government policies and cultural trends—but they ultimately trace all these to the frailty of imperfect human nature. If things have gone wrong, it is probably because fallible men and women, acting through government, have tried to do more than humans are capable of doing. If things have gone well, it is because they have kept their hopes and expectations low and proceeded with caution.

Evaluative Function. But how do people know when things have gone well or poorly? Conservatives evaluate social conditions by appealing to social peace and stability. If the relations between the different classes or levels of society are harmonious, then the social fabric is in good condition. If relations are torn by conflict, strife, and bitterness, then action must be taken to repair the fraying social fabric.

Orientative Function. Conservatism believes that people are not simply individuals. Each person is part of a greater whole, and people should realize that they must act with the good of the whole society in mind. The best way for them to do this is to play their part in society—to be a good parent or teacher or engineer or plumber—and to recognize how each part must blend with all of the others to provide social harmony. Individualist conservatives sharply differ from the others on this point, for they favour competitive individualism. But in this respect, they are simply closer to the liberal tradition than the traditional conservative tradition of Burke and his heirs.

Programmatic Function. Conservative policies focus on slow change on the grounds that it is better to do a little good than a lot of harm. Conservatives warn that it is too easy to lose sight of the good things that a society already enjoys. We should take our eyes off distant horizons in order to appreciate what we have here and now. Once we see this clearly, conservatives say, we will cherish and conserve what we already have.

Conservatism and the Democratic Ideal

The conservative desire to preserve the good things a society currently enjoys explains how conservatism, which began with a distinctly antidemocratic attitude, has in the past century come to accept the democratic ideal. In societies where democracy has become an integral part of the social fabric, of the traditional and customary way of life, conservatives support democracy. But it will always be a chastened or modest form of representative democracy.

The conservative view of human nature leads to a modest view of what is possible in any political society, including a democracy. Given the weakness of human reason and the strong tendency toward selfishness, conservatives will expect any pure democracy to degenerate into anarchy, followed shortly by dictatorship or despotism. Democracy is acceptable to conservatives only when the people generally have limited power and make limited demands. The people must learn self-restraint, or learn at least to place sufficient power to restrain themselves in the hands of those prudent and virtuous women and men who form the natural aristocracy of their society. Instead of turning to demagogues and rabble-rousers, the people must elect cautious, conservative leaders who will exercise their duties with great care for the needs of the people and the delicacy of the social fabric. To do more might be democratic, but it could not be conservative.

For Further Reading

Berlin, Isaiah. "Joseph de Maistre and the Origins of Fascism," in Isaiah Berlin, ed., *The Crooked Timber of Humanity: Chapters in the History of Ideas.* New York: Vintage, 1992.

Buckley, William F., Jr., and Charles R. Kesler, eds. *Keeping the Tablets: Modern American Conservative Thought.* New York: Harper, 1987.

Cheney, Dick. *In My Time: A Personal and Political Memoir.* New York: Threshold Editions, 2011.

Dunn, Charles W., and J. David Woodard. *The Conservative Tradition in America.* Lanham, MD: Rowman, 1996.

Easton, Nina. *Gang of Five: Leaders at the Center of the Conservative Crusade.* New York: Simon, 2000.

Farthing, John. *Freedom Wears a Crown.* Toronto: Kingswood, 1957.

Flannagan, Tom. *Harper's Team: Behind the Scenes in the Conservative Rise to Power.* Montreal: McGill-Queen's UP, 2007.

———, ed. *The Essential Neoconservative Reader.* New York: Addison, 1996.

Grant, George. *Lament for a Nation.* Toronto: McClelland, 1965.

Harris, Mike, and Preston Manning. *Caring for Canada.* Vancouver: Fraser Institute, 2005.

Hodgson, Godfrey. *The World Turned Rightside Up: A History of the Conservative Ascendancy in America.* New York: Houghton, 1996.

Hogg, Quintin. *The Case for Conservatism.* Harmondsworth, UK: Penguin, 1947.

Kekes, John. *A Case for Conservatism.* Ithaca, NY: Cornell UP, 1998.

Kirk, Russell. *The Conservative Mind: From Burke to Eliot.* 4th ed. New York: Avon, 1968.

———, ed. *The Portable Conservative Reader.* Harmondsworth, UK: Penguin, 1982.

Laycock, David. *The New Right and Democracy in Canada.* Toronto: Oxford UP, 2002.

Martin, Lawrence. *Harperland: The Politics of Control.* Toronto: Penguin Canada, 2010.

Minogue, Kenneth, ed. *Conservative Realism: New Essays in Conservatism.* London: Harper-Collins, 1996.

Minogue, Kenneth. *The Servile Mind: How Democracy Erodes the Moral Life.* Jackson: Encounter Books, 2010.

Mulroney, M. B. *Memoirs: 1939–1993.* Toronto: McClelland and Stewart, 2007.

Nash, George H. *The Conservative Intellectual Movement in America: Since 1945.* New York: Basic, 1979.

O'Gorman, Frank. *Edmund Burke: His Political Philosophy.* London: Allen, 1973.

O'Hara, Kieran. *Conservatism.* London: Reaction Books, 2011.

Orchard, David. *The Fight for Canada.* Toronto: Stoddart, 1998.

O'Sullivan, Noel. "Conservatism." *The Cambridge History of Twentieth-Century Political Thought*, ed. Terence Ball and Richard Bellamy. Cambridge: Cambridge UP, 2003.

Rossiter, Clinton. *Conservatism in America: The Thankless Persuasion,* 2nd ed. New York: Random, 1962.

Steinfels, Peter. *The Neoconservatives.* New York: Simon, 1979.

Taylor, Charles. *Radical Tories.* Toronto: Anansi, 1982.

Wills, Garry. *Nixon Agonistes: The Crisis of the Self-Made Man.* New York: New American Library, 1971.

Useful Websites and Social Media

www.conservative.org American Conservative Union

www.aei.org American Enterprise Institute

www.chp.ca Christian Heritage Party of Canada

www.conservative.ca Conservative Party of Canada

http://www.focusonthefamily.com/ Focus on the Family

www.fraserinstitute.org Fraser Institute

www.heritage.org The Heritage Foundation

http://libertycounselaction.org Liberty Counsel Action

www.nationalcitizens.ca National Citizens Coalition

www.newamericancentury.org Project for the New American Century

http://pm.gc.ca/eng/pm.asp?featureId=7&pageId=27 Prime Minister of Canada Stephen Harper

Twitter:

@pmharper Prime Minister Stephen Harper

@FraserInstitute The Fraser Institute

@GOP Republican Party

@Conservatives Conservative Party (UK)

Facebook:

www.facebook.com/pmharper

From the Ball and Dagger Reader *Ideals and Ideologies,* US Eighth Edition

Part Four: Contemporary Conservatism

Discussion Questions

1. Do you believe in the concept of the masses and, if you do, are you part of the masses?

2. Is a monarchical form of government valid in the modern world?

3. What role does religion have in politics? (In this context, focus on Christianity and the West.)

4. Is the most pressing need in contemporary society to reduce the size of government and limit its role in society and the economy?

MySearchLab   MySearchLab with eText offers you access to an online interactive version of the text, additional quizzes and assessment, extensive help with your writing and research projects, and provides round-the-clock access to credible and reliable source material. Go to **www.mysearchlab.com** to access these resources.

CHAPTER 7

Socialism, Communism, and Anarchism: The Dream of an Equal Society

Wherever men have private property and money is the measure of everything, there it is hardly possible for the commonwealth to be governed justly or to flourish in prosperity.

Sir Thomas More, *Utopia*

LEARNING OBJECTIVES

After completing this chapter you should be able to

1. Explain the differences between a planned economy and a free market.
2. Differentiate the ideological positions of the various precursors to Karl Marx.
3. Critically assess Marx's theory of history.
4. Present an overview of Marx's revolutionary process.
5. Differentiate anarchism from communism.

Modern **socialism**, like traditional conservatism, began as a critique of liberalism. Like conservatives, socialists objected to the liberal emphasis on self-interest, competition, and individual liberty. Like traditional conservatives, socialists shared the belief that human beings are by nature social or communal creatures. Individuals do not live or work in isolation, but in cooperation with one another. It is cooperation among individuals, not competition between them, that both see as the foundation of a society in which everyone can enjoy a decent measure of liberty, justice, and prosperity.

Unlike traditional conservatives, socialists assign no particular value to tradition or custom. Nor do they share conservatives' fondness for private property and the hierarchy that accompanies it. From the socialist viewpoint, private property is the source of the class divisions that place some people in positions of power and privilege while condemning others to poverty and powerlessness. Indeed, socialists usually call for programs that will distribute wealth and power more evenly throughout society—programs that conservatives typically deplore as levelling. In a sense, socialists share a belief in equality with liberals. However, liberals believe in equality of status, the kind of equality that produces an unequal society. By contrast, socialists want equality of condition. Everything that people produce, socialists say, is in some sense a social product, and everyone who participates in producing a good is entitled to a share in it. This means that society as a whole, and not private individuals, should own or control the means of production for the benefit of all. This is a fundamental conviction shared by many socialists.

But what exactly does it mean? Some suggest that most goods should be regarded as public property; others maintain that only the major means of production should be regarded this way. Still others believe that ownership is not necessary and that the same goals can be achieved through extensive and detailed government regulation and control. There is no clear point of agreement except on the general principle that anything that contributes significantly to the production, distribution, and delivery of socially necessary goods must be socially controlled for the benefit of all.

This raises a second question: How can society exercise control over the means of production? It is one thing to say that society as a whole should own and control a power plant, but quite another to say just *how* society is to operate this plant. Is *everyone* to take a turn working in the plant or having a say in its daily operations? No socialist goes that far. Instead, socialists have generally argued for either **centralized control** or **decentralized control** of public property. Those who favour centralized control want to see the state or government assume the responsibility for managing property and resources in the name of the whole society. This was the approach followed in the Soviet Union. Centralists believe this approach promotes efficiency because it gives the state power to plan, coordinate, and manage the whole economy in the interests of every member of society. Other socialists dispute this claim by pointing to the top-heavy and sluggish bureaucracies that dominate centrally planned economies. As they see it, the best way to exercise control over public property is to decentralize—to vest this control in groups at the local level, especially groups of workers who labour in the factories, fields, and shops and the consumers who purchase and use the workers' products. These are the people who feel most directly the effects of the use of social property, so they should decide how the property is to be used.

In short, like conservatives and liberals, socialists differ among themselves on important issues. But they are united in their opposition to **capitalism**, which they believe determines the distribution of power in every society in which it is the dominant form of economic exchange. Poor people have a good deal less power than the rich because they have less ability to control and direct their own lives and to choose where and how to live. In a capitalist society, socialists charge, a term such as *freedom* is hollow for many working people, and equality of opportunity needs to be replaced by equality of condition, a situation where people are more or less equal in their wealth and power. To see why socialists object to capitalism, we need to examine their view of freedom. With that as background, we can then explore the history of socialism.

SOCIALISM, HUMAN NATURE, AND FREEDOM

Liberals and conservatives often say that socialism is opposed to freedom. Yet this claim requires clarification and qualification. Socialists are certainly opposed to the liberal-individualist understanding of freedom, as described in Chapter 3, and to the conservative's notion of ordered liberty, as described in Chapter 4. This is because socialists propose an alternative conception of freedom, not because they consider freedom undesirable or unimportant. Their alternative view can be most readily understood by referring once again to the triadic model (see Figure 7.1.) For socialists, the *agent* who is to be free is not the abstract or isolated individual, but individuals in relations. Human beings are social or communal creatures, socialists say, so we should think of an agent as someone who is connected to and dependent upon other people in various ways. In particular, we should think of agents as individuals engaged in **relations of production**, distribution, and exchange with others. In other words, the agent is the producer, or worker, viewed not as an isolated individual, but as a member of a class—the working class. Members of the working class share several common *goals* including (but not restricted to) fulfilling work, a fair share of the product they produce (or the profits thereof), a voice in the management of their affairs, and an equal opportunity to develop and use their talents to their full extent. The system of capitalist production thwarts these aspirations by throwing various *obstacles* in their way.

FIGURE 7.1	The Socialist View of Freedom

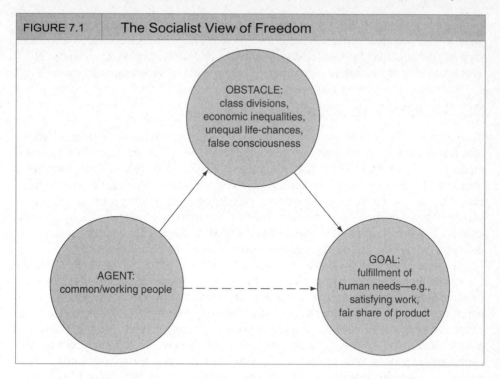

These obstacles can be either material or mental. One example is the division of society into a wealthy class of owners and a poorer class of producers who are forced to sell their labour to eke out a subsistence living. People who must devote most of their time and energy merely to making a living can scarcely hope to fully develop their talents. The division of society into classes of unequal political power and economic wealth also results in the sharpening and hardening of class differences that perpetuate these inequalities from one generation to the next. In the words of a Co-operative Commonwealth Federation (CCF) document from 1957, "The CCF presents an alternative to the people of Canada. It offers a programme designed to ensure that every person—regardless of occupation, sex, colour or creed—will have full opportunity to share in the nation's progress and to develop his talents in a society free from the exploitation of man by man or class by class."[1] "The rich get richer," the old saying goes, "and the poor get poorer." Another example: To the extent that the rich own or control the system of education and information (radio and television stations, newspapers, and so on), they are able to raise and maintain still other obstacles. They can erect and maintain mental barriers by keeping the poor in ignorance of radical alternatives to the status quo. In this way the members of the poorer classes may be kept in ignorance of their true or real interests and of the alternative political visions and economic arrangements that might better serve those interests.

To be truly free, then, is to be free from such obstacles and to be free to pursue one's aims and aspirations—as long as they are not detrimental or harmful to others. Thus, one should not be free to make a private profit off the labour of another. Since humans are social and communal creatures, it makes no sense to speak of one person's being free and

---

[1]Co-operative Commonwealth Federation, *Share Canada's Wealth!* (Ottawa: CCF, 1957).

another's not. Either all are free or none are. Karl Marx and Friedrich Engels made this point in *The Manifesto of the Communist Party* when they proclaimed that in a socialist society, "the condition for the free development of each is the free development of all."[2] This conception of freedom is quite different from the liberal view examined earlier.

SOCIALISM: THE PRECURSORS

The first name likely to be associated with the ideology of socialism, or at least with its communist variant, is Karl Marx. Yet some aspects of socialism predated Marx by many centuries.[3] In *The Republic* (c. 380 BCE), Plato imagines a society in which the ruling class would share its property communally and marriage would no longer exist.[4] As well, early Christians in the first and second centuries CE espoused a rather different version of socialism: that Christians had a duty to share their labour and their worldly goods with one another. This simple form of communism continued in the practices of certain monastic orders up through the Middle Ages and still survives in some monasteries today.

At the beginning of the sixteenth century, Sir Thomas More (1478–1535), a Roman Catholic saint and martyr, wrote *Utopia*.[5] In this book, More created a society with no parasitic lords and ladies (and their servants and retainers), where everyone gave a fair day's work and wanted no more than he or she needed in terms of food, shelter, clothing, and the other necessities of life. Everyone lived a reasonably comfortable life. But it was a very severe society that combined intrusive government, severe punishments, and communal ownership as an antidote to the sins of pride, envy, and greed. Sinful human nature was such that this type of society could never exist, so More called his society *Utopia,* which means "nowhere" in classical Greek.

Initially, views of communist or socialist society were agrarian visions. The workers were agricultural labourers tilling the land together and sharing in the harvest. But this older agrarian vision was rendered quaint by the Industrial Revolution. In the late eighteenth and early nineteenth centuries, European farmers left, or were forced off, the land to work in factories, mills, and mines. Steam power replaced horsepower; the steamship, the sailing ship; the locomotive, the stagecoach. The power loom and the spinning jenny put thousands out of work. Workers were no longer tied to the seasonal rhythms of the land but to the harsher and more insistent rhythms of the factory. Entire families— fathers, mothers, and small children—worked seventy to eighty hours a week in dirty and dangerous conditions. The tenements in which they lived were squalid, overcrowded, and unsanitary.

Many in the ruling class accepted the social disruptions and dislocations brought about by early capitalism, but others rejected them as inhuman and unnecessary evils. For example, British journalist Henry Mayhew chronicled the miserable life of the poor in the Victorian era. He reported the story of a young London girl who had been lucky because her parents had not turned her out into the street at twelve to survive as best she could. Her mother insisted, however, that the girl must take on the trade of selling apples

---

[2]Leszek Kolakowski, *Main Currents of Marxism, vol. 2: The Golden Age* (Oxford: Clarendon, 1978).

[3]For two histories of socialism with very different emphases, see Alexander Gray, *The Socialist Tradition: Moses to Lenin* (London: Longman, 1947), and George Lictheim, *A Short History of Socialism* (New York: Praeger, 1970).

[4]Plato, *The Republic* (Books III and IV, 412–421 BCE).

[5]Thomas More, *Utopia*, ed. J. Churlton Collins (Oxford: Clarendon, 1904); see Terence Ball and Richard Dagger, eds., *Ideals and Ideologies: A Reader*, 8th ed. (New York: Longman, 2011) selection 5.32.

from a basket. It was common for a girl to be put to work in this way at seven years old and to be punished by her mother if she failed to sell her basket of fruit.[6] Similarly, Charles Dickens's popular serial novels increased awareness of the plight of the poor working class. He embodied in the character of Ebenezer Scrooge the evils of a system that rewarded greed and selfishness. Moral outrage over the excesses of early capitalism led some people to become reformers and others to become radicals and revolutionaries. Reform-minded liberals wished to improve working conditions and raise wages, but more radical critics of capitalism advocated abolishing the entire system that produced such vast inequalities of opportunity, freedom, and wealth.

Most, though not all, of these critics were socialists of one stripe or another. In their assault on capitalism, they sounded one or both of two basic themes. One, as described above, was moral outrage. The other was an appeal to science and history—claims that half-hidden historical processes were at work undermining capitalism and paving the way for a future socialist society.

Count Claude-Henri de Saint-Simon

One of the first reformers to describe the scientific basis for socialism was French aristocrat Count Claude-Henri de Saint-Simon (1760–1825). He held that human history is divided into successive stages or periods. As an older form of society disappears, a new one necessarily arises to take its place. Each is marked by the presence of particular classes and depends upon certain beliefs. As these beliefs lose credibility, so too does the social and economic system that rests upon them. Thus, said Saint-Simon, **feudalism** depended upon the presence of landed nobility and a clergy who articulated the religious assumptions and beliefs upon which feudalism rested. These classes were undermined and eventually replaced by philosophers of the **Enlightenment,** with their emphasis on reason, and the coming of industrial society, with its emphasis on science and technology. A new class of scientists, engineers, and industrialists became increasingly important, said Saint-Simon, because without them, there could be no industrial society. This new society was enormously complex, depending as it did on the coordinated knowledge and skills of many different types of technicians and experts. In such a society it made no sense to speak, as liberals did, of "the individual." The isolated individual is a fiction. In the real world of the industrial society, individuals are reduced to their social roles and productive functions. In Saint-Simon's version, socialism involves the recognition and appreciation of the fact that social complexity and interdependence leads to the application of "positive" scientific knowledge to social and economic planning by an elite of experts.[7]

Saint-Simon did not explicitly call for the transfer of property from private to public control, but he did argue that **laissez-faire** capitalism was inefficient because it led to gluts and waste, as people competing for profits produced too much of one good and too little of another. Saint-Simon believed that through planning, experts could anticipate and thus meet social needs, providing an economic system that was both more efficient and more just than capitalism.

---

[6]Donald Thomas, *The Victorian Underworld* (London: John Murray, 1998).
[7]Claude-Henri de Saint-Simon, *Social Organization, The Sciences of Man, and Other Writings,* ed. Felix Markham (New York: Harper, 1964).

Saint-Simon's disciple Auguste Comte (1798–1857) carried this idea even further. Comte called himself a *positivist* and emphasized the importance of scientific planning, prediction, and social control in a society. "From science," he said, "comes prevision; from prevision comes control."[8] With its emphasis on social control, Comte's positivist version of socialism was characterized by a deep aversion to democracy and a fondness for technocracy, or rule by experts. Like Saint-Simon, Comte equated socialism with systematic scientific social planning, which was in turn justified by a new "religion of humanity" in which scientists were the high priests (and Comte the pope).[9]

Although Saint-Simon and Comte favoured centralized control of social production, other socialists in the early 1800s took the opposite position. Two prominent proponents of a decentralist version of socialism were Charles Fourier and Robert Owen, both of whom inspired disciples to establish short-lived utopian communities in the United States. Fourier and Owen devised schemes for a socialist society that were as visionary as Saint-Simon's and Comte's, but their visions were of small, self-sufficient, self-governing communities where decisions were made not by experts but by all adult members of the community.

Charles Fourier

Charles Fourier (1772–1837) was a French socialist whose vision of utopia derived from a mixture of mysticism, numerology, and a crude psychological theory. Modern society, Fourier said, is not so far from barbarism as its inhabitants are inclined to believe. It is afflicted with the evils of commerce, selfishness, and deception, among many others (144 of them, to be exact). Humans deceive not only others, but also ourselves by holding false or mistaken beliefs—especially the belief that wealth brings happiness. The evils of commercial society, with its mad pursuit of wealth, are embodied in its institutions. The institutions of marriage, the male-dominated family, and the competitive market prevent the satisfaction of the twelve passions. The five senses, along with those of familism, friendship, love, and ambition, are the first nine of these passions; to these Fourier added the thirsts for variety (the "butterfly" passion), for plotting and intrigue (the "cabalistic" passion), and for combining physical and mental pleasures (the "composite" passion). There is also a thirteenth, the passion for "harmony" that comes from the proper balance of the twelve basic passions.

Fourier believed that a competitive commercial society frustrates our desire for harmony. We can never satisfy our passion for harmony when we are divided against each other—and against ourselves—by competition for jobs and profits. Only when the evils of this society are overcome will humanity reach its highest stage, "harmonism," in which human beings will cooperate freely for the common good.

Fourier's vision of a harmonious society was captured in his account of the *phalanstery*, a type of community of about 1600 (he believed that the ideal population is 1610) in which the residents would produce all they needed and all the passions would be fully

---

[8]Auguste Comte, *Auguste Comte and Positivism: Selections from His Writings,* ed. Gertrude Linzer (New York: Harper, 1975) 88.

[9]See Frank E. Manuel, *The Prophets of Paris* (Cambridge, MA: Harvard UP, 1962). For a scathing liberal-individualist critique of Comte, see John Stuart Mill, *Auguste Comte and Positivism* (Ann Arbor, MI: U of Michigan P, 1961). Karl Marx was no less critical of Comte's *"Scheiss positivismus"* (shit positivism): Marx to Engels, 7 July 1866, in Karl Marx and Friedrich Engels, *Werke,* vol. 31 (Berlin: Dietz Verlag, 1968) 234.

satisfied. The phalanstery was based on the principle of *attractive labour*, which holds that people will work voluntarily if only they find an occupation that engages their talents and interests. Those who like to grow things will be the gardeners. Those who like children will provide daycare. Children, who like to play in the dirt, will sweep the streets and collect the garbage. Since people will work freely and spontaneously in these circumstances, the coercive apparatus of the state—laws, police, courts, prisons—will not be needed. Fourier envisioned that socialist society will be productive, prosperous, and free.

Robert Owen

Robert Owen (1771–1858) was a British capitalist who was appalled by the effects of early capitalism and became an ardent socialist. Drunkenness, debauchery, theft, and other evils were not, he believed, the result of original sin or of individual character defects, but, rather, the consequences of a deformed social system. By rewarding the greed and selfishness of the capitalist, the capitalist system sent the wrong message to young people. Little wonder, then, that so many people tried to advance themselves at other people's expense. The cure for the evils of capitalism was a new system of production—cooperative production for public profit—and a new system of education. Owen believed that deformed character was the result of defective education—where "education" is understood in the broadest possible sense as the sum of all the formative influences in one's life.

In 1800 in New Lanark, Scotland, Owen established a model textile factory that was radical by the standards of the day. The factory was clean and working conditions were relatively safe. The workweek was reduced. Children under ten were not only forbidden to work but also educated at the owner's expense. Besides learning the three Rs, children learned the value and necessity of cooperation in all aspects of life.

Owen described and defended these and other practices in *A New View of Society* (1813).[10] Over the next ten years, he laboured tirelessly to persuade his fellow capitalists to see the merits of his scheme. He also appealed to workers to share his vision of a network of small, self-sufficient communities that would spread around the globe. He was more successful with the workers than with the capitalists, who were understandably worried by Owen's attacks on private property and religion and by his growing popularity among the working class. In 1824 Owen took his ideas to North America. On 12 000 hectares in southwest Indiana, he established the socialist community of New Harmony, which he intended as a model of social organization. Within four years, however, New Harmony had failed, and Owen lost most of his fortune in the venture. He spent the remainder of his life promoting trade unionism and advocating the establishment of worker-owned cooperatives as the nucleus from which a larger and more comprehensive socialist society might grow.

Many other thinkers also dreamed dreams and fashioned schemes for a socialist society. Important though these proponents of **utopian socialism** were, none of their efforts proved to be as long-lived and influential as those of Karl Marx. In fact, by the middle of the twentieth century, roughly one-third of the world's population lived under regimes that claimed to be Marxist. It is safe to say that Marx is not only the most important thinker in the history of socialism, but also one of the most important in all history. That is reason enough to study his views closely and carefully.

---

[10]Robert Owen, *A New View of Society and Other Writings*, ed. G. D. H. Cole (London: Dent, 1927); see Ball and Dagger, selection 34.

THE SOCIALISM OF KARL MARX

Karl Marx (1818–1883) was the most influential of all socialist thinkers. An intellectual who studied law and earned a doctorate in philosophy, he was deeply influenced by the German philosopher Georg Wilhelm Friedrich Hegel.

The Influence of Georg Wilhelm Friedrich Hegel

During his lifetime and for some two decades after his death, Georg Wilhelm Friedrich Hegel (1770–1831) had a virtual monopoly on the German philosophical imagination. It was largely within the framework of his philosophy that educated Germans, especially the young, discussed history, politics, and culture.

Hegel's philosophy of history proved to be particularly influential. Human history, Hegel maintained, consists of human beings becoming more and more free and depends on their attaining greater awareness of that freedom. History is the story of this evolution of "spirit," or *Geist* in German.

At this point another key concept in Hegel's philosophy—estrangement or alienation (*Entfremdung*)—comes into play. Each step toward greater freedom requires breaking free from a way of life that was familiar and comfortable, but which spirit (*Geist*) now knows restricts its progress toward greater freedom. In the Middle Ages, for example, the church, the village, and the family provided a sense of comfort and community, but they

Karl Marx (1818–1883)

stood in the way of greater individuality. To achieve greater freedom, they had to be overcome. This alienation was painful, but necessary. The various stages through which spirit passes reveal what Hegel called the **cunning of reason** (*List der Vernunft*) and the operation of the **dialectic**. Individual human beings, and even entire nations, are characters in a vast unfolding drama whose plot—the progress of spirit and the growth of freedom—is unknown to them. Each plays his or her part, unaware of how that part fits into the greater whole. The story unfolds dialectically through the clash of opposing ideas and ideals. Out of this conflict emerge new and more comprehensive ideas and ideals.

To show how this dialectical process works to promote human freedom, Hegel imagines the essential conflict between a master and slave, the famous **master-slave dialectic**.[11] Imagine, Hegel proposed, a battle to the death between two men. One is prepared to risk his life and fight to the end. The other is not and submits. The first becomes the master, the second the slave. At first the slave is grateful for having his life spared and fearful that the master might yet take it from him. He sees himself through his master's eyes as inferior, degraded, and dependent. The master, likewise, sees himself through the slave's eyes as superior, ennobled, and independent. The slave, in other words, wants the master to recognize and acknowledge his humanity, which would in turn require the master to treat the slave as an equal—that is, to free him. Yet the master cannot free the slave without ceasing to be who he is, socially speaking—namely, a master. The master can never attain his full dignity as a human being, since what recognition he receives comes only from a cowardly slave and not from an equal.

The master at first appears to have the upper hand. He has all the power. And yet, when the slave refuses to recognize the master's moral or social superiority, *he* gains the upper hand. He withholds from the master the one thing that the master wants but cannot compel. From the moment of the slave's refusal, their positions are effectively reversed. The master is shown to have been dependent upon the slave all along. Not only did he depend upon the slave's labour for his livelihood, but also his very identity depended upon the presence and continued subservience of the slave—since without a slave he could not even *be* master. So, appearances aside, the master was in fact no more free than the slave, since his social role was in its own way restrictive and confining, keeping the master morally stunted and cut off from the humanity that he shared with the slave. Once they both recognize this, they cease to be master and slave and the institution of slavery is superseded or surpassed. Stripped at last of their *particularity* (their historically specific social roles), the former master and the former slave confront each other in their *universality*, or common humanity, as free and equal human beings. In freeing himself, the slave has freed his master as well.

Marx's Theory of History

After Hegel's death, his followers split into two main camps. On one side were the conservative Right Hegelians, who interpreted Hegel's philosophy of history in theological terms. For them, *spirit* meant God or the Holy Spirit, and human history is the unfolding of God's plan. On the other side were the Young or Left Hegelians (Marx among them), who held that Hegel's philosophy was open to a more radical interpretation than Hegel had perhaps realized. So with the hope of revealing "the rational kernel within the mystical shell" of Hegel's philosophy, Marx renewed his study of Hegel in 1843–1844.[12]

---

[11]Georg Wilhelm Friedrich Hegel, *Phenomenology of Mind,* trans. J. B. Baillie (New York: Harper, 1967) 228–240.
[12]Karl Marx, afterword to the second German edition, *Capital,* vol. 1 (New York: International, 1967) 20.

Like Hegel, Marx saw history as the story of human labour and struggle. But for Marx, history is the story not of the struggle of disembodied *spirit* but of human struggles in and against a hostile world. Humans have to struggle to survive heat and cold and the ever-present threat of starvation in order to wrest a living from a recalcitrant nature. But they also struggle against each other. Historically, the most important of these conflicts is the struggle of one class against another. "The history of all hitherto existing society," Marx and Engels wrote in the *Communist Manifesto*, "is the history of class struggles."[13] Different classes—masters and slaves in slave societies, lords and serfs in feudal society, and later capitalists and workers in capitalist society—have different, if not diametrically opposed, interests, aims, and aspirations. So long as societies are divided into different classes, class conflict is eventually inevitable.

To understand Marx's position here, we need to examine what Marx meant by **class**, how he thought different classes come into being and into conflict, and how he expected a classless communist society to arise. In short, we need to look closely at Marx's **materialist conception (or interpretation) of history**, which he called the "leading thread in my studies."

Marx called his interpretation of history materialist to distinguish it from Hegel's idealist interpretation. Where Hegel had seen history as the story of spirit's self-realization, Marx saw history as the story of class struggles over opposing material (or economic) interests and resources. This does not mean that Marx was, as he has sometimes been charged, an *economic determinist* who wished to "reduce everything to economics"; but he did emphasize the primary importance of material production. "Before men do anything else," he said, "they must first produce the means of their subsistence"—the food they eat, the clothing they wear, the houses they live in, and so on. Everything else follows from the necessity to produce the material means of our subsistence.[14]

Marx maintained that material production is based on two principles: the **material forces of production** and the **relations of production**. The material forces of production consist of the means of labour, which is "all those things with the aid of which man acts upon the subject of his labor, and transforms it" and the subject of labour, which "everything to which man's labor is directed," such as wood in a furniture factory or steel in an automotive plant. But human beings have to organize themselves in order to extract the raw materials; to invent, make, operate, and repair the machinery; to build and staff the factories; and so on. However primitive or sophisticated, material production requires a degree of specialization—what Adam Smith called the *division of labour*. Out of these social relations of production the different classes arise. Marx suggested that for purposes of scientific social analysis, we can simplify somewhat by imagining any society to contain two antagonistic classes, one of which dominates the other. According to Marx, in an industrial capitalist society these classes are the *capitalists*, or **bourgeoisie**, and the *wage-labourers*, or **proletariat**. Which class you belong to depends upon your relation to the forces of production. In every class-divided society, Marx noted, the dominant class tends to be much smaller than the dominated class.

---

[13]Karl Marx and Friedrich Engels, "The Manifesto of the Communist Party," *Marx and Engels: Basic Writings on Politics and Philosophy,* ed. Lewis Feuer (Garden City, NY: Doubleday, 1959) 7; see Ball and Dagger, selection 35.

[14]All quotations in this paragraph are from Karl Marx and Friedrich Engels, *The German Ideology,* part I (New York: International, 1947).

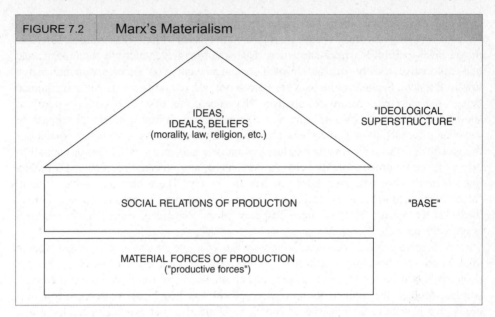

FIGURE 7.2 | Marx's Materialism

IDEAS,
IDEALS, BELIEFS
(morality, law, religion, etc.)

"IDEOLOGICAL
SUPERSTRUCTURE"

SOCIAL RELATIONS OF PRODUCTION

"BASE"

MATERIAL FORCES OF PRODUCTION
("productive forces")

Marx emphasized, however, that the ruling class does not rule by brute force alone. If it did, it would not rule for long. The longevity and stability of the ruling class's dominance is due to a second and arguably more important factor: It controls the thoughts, beliefs, and ideas—the "consciousness"—of the working class. Thus, the material-economic **base** of every society is capped by an **ideological superstructure**—a set of ideas, ideals, and beliefs that legitimizes and justifies the arrangements and institutions of that society. These ideas characteristically take several forms—moral, legal, theological, political, economic—but their function, in the final analysis, is the same: to explain, justify, and legitimize the division of labour, class differences, and vast disparities of wealth, status, and power that exist within a particular society. In a class-divided society, said Marx, we will always see ideology operating for the benefit of the dominant class and to the detriment of the subservient class. (See Figure 7.2.)

In all these ways, Marx maintained, the working class is kept from forming a true picture of its real situation. It mistakenly takes the ideas of the ruling class as its own. In short, the working class suffers from **false consciousness**. And as long as it does so, it will be a class "in itself"—that is, a class as yet unaware of its own interests and revolutionary political possibilities—but not yet "for itself." To see how the working class might overcome its false consciousness and in the process become a class for itself ready to make a **revolution** against the ruling class, we need to examine Marx's critique of capitalism and his theory of revolution.

Marx's Critique of Capitalism

Although an outspoken critic of capitalism, Marx admitted that capitalism was at one time a progressive and even radical force: "The bourgeoisie, historically, has played a most revolutionary part."[15] In its early phase, he said, capitalism had performed three important and historically progressive functions. First, in the late feudal period, merchant

---

[15]Marx and Engels, "Manifesto" 9.

capitalists hastened the demise of feudalism by breaking down domestic restrictions on trade and opening new trade routes. Strange as it may seem, Marx viewed these moves as progressive—painful but necessary steps that would lead eventually to a more just and non-exploitative society, just as Hegel had seen alienation as necessary in the march toward freedom. Second, capitalism has been a progressive force because it made human beings masters over nature. Capitalism "has been the first [economic system] to show what human activity can bring about. It has accomplished wonders far surpassing Egyptian pyramids, Roman aqueducts, and Gothic cathedrals; it has conducted expeditions that put in the shade all former exoduses of nations and crusades."[16] Third, capitalism proved to be progressive in its need for innovation and change. To remain profitable, industry must have new and more efficient machinery. These changes in the material forces of production bring about changes in the social relations of production, and thereby in the wider society. In these three respects, Marx contended, capitalism has been a progressive force for the good.

But if capitalism has been beneficial, why was Marx so critical of it? And why did he think capitalism should be overthrown and replaced? Of the many reasons Marx gave for doing so, the following three are of special importance. First, Marx claimed that capitalism had reached the limit of its productive power and had to be transcended for new productive powers to be unleashed. Second, he contended that capitalism created alienation in four distinct ways:

- Because workers are forced to sell their labour and do not own what they produce, they are alienated from the product of their labour.
- Because the capitalist system of mass production kills the creative spirit, workers cannot find satisfaction in their labour and are therefore alienated from the activity of production itself. The worker becomes "an appendage of the machine."[17]
- Workers are alienated from their distinctively and uniquely human potentials or powers—particularly the power to create and enjoy beauty—which are dulled or remain undeveloped in capitalist society.
- Capitalism alienates workers from each other inasmuch as it makes them compete with one another for jobs and wages.

Third, the sense of alienation felt by the working class would eventually help bring about the downfall of capitalism and the coming of communism, since capitalism is self-subverting in that it created conditions and unleashed forces that would one day destroy it.

Marx's Dialectic of Change

How exactly did Marx view the process that would bring about the momentous change from a competitive capitalist society to a cooperative communist society? Here we need to remember Marx's debt to Hegel, and particularly to Hegel's notion that history, in moving dialectically, exhibits the *cunning of reason*. Capitalists and proletarians are characters enmeshed in a drama whose plot and ending they do not know. And, as we

---

[16]Marx and Engels, "Manifesto" 12.
[17]Marx and Engels, "Manifesto" 14.

noted earlier, Marx drew his analysis from Hegel's master–slave dialectic. Now the actors are not individuals but two great contending classes, replacing master and slave with bourgeoisie and proletariat.

In capitalist society, workers are in fact enslaved, although they do not know it. Grateful to the capitalists for jobs and fearful of losing them, workers feel indebted to and dependent upon capitalists. The workers also accept the capitalist worldview and their respective places in it. In this view, capitalists are credited with creating jobs that they then give to the lucky workers. And since capitalists pay wages in exchange for the workers' labour, the relationship looks like a reciprocal one. But the appearance is misleading. Capitalists exploit workers by paying less than their labour is worth. By "extracting surplus value" (Marx's phrase for making a profit), capitalists are able to live luxuriously, while workers barely eke out a living. Their relationship, though ostensibly reciprocal, is far from equal. The worker is impoverished even as the capitalist is enriched. At the same time, the capitalist class grows smaller as the proletariat grows larger.

In Marx's view, the proletariat is the *universal class* because, in serving its interests, it serves the interests of all humanity.[18] It is in the workers' interest to abolish the working class—a class that is impoverished, despised, and degraded—and to become free and equal human beings. In freeing themselves, moreover, they free their former masters as well. They achieve at last "the full and free development of all."[19]

For Marx, true freedom—freedom from exploitation and alienation, the freedom to develop one's human powers to their fullest—can flourish only in a classless society. It is just this kind of society that workers have an interest in bringing about. But how, according to Marx's account, are they able to overcome false consciousness and to discover what their true interests are? How does the proletariat come to be a class for itself, equipped with a revolutionary consciousness? What are the actual steps or stages in the revolutionary sequence that lead to the overthrow of capitalism and the creation of a classless communist society? And, not least, what will communist society look like?

Marx's Revolutionary Sequence

Marx predicted that proletarian revolution, though eventually worldwide, would begin in the more advanced capitalist countries and proceed in a fairly definite order. The revolutionary sequence would follow seven stages. (See Figure 7.3.)

1. **Economic Crises.** Marx was by no means the first to observe that capitalism is plagued by periodic economic downturns—recessions and depressions. Bourgeois economists call these fluctuations in the business cycle that will, in time, correct themselves. Marx, by contrast, believed that these crises were due to the *anarchy of production* that characterizes a capitalist economy.[20] The more mature or advanced a capitalist society becomes, the more frequent and severe these crises will be—and the less likely they are to correct themselves. The process toward a socialist society starts with economic crises.

---

[18]"Critique of Hegel's Philosophy of Right," in Feuer, *Marx and Engels* 141–142.
[19]Marx and Engels, "Manifesto" 29.
[20]Marx and Engels, "Manifesto" 32.

FIGURE 7.3	Marx's View of the Revolutionary Sequence

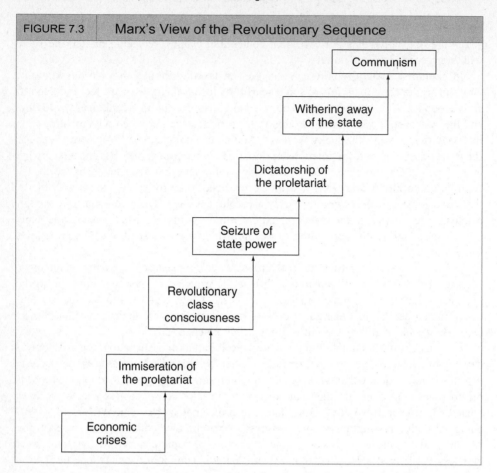

2. **Immiseration of the Proletariat.** The bourgeoisie, being wealthier, is better able to weather these crises than are the workers. Recessions and depressions deprive workers of their jobs, their income, and finally their food and shelter. Unable through no fault of their own to find work, some resort to begging, others to petty thievery for which they risk imprisonment or even death, and still others die of starvation. However miserable their lot as workers, they become even more miserable when they lose their jobs. This process, the **immiseration of the proletariat**, is inescapable in capitalist society, according to Marx.

3. **The Rise of Revolutionary Class Consciousness.** The workers in their misery begin to realize that the fault lies not with them but with the system—a system beset by contradictions too glaring to pass unnoticed. Workers are willing to work, but there are not enough jobs to go around. The bourgeois "coupon clippers" who do not work are nevertheless comfortable and affluent. Their children, well fed and warmly clothed, go to school; the workers' children—malnourished, hungry, and ill clad— beg in the streets and dig through garbage for scraps of food. Seeing these contradictions leads workers to reflect critically on the causes of their misery. At this point, Marx's theory intervenes to make a contribution by supplying an explanation of how

things came to be this way. It also proposes a solution: the overthrow of the ruling bourgeoisie. Because Marx believed that the workers would sooner or later arrive at this conclusion on their own, he saw himself as merely a "midwife," reducing the "birth pangs" by hastening the revolutionary process along the most direct and least painful course.

4. **Seizure of State Power.** Marx predicted that "objective" economic conditions (the economic crises resulting in the immiseration of the proletariat) and "subjective" conditions (revolutionary class consciousness) would combine to form a politically explosive mixture. Beginning with apparently unrelated, small, spontaneous strikes, boycotts, demonstrations, and riots, the revolutionary movement quickly coalesces into a more militant, organized, and unified force for the overthrow of the ruling class. Marx believed that the rule of the proletariat could come about in a number of ways. One possibility is that a nationwide "general strike" will cripple the economy and bankrupt the capitalists almost overnight. Another possibility is a bloody civil war pitting capitalists, soldiers, and police against armed proletarians. A third possibility, albeit an unlikely one (except perhaps in Holland and the United States, Marx said), is that the bourgeoisie will be overthrown not by bullets but by ballots in a free and fair election. In any case, the workers have the advantage of solidarity and sheer force of numbers. The struggle will be protracted, difficult, and probably violent. But, by whatever means, the proletariat will at last take state power out of the hands of the bourgeoisie and into its own.

5. **Dictatorship of the Proletariat.** Having seized state power, the proletariat proceeds to establish what Marx called the **revolutionary dictatorship of the proletariat**. By this inflammatory phrase, Marx meant merely that the bourgeois state, being a system of class rule, amounts to the dictatorship of the bourgeoisie over the proletariat. When the workers take state power into their hands, they become the new ruling class. In other words, the workers will rule in their own interest. Their most pressing interest is to preserve the gains of the revolution and prevent the defeated bourgeoisie from regrouping and mounting (possibly with outside assistance) a counterrevolution to regain power. As a result, the working class must use the apparatus of the state—the schools, courts, prisons, and police—in as dictatorial a manner as necessary to prevent this counterrevolution. Marx expected the victorious workers to be democratic and open in their dealings with each other. Theirs is to be a dictatorship of and by, not over, the proletariat.

6. **Withering Away of the State.** In one of his later writings, *Critique of the Gotha Programme,* Marx stated that the proletariat's defeat of the bourgeoisie will inaugurate a transitional period that will take society from capitalism to full-fledged communism. Because the old competitive ways of thinking typical of bourgeois society will not disappear immediately, this first or transitional form of communism will include not only the dictatorship of the proletariat but also continued use of wage incentives to encourage people to work hard. According to Marx, in this first phase of communism the guiding maxim should be "from each according to his ability, to each according to his labour." But the abiding interest of the proletariat, the universal class, is abolishing

classes and class distinctions. This abolition will begin once the workers take control of the workplace and transform the conditions of labour, ending exploitation and alienation. As the bourgeoisie dies out, or sees the errors of its ways, the need for coercion will gradually fade. Marx expected the result would be the **withering away of the state**: the dictatorship of the proletariat would lose its reason for being and simply wither away as communism achieves its full or mature form.

7. **Communism.** In spite of Marx's belief that this dialectic would end in communism, he said remarkably little about the specific features of this future communist society. One reason for this is that he—unlike earlier utopian socialists, with their detailed blueprints for building a perfect society—refused to write "recipes for the kitchens of the future."[21] The shape of any future society, Marx thought, could be decided only by the people who would inhabit it. Even so, Marx did hint at several features that he thought such a society would have. For one, it would be open and democratic, with all citizens taking an active part in governing it. For another, the major means of production—mills, mines, forests, factories, and so on—would be publicly owned. Economic production would be planned and orderly. And distribution of goods and services would be based not on privilege or wealth, but on ability and need. Under **communism**, then, the rule would be "from each according to his ability, to each according to his need." People living in a communist society would at last be truly free. Having overcome the obstacles of exploitation, alienation, and ideological illusions, they would be free to develop their many-sided personalities. Marx thus envisioned a future society in which every human being, not just a fortunate few, would be free to become well-rounded Renaissance men and women:

> In communist society, where nobody has one exclusive sphere of activity but each can become accomplished in any branch he wishes, society regulates the general production and thus makes it possible for me to do one thing today and another tomorrow, to hunt in the morning, fish in the afternoon, rear cattle in the evening, criticize after dinner, just as I please, without ever becoming hunter, fisherman, shepherd or critic.[22]

Marx died in 1883, too early to witness attempts to put his ideas into political practice. Others calling themselves Marxists and claiming to speak in his name were soon busy interpreting, reinterpreting, and adapting his ideas in ways that would almost certainly have astonished—and in some cases appalled—Marx. Whether Marx would have liked it or not, he gave rise to Marxism. And Marxism after Marx, as we shall now see, has had an interesting career of its own.

Several years before his death, Marx learned that a group of admiring French workers were calling themselves Marxists. The idea that anyone would reduce his complex and supposedly scientific theory to a simplistic "ism" appalled the old man. As Marx told his son-in-law, "What is certain is that I am not a Marxist."[23] But if Marx did not regard himself as a Marxist, many others were happy to claim the title. Chief among these was Marx's old friend and co-author, Friedrich Engels.

---

[21]Marx, *Capital* 17.
[22]Marx and Engels, *German Ideology* 22.
[23]Quoted in David McLellan, *Karl Marx: His Life and Work* (London: Macmillan, 1973) 443.

Friedrich Engels's Marxism

Although a fierce critic of capitalism, Friedrich Engels (1820–1895) was himself a capitalist. In the mid-1840s, Marx the radical philosopher teamed up with Engels the capitalist. Their partnership was in many ways unique. Each was strong where the other was weak. Marx quickly came to depend on Engels, not least for financial assistance during the early years of his exile in England, where the Marx family had moved in 1849 and where they lived for years in dire poverty. For his part, Engels depended on Marx for political inspiration and intellectual stimulation. Marx, as Engels readily acknowledged, was the deeper and more original thinker. But Engels was the better writer, with a knack for turning memorable phrases and writing with ease and speed in several languages. In the works they wrote together—including the *Communist Manifesto* (1848)—the ideas were mainly Marx's, but much of the prose was Engels's. During Marx's lifetime, Engels did much to simplify and popularize his friend's ideas.

In the years immediately following Marx's death, however, Engels added his own ideas to Marx's. Engels adapted and interpreted—one might even say radically reinterpreted—Marx's theory. Indeed, some scholars have suggested that it was Engels, not Marx, who invented Marxism, such that later Soviet Marxism (Marxism-Leninism) owes more to Engels than to Marx.[24]

The political situation in which Engels found himself in the 1880s was peculiar. After Marx's death in 1883, Engels claimed to speak for Marx on a wide variety of subjects, including the direction in which the German Social Democratic Party (SPD) should be heading. The SPD had been formed in 1875 by an alliance of two rival German socialist parties—the United German Labour Party, founded in 1863 and led by Ferdinand Lassalle (1825–1864), and the Social Democratic Workers' Party, established in 1869 by Marx's disciples August Bebel and Wilhelm Liebknecht. Lassalle had been Marx's main rival for the theoretical and intellectual leadership of the German socialist movement, and each devoted considerable energy to criticizing the other.

Unlike Marx, an internationalist who held that the working class has no homeland, Lassalle was an ardent advocate of **nationalism.** He believed that workers of every nation should seek their own path to socialism. The political tactics that would work for German socialists, for example, would not necessarily work for the French. Moreover, Lassalle believed that working people tend to be deeply patriotic and protective of their respective countries. To try to weld them into a unified international movement would therefore be ill conceived and bound to fail. Also unlike Marx, Lassalle held that the state could not, should not, and would not "wither away." It must instead be captured electorally and controlled democratically by workers and their elected representatives. Socialism was to be imposed from above by a beneficent and all-powerful state.

Even after Lassalle's premature death in 1864, the Lassallean wing of the SPD continued to be a thorn in Marx's side. Its reformist tendencies, its eclecticism and romanticism, and its German nationalism all ran counter to Marx's vision of a broad, unified, and international workers' movement.

From Marx's death in 1883 until his own in 1895, Engels was the guardian of Marxian orthodoxy to whom Marxists in Germany and elsewhere looked, not only for theoretical

---

[24]See Terrell Carver, *Engels* (Oxford: Oxford UP, 1981); and Terrell Carver, *Marx and Engels: The Intellectual Relationship* (Brighton, UK: Harvester, 1983); Terence Ball, "Marxian Science and Positivist Politics," in *After Marx,* ed. Terence Ball and James Farr (Cambridge: Cambridge UP, 1984) chapter 11.

inspiration and clarification but also for practical advice. In addition to offering advice about political tactics, Engels supplied a simplified version of Marx's theory that is in several respects difficult to square with Marx's own views. In particular, Engels made two very important moves. First, he claimed for Marxism the honorific title of **scientific socialism**. And second, Engels reinterpreted what Marx meant by **materialism**.

Scientific Socialism. In his speech at Marx's graveside, Engels called Marx "the man of science," comparing his achievement to that of Charles Darwin. "Just as Darwin discovered the law of development of organic nature, so Marx discovered the law of development of human history."[25] There is at first sight an air of plausibility about the comparison. After all, Marx did believe that his inquiries were scientific. By science (the German word is *Wissenschaft*) Marx meant a body of organized knowledge that can be tested and found to be true or false. Scientific knowledge, he held, is not static and closed, but open to criticism and refutation. Marx was highly critical of earlier thinkers—including Adam Smith and many others—for being insufficiently scientific. But he could also be quite critical of himself, and he repeatedly revised and amended his theory in the light of new evidence.

Marx's open and self-critical conception of science contrasts sharply with Engels's closed and uncritical view. Consider, for example, their respective views of the nature and function of scientific generalizations, or laws. Some nineteenth-century thinkers maintained that just as there are immutable laws of gravity, thermodynamics, and other natural phenomena, so too are there unchangeable laws governing history and human society. Marx agreed that there are social and historical laws, but he believed that these were historically changeable artifacts—mutable features characteristic of particular social formations rather than fixed features of all past, present, or possible societies. The so-called law of supply and demand, for example, is not a timelessly true law, but merely an artifact of capitalist market society. When capitalist society is superseded, that law will no longer be valid. In this respect, the laws social scientists seek are quite unlike the laws discovered by physicists, chemists, and other natural scientists.[26]

Engels, by contrast, believed that the new science of dialectics showed that the laws governing nature and society were one and the same. According to dialectics, everything—nature, history, even human thought—is nothing more than matter moving in accordance with the timeless laws of dialectics. And dialectics, he wrote, is "the science of the most general laws of all motion. Therein is included that their laws must be equally valid for motion in nature and human history and for the motion of thought." Just as "all true knowledge of nature is knowledge of the eternal, the infinite, and hence essentially absolute," so, too, Engels claimed, is all true knowledge of human beings and their history absolute and unchanging.[27]

On this dogmatic and rigid science of dialectics, Engels erected his claims for scientific socialism. Engels maintained that scientific socialism—that is, his (and, he claimed, Marx's) version of socialism—was not simply one ideology among many competitors, but an unchallengeable scientific account of how things were and must be. Any socialist

---

[25]Friedrich Engels, "Speech at Marx's Graveside," *Selected Works*, 1 vol., ed. Karl Marx and Friedrich Engels (New York: International, 1968) 435. For an inquiry into the Marx–Darwin myth, see Terence Ball, *Reappraising Political Theory* (Oxford: Clarendon, 1995) chapter 10.

[26]See James Farr, "Marx's Laws," *Political Studies* 34 (1986): 202–222; and "Marx and Positivism," *After Marx*, ed. Ball and Farr, chapter 10.

[27]Friedrich Engels, *Dialectics of Nature* (New York: International, 1963) 314.

Chapter 7: Socialism, Communism, and Anarchism: The Dream of an Equal Society   139

who argued otherwise was merely a utopian whose views rested more on sentiment or opinion than on science.[28] Such dogmatic self-certitude represented a dramatic departure from the young Marx's call for a "relentless critique of all that exists"—including existing conceptions of science.

Materialism. As we saw, Marx called himself a materialist, largely in order to distinguish his views from those of Hegel and other philosophical idealists of whom he was highly critical. But he was no less **critical** of earlier crude materialists like Thomas Hobbes, who believed that the world and everything (and everyone) in it consists of nothing but physical matter in motion. According to Hobbes, human thoughts and actions are merely the effects of physical forces beyond human control. In the "Theses on Feuerbach," Marx heaped ridicule upon this kind of crude materialism: "The materialist doctrine that men are products of circumstances and upbringing, and that, therefore, changed men are products of other circumstances and changed upbringing, forgets that it is men that change circumstances and that the educator himself needs educating."[29]

Marx was a materialist in another and altogether different sense. He was not concerned with matter per se but with the ways in which human beings organize themselves in order to survive and flourish by transforming raw materials into humanly useful objects, artifacts, and commodities. These ways of organizing influence or condition (*bedingen*) the way in which people think about themselves and their world.

In contrast, Engels's version of materialism has more in common with the materialism of Hobbes than with that of Marx. Engels asserted that everything is reducible to matter and its transformations. However extensive the changes, matter remains eternally the same, its "motions" governed by timeless "iron laws":

> We have the certainty that matter remains eternally the same in all its transformations, that none of its attributes can ever be lost, and therefore, also, that with the same iron necessity that it will exterminate on the earth its highest creation, the thinking mind, it must somewhere else and at another time again produce it.[30]

Thus, Engels's emphasis on matter in motion stands in curious contrast to Marx's emphasis on human beings in motion, making and remaking their world into a more humanly habitable place.

Engels reduced Marx's very subtle and complex philosophy into a much more simplistic ideology. As we will see, this simplification had considerable appeal in the hundred years that followed, as many thinkers who claimed to be socialists argued about which of them came closest to the spirit or letter of Marx's legacy. Great though Marx was, there were other socialists who either fought to free themselves from his influence or whose socialism arose from a different tradition.

ANARCHISM

Anarchism is a very old word. It comes to us from the ancient Greek *anarchia*. Literally, it means "without a leader," since leaderlessness, or lack of government, normally produces lawlessness and chaos, which was the meaning it held for Aristotle and for most political

---

[28]Friedrich Engels, "Socialism, Utopian and Scientific," in *Selected Works*, ed. Marx and Engels.
[29]Karl Marx, "Theses on Feuerbach," *Selected Works,* ed. Marx and Engels 28.
[30]Engels, *Dialectics* 25.

thinkers of his time. It is also what most people mean when they use the word today. The first known use of it in English occurred in the 1530s and the word "anarchist" was first recorded in 1679.

The English Peasants' Rebellion of 1381, led by Wat Tyler, marched to the slogan, "When Adam delved [dug the ground] and Eve span [spun wool], / Who was then the gentleman?" They demanded relief from serfdom, controlled wages, and reduced taxes. Although their slogan was egalitarian, they were quite happy to accept the continuation of the monarchy.

The first political movements that might be plausibly considered anarchist were the Levellers and Diggers of the English Civil War (1641–1660). The Levellers were democratic and egalitarian; but a more radical offshoot led by Gerald Winstanley, the Diggers, or True Levellers as they called themselves, might more realistically be deemed the first anarchists. In 1649 they took over some common land just outside London. Their act of reclaiming it, they believed, was the first step toward making the Earth a common treasury again, initiating a new order in the world. In Winstanley's words:

> Then this Enmity in all Lands will cease, for none shall dare to seek a Dominion over others, neither shall any dare to kill another, nor desire more of the Earth than another; for he that will rule over, imprison, oppresse, and kill his fellow Creatures, under what pretence so ever, is a destroyer of the Creation, and an actor of the Curse, and walks contrary to the rule of righteousness.[31]

The Levellers and the Diggers also believed that if they could free England from something they called the Norman yoke, they could restore the country to a state of political freedom. The "Norman yoke" referred to William the Conqueror's invasion of England in 1066. Their argument was that the Norman invaders had robbed the Anglo-Saxons of their rights and that, once the oppressive regime was overthrown, a free and happy people could thrive again.

In one form or another, variations of these two themes run through anarchist thought. The first deals with the issue of scarcity. Some anarchists are collectivists, even communists; some are individualists who believe in private property ownership. What they share in common is the view that the problem of distributive justice has been solved. Ever since Aristotle, political thinkers have believed that there would always be scarcity in some of the things that people value in life, and perhaps even in some of the goods that were necessary to sustain existence. A central question of politics was how most fairly to distribute scarce resources among competing wants. Capitalists had one answer; communists had another. Indeed this is the central question that many ideologies address.

However, anarchists deny that scarce resources are a problem. They say that either or both of two things can happen. First, as the Diggers believed, the productive capacities of the earth can be almost limitlessly increased if the old regime is overthrown, providing enough of the previously scarce resources so that there is no need to ration them. Then people's vices—avarice, gluttony, pride—will be transformed. Before such a transformation, people would want luxury or want to compete with their neighbour, and their demand for resources would soar. But when their requirements are paired to their needs, the demands on society's resources are dramatically reduced. The state, which previously had

---

[31]Gerald Winstanley. *'The Law of Freedom' and Other Writings.* Ed. Christopher Hill (Cambridge: Cambridge UP, 1983). Digitally printed version 2006.

been necessary as a repressive instrument to enforce decisions about distributive justice, no longer was necessary because distributive justice no longer was necessary. The garbage would still need to be picked up and the streets paved, but these were matters of detail.

Anarchists also believed that the state was like the Norman yoke, an unnecessary and artificial infringement on human freedom. They believed that it corrupted the individuals who lived under its domination. How badly they were damaged and how quickly they might recover was a matter about which they disagreed, and they also disputed whether it was possible to destroy the state by eliminating its agents (such as by the assassination of American President William McKinley in 1901) or whether a more comprehensive revolution was necessary. However, there was agreement that the destruction, or deconstruction, of the state and its institutions was necessary if human beings were ever going to attain their full development as human beings.

The first thinker who systematically elaborated these principles was an Englishman, William Godwin (1756–1836), who was married to Mary Wollstonecraft (1759–1797), whom many consider the first feminist theorist. In 1793, Godwin published *An Enquiry Concerning Political Justice*. The government of the day seriously considered prosecuting him for treason, but decided that the high price and length of the book put it beyond the reach of the working class. Godwin put forward two fundamental propositions. The first was that the fundamental motivation for most men and women was not greed, but benevolence or a wish to do good to their fellow human beings. It was society, not human nature, that made them behave selfishly. The second proposition was that the state existed as an instrument to protect private property. Private property was not only unnecessary, but also harmful. It encouraged the production of luxuries for the rich at the expense of necessities for the poor, and it led to an unequal distribution of wealth that led to widespread starvation and misery side by side with great wealth. Without private property, Godwin thought, everyone's basic needs for food, shelter, clothing, and the like could be easily satisfied. Small communities would replace large cities and, if quarrels or minor troubles arose, they could be easily settled by the disapproval of neighbours.

In revolutionary France, Godwin's contemporaries were making similar points more forcefully. In 1796, Gracchus Babeuf led a movement called "The Conspiracy of Equals." It prepared a document "Analysis of the Doctrine of Babeuf," part of which stated the anarchist case quite clearly.

1. We mean by society an association guided by agreed upon rules . . .
2. . . . Whatever the case, the preservation of equality is the goal of association, because it's only through it that men gathered together can be happy.
3. In uniting their forces, mankind surely wanted to assure itself the maximum of pleasure with the minimum of pain.

. . . The abundance of necessary things assures these pleasures, and is itself assured by the labor of those who are leagued together. This labor is reduced to the minimum for each of them only when it is shared by all.

The first important thinker to call himself an anarchist was Pierre-Joseph Proudhon (1809–1865). Proudhon is most famous today for the phrase "property is theft" from his 1840 book *What is Property?* What he really opposed were large manufacturers and large landowners. His ideal society was probably not anarchist at all by most people's standards. His ideal was a community composed of people owning small farms. The downfall and death of societies are due to the power of accumulation possessed by property. Resolve this, and you resolve the problem of scarcity.

Proudhon's belief in private property and his hope for peaceful social change made him the target for powerful thinkers of the nineteenth century. Marx largely dismissed him for his failure to understand the need to eliminate private property. In contrast, Mikhail Bakunin (1814–1876) described him as the father of anarchism. In the middle of the nineteenth century, anarchism became a political movement. Most anarchists shared Godwin's vision that the ideal form of social organization is a small community and that this way of life would be possible once the repression of capitalism was overcome. Most anarchists, such as Bakunin and novelist Leo Tolstoy (1828–1910), believed that it is possible and necessary to achieve this ideal without violence. Peter Kropotkin (1842–1921) tried to turn social Darwinism against itself by arguing that animals had a biological tendency to cooperate. As he wrote in *Mutual Aid: A Factor of Evolution* (1902), "In all these scenes of animal life which passed before my eyes, I saw Mutual Aid and Mutual Support carried on to an extent which made me suspect in it a feature of the greatest importance for the maintenance of life, the preservation of each species, and its further evolution."

In the United States, one of the most controversial anarchist theorists was Emma Goldman (1869–1940), known as Red Emma. She became an especially controversial figure. Like others who followed the ideas of anarcho-communism, Goldman thought of anarchism as "the great liberator of man from the phantoms that have held him captive"—phantoms such as God, the state, and private property. Anarchism, she declared, "really stands for the liberation of the human mind from the dominion of religion; the liberation of the human body from the dominion of property; liberation from the shackles and restraints of government." To these concerns she added the feminist theme of liberation of women from the exploitation of men. Just as capitalism oppresses working men (and women), she argued, so marriage oppresses women. Goldman believed capitalism robs man of his birthright; stunts his growth; poisons his body; keeps him in ignorance, in poverty, and in dependence; and then institutes charities that thrive on the last vestige of man's self-respect. The institution of marriage makes a parasite of women, who become absolute dependents. It incapacitates her for life's struggle, annihilates her social consciousness, paralyzes her imagination, and then imposes its gracious protection, which is in reality a travesty on human character.

As an advocate of free love, Goldman also championed the cause of birth control—and, as a result, served a prison term.

Anarcho-syndicalism became the model for the powerful, though relatively short-lived, American organization called the International Workers of the World (IWW or Wobblies). The Wobblies refused any alliance, direct or indirect, with any political party and aimed at creating a revolution that would practise community and worker self-management.

The success of Leninism and Stalinism in the Soviet Union sounded the death knell for anarchism as a political force. Although the black and red flag of anarchism was a significant force in the Spanish Civil War in the 1930s, in effect both the fascists and the communists combined indirectly to destroy the power of the anarchists. George Orwell's *Homage to Catalonia* (1938) chronicles the struggles between its various factions. Since then, there have been mostly isolated incidents of anarchist activity. One was perpetrated by a former American academic, Ted Kaczynski (1942–), known as the Unabomber. In 1969 Kaczynski resigned his position as assistant professor of mathematics at Berkeley and moved to a remote cabin in Montana. Over a period of seventeen years starting in 1978, he sent sixteen letter bombs that caused extensive injuries and two deaths. In 1995 he released a 35 000 word manifesto, "Industrial Society and Its Future," in which he denounced the industrial-technological system and called for a revolution that might or might not be violent. Section 94 reveals the anarchist nature of his goals:

> Freedom means being in control (either as an individual or as a member of a small group) of the life-and-death issues of one's existence: food, clothing, shelter, and defense against whatever threats there may be in one's environment. Freedom means having power; not the power to control other people but the power to control the circumstances of one's own life. One does not have freedom if anyone else (especially a large organization) has power over one, no matter how benevolently, tolerantly, and permissively that power may be exercised.

Canada witnessed an attempt at violent revolution in October 1970 with the kidnapping of British trade commissioner James Cross and Quebec provincial cabinet minister Pierre Laporte, both of whom were seen as symbols of oppressive state power. The kidnappers were members of the Front de Libération du Québec (FLQ), an anarcho-syndicalist group that was trying to create a separate Quebec country by waging a terrorist campaign. Members of the group drew their theoretical inspiration from Pierre Vallières's Negres Blancs d'Amérique (White Niggers of America). Vallières argued that the workers of Quebec were a colonized and oppressed people, analogous to the Blacks in the American South after the Civil War. The ruling class had consolidated its power and was highly resistant to change. A war of liberation was needed. They believed that their terrorist acts would provoke massive repression on the part of the bourgeois federal state, which in turn would reveal its true repressive character, sparking a revolution of the oppressed. They were correct about the repression, but most Canadians, including most Quebecers, approved of the subsequent use of force.

Probably the most influential anarchists in the second half of the twentieth century were writers. George Woodcock (1912–1995), a Canadian poet and historian, was an anarchist in the tradition of Kropotkin and Proudhon. His most important book, *Anarchism* (1962), is perhaps the best history of the movement, though contemporary critics criticized it as being too backward looking. Internationally renowned MIT linguist Noam Chomsky (1928–) describes himself variously as "a kind of voluntary socialist, that is, as libertarian socialist or anarcho-syndicalist or communist anarchist." He opposes representative democracy because it centralizes power in the state and because it does not effectively control the economy. He envisages a society organized on the basis of interconnected organic communities.

Robert Nozzick's views are similar. In *Anarchy, State, and Utopia* (1974), he argues that theorizing about the state should begin with the assumption that the individual is free and rational. Building on that, he says, "Out of anarchy, pressed by spontaneous groupings, mutual-protection associations, division of labor, market pressures, economies of scale, and rational self-interest there arises something very much resembling a minimal state or a group of geographically distinct minimal states' will arise."

Nozzick has been criticized for claiming to be an anarchist but actually being a libertarian. Thomas Jefferson, an early nineteenth-century American president, is thought to have said, "That government is best that governs least." This sums up the view of the libertarians. It is often difficult to know where to draw the line between these two ideologies. Novelist Ayn Rand (1905–1982), author of *The Fountainhead* (1943) and *Atlas Shrugged* (1957), calls her own philosophy objectivism, but she was often described both as an anarchist and as a libertarian, though she rejected these labels. She believed that free market capitalism was the only morally defensible form of economics, and she was strongly anticommunist because communism suppressed individual creativity.

For Further Reading

Ackroyd, Peter. *The Life of Thomas More.* New York: Doubleday, 1998.

Avineri, Shlomo. *The Social and Political Thought of Karl Marx.* Cambridge: Cambridge UP, 1993.

Ball, Terence, and James Farr, eds. *After Marx.* Cambridge: Cambridge UP, 1984.

Berlin, Isaiah. *Karl Marx: His Life and Environment.* 4th ed. Oxford: Oxford UP, 1978.

Carver, Terrell. *Engels.* Oxford: Oxford UP, 1981.

———. *Marx's Social Theory.* Oxford: Oxford UP, 1982.

Cohen, G.A. *Karl Marx's Theory of History: A Defense.* Princeton, NJ: Princeton UP, 2001.

Gilbert, Alan. *Marx's Politics: Communists and Citizens.* New Brunswick, NJ: Rutgers UP, 1981.

Hunley, T. *Friedrich Engels: A Reinterpretation of His Life and Thought.* New Haven: Yale UP, 1991.

Kolakowski, Leszek. *Main Currents of Marxism.* 3 vols. Trans. P.S. Falla. Oxford: Clarendon, 1978.

Manuel, Frank E. *The Prophets of Paris.* Cambridge, MA: Harvard UP, 1962.

McLellan, David. *Karl Marx: His Life and Thought.* London: Macmillan, 1973.

Rockmore, Tom. *Marx after Marxism.* Oxford: Blackwell, 2002.

Singer, Peter. *Marx.* Oxford: Oxford UP, 1980.

Taylor, Charles. *Hegel.* Cambridge: Cambridge UP, 1975.

Taylor, Keith. *The Political Ideas of the Utopian Socialists.* London: Cass, 1982.

Wheen, Francis. *Karl Marx: A Life.* New York: Norton, 2000.

Wilson, Edmund. *To the Finland Station.* New York: Doubleday, 1953.

Wood, Allen. *Karl Marx.* London: Routledge, 2004.

Woodcock, George. *Anarchism.* Harmondsworth, UK: Penguin, 1963.

Useful Websites and Social Media

www.marxists.org/archive/marx Marx and Engels Internet Archive

www.anu.edu.au/polsci/marx/classics/manifesto.html The Communist Manifesto

www.marxism.org.uk What is Marxism?

http://anarchism.net/books.htm Anarchism.net

Facebook :

      www.facebook.com/karl.marxist

      www.facebook.com/pages/Anarchy/14067324330

From the Ball and Dagger Reader *Ideals and Ideologies*, US Eighth Edition

Part Five: Socialism and Communism: More to Marx

Discussion Questions

1. Tories believe social hierarchy is natural. Socialists believe human beings are by nature equal. Who's right?

2. Marx was an historical determinist. Do you believe it's possible to foresee the future?

3. Political thinkers like Republican presidential candidate Ron Paul believe that the role of government should be severely limited. Anarchists believe that government should be (largely) eliminated. Is either of these positions practical?

4. Communists were persecuted in Canada and the United States in the nineteenth century and most of the twentieth. Is persecution of an individual or group ever justified?

MySearchLab MySearchLab with eText offers you access to an online interactive version of the text, additional quizzes and assessment, extensive help with your writing and research projects, and provides round-the-clock access to credible and reliable source material. Go to **www.mysearchlab.com** to access these resources.

CHAPTER 8

Socialism and Communism after Marx

Capitalism in Canada and the world today is a crisis-ridden and decaying system. But, it is pregnant with its opposite—socialism.

Communist Party of Canada

LEARNING OBJECTIVES

After completing this chapter you should be able to

1. Describe the paths of Marxism in Russia and China and socialism in Britain.

2. Analyze why socialism has been more successful in Canada than in the United States.

3. Define market socialism and critical Western Marxism.

4. Discuss how the core assumptions of socialism perform the four functions of an ideology.

In the early twenty-first century, socialism—especially of the top-down, authoritarian, central-planning variety—seems to be an idea whose time has passed. In the early twentieth century, by contrast, socialism seemed to many in Europe and North America to be an idea whose time had come. The period from Karl Marx's death in 1883 until the outbreak of First World War in 1914 was a time of political and theoretical ferment—and growing popular support for socialism and socialist parties. One observer has called this the "golden age" of socialism and of Marxism in particular.[1]

It was an age of Marxian socialism, to be sure, but it was also an age of Christian socialism, **Fabian socialism**, **anarcho-communism**, and other non-Marxian variants. While some socialists considered themselves Marxists, others were highly critical of various aspects of Marx's theory. Even those who called themselves Marxists often subscribed to different interpretations of what Marx meant and what Marxism was. Engels advanced his own distinctive interpretation of Marxism, as later did Lenin and the **Bolsheviks** (meaning "majority"—that is, the majority within the Russian Communist Party), who thought of themselves as scientific socialists remaking the world in the fiery forge of **revolution**. Others were skeptical or critical or both. The **revisionists**, for example, criticized the revolutionary thrust of Marx's theory. They thought that socialism, and later communism, would come about peacefully, by evolutionary means.

Such faction and ferment characterized socialism throughout the twentieth century. There have been many voices in the socialist chorus—not all singing in the same key, and some marching to different drummers and singing altogether different songs. Even so, Marx's voice has until recently boomed louder than anyone else's. Many European and Asian socialists since his time have thought it necessary to come to terms with Marx's theory, to accept it, to reject it outright, or to modify it almost beyond recognition. Something of the variety of Marxisms and other forms of socialism are presented in Fig 8.1.

---

[1]Leszek Kolakowski, *Main Currents of Marxism,* vol. 2, *The Golden Age* (Oxford: Clarendon, 1978).

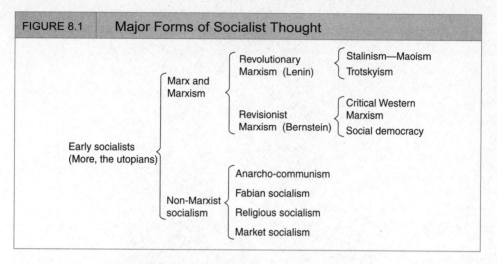

FIGURE 8.1   Major Forms of Socialist Thought

MARXISM AFTER KARL MARX

As we saw in the last chapter, on several occasions Marx changed his view about how the transition from socialism to communism was likely to occur. At the time of the *Communist Manifesto* in 1848 and the uprising called the Paris Commune in 1870, he thought a violent revolution was likely. At other times, he suggested that advanced industrial countries such as the United States, the United Kingdom, and Holland might make the transition almost seamlessly. Which one was the real Marx? Opinions clashed violently in answer to that question, and countless men and women died as a consequence. Ideological struggles and academic debates are often very different things.

REVOLUTIONARY MARXISM

Soviet Marxism-Leninism

The Russian Context. At first glance, the last place in Europe that a communist revolution should have taken place was Russia. Compared with North America and most of the countries of Western Europe, Russia in the late nineteenth century was economically and politically backward. Its economy was mainly agricultural, its industrial base relatively small, and its factories few and inefficient. The vast majority of its people were not proletarian wage-labourers working in factories, but peasants who tilled the land in exchange for a portion of the produce. Further, Russia was as politically primitive as it was economically backward. Its institutions were undemocratic, its tsar an autocratic ruler, and its hereditary nobility oppressive and largely indifferent to the suffering of the common people. Such a semi-feudal society seemed singularly unlikely to spawn the kind of revolution that Marx had expected. Proletarian revolution, after all, required a large proletarian class, not a class of peasants afflicted with what Marx and Engels called "the idiocy of rural life."[2]

---

[2]Karl Marx and Friedrich Engels, "The Manifesto of the Communist Party," *Marx and Engels: Basic Writings on Politics and Philosophy,* ed. Lewis Feuer (Garden City, NY: Doubleday, 1959) 11; see Terence Ball and Richard Dagger, eds., *Ideals and Ideologies: A Reader*, 8th ed. (New York: Longman, 2011) selection 5.34.

Vladimir Ilich Lenin (1870–1924)

Vladimir Ilich Lenin's Contributions. With the help of Russian Marxist philosopher Georgi Plekhanov (1856–1918), Vladimir Ilich Lenin (1870–1924) plunged into an intensive study of the few works of Marx and Engels then available in Russian. The main lesson that Lenin learned from his studies, and subsequently sought to apply in practice, was that class struggle is the chief driving force of historical development. For the revolutionary, rational political action consists of following strategies for intensifying and taking advantage of class divisions and differences. Anything that helps to accomplish that end is justifiable.

Lenin's view of the hardened revolutionary personality carried over to his vision of the Communist Party. Marx had viewed the communist movement as a large, inclusive, and broadly based organization of working people from many countries. Yet Lenin believed that the Communist Party should be small, exclusive, highly organized, tightly disciplined, and conspiratorial. No other party, he argued, could succeed in overthrowing the Russian police state. Lenin's view was put to the test in 1903, when a rival wing of the Russian Communist Party wanted a less exclusive and more open party. Through some adroit manoeuvring in this internal party struggle, Lenin's wing gained control. At this point, members of the Communist Party began calling themselves *Bolsheviks*.

In Lenin's view, the party's role is to agitate, organize, and educate the workers, teaching them where their true interests lie. The "function of the proletarian vanguard," Lenin wrote, "consists in training, educating, enlightening and drawing into the new life the most backward strata and masses of the working class and the peasantry."[3] Moreover, revolutionary class consciousness cannot, or should not, be allowed to come about spontaneously and by itself. It must instead be imported into the working class from outside, by a **vanguard party**, whose leadership was to consist primarily of revolutionary intellectuals. Without such a vanguard, Lenin feared, the working class would not only fail to become a revolutionary force but would also become downright reactionary. This vanguard party was to be democratic in two rather restricted respects. First, it must claim to represent the real or true interests of the modern *demos,* the **proletariat,** and the peasantry. Second, the party had to be, in itself, a microcosm of the democratic society that was to come. Thus, inside the party, free discussion was to be permitted. Yet once a vote was taken and an issue decided, discussion was to cease and everyone was to follow the orders of the central leadership. Lenin called this notion of internal party democracy **democratic centralism**. Democracy throughout society was not yet feasible, Lenin believed, because the masses could not yet be trusted to know their own real interests. Left to their own devices without a vanguard party to tutor and guide them, the workers would make wrong or even reactionary decisions.

With the outbreak of the First World War, Marxism came under question as workers volunteered in droves to fight other workers in other countries, thereby undermining Marx's analysis of workers as fellow proletariats. In *Imperialism, the Highest Stage of Capitalism* (1916), Lenin argued that the workers in the advanced capitalist countries— England, Germany, Italy, France, Belgium, and eventually the United States—were willing to go to war against their fellow proletarians because they had come to have a stake in their respective countries' colonization and exploitation of peoples in Africa, Asia, and South America. Each country had carved out *spheres of influence*—a polite phrase they used to mask brutal exploitation that exceeded even that of early capitalism in the West. The First World War was a war for cheap labour, cheap raw materials, and foreign markets. The scene of the most brutal capitalist oppression had shifted from Europe and North America to the countries on the capitalist periphery (known today as *developing countries*). Meanwhile, according to Lenin, European and American workers were being allowed to organize into trade unions to demand a larger share of an ever-expanding economic pie—an expansion made possible by the "super profits" that their countries' capitalists were extracting from the land, labour, and resources of these poorer nations. The capitalists were thus able to bribe their own workers and trade unionists with higher wages, shorter hours, better working conditions, health insurance plans, and other benefits. This, said Lenin, is the real source of the rising wages and standard of living touted by Eduard Bernstein and the revisionists.[4]

Four important and far-reaching conclusions followed from Lenin's analysis of **imperialism**. First, imperialism reconfirmed Lenin's suspicion of and hostility toward the revisionists, whom he saw as the allies and apologists for the capitalist class that they claimed to oppose. Second, he concluded that members of the working class in the advanced capitalist countries had been infected with *trade-union consciousness*; they had, in effect, become bourgeois and could not be counted on to lead the revolution that

---

[3]Vladimir Ilich Lenin, "'Left Wing' Communism—An Infantile Disorder," *Selected Works,* vol. 2 (Moscow: Progress, 1968) 535.

[4]Vladimir Ilich Lenin, "Imperialism, the Highest Stage of Capitalism," *Selected Works*, ed. V.I. Lenin (New York: International, 1969) 171–175, 240–247.

Marx had predicted—at least not without the help of a vanguard party to show them the way. Third, he believed that the Communist Party had the important, indeed indispensable, role of raising the consciousness of the working class. Fourth—and, as we shall see, especially significantly—Lenin concluded that the revolution would come first to those areas in which the proletariat was both immiserated and led by an active vanguard party. Instead of occurring first in the most advanced capitalist countries, as Marx had expected, proletarian revolutions would begin in the more backward nations of the world—in Russia and China, for example.

Revolution came to Russia in 1917. The Bolsheviks violently seized power in October 1917, murdered the tsar and his whole family, and waged a fierce civil war to gain control. Lenin was named premier, and a government based on "soviets" (workers' councils) was set up. The Bolshevik government attempted to restructure Russian society from the ground up. It seized mines, mills, factories, and other large manufacturing facilities and put them in the hands of the soviets. With the help of a brutal secret police, it began to lay the groundwork for a totalitarian state. In all this it claimed that Marxism-Leninism was a creative but faithful adaptation of Marxist revolutionary doctrines to twentieth-century circumstances. When Lenin died in 1924, the party he created was called Communist, but it was a far cry from the utopian-anarchist vision of communism that Marx had sketched out in *The German Ideology* eighty years earlier.

Chinese Communism

In the early twenty-first century, the only remaining major global power whose ruling party calls itself communist is the People's Republic of China. With its increasing industrial might and a population of more than a billion—one out of five people alive today is Chinese—China plays an increasingly important role on the world's stage. If we are to understand current Chinese thinking and actions, we need to know something about China's past and its revolutionary path to the present.

The Chinese Context. The ideological thread of Chinese history over the past century consists of several complex strands. The oldest is Confucianism, a body of doctrine drawn from the teachings of Confucius (551–479 BCE). From a political perspective, Confucianism stresses order, hierarchy, respect for the monarchy and one's parents, and a bureaucracy managed by a learned elite, the mandarins. A second strand, Chinese nationalism, was born of a reaction against nineteenth-century European, American, and Japanese colonialism and foreign occupation. For a proud and ancient people to be economically dominated by "barbarians" was especially galling. Repeated attempts by the Chinese to drive the foreigners out—as in the Boxer Rebellion of 1899, for example—were suppressed by better-armed foreign forces. In 1905 the Nationalist Party, under Sun Yat-sen, established a nominally independent Chinese Republic. After a series of setbacks, China was unified under Nationalist leader Generalissimo Chiang Kai-shek in 1928.

Chiang's Nationalist Party was not without rivals. The still-new Chinese Communist Party (CCP), founded in 1921, represents a third strand in China's ideological configuration. A young library assistant at Beijing University, Mao Zedong (1893–1976), was among the first to join the newly formed CCP. Mao had been electrified by the news of the 1917 Russian Revolution and had set about studying the works of Marx, Engels, and Lenin to see what lessons they might contain for China. Unable to read any language other than Chinese, however, Mao's choice of readings was severely restricted. Most of the works of Marx and Engels—with the exception of the *Communist Manifesto* and several other short works—had not yet been translated into Chinese. But a number of Lenin's essays were beginning to appear in translation. One of these, Lenin's *Imperialism,* was to have a decisive influence on Mao's thinking. Mao was drawn to Lenin's theory of imperialism for several reasons. First, it seemed especially well suited to Chinese conditions. China had no sizable industrial proletariat; the vast majority of its people were peasants who tilled the soil. For another, the imperialist powers found in China vast resources—abundant raw materials and cheap labour—and a large foreign market for their own manufactured goods. Little wonder, Mao reasoned, that the advanced capitalist countries sought "super profits" in China. Yet Lenin's analysis not only served to explain several puzzling features of modern Chinese history but also offered a prescription— revolution not as the internal class war that Marx had predicted, but as an anti-imperialist "war of national liberation" waged by the people of an economically backward nation against their foreign capitalist oppressors.

Certainly China in the 1920s was neither prosperous nor powerful. Most of its people were pitifully poor. Nearly three out of four were poor peasants who owned little or no land and survived by working the landlords' vast estates. There was little heavy industry. Only about one of every 200 Chinese could be classified as proletarians in Marx's sense. Those who were not poor peasants or industrial workers were mostly "rich" peasants who, like Mao's parents, owned and farmed small plots. Mao's most original contribution to—or perhaps departure from—Marxism was his proposal to make a revolution that would downplay the importance of the urban proletariat and concentrate instead on harnessing the pent-up resentments of rural peasants.

Mao Zedong (1893–1976)

The Rural Proletariat. Mao's reliance on the Chinese peasantry rested on several factors. First and most obviously, poor peasants constituted an overwhelming majority of the Chinese population. Once organized and mobilized, they would be an almost irresistible force. Second, they were not only the poorest but also the most oppressed sector of the populace. They therefore had everything to gain and little to lose by waging an all-out struggle against their oppressors. Finally, Mao believed that the peasants were endowed with a kind of practical wisdom or common sense that comes not from books or theories, but from experience. If a revolution were to be made in China, it must be made by peasants led by a party whose leaders spoke their language and thought as they thought. Many of Mao's speeches and writings were, accordingly, directed against abstract theorizing and couched in a folksy style calculated to appeal to peasants:

> Marxism-Leninism has no decorative value, nor has it mystical value. It is only extremely useful. It seems that, right up to the present, quite a few have regarded Marxism-Leninism as a ready-made panacea: once you have it, you can cure all your ills with little effort. This is . . . childish. . . . Those who regard Marxism-Leninism as religious dogma show this type of blind ignorance. We must tell them openly, "Your dogma is of no use," or to use an impolite phrase, "Your dogma is less useful than shit." We see that dog shit can fertilize the fields, and man's can feed the dog. And dogmas? They can't fertilize the fields, nor can they feed a dog. Of what use are they?[5]

In the late 1920s, Mao helped lead several uprisings in the countryside and created the Red Army. By the early 1930s, he was a key figure in the new People's Republic of China.

Mao Zedong's Amendments. Although many of Mao's writings are concerned with practice—particularly with ways to mobilize the peasantry and the appropriate military strategy and tactics to use in different situations—he did amend Marxian theory in several significant ways. The first, as we have noted already, was to downplay the importance of the urban proletariat and to mould the peasantry into a revolutionary force. Revolution was to begin in the countryside. As the rural revolutionary forces gained strength, they could then encircle and force the cities into submission. A second significant amendment was to downplay the importance of objective conditions, such as the size of the industrial working class, and to stress instead the central role of subjective factors. Especially in Mao's later life, his revision of Marxian theory placed consciousness or political will above material or objective conditions. A third significant amendment was Mao's recasting of the concepts of **class** and class struggle. In Mao's hands the concept of class, which was of course central to classical Marxism, was largely replaced by the concept of nation. Specifically, Mao redescribed international relations in class terms. China, he claimed, was a poor and oppressed "proletarian" nation that needed to throw off the yoke of the wealthy "bourgeois" oppressor nations. Far from being a purely internal struggle, the Chinese Revolution pitted proletarian nationalist forces against the representatives of international capitalism.

Reds and Experts. By the mid-1960s, Mao's cult of personality was building toward a disruptive and in many ways disastrous conclusion—the so-called Cultural Revolution. To understand the theoretical roots of the Cultural Revolution, we must take note of

---

[5]Mao Zedong, "The Chen-Feng Movement," *A Documentary History of Chinese Communism,* ed. Conrad Brandt, Benjamin Schwartz, and John King Fairbank (New York: Atheneum, 1966) 384–385. We have modified the sanitized translation to reflect Mao's earthy prose.

Mao's distinction between being *red* and being *expert*. To be **red** was to be ideologically pure and correct; to be **expert** was to emphasize increased agricultural and industrial production by techniques that might impede or even negate the goals of the revolution. Mao, who favoured reds over experts, believed that by the mid-1960s the pendulum had swung too far in the direction of experts. Ideological purity was in danger. So he called for a Cultural Revolution that would oust the experts and restore the reds to their rightful role. Workers were encouraged to humiliate managers and engineers, and students to humble their professors. Many experts were killed or imprisoned or removed from their posts and sent to work in the fields. What had been up was now down, and vice versa. In this topsy-turvy situation, industrial and agricultural production fell drastically, and widespread suffering resulted. So disruptive was the Cultural Revolution that Mao finally agreed to call the army in to restore order in factories and universities and throughout society.

The Cultural Revolution left many of China's institutions and its economy in a shambles. It also tarnished Mao's reputation among the Chinese. The radicals, including Mao's wife, were discredited, and pragmatists such as Deng Xiaoping (1904–1997) gained the upper hand after Mao's death in 1976. Since then China has concentrated its energies on building its economic infrastructure. Under Deng's leadership, China began to reintroduce some features of a free-market economy, including extensive commerce with capitalist countries. He also took some steps in the direction of freedom of speech, especially the freedom to criticize the Chinese Communist Party leadership, but these reforms were halted when the tanks and troops of the People's Liberation Army crushed the peaceful demonstration of Chinese students and their supporters in Beijing's Tiananmen Square in June 1989. In 1993, on what would have been Mao's hundredth birthday, Chinese authorities paid particular homage to Mao's thought and advocated its close and careful study by young people—a clear signal that the government would tolerate dissent or liberal-democratic ideas no more than Mao did during his lifetime.

Yet even as the Chinese government cracked down politically, it continued to relax its grip economically. Currently, it openly courts foreign investors and encourages Chinese entrepreneurs to build their own businesses. However, the government emphasizes that economic liberalization is not to be linked to liberalization in political matters. During his state visit in 1997 to the United States, in fact, Chinese President Jiang Zemin defended his government's bloody suppression of the Tiananmen Square protestors as the "correct conclusion" to the affair.[6] Whether the Chinese Communist Party's attempt to decouple economic and political liberty can or will succeed in the long term is unclear.

What will become of communism in China? With Deng's death in 1997, the last of the older revolutionary generation passed from the scene, and younger party members are appearing in important posts. Some of these new leaders almost certainly hold beliefs and ideas with which their elders disagree. Exactly what those ideas may be and how they may change the character of Chinese communism remain to be seen. In what sense, if at all, current Chinese leader Hu Jintao is communist is not clear. But modern China, on the verge of becoming one of the great economic powers of the world, is not a place that Mao would recognize—or like. It still rejects the idea of individual and group rights, though, and foreign governments such as Canada criticized it for its civil rights abuses domestically and in Tibet during the 2008 Olympics.

If Mao Zedong ideology is passé in China, it is still attractive to guerrilla movements in developing countries. In Peru, the *Sendero Luminoso,* or "Shining Path," movement is

---

[6]Terence Hunt, "Clinton, China Leader Spar Over Human Rights," *Arizona Republic* 30 Oct. 1997: A1.

inspired by the strategy and tactics of Mao Zedong. In Nepal, a small but powerful Maoist guerrilla movement threatens to destabilize the country's undemocratic government. There are many other such movements around the world. Perhaps the most important remaining communist government is in Cuba. It remains to be seen whether it can survive the death of Fidel Castro.

REVISIONIST MARXISM

The Social Democrats

Lenin in Russia and Mao in China took one strain of Marx's thought and creatively adapted it to the revolutionary circumstances of Russia and China. One common thread ran through their view of socialism and communism: they saw it as a goal to be pursued. They knew where they were headed and they knew that when they got there, workers would have a condition of economic equality.

Other thinkers drew their inspiration more from the more dialectical and progressive aspects of Marx's thought. Their chief distinction from the revolutionaries was their belief that it mattered a great deal how you achieved a society of free and equal men and women. For them, socialism was a way of life, a manner in which people learned to relate to one another. Socialism was as much about education as it was about elections. Mao might have said that political power grows out of the barrel of a gun. For the social democrats, it grew out of seemingly endless discussions at workers' clubs and hours spent distributing pamphlets in public squares.

The leading theorist among this group was Eduard Bernstein (1850–1932). A prominent member of the German Social Democratic Party (SDP), Bernstein believed that some aspects of Marx's theory, especially the polarization of the classes and the concentration of capital in an increasingly smaller number of people, had not happened. Therefore, he said, Marx's theories needed revision. For this reason, Bernstein's school of thought was called the **revisionist**.

An active and outspoken socialist, Bernstein fled Germany to avoid imprisonment under Bismarck's antisocialist laws in effect from 1878 to 1890. Bernstein's temporary exile in Switzerland and England was to last thirteen years. He had previously met Marx and Engels, whom he found to be a good deal less dogmatic than many Marxists were. While in England, Bernstein also came under the influence of **Fabian socialism**, which favoured a strategy of gradual reform as the best way of creating a socialist society in the United Kingdom. Like the Fabians, Bernstein came to believe that an evolutionary path to socialism was morally and politically preferable to a violent revolutionary one—as the title of his *Evolutionary Socialism* (1899) implies.

Bernstein regarded himself as a Marxist, in spirit if not always in letter. To reject those aspects of Marx's theory that were false and to revise those that were outmoded was, he thought, in the best critical scientific spirit of Marx himself, as the mark of a genuinely scientific theory is that its truth is open to question and criticism. Just as Marx had criticized his predecessors, so Bernstein did not flinch from criticizing Marx. His criticisms fall into three categories: moral, political, and economic.

Moral Criticism. Bernstein believed that Marx and later Marxists had been too little concerned with ethics or morality. This omission had two implications. First, Marx had maintained that ethical values and beliefs belong to the **ideological superstructure** of society and therefore depend upon the economic **base**. Thus to Marx, ethics and values depend upon non-ethical factors; they can be effects, but never causes, of social actions and institutions. Bernstein rejected this perspective and followed German philosopher Immanuel Kant (1724–1804), who held that the human will is free of outside influences or causes. In short, people are free to choose (or *will*) as they please; as a result, they have a duty to make morally responsible choices. For Bernstein, as for Kant, morally responsible choices start from the conviction that human beings belong to the *kingdom of ends*. That is, individuals are ends in themselves, and it is wrong to treat anyone as if he or she were merely an instrument or means for the fulfillment of some other person's desires or purposes. Thus, capitalists are immoral in using workers as human machines, and communists are immoral in proposing to use them as cannon fodder in the coming revolution.

A second and even more worrying implication for Bernstein was that Marxian socialists focused on the ultimate goal or end—the coming of a communist society—without worrying about the morality or immorality of the means used to arrive at that end. "To me," Bernstein wrote, "that which is generally called the ultimate aim of socialism is nothing, but the movement is everything."[7] By this Bernstein meant that socialists should think about the morality of the means by which they propose to bring about a socialist society. A society born in blood is unlikely to be as peaceful and democratic as one that evolves by nonviolent means. Since ends and means are inextricably bound together, a just society cannot be created by unjust means. Nor can a democratic society come about by undemocratic means. Socialism without democracy is not worth having—indeed, without democracy, socialism cannot exist.[8] Moreover, Bernstein believed that Marxists who focus on distant aims rather than on shorter-term goals are being naively and dangerously utopian. To the extent that Marxists—including Marx himself—fix their gaze exclusively on the final victory of socialism, there "remains a real residue of Utopianism in the Marxist system."[9] His own brand of *practical political socialism*, by contrast, "places near aims in front of distant ones."[10] In these respects, Bernstein was echoing what Lassalle had said earlier about the relation between ends and means:

> Show us not the aim without the way.
>
> For ends and means on earth are so entangled
>
> That changing one, you change the other too;
>
> Each different path brings different ends in view.[11]

Political Criticism. Besides these ethical reservations, Bernstein expressed doubts about some of Marx's political predictions. He pointed to a number of remarkable developments since Marx's death—developments that ran counter to Marx's expectations. For one, the labour movement in Germany and elsewhere had grown larger and stronger,

[7]Eduard Bernstein, *Evolutionary Socialism* (New York: Schocken, 1961) 202. See, also Kolakowski, chapter 4; and Peter Gay, *The Dilemma of Democratic Socialism,* 2d ed. (New York: Collier, 1962); see Ball and Dagger, selection 37.

[8]Bernstein 106.

[9]Bernstein 210.

[10]Bernstein 202.

[11]Ferdinand Lassalle, *Franz von Sickingen* (1859), act III, scene 5; quoted from Arthur Koestler, *Darkness at Noon,* trans. Daphne Hardy (New York: Macmillan, 1941) 241.

partly because working-class males in most industrial countries could now vote. The socialist parties that maintained close ties with trade unions and other working-class organizations had also grown larger and stronger. Bismarck's antisocialist laws of 1878 had been repealed in 1890, making it possible for socialist parties to organize, to recruit members openly, and to send representatives to the *Reichstag* (the German Parliament). They could then propose legislation favouring working-class interests, including the graduated income tax and a shorter workweek. For the first time it appeared that instead of suppressing the workers, the state could—as Lassalle had insisted—be their ally and guardian. In Bernstein's view, these were hopeful developments pointing toward the possibility of a peaceful transition to socialism.

Economic Criticism. No less important, Bernstein claimed, were certain newly emergent economic facts and trends that tended to undermine Marx's theory. Indeed, he charged that "certain statements in *Capital* . . . are falsified by facts."[12] For example, Marx had predicted that wealth would be concentrated in fewer and fewer hands until the few were very rich and the many were very poor. Bernstein noted that this had not yet happened in the advanced capitalist countries. Far from growing poorer and more miserable, the workers had, on the whole, become better off. Citing statistics, Bernstein showed that the real income of workers had risen in the latter part of the nineteenth century. Consequently, more workers were able to afford decent housing, better food and clothing, and other life amenities. These developments were not due to the generosity of the **bourgeoisie** but to the success of trade unions in raising wages and improving working conditions.

To critics who complained that comfortable workers suffer from false consciousness and are apt to lose sight of socialist goals and aspirations, Bernstein replied,

> One has not overcome Utopianism if one assumes that there is in the present, or ascribes to the present, what is to be in the future. We [socialists] have to take working men as they are. And they are neither so universally pauperized as [Marx and Engels had predicted] in the *Communist Manifesto,* nor so free from prejudices and weaknesses as their courtiers wish to make us believe. They have the virtues and failings of the economic and social conditions under which they live.[13]

For his part, Bernstein had no doubt that these conditions were gradually improving and would continue to improve so long as workers continued to organize themselves into trade unions and political parties that would promote their interests.

When Bernstein brought these ideas back to Germany in the late 1890s, they proved to be both influential and controversial. The German SDP did, in the end, come to favour a peaceful parliamentary path to socialism, but not without a good deal of fighting and feuding within party ranks. Former friends and allies, including Karl Kautsky (1854–1938), broke with Bernstein over the issue. Some years later, Kautsky, who initially maintained that revolution remained a viable possibility for socialists, finally came to share Bernstein's view.[14] Other breakaway socialist factions, such as the Spartacus League led by Rosa Luxemburg and Karl Liebknecht, remained revolutionists who were adamantly opposed to Bernstein's revised version of Marxism. Meanwhile, Russian Marxists

---

[12]Bernstein 211.
[13]Bernstein 219.
[14]See Gary P. Steenson, *Karl Kautsky, 1854–1938: Marxism in the Classical Years* (Pittsburgh: U of Pittsburgh P, 1978), esp. 116–31, 186.

branded Bernstein a traitor to Marxism.[15] While revisionist Marxism carried the day in Germany and other advanced capitalist countries, a very different variant had taken shape to the east.

NON-MARXIST SOCIALISM

Marx and his followers have been the most influential of all socialists. For much of the twentieth century, in fact, roughly one-third of the world's population lived in countries governed by regimes that claimed to be Marxist. Yet Marx and the Marxists have by no means been the only founts of socialist or communist theory and practice. As we noted at the beginning of this chapter, there have been and continue to be many non-Marxian voices in the socialist chorus. Indeed, there are so many varieties of non-Marxian socialism that we can scarcely list them, much less describe them in any detail. Nevertheless, we can conclude our history of socialism with brief discussions of several of the more important and influential varieties of non-Marxist socialism.

Fabian Socialism

The Fabian Society was founded in London in 1884 to pursue socialism by peaceful parliamentary means. Fabian socialists sought to nudge England in an ever more markedly socialist direction.[16] Its leading members—including George Bernard Shaw, H. G. Wells, Graham Wallis, and Sidney and Beatrice Webb—were mostly middle-class writers and social reformers. They put their considerable talents to political use in the socialist cause, mainly by writing popular essays, plays, and books. Shaw's play *Pygmalion* (which, relieved of its socialist message, later became the Broadway musical and then the movie *My Fair Lady*) pokes fun at the English class system, and his *The Intelligent Woman's Guide to Socialism and Capitalism* (1928) explains socialist economic and political principles in a clear and witty way. The society's members also founded what is now one of the most famous educational social policy institutions in the world: the London School of Economics.

The British Labour Party, founded in 1900, generally accepted the Fabian ideal of a peaceful parliamentary path to a social democratic society. The party incorporated a number of organizations, such as the Social Democratic Federation, the Independent Labour Party, and many important trade unions; it elected Keir Hardy as one of its first two MPs. The Labour Party first won control of the government in the election of 1924, when Ramsay MacDonald became the United Kingdom's first social democratic prime minister, though his government enacted few socialist measures. Since then, the Labour Party has been in and out of office many times and has succeeded in implementing such policies as the *nationalization* (that is, government ownership and operation) of certain services and industries, such as coal and steel, railways, airlines, telecommunications, and others. The Labour Party also instituted a comprehensive social welfare system that includes a national health program providing free medical and dental care. In the 1980s

---

[15]See, for example, Vladimir Ilich Lenin, "Marxism and Revisionism," *Selected Works,* ed. V.I. Lenin 25–32; see Ball and Dagger, selection 38.

[16]See Norman MacKenzie and Jean MacKenzie, *The First Fabians* (London: Weidenfeld, 1977); A. M. McBriar, *Fabian Socialism and English Politics, 1884–1914* (Cambridge: Cambridge UP, 1966); Margaret Cole, *The Story of Fabian Socialism* (Stanford, CA: Stanford UP, 1961). See also Ball and Dagger, selection 43, for excerpts from George Bernard Shaw's preface to *Fabian Essays.*

the British Conservative Party under the leadership of Prime Minister Margaret Thatcher curtailed many social services and *privatized* (that is, sold to private investors) a number of industries that had been nationalized by the Labour Party. Unable to agree about the best way to oppose the Conservatives, the opposition Labour Party was for a time torn by internal disagreements and differences. That situation began to change in the 1990s under the moderate leadership of Tony Blair. Although criticized by more traditional socialists in his party, Blair's "Third Way," a blend of Christian socialism and **communitarianism**, led to a resounding victory that returned the Labour Party to power in 1997 (and again in 2001 and 2005) and made him prime minister.

American Socialism

Why has socialism never taken hold in the United States? The United States is a fundamentally liberal society and has been since its founding. But as we saw in Chapter 3, it was a liberal fragment. It did not inherit the full range of the European ideological foundation, but was limited to the liberal concern with individualism and freedom. Thus, in America, socialism was marginalized and vilified. An early American socialist was Edward Bellamy (1850–1898), the author of a best-selling utopian novel, *Looking Backward* (1888). The novel's hero, Julian West, falls into a deep coma-like sleep and awakens in the year 2000 to find an America vastly different from the one he knew at the end of the nineteenth century. The United States has become a cooperative socialist society. When he tells his newfound friends about life in the old competitive capitalist society, they can hardly believe their ears. Why, they want to know, would anyone willingly live in a dog-eat-dog society? The United States in the year 2000 has no poverty and no unemployment. All able-bodied people work willingly, and all are compensated equally for their labour. Those who work at unpleasant jobs, such as garbage collecting, work fewer hours per week than those with easier or more pleasant jobs. There are no wages, for there is no money. Instead, everyone has a debit card (remarkably prophetic, that!) with which one "buys" from state-owned stores what is required to satisfy one's basic needs. Through these and other ingenious arrangements, people live in equality, harmony, and freedom. Bellamy's novel was well read, but his ideas were not followed.

There are also institutional explanations for the absence of American socialism. One is that the United States is essentially a two-party political system in which third parties have little chance of significant electoral success. Although in 1920, Socialist Party presidential candidate Eugene V. Debs received nearly a million votes—more than 3 percent of the votes cast, in 1936, Socialist Party presidential candidate Norman Thomas received only 0.4 percent. A second explanation is that socialism is a working-class movement and ideology, and surveys show that most Americans—whether blue- or white-collar—think of themselves as belonging to the middle class. A third and closely related explanation is that the fluidity of class distinctions and a corresponding possibility of moving up socially and economically renders socialism unappealing to people who think of themselves as upwardly mobile. A fourth explanation is that the long and still-strong tradition of liberal individualism in the United States makes collectivist ideologies unappealing. The idea of "rugged individualists" who "pull themselves up by their bootstraps" retains a powerful appeal among many Americans.

However, the intolerance of American political society cannot be overlooked as an explanation. For example, in the late 1940s and early 1950s the House Un-American

Activities Committee launched a witch-hunt against Hollywood and other areas of American society in an attempt to drive out what they considered communist activities. At the same time, Senator Joseph McCarthy launched attacks on the army and the state department, especially those whom he blamed for Mao Zedong's victory in China. Programs like *I was a communist for the FBI* were popular on the new medium of television. The Cold War created an atmosphere in which socialism was confused with communism, and anticommunism was equated with patriotism.

The increasing American involvement in Vietnam in the 1960s, however, provoked an increasingly intense left-wing reaction. Groups like Students for a Democratic Society (SDS) advocated peaceful civil disobedience to the war, a more communitarian society ("the greening of America"), and greater social cohesion through the use of drugs such as cannabis and LSD. Other groups like the Weathermen sought more extreme social and political changes. They described themselves as a "revolutionary organization of communist men and women,"[17] and in 1970 they issued what they called a declaration of war against the United States.

A few groups sought to destroy capitalism through terrorism. In 1974 one such group, which called itself the Symbionese Liberation Army, kidnapped heiress Patty Hearst and engaged in a number of bank robberies to finance its terrorist activities. In the words of one of the group's press releases:

> The explosion at the Emeryville Station of Fascist Pig Representation is a warning to the rabid dogs who murder our children in cold blood. Remember, pigs: every time you strap on your gun, the next bullet may be speeding towards your head, the next bomb may be under the seat of your car. The people and the people's armed forces will no longer quietly submit to the occupation of our communities . . .[18]

By the end of the 1970s, effective government action had suppressed these radical groups, who lost public support after the United States withdrew from Vietnam. However, left-wing voices were not silenced. Nobel Prize winner Noam Chomsky challenged the objectivity of the media with *Manufacturing Consent*, a film that had a major impact on college and university students, as did Michael Moore's film *Roger and Me*, a study of the decay of American capitalism, and, most recently, *The Corporation*, a scathing critique of the pathological pursuit of power by corporations.[19] The collapse of the dot.com bubble, the accounting scandals of the 1990s, and the corporate ethics scandals in the early twenty-first century brought forth a great many critiques of American capitalism and corporate governance. Kevin Phillips, a best-selling American political commentator, argues that the imbalance between the rich and the poor has grown so great in the United States over the course of the twentieth century that it threatens the survival of democracy itself.[20] This is a point that was central to consumer advocate Ralph Nader's presidential campaign in 2004:

> The U.S. needs to crack down on corporate crime, fraud and abuse that have just in the last four years looted and drained trillions of dollars from workers, investors, pension holders and

---

[17]See "Weathermen," *The Free Dictionary* 6 May 2004. http://encyclopedia.thefreedictionary.com/Weathermen.

[18]See www.startribune.com/local/16894551.html.

[19]*Manufacturing Consent,* a film based on Noam Chomsky's and Edward Herman's book *Manufacturing Consent: The Political Economy of the Mass Media* (New York: Pantheon, 1988). Other films that had major impact were Michael Moore's *Roger and Me,* Warner Bros., Dog Eat Dog Films, 1989, and Mark Achbar, Jennifer Abbott, and Joel Bakan's *The Corporation,* Big Picture Media, 2004.

[20]Kevin Phillips, *Wealth and Democracy: A Political History of the American Rich* (New York: Broadway, 2002).

consumers. Among the reforms needed are resources to prosecute and convict the corporate executive crooks and to democratize corporate governance so shareholders have real power; pay back ill-gotten gains; rein in executive pay . . .[21]

It is true that socialism has never been a mainstream electoral force in American politics, but there have been articulate men and women who have effectively pointed to deep problems in American capitalism and American society from a socialist perspective. They have, as during the Vietnam era, had a profound effect on American policy.

Canadian Socialism

In Canada, socialism has been more mainstream and more enduring than in the United States. In the late nineteenth and early twentieth centuries, much of Canadian socialism consisted of small Marxist parties concentrated in Montreal and Winnipeg and, to a lesser extent, Toronto. The Marxists in Montreal and Winnipeg were mostly immigrants from central Europe whose Marxism had originated in opposition to Russian domination of their homeland. There were also Marxist elements in the mining areas of British Columbia and Northern Ontario. In these areas there was a direct clash of interests between mine owners and miners. A certain amount of gold or nickel was mined and the question was: Who got what percentage of the profit? The situation seemed very much like the class conflict between bourgeoisie and proletariat that Marx had theorized, and Marxist union organizers had an easy time signing up members and selling Marxist literature.

In spite of the success that Marxism had elsewhere in the world, it had little appeal in twentieth-century Canada. The first reason for this lack of success was the effect of the Social Gospel movement. Starting in the 1880s, members of several religious denominations, mostly evangelicals, began to think about Darwinian science, the new biblical criticism, and liberal philosophy. As their faith weakened, members concluded that the real role of the church lay not in salvation in heaven but in making conditions better for people here and now. So they set out to undertake such practical work as advocating temperance and creating the Fred Victor Mission in Toronto, a hostel for homeless men. Their concerns were pragmatic and peaceful, not theoretical and revolutionary. They had no hesitation in working in partnership with government at any level. A number of employers followed the principles of the Social Gospel movement, including Timothy Eaton, a devoutly religious man who introduced fair labour practices and closed his stores two hours earlier than his competitors to give his staff more time for rest and relaxation.[22]

The second reason Marxism wasn't politically successful in Canada was the influence of the American trade union movement. As we saw in the United Kingdom, the trade unions joined with social democrats to create the British Labour Party, which took power within a quarter century after it was founded. In the United States, by contrast, Samuel Gompers (1850–1924), the president of the American Federation of Labor (AF of L), believed that the primary responsibility of trade unions was to pursue better wages and other benefits for their workers. He did not believe that they should form their own political party. They should lobby or vote for whichever candidate was most sympathetic to the cause of labour. Gompers led the AF of L into Canada, displacing the Knights of

---

[21]See Nader/Camejo 2004 8 May 2004 www.votenader.org/issues/market/corporate-crime.
[22]J. M. S. Careless, *Timothy Eaton,* www.biographi.ca/009004-119.01-e.php?BioId=40819.

Labor. The Knights of Labor, also American-based, had come to Canada around 1875. Its members believed that all workers, male and female, regardless of industry, trade, or craft, should belong to the same union and politically seek to create a labour party. The success of Gompers's craft-based, antipartisan model for the trade union movement meant that Canadian trade unions followed the American pattern and avoided direct involvement in political activity. Wilfrid Laurier created a ministry of labour in 1900 and thus gave the labour movement leverage in government. Therefore, there was less need for labour to create a party of its own that would put them at odds with the party in power.

The First World War radicalized many workers. Labour leaders began to demand the conscription of the wealthy, and not just men. When the Russian Revolution took place in 1917, some socialist leaders hoped they could imitate it in Canada. The end of the War in 1918 caused social dislocation as soldiers were discharged from the army. Social discontent reached its peak in Winnipeg in 1919, a city that was one of the centres of Canadian Marxism and other extreme movements of the left. The Winnipeg General Strike broke out and delegates from western Canadian trade unions met, proclaimed their support for the Bolshevik revolution, and formed what they called the One Big Union (OBU). Their aim was to trigger a revolutionary wave that would sweep the country and usher in a socialist government. In the aftermath of Lenin's revolution, the idea was not as absurd as it might now seem. The government sent troops to put down the strike, and they did, though not without some bloodshed.

The Winnipeg General Strike was the last time socialists in Canada attempted to achieve their aims through revolutionary violence. The path of Canadian socialism was altered by a man who had been a voice of moderation in Winnipeg: J. S. Woodsworth (1874–1942). Woodsworth was an ordained minister and came from the social gospel tradition, but he had increasingly come to see that piecemeal social reform would not be enough. Something more comprehensive was necessary. Within two years after the strike, he had founded the Independent Labour Party and was in the House of Commons as a Member of Parliament, calling for the abolition of capitalism and its replacement by a *co-operative commonwealth*. By 1926, with the support of a handful of other social democratic members of Parliament, he allied with Liberal Prime Minister William Lyon Mackenzie King to enact Canada's first old-age pension legislation.

The Founding of the Co-operative Commonwealth Federation. The Depression of 1929–1939 caused great hardship in the industrial areas of central Canada, but the farming areas of the West were particularly devastated. In 1932, Woodsworth gathered together social democrats, farmers' groups, and socialist intellectuals to form a new political party, the Cooperative Commonwealth Federation (CCF). He was clear that the new party should be distinctively Canadian:

> Undoubtedly we should profit by the experience of other nations and other times, but personally I believe that we in Canada must work out our own salvation in our own way. Socialism has so many variations that we hesitate to use the class name. Utopian Socialism and Christian Socialism, Marxian Socialism and Fabianism, the Latin type, the German type, the Russian type—why not a Canadian type?[23]

---

[23]J. S. Woodsworth, quoted in Grace MacInnis, *J. S. Woodsworth: A Man to Remember* (Toronto: Macmillan, 1953) 274.

J. S. Woodsworth (1874–1942)

At its core, the CCF was fundamentally committed to following a peaceful, parliamentary path to power. The changes it sought were radical, but it did not seek them by revolutionary means. The most controversial clause in its manifesto was the assertion that no CCF government would rest content until capitalism had been eradicated and a system of socialized planning put in its place. In spite of the Depression, the CCF won only seven seats in the 1935 election.

Tommy Douglas (1904–1986) became the head of the first democratically elected social democratic government in North America in 1944, as premier of Saskatchewan. Douglas's CCF administration was inspired by religious, moral, and ethical principles. A great communicator and clergyman, Douglas spoke in the style of the Baptist minister. He introduced many social programs to Saskatchewan, always balancing his provincial budget. His most notable achievement was the introduction of free hospital care. His policies eventually led to the introduction of national health care under Lester Pearson's Liberal government in the 1960s.

In spite of the CCF's success in Saskatchewan, it never enjoyed electoral success at the federal level. By the mid-1950s, Canadian **social democracy** had lost its intellectual and moral direction, and in 1958 the CCF was virtually annihilated by Progressive Conservative John Diefenbaker's landslide victory. CCF members decided to attempt what had always eluded them in the past—an alliance with organized labour. They hoped that the Canadian Labour Congress, formed in 1956, was more favourably disposed toward active political involvement. In 1961 the remnants of the CCF formally joined

Tommy Douglas (1904–1986)

with organized labour and what they called "other progressive individuals" to create the New Democratic Party (NDP). Tommy Douglas became the NDP's first leader, and his moral, reforming zeal helped push Liberal Prime Minister Lester Pearson's minority governments to enact the Canada Pension Plan and a universal health care system.

Douglas's successor, David Lewis, represented a different strain of Canadian socialism. An immigrant from eastern Europe who had studied in the United Kingdom, he saw social democracy more as a conflict between big business and ordinary Canadians, and waged the 1972 election against what he called the "corporate welfare bums." One of the candidates to succeed him was Rosemary Brown. She offered a radically different vision of democratic socialism. Like Reverend Jesse Jackson in the United States, who describes his movement as a "Rainbow Coalition" or a "Big Tent," Brown sought to move away from the politics of class. Instead, she wanted to bring together the oppressed groups of societies—women, gays and lesbians, blacks, Aboriginal peoples, the poor. United, she believed they constituted such a majority that they could bring the party to victory and social justice to the country. For the next thirty years, though, the party was led by electoralists—social democrats who thought that the primary role was to gain power, since without power there was little chance of seeing significant change in capitalist society.

The NDP's electoralist strategy proved successful in several provincial elections. The NDP has been elected to government in Manitoba, Saskatchewan, British Columbia, and Yukon, and it generally followed moderate programs in office. In 1990 the party came to power in Canada's largest province, Ontario, under Bob Rae. Although Rae pursued a radical social agenda when he first assumed power, after 1991 the province was facing a very serious economic recession. The NDP government introduced what it called the *Social Contract*, freezing public service wages and forcing many civil servants, plus doctors, nurses, teachers, and others, to take unpaid days of leave each year. These policies were bitterly opposed by OPSEU, the public service union, and by Buzz Hargrove, the powerful leader of the Canadian Autoworkers Union. Rae's government's policies led many in the trade union movement to question the desirability of continued union affiliation with the party and seriously hurt the party's support nationally.

Although the national NDP had elected forty-three MPs in the 1988 election, its highest total ever, its support began to weaken as a consequence of the Rae government's unpopularity. Then it made what turned out to be a serious strategic mistake. In 1993 the Mulroney government held a referendum on the Charlottetown Accord, a series of measures intended, as people said, to get Quebec back into the constitution. The NDP had bargained very hard for the inclusion of a social charter that protected and promoted health care, the environment, education, welfare, and collective bargaining. In order to ensure passage of the Accord, Audrey McLaughlin, the party's new leader, agreed to campaign with the leaders of the Conservative and Liberal parties on the Yes side. Preston Manning of the Reform party was the only leader to campaign against. Instantly McLaughlin reinforced the image that Rae had presented: The NDP had become part of the establishment and was no longer a voice for change. In the 1993 election, it fell to nine seats and lost official party status.

McLaughlin's successor, Alexa McDonough, was a moderate in the Third Way tradition of Bill Clinton and Tony Blair. Although she modestly improved the NDP's seat totals, the party seemed to stagnate politically and ideologically. When the party met to elect her successor in 2002, it faced a difficult choice. The two leading candidates came from two different traditions in the party and appealed to two different constituencies. Bill Blaikie, a highly experienced and respected parliamentarian, represented the Christian and Western roots of the party. Jack Layton, a lively Toronto municipal councillor who had never run successfully for federal office, represented a province that had regularly provided the party with a majority of its votes, but usually with few of its seats. Layton won and, in 2006, led the party to twenty-nine seats.

Ideologically, Layton had to concern himself with two problems. The first was that the Green Party posed a serious threat to his electoral support, at times coming even with the NDP in public opinion polls. In response the NDP moved to emphasize a moderate, environmentally conscious agenda. Unlike the Greens, though, the NDP thinks of itself as a possible alternative government, and Layton shifted the party more toward welfare liberalism in the hope of displacing the Liberal Party as the official opposition. Some people on the left consider this an abandonment of social democratic principles and describe it as **electoralism.**

Since the Ontario NDP was in office, there has been a vigorous debate between New Democrats, academics, and trade unionists about the future of social democracy in Canada. Some trade unionists believe it is in the best interests of their members to retreat from active involvement in partisan politics. At the other extreme, trade unionists such as Buzz Hargrove of the Canadian Auto Workers' Union think that unions should be in the vanguard of social change and that they should take their protests to the street to achieve their aims. As well, a very small number of socialists still believe that the NDP should pursue a social and economic egalitarian condition for all Canadians, regardless of the electoral consequences. A majority of NDP members of Parliament continue to be descendents of the social gospel tradition. They believe that their role is to bear witness to what is morally wrong and to continuously be the conscience of Canadians. There are some on the Canadian left who are no longer convinced that parliamentary activity is the appropriate means to achieve significant social change. Passing laws, they say, may be important, but being permanently in the opposition is futile. What is important is to form alliances with groups outside Parliament and perhaps outside the country to serve peace, the environment, or antiglobalization movements. Election merely gives a platform and publicity.

Canadian social democracy has also frequently been associated with nationalism. George Grant's *Lament for a Nation* (1965), a seminal **Red Tory** and nationalist work, had a profound effect on the socialist left. The Watkins Report (1967) on foreign ownership of Canadian industry reflected Grant's concerns. The Waffle movement, formed within the NDP in 1969 to agitate for an independent socialist Canada, was inspired by the same ideals. In 1973 the NDP pushed Pierre Elliott Trudeau's minority Liberal government to create the Foreign Investment Review Agency (FIRA) to screen foreign (usually American) takeovers of Canadian businesses. In 1988 the NDP campaigned against the Canada–U.S. Free Trade Agreement (FTA), and in 1991 it campaigned against the North American Free Trade Agreement (NAFTA). As well, socialist intellectuals like Naomi Klein and Judy Rebick actively oppose the international homogenizing powers of the World Trade Organization (WTO).

The Communist Party of Canada. In 1921 at a secret meeting in a barn in Guelph, Ontario, the Communist Party of Canada (CPC) was formed. Never large in size, it was regularly harassed by the government and the police. Since it was a member of the Moscow-directed Communist International (Comintern) and depended on it for financing, the CPC was particularly servile, and it followed every twist and turn of Stalin's policies with regard to Adolf Hitler. It opposed Hitler in the 1930s, supported him in 1939 when Stalin signed a treaty with him, and then opposed him again when Hitler attacked the Soviet Union in 1941. After the Second World War, the CPC supported the Soviet invasions of Czechoslovakia and Hungary, each time splitting the party. Ideologically, the CPC followed Moscow's lead. A breakaway faction called the Communist Party of Canada (Marxist–Leninist) (now the Marxist Leninist Party of Canada) looked for countries with more ideological purity than the Soviet Union; it admired Cuba, China, Albania, and North Korea, but was continuously disappointed by them because they all seemed too moderate.

SOCIALISM TODAY

If the late nineteenth century was the golden age of Marxism, as Leszek Kolakowski has claimed, then how should we regard the end of the twentieth century, a time of dramatic and astonishingly swift change in the socialist world? From one point of view, these decades seem to signal the end of socialism as a compelling ideology; from another, the turbulence of these years may mark a revival of socialism. As old institutions and dogmas are discredited and overturned, socialists confront new opportunities and challenges— especially the challenge of deciding what forms and directions socialism should take.

At this point it seems that the Marxist-Leninist version of communism is dead. In 1989, a year that future historians may consider as significant as 1789, the Soviet Union and Poland began to allow noncommunist parties to compete for political office. Most communist regimes by this point had long since ceased to take their Marxism-Leninism seriously. For the most part, they had become simply repressive authoritarian states whose **command economies** made their citizens far poorer and less free than they needed to be, particularly when compared with their neighbours in Western Europe. The ideology was something to which most individuals merely paid lip service, and the Communist Party was an institution that people had to join if they were ambitious.

But it would be a great mistake to conclude that the death of communism automatically marked the triumph of capitalism. In the former Soviet Union and Eastern Europe, many former communists remained in positions of influence because they were the only people with the technical skills to run the economy. Early attempts by reformers in countries like Poland to move quickly to a free market economy imposed unacceptable levels of economic hardship and were abandoned. Marxism had long since ceased to have any serious intellectual hold, and serious political disputes in countries such as the Czech Republic and Russia were between social democrats and defenders of a vision of a strong welfare state very similar to that expressed by former U.S. President Bill Clinton or by UK Prime Minister Tony Blair in his party's Third Way. The remnants of the communist parties in these countries are not committed to the return of a command economy and a one-party dictatorship. Instead, they see their role as the defenders of those citizens, like old age pensioners and former soldiers, who they think have been abandoned by the new postcommunist regime. In the sense that we describe one aspect of conservatism as a nostalgia for the past, some communists, especially in the former East Germany, think affectionately of the days when their country was a proud independent state winning medal after medal in the Olympics, instead of an economic backwater with high unemployment in a united Germany.

As we noted at the beginning of our discussion of socialism in Chapter 5, socialists have long been divided over two questions: How much and what kind of property is to be in public hands? And how is society to exercise control over this property? From Count Claude-Henri de Saint-Simon to the Soviet communists, some socialists have responded by calling for centralized control of most forms of property—factories and farms, mills and mines, and other means of production. Yet from the beginning, other socialists have responded to one or both of these questions in a more modest fashion. Robert Owen and Charles Fourier, with their visions of societies divided into small, self-sufficient, self-governing communities, called for highly decentralized forms of socialism. Since the late twentieth century, a growing number of socialists advocate **market socialism**.[24] As the name implies, market socialism attempts to blend elements of a free-market economy with social ownership and control of resources. Although different socialists propose to blend these elements in different ways, the basic idea is that the major resources—large factories, mines, power plants, forests, mineral reserves, and so on—would be owned and operated directly for the public good, while private individuals would be free to own small businesses, farms, houses, cars, and so on. Mid-sized firms would be owned by those who work in them. All businesses, even the publicly owned firms, would compete in the marketplace for profits. If there were four or five steel factories in a country, for example, the workers in each factory would choose their supervisors, control their working conditions, and set the price of the finished steel, which they would then try to sell in competition with the other factories—and perhaps foreign competitors too. Any profits would then be shared among the factory's workers as they saw fit. If the factory lost money, it would be up to the workers to decide how to cope with the losses and become more competitive.

Some form of market socialism may well be the future of socialism. It promises neither the utopia of the early socialists nor the brave new world that Marx and his followers

---

[24]See, for example, Alec Nove, *The Economics of Feasible Socialism* (London: Allen, 1983); and David Miller, *Market, State, and Community* (Oxford: Clarendon, 1989).

envisioned as the ultimate result of historical development. It does promise to promote cooperation and solidarity rather than competition and individualism, even as it aims at reducing, if not completely eliminating, the class divisions that spawn exploitation and alienation. In these respects, the modest, decentralized version of socialism that seems to be emerging continues to draw on themes that have long inspired people to seize the socialist banner. In short, if communism is dying, it need not take socialism to the grave with it. On the contrary, communism's death could conceivably breathe new life into other forms of socialism.

That would certainly be agreeable to the thinkers, principally European, who have come to be identified with **critical Western Marxism**. These thinkers—especially those connected to the Frankfurt School of *critical theory*, such as Herbert Marcuse and Jürgen Habermas—have been "critical" in two main respects. First, they have followed Marx's example in criticizing capitalism, which continues, they argue, to dominate and repress people. Rather than concentrate on capitalism as a form of economic exploitation, however, the critical theorists tend to focus their criticism on capitalism as a form of *cultural* domination. Capitalism turns everything into a commodity so that even those activities in which people should be freest and most creative—art, literature, music, and play among them—are subjected to the demands of the marketplace. Films, television, pop music, professional sports, and other forms of entertainment have supplanted religion as the **opium of the masses**.

If it is true that capitalism has this narcotic effect, what should be done to free people from its grip? Here, the second respect in which the critical Western Marxists are critical theorists becomes evident: Western Marxian theorists have levelled criticism at other Marxists, particularly the revolutionary Marxists who put their faith in the Communist Party. According to the critical Western Marxists, Communist Party rule in the Soviet Union, China, and elsewhere has been worse—less productive and more repressive—than the capitalist disease it was supposed to cure. In place of the revolutionary over-throw of capitalism, critical theorists propose to use the tools of analysis to break the capitalist-induced cultural addiction that people in modern societies endure. That is, in the same way that a psychoanalyst tries to help his or her patients identify the source of their fears and anxieties so that they may overcome them, so the scholarly analysts of critical Western Marxism try to show people how the apathy, boredom, and depression that plague them are all ultimately caused by the repressive capitalist system. Once people understand this, they will then be able to emancipate themselves from the cultural addiction of capitalism. What form society would then take is not clear. Like Marx himself, these critical Marxists are more concerned with analyzing the causes of social conditions than with drafting blueprints for future societies. In the work of these Frankfurt School theorists, then, Marxian theory survives as a branch of social science.

To sum up: If *socialism* were identical with *Marxism-Leninism,* then socialism would be dead or dying. But socialism comes in several varieties, some of which are Marxist, but many of which are not. Some socialists have heartily welcomed the end of communism, claiming that real or true socialism can now be given a chance to succeed. Critics, by con-trast, say that socialism of any sort bears a stigma that it will not soon shed—and that will prevent it from being a contender in the ideological contests of the twenty-first century.

Socialism in Western Europe and Canada seems to have lost its direction again. Gordon Brown's succession to Tony Blair proved very rocky; he showed no clear vision of where he wanted to take the country. Ségolène Royal, the socialist candidate for the French presidential election, revealed much about the many divisions within the French left during her candidacy. Angela Merkel, the Social Democratic Chancellor of Germany, presides over a state that is more dominated by the bureaucracy than by social democratic principles. In 2011, Jack Layton, who passed away shortly after the election, led the NDP to its greatest electoral success—30.6 percent of the vote, 103 seats, and status as the Official Opposition. His campaign focused on the hardships endured by marginalized groups such as the poor and First Nations. Layton's social democratic perspective and fluent French brought the NDP a historic breakthrough in Quebec.

Conclusion

Socialism as an Ideology

Like liberalism and conservatism, socialism comes in so many varieties that it sometimes seems to be not one but many different ideologies. Socialists do share certain core assumptions or beliefs, however, just as liberals and conservatives do. To see what these are, we must note how socialism performs the four functions that all ideologies perform.

Explanatory Function. How do socialists try to explain social conditions? In general, they explain them in terms of economic and class relations. Rather than appeal to the choices of individuals, as liberals typically do, socialists are inclined to say that individuals are always caught up in social relations that shape and structure the choices available to them. Individuals may make choices, but they cannot choose to do just anything they wish. As Marx put it, "Men make their own history, but they do not make it just as they please."[25] Some will have more to choose from than others. In particular, capitalists will have more options than the workers, and the choices that capitalists make will sharply limit the choices available to the workers. A capitalist faced with declining profits can decide to expand or reinvest in his or her business, for instance, or move it to a different region or country, or simply sell or close down. Within the limits of his or her resources, the capitalist can do as he or she sees fit. But the workers can usually do nothing more than react to the choice the capitalist makes. Hence, when the capitalist decides to close the business, the workers have little choice but to look elsewhere for work.

For these reasons, socialists maintain that social conditions must be explained by referring to economic or class relations. So much depends upon the way people organize themselves to work and produce goods and services, beginning with the food they need to live, that much of what happens in society can be accounted for only in terms of the division of society into classes. So to explain the problem of crime, for example, socialists are not likely to point to the weakness of human nature, as conservatives do. Instead, they are inclined to say that much criminal activity is the result of the exploitation and alienation of working-class people who lack the power to improve their condition in a class-divided society.

Evaluative Function. The emphasis on social class carries over to the second function of ideologies—that of evaluating social conditions. The key factor socialism evaluates is the sharpness of class divisions in a society. If one class of people clearly has firm control of

---

[25]Karl Marx, "The Eighteenth Brumaire of Louis Bonaparte," *Selected Works,* ed. Marx and Engels 97.

the wealth so that it is able to limit sharply the choices open to the working class, then conditions are, from the socialist point of view, exploitative and unjust. If class divisions are slight, or if there are no apparent classes at all, then conditions will be much better. This can happen, socialists say, only when all members of society somehow share control of the major means of production.

Orientative Function. Socialists tell people that they should think of themselves mainly in terms of their position in the class structure. Some socialists have taken this to the extreme, saying that class differences are the only differences that matter. When Marx said that the workers have no fatherland, for instance, he seemed to say that nationality or citizenship should play no real role in one's identity. Race, religion, and nationality are not important; only class position really makes a difference to one's identity in the world. Most socialists do not go this far. As we saw, J. S. Woodsworth specifically wanted to create a unique socialism in Canada, and so have many socialists in other countries, based on the belief that socialism has to respond to national circumstances. However, all believe that our position in the class structure is an important factor in shaping people's identities. We see things as we do and we are who we are largely because of our class position.

If the preceding claim is true, then what is the point of telling people that they should see themselves as members of this or that class? According to socialists, the point is that class consciousness is a necessary step on the path to a classless society. Before a capitalist can see the error of his or her ways, the capitalist must first understand that he or she is a member of the class that exploits and oppresses the workers. Only then is there any chance that the capitalist will surrender control of wealth and resources to their rightful owner— society at large. More important, only when the workers see that they form a large and oppressed class will they be able to take action to free themselves. If they fail to develop this awareness of their social position, they will have no more chance of liberating themselves than the slave who thinks that his or her slavery is altogether natural and proper.

Programmatic Function. For most socialists, orientation is necessary to the programmatic function of their ideology. The socialist goal is simple: to bring about a society that is as nearly classless as possible. Exactly how socialists propose to do this varies from one time and place to another, of course. Some look for an almost spontaneous revolution, as we have seen, while others believe a single highly disciplined party must lead the way; some rely on persuasion and the force of argument, while others favour violent revolution and the force of arms. Social democrats are convinced that only if people are persuaded of the merits of a socialist way of life will a socialist society be worthwhile. They believe that persuasion and elections are perfectly adequate to achieve the goal of a more equal and just society. Perfect equality might never be achieved, but as long as society is moving in that direction, they are content. But in all cases, they maintain that steps must be taken to promote equality and cooperation among all members of society in order to give everyone greater control over his or her own life.

Socialism and the Democratic Ideal

In its pursuit of equality, socialism is an ideology committed to democracy in one or another sense of that contested term. As most socialists will quickly admit, leaders like Stalin have been more interested in acquiring personal power than in promoting democracy; but these leaders, they say, were not true socialists. True socialism requires government of, by, and for the people. It aims to give everyone an equal voice in the decisions that affect his or her life in direct and important ways. But this can happen, socialists say, only if no one person or class controls most of the wealth and resources—and thus most of the power—within a society. Wealth and resources must be shared evenly and owned and controlled for the benefit of the whole society if true democracy is ever to take shape. Otherwise, they insist, we shall have nothing but government of the wealthy, by the wealthy, and for the wealthy.

For Further Reading

Ball, Terence, and James Farr, eds. *After Marx.* Cambridge: Cambridge UP, 1984.

Broadbent, Ed, ed. *Democratic Equality: What Went Wrong?* Toronto: U of Toronto P, 2001.

Carr, E.H. *Michael Bakunin.* London: Macmillan, 1937.

Cole, Margaret. *The Story of Fabian Socialism.* Stanford, CA: Stanford UP, 1961.

Crick, Bernard. *Socialism.* Minneapolis: U of Minnesota P, 1987.

Garton Ash, Timothy. *The Magic Lantern: The Revolution Witnessed in Warsaw, Budapest, Berlin, and Prague.* New York: Random, 1990.

Gay, Peter. *The Dilemma of Democratic Socialism: Eduard Bernstein's Challenge to Marx,* 2d ed. New York: Collier, 1962.

Glaser T. Glaser. *Twentieth-Century Marxism: A Global Introduction.* New York: Routledge, 2007.

Graf, William D. *The German Left Since 1945: Socialism and Social Democracy in the German Federal Republic.* Cambridge: Oleander, 1976.

Gray, Alexander. *The Socialist Tradition: Moses to Lenin.* London: Longmans, 1947.

Hunt, Tristram. *Marx's General: The Revolutionary Life of Friedrich Engels.* Tantor Media: Old Saybrook, CT, 2010.

King, Preston, ed. *Socialism and the Common Good: New Fabian Essays.* London: Frank, 1996.

Knight, Amy. *How The Cold War Began: The Gouzenko Affair and the Hunt for Soviet Spies.* Toronto: McClelland and Stewart, 2005.

Kolakowski, Leszek. *Main Currents of Marxism.* 3 vols. Trans. P. S. Falla. Oxford: Clarendon, 2005.

Layton, Jack. *Speaking Out Louder: Ideas That Work For Canadians.* Toronto: McClelland and Stewart, 2011.

Layton, Jack. *Homelessness.* Toronto: Penguin, 2008

Lichtheim, George. *A Short History of Socialism.* New York: Praeger, 1970.

Lukes, Steven. *Marxism and Morality.* Oxford: Oxford UP, 1985.

Medvedev, Roy A. *Let History Judge: The Origins and Consequences of Stalinism.* Trans. Colleen Taylor. New York: Knopf, 1972.

Miller, David. *Anarchism.* London: Dent, 1984.

Mills, Allen. *Fool for Christ: The Political Thought of J. S. Woodsworth.* Toronto: U of Toronto P, 1991.

Pierson, Christopher. *Socialism after Communism: The New Market Socialism.* University Park, PA: Pennsylvania State UP, 1995.

Rebick, Judy. *Imagine Democracy.* Toronto: Stoddart, 2000.

Roemer, John. *A Future for Socialism.* Cambridge, MA: Harvard UP, 1994.

Spence, Jonathan. *Mao Zedong.* New York: Viking, 1999.

Starr, John B. *Continuing the Revolution: The Political Thought of Mao.* Princeton, NJ: Princeton UP, 1979.

Tucker, Robert C., ed. *Stalinism.* New York: Norton, 1977.

Wolfe, Bertram D. *Three Who Made a Revolution.* New York: Dell, 1964.

Woodcock, George. *Anarchism: A History of Libertarian Ideas and Movements* Toronto: U of T Press, 2004.

Useful Websites and Social Media

http://dwardmac.pitzer.edu/Anarchist_Archives Anarchy Archives

www.cpusa.org Communist Party USA

www.dcf.ca Douglas-Coldwell Foundation

www.fabians.org.uk Fabian Society

www.monthlyreview.org *Monthly Review*

www.ndp.ca Canada's New Democrats

www.pes.eu Party of European Socialists

www.plp.org Progressive Labor Party

http://sp-usa.org Socialist Party USA

www.themilitant.com *The Militant*

www.swp.org.uk Socialist Workers Party

www.parti-communiste.ca/ Communist Party of Canada

http://cpcml.ca/ Marxist-Leninist Party of Canada

From the Ball and Dagger Reader *Ideals and Ideologies,* US Eighth Edition

Part Six: Socialism and Communism After Marx

Discussion Questions

1. Is the NDP a socialist party, a social democratic party, or a welfare liberal party?
2. Ronald Reagan once described the USSR and an "evil empire." Do you agree?
3. Was Eduard Bernstein the intellectual father of the NDP?
4. Were the Occupy Wall Street protestors socialists or anarchists?

MySearchLab   MySearchLab with eText offers you access to an online interactive version of the text, additional quizzes and assessment, extensive help with your writing and research projects, and provides round-the-clock access to credible and reliable source material. Go to **www.mysearchlab.com** to access these resources.

CHAPTER 9

Nationalism and Fascism

Vive le Québec libre!

Charles de Gaulle, in Montreal, July 24, 1967

The sleep of reason brings forth monsters.

Francisco Goya

LEARNING OBJECTIVES

After completing this chapter you should be able to

1. Differentiate nationalism, Nazism, and fascism from liberal and conservative ideology.
2. Understand the historical origins of nationalism in Europe.
3. Explain Kedourie's definition of nationalism.
4. Distinguish between nationalism and patriotism as well as ethnic and civic nationalism.
5. Understand the history of nationalism in Canada and the differences between Quebec and Canadian nationalism.
6. Explain how nationalism as an ideology performs the four functions of an ideology: explanatory, evaluative, orientative, and programmatic.
7. Define totalitarianism.
8. Explain how the attitudes of the Counter-Enlightenment, ethnic nationalism, elitism,
and irrationalism influenced the development of fascism in the twentieth century.
9. Illustrate the rise of the fascist party in Italy.
10. Understand fascist conceptions of human nature and freedom.
11. Discuss the origins of Nazism in Germany and explain how it is different from Italian fascism.
12. Explain the views of Gobineau and the social Darwinists on human nature, and discuss how they contributed to Nazi racism and views of freedom.
13. Explain how fascism and Nazism found expression in Canada.
14. Illustrate how fascism and Nazism perform the four functions of an ideology: explanatory, evaluative, orientative, and programmatic.

Nationalism and fascism are distinct and different ideologies, but both have certain resemblances and it is useful to consider them together. Both are ways of thinking that focus on the group—the nation or racial or ethnic group—rather than on the individual, which distinguishes them from liberalism and conservatism. Unlike socialists, nationalists and fascists reject class as an organizing concept in society and look not for equality as the ultimate goal but for the welfare and status of the nation. Individual freedom and fulfillment is identified with the freedom and fulfillment of the nation. That said, there are significant differences between the two ideologies, and many nationalists would be surprised (and outraged) to be identified with fascism.

NATIONALISM

Nationalism, one of the most powerful forces in modern politics, grows out of the sense that the people of the world fall more or less naturally into a unique type of group called a *nation*. In this view, a person's nationality is not something he or she chooses but something acquired at birth. Indeed, *nation* and *nationality* come from the Latin word *natus,* meaning "birth." A *nation* is a group of people who in a sense share a common birth. Consequently, a person's nationality may be distinct from his or her citizenship. For example, a person born in the nation of Scotland may also be a citizen of the United Kingdom. However, from the perspective of the ardent nationalist, nationality and citizenship *should not* be separate. People who share a common birth—who belong to the same nation—should also share citizenship in the same political unit or state. This is the source of the idea of the nation-state—a sovereign, self-governing political unit that binds together and expresses the feelings and needs of members of a single nation.

Nationalist sentiment became especially powerful following the Napoleonic Wars of the early 1800s. As Napoleon's armies conquered most of Europe, they stirred the resentment—and sometimes the envy—of many of the conquered peoples. This was particularly true in Germany and Italy, neither of which was then a unified country. Germany was a scattered collection of separate political units, ranging in size and strength from the Kingdom of Prussia and the Austrian Empire to tiny duchies or baronies ruled by the local nobility. Even so, the people of these separate political units shared a common ethnicity, spoke a common language, and shared a common literature as well as many customs and traditions. The case in Italy was similar. The victories of Napoleon's armies—the victories of the French *nation*—created a backlash of sorts by inspiring many people in Germany, Italy, and elsewhere to recognize their respective nationalities and struggle for unified nation-states of their own. In the nineteenth and twentieth centuries, this struggle spread to virtually every part of the globe. For example, nationalist sentiments and antagonisms provided fertile ground for the First and Second World Wars, as well as the anticolonial wars of national liberation in Asia and Africa.

For all their emotional power and political force, the concepts of nation and nationalism are difficult to define. First, it is difficult to identify the distinguishing characteristics of a nation. What is it that marks a group of people as members of the same nationality? There is no clear answer to this question, although nationalists often appeal to such traits as shared race, ethnicity, culture, language, religion, customs, or history. These traits are themselves notoriously difficult to define, however.

In addition to global warfare and nuclear weapons, the twentieth century produced a new kind of political regime and a new kind of political thinking—totalitarianism. Totalitarianism is ideological thinking at its most complete because it represents the attempt to take complete control of a society—not just its government but all of its social, cultural, and economic institutions—in order to fulfill an ideological vision of how society ought to be organized and life ought to be lived. This is what happened in the former Soviet Union when Stalin imposed his version of Marxist socialism on that country. It is also what happened in Italy and Germany when Benito Mussolini and Adolf Hitler imposed varieties of a new and openly totalitarian ideology called fascism.

In fact, Mussolini and the Italian fascists coined the word *totalitarian.* They did this to define their revolutionary aims and to distinguish their ideology from liberalism and socialism, which they saw as defenders of democracy. Democracy requires equality of some sort, whether in the liberals' insistence on equal opportunity for individuals or the socialists' insistence on equal power for all in a classless society. Mussolini and his followers regarded these ideals with contempt, as did Hitler and the Nazis. They did appeal to the masses for support, to be sure, but in their view the masses were to exercise power not by thinking, speaking, or voting for themselves, but by blindly following their leaders to glory. As one of Mussolini's many slogans put it, *credere, obbedire, combattere*— "believe, obey, fight." Nothing more was asked; nothing more was desired of the people. By embracing totalitarianism, fascists rejected democracy.

In this respect, fascism is a reactionary ideology. It took shape in the years following the First World War as a reaction against the two leading ideologies of the time: liberalism and socialism. Unhappy with the liberal emphasis on the individual and with the socialist emphasis on contending social classes, the fascists provided a view of the world in which individuals and classes were absorbed into an all-embracing whole under the control of a single party and a supreme leader. Like the reactionaries of the early 1800s, they also rejected faith in reason because they believed it formed the foundation for liberalism and socialism. Reason is less reliable, both Mussolini and Hitler declared, than intuition and emotion.

Even if we can define the distinguishing characteristics of a nation, a significant difficulty remains. Many states—Canada, Switzerland, and the United States among them—include people of apparently different nationalities. Should each nationality have its own state? Should Switzerland be taken apart, for instance, with France, Germany, and Italy absorbing the French-speaking, German-speaking, and Italian-speaking parts, respectively? Should this happen even though the Swiss seem to be prospering under their present arrangement? Or should we say that together these groups form a distinct nation: the Swiss nation? Should Canada be split into two states, one French speaking and the other English speaking?

Despite these difficulties of definition, there is no doubt that many people not only feel the pull of national sentiment but also identify and orient themselves primarily in terms of nationality. This sentiment has been especially evident in the events following the collapse of communism in Eastern Europe. When the communist regimes that held together the Soviet Union and Yugoslavia fell, both countries split apart into states divided largely along lines of nationality. In those areas where no national group was powerful enough to establish an independent state, as in the Bosnian section of the former Yugoslavia, bitter warfare between former neighbours resulted. In areas where one group dominated, ethnic and linguistic minorities were attacked and driven out. The tug of nationalism even pulled apart Czechoslovakia, which in the 1990s peacefully divided itself into the Czech and Slovak states. Thus, despite all the difficulties of defining what a nation is, nationalism remains a real and powerful force in politics in the twenty-first century. Figure 9.1 shows the nationalist conception of freedom using the triadic definition of freedom.

Two important points must be made about nationalism: nationalism is limited by its nature, and there are different types of nationalism.

First, nationalism is concerned specifically with issues of national identity and the creation or defence of a nation-state. Because nationalism deals with a relatively narrow range of social and political issues, it does not offer an obvious approach to many political issues. For example, nationalism has little direct bearing on the design of child care policies, which have minimal relevance to issues of national identity or independence.

FIGURE 9.1	The Nationalist View of Freedom

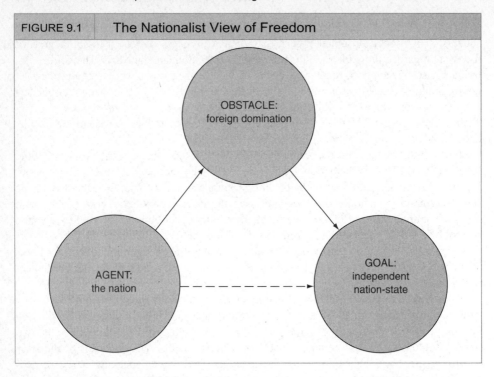

Further, while some public policy areas, such as foreign policy or language laws, are direct nationalist concerns, nationalism does not provide the same broad framework for understanding them that liberalism, conservatism, or socialism do. Therefore, nationalism tends to ally itself with other ideologies or act as a force that influences or interacts with other ideologies. Thus, it is possible to say that there are liberal, conservative, or socialist forms of nationalism or, conversely, nationalist forms of those ideologies. For example, while the central goal of the Parti Québécois has been the nationalist goal of independence for Quebec, the party has shown significant democratic socialist and welfare liberal elements in the policies it has espoused or taken when in government.

Second, there are different types of nationalism, ranging from full-blown ethnic nationalism on the one hand to a much less extreme communitarian or patriotic nationalism on the other. Probably the best definition of ethnic nationalism is that of Elie Kedourie (1926–1992), a political philosopher who lived in England and whose views on nationalism had a significant influence on many, including Pierre Elliott Trudeau. Kedourie defined *nationalism* as the ideology that "holds that humanity is naturally divided into nations, that nations are known by certain characteristics which can be ascertained, and that the only legitimate type of government is national self-government."[1] In this view, since the world is naturally divided into nations, nationalism seeks to remake the world on that basis, regardless of geography, history, economics, or any other factor.

Kedourie argued that this kind of nationalism was based on the argument of Immanuel Kant, the German philosopher, and that moral behaviour flowed from the free person acting consciously on the basis of an internalized moral law, the categorical imperative.

---

[1]Elie Kedourie, *Nationalism* (London: Hutchinson, 1966) 9.

While Kant's views had an obvious effect on the development of liberal thinking, they were turned to nationalist ends through subsequent thinkers such as German ethnologist Johann Gottfried von Herder and German philosopher Johann Gottlieb Fichte.

Nationalism in Europe

Johann Gottfried von Herder (1744–1803) and Johann Gottlieb Fichte (1762–1814) moved the emphasis of nationalism from the individual to the group, promoting collective or national self-determination and consciousness as the source of moral behaviour. Both Herder and Fichte appealed to the sense of German nationality, with Fichte placing particular stress on the distinctiveness of the German language—the only truly original European language, he said, for Latin had smothered the originality in the others.[2] In Berlin in the winter of 1807–1808, still smarting from Napoleon's defeat in 1806 of the army of Prussia, the largest of the Germanic kingdoms, Fichte delivered his *Addresses to the German Nation*. In the *Addresses,* he maintained that the individual finds much of the meaning and value of life in being connected to the nation into which he or she was born. Rather than think of ourselves merely as individuals, in other words, we must think of ourselves as members of the larger and lasting community of the nation. Hence, Fichte said,

> The noble-minded man will be active and effective, and will sacrifice himself for his people. Life merely as such, the mere continuance of changing existence, has in any case never had any value for him; he has wished for it only as the source of what is permanent. But this permanence is promised to him only by the continuous and independent existence of his nation. In order to save his nation he must be ready even to die that it may live, and that he may live in it the only life for which he has ever wished.[3]

Johann Gottfried von Herder.

Johann Gottfried von Herder (1744–1803)

---

[2]Hans Kohn, *Nationalism: Its Meaning and History* (Princeton, NJ: Van Nostrand, 1955) 36.
[3]As reprinted in William Y. Elliot and Neil McDonald, eds., *Western Political Heritage* (New York: Prentice-Hall, 1949) 797.

Each individual seeks meaning for his or her life in a larger community, and for Fichte that community was the nation. Although Fichte thought the German nation was especially worth defending, he and Herder believed that all nations have value because each gives shape and significance to the lives of its people. Against the universalism of the Enlightenment, which wanted all nations to be identical in their political systems and doctrines of rights, Herder and Fichte argued that every nation brings something distinct or unique to the world—something for which it deserves to be recognized and respected.

Yet neither Herder nor Fichte called for every nation to be embodied politically in its own distinct state. That development came later, most notably in the words and deeds of Italian nationalist Giuseppe Mazzini (1805–1872) and German nationalist "Iron Chancellor" Otto von Bismarck.

In the early 1800s, Italy was as fragmented as Germany. Since the fall of the Roman Empire around CE 500, the word *Italy* had referred to a geographical and cultural region but never to a politically united country. Divided into kingdoms, duchies, and warring city-states, and often overrun by French and Spanish armies, Italy became the centre of commerce and culture during the Renaissance, but it was far from the centre of European political power. Niccolò Machiavelli called attention to this in the sixteenth century when he concluded his best-known book *The Prince* with "An Exhortation to Liberate Italy from the Barbarians"—but to no avail. Italy remained divided until the 1800s, when Giuseppe Mazzini (1805–1872) and others made it their mission to unify the country. Other nations had found statehood—for instance, England, France, and Spain—and now, Mazzini said, it was time for Italy to join their ranks as a nation-state. Italy must be united not only geographically and culturally but also politically. A nation cannot truly be a nation unless it can take its place among the powers of the earth. So Mazzini argued that Italians must be brought together as citizens under a common government. Only then could they achieve freedom and fulfill their destiny as a people.

Mazzini did not believe nationalism should be an ideal for his native country only. Like Herder and Fichte, he supported nationalism as an ideal for all nations. Mazzini sometimes suggested that geography testified to God's intention of creating a world of distinct nations. Why else, he asked, did rivers, mountains, and seas separate groups of people from one another and foster the development of separate languages, cultures, and customs? Mazzini even envisioned a world in which each nation had its state and every nation-state lived in harmony with all the others—all following the example of a politically united Italy.

Kedourie believed that when the ideas of ethnic and national diversity were joined to the belief in the moral value of collective self-determination in the nineteenth century, an overriding commitment to national self-determination as the highest temporal value arose in members of the national group. The moral strenuousness of Kant's philosophy absorbed by this kind of nationalism had an appeal that was both strong and almost religious in nature. In addition, American political scientist Carlton Hayes documented the sacralization of the nation and its symbols, such as flags and national anthems, which provided a basis for nationalist fanaticism and inspired numerous wars and acts of terrorism and violence in the name of national self-determination.[4] In *Paris 1919: Six Months That Changed the World* (2002), Margaret MacMillan argued that U.S. President Woodrow Wilson was determined to redraw the post–First World War political arena largely

---

[4]See J. H. Hayes, *Nationalism: A Religion* (New York: Macmillan, 1960).

on the basis of this principle. Instead of peace and harmony, MacMillan argues that he caused social turmoil, which was a significant contributing factor to the outbreak of the Second World War just twenty years later. A similar tragedy occurred following the breakup of the former Yugoslavia in the 1990s. The various former components of Yugoslavia, which had previously coexisted reasonably peacefully, engaged in racially inspired **ethnic cleansing** to achieve ethnically homogeneous nation-states. The ethnic nationalist impulses that prompted this conflict and its consequences are well documented in Michael Ignatieff's *Blood and Belonging.*[5] Ignatieff's description of this type of nationalism as **ethnic nationalism** is apt, and we will use it in this text for that purpose.

Another quite different type of nationalist thinking, which Ignatieff labels **civic nationalism**, is perhaps closer to the love of country generally referred to as *patriotism*. Civic nationalism is the belief that the nation is defined not in terms of a particular ethnic, linguistic, or religious identity, but on the basis of loyalty to a particular geographic unit with a common history or a common political allegiance. Canadian Conservative leader Robert Stanfield called this "simply a feeling for the nation," which is not limited to a restricted view of what or who constitutes the nation and which does not impose any particular moral claim on the individual.[6] Canadian political philosopher George Heiman described the more tolerant and less demanding nature of patriotism in these terms:

> Nationalism, as opposed to patriotism, commands the ultimate loyalty and devotion to the nation-state. Patriotism, on the other hand, is pluralistic in its inclinations. A patriot can have ties with other associations besides those he has with the nation. He may show loyalty towards a religious group, a political party, a trade union, not to mention the traditional ties of family and kin. These loyalties are not looked upon as being incompatible with the loyalty he shows towards the nation. Where patriotism rather than nationalism prevails, the political structure of the native land, the nation-state, does not encompass or subjugate all of the individual's interests.[7]

Civic nationalism is obviously more suited to multi-ethnic and multicultural states such as Canada. The existence of states that encompass different ethnic groups concentrated in different parts of their territory, such as Canada, Switzerland, the United Kingdom, and Spain, is incompatible with the doctrine of ethnic nationalism (and the disruptive potential of ethnic nationalism is increased by the fact that so many states have ethnic minorities). As a result, ethnic nationalism has been espoused in Canada only by those who seek to disrupt or radically change the Canadian state, either by achieving independence for Quebec or assimilating French-speaking Canadians into the English-speaking majority. The quite different tone of civic nationalism is encapsulated well in the observation of Mitchell Sharp, a cabinet minister in the Lester Pearson and Pierre Elliott Trudeau governments in the 1960s and 1970s:

> I am not an economic nationalist in the accepted Canadian sense of that phrase. I confess, however, to be an ardent Canadian patriot and even to being somewhat sentimental on the subject. I want my fellow citizens to take pride in their country. I want foreigners to recognize us as a

---

[5]Michael Ignatieff, *Blood and Belonging: Journeys into the New Nationalism* (Toronto: Penguin, 1993).
[6]Robert Stanfield, Notes for the 1978 Josiah Wood Lectures, "Nationalism: A Canadian Dilemma," Mount Allison University, February 7–8, 1978. First lecture.
[7]George Heiman, "The 19th Century Legacy: Nationalism or Patriotism," *Nationalism in Canada*, ed. P. Russell (Toronto: McGraw-Hill, 1966).

distinct society, even if we cannot call ourselves *nation* in the French sense of the word because of our bilingual and bicultural nature.[8]

Nationalism in Canada

Canada demonstrates the distinction between ethnic nationalist and civic nationalist tendencies. French-Canadian nationalism, while almost entirely nonviolent, exhibits the classic features of ethnic nationalism: Many francophones in Quebec view themselves as a distinct nation defined by language, culture, and ethnicity; occupying a common territory; and having a right to national self-determination in the form of an independent state of Quebec. Like other forms of ethnic nationalism, French-Canadian nationalism rejects the idea of a state that contains more than one linguistic or cultural group and seeks to disrupt such arrangements in the pursuit of national self-determination (in the same way that nineteenth-century central European and Balkan nationalists sought to disrupt the Austro-Hungarian Empire).

The roots of nationalism in Quebec extend well back into the nineteenth century. By the time of Confederation, Quebec nationalist thinkers were identifying Quebec as a distinct nation on the basis of language and ethnicity. For example, in 1886, Bishop Louis-François Laflèche concluded,

> French Canadians in this country are a real nation, and the vast expanse of territory irrigated by the majestic St. Lawrence is their own legitimate homeland. For here we have a population of close to one million rising up as one man upon hearing their name called out, speaking the same language, confessing the same faith . . . We French Canadians have become a nation.[9]

By the turn of the twentieth century, Quebec nationalists were calling for self-determination, and in the 1920s, they began explicitly advocating separatism. These developments were encouraged by linguistic conflicts surrounding the Riel Rebellion in 1885, the controversy over French-language schools in Manitoba in 1896, and the conscription crisis in 1917. In 1924 Antonio Perrault called for "the establishing of a French state in eastern Canada."[10]

As noted above, nationalism is a limited ideology and usually acts in alliance with other ideological views. Early Quebec nationalists allied themselves principally with conservative and Roman Catholic views in Quebec and generally ignored demands for a secular, urban, and industrial society. In 1924, J.-M.-R. Villeneuve stated, "That a French and Catholic State should, during the course of the present century, be established in the St. Lawrence Valley is . . . no longer a utopian dream."[11]

In the 1960s, Quebec nationalists began to identify themselves not with conservatism, but with democratic socialism and welfare liberalism. Indeed, one prominent nationalist argument was that an independent Quebec could better put into effect democratic socialist

---

[8]Mitchell Sharp, *Which Reminds Me . . . A Memoir* (Toronto: U of Toronto P, 1993) 125.

[9]Louis-François Laflèche, *Quelques considérations sur les rapports de la société civile avec la religion à la famille* (1866). Translated and reprinted in Ramsey Cook, ed., *French-Canadian Nationalism* (Toronto: Macmillan, 1969) 96.

[10]Antonio Perrault, "Enquête sur le nationalisme," *L'action Française*, February 1924. Translated and reprinted in Cook 220.

[11]J.-M.-R. Villeneuve, "Et nos frères de la dispersion," in Bibliotheque de l'action francaise, *Notre avenir politique: Enquête de l'action française* (1923), Translated and reprinted in Cook 202–208.

or welfare liberal policies. This new ideological alliance broadened nationalism's ideo-logical appeal by combining traditional nationalist concerns for the ethnic-linguistic nation with new concerns about economic and social development and reform. The main vehicle for Quebec nationalism was the Parti Québécois, formed by a merger of other sepa-ratist groups in 1968. Under the charismatic leadership of René Lévesque (1922–1987), the party adopted policies very similar to those of New Democratic Party (NDP) provin-cial governments elsewhere in Canada, while at the same time pursuing the traditional nationalist policies of promoting French language and culture in seeking an independent Quebec. Their policies included expanded social welfare programs, greater rights for organized labour, government auto insurance, and broader planning and land use rules, as well as the Charter of the French Language, intended to make French the only official language in Quebec. The breadth of its appeal was reflected in Parti Quebecois victories in the 1976, 1981, 1994, and 1998 provincial elections.

Nationalist criticism of the Meech Lake Accord of 1988, and criticism and rejection of the Charlottetown Accord in 1992 were accompanied by the emergence of a national-ist party on the federal level: the Bloc Québécois (BQ), led by former Conservative cabinet minister Lucien Bouchard, who later became the PQ premier of Quebec. The goal of the BQ was to support and promote Quebec sovereignty at the federal level and to pre-vent federal politicians from co-opting Quebec nationalist voters at the federal level. It initially attempted to take positions only on specifically nationalist matters, but the inher-ently limited nature of nationalism soon forced the BQ to take positions on other issues, generally in a way that mirrored the PQ's amalgam of nationalism and social democracy.

The resurgence of free market, so-called neoconservative, ideas in the English-speaking world also reached Quebec in the 1990s, notwithstanding its long-standing inclination to more collectivist ideas. This resulted in a new nationalist alliance and a new political party, Action Démocratique du Québec (ADQ), which first emerged in the 1994 provincial election and was led by an ex-Liberal, Mario Dumont. In some ways a throwback to the Union Nationale Party of the 1930s to 1950s, the ADQ combined tradi-tional nationalist ideas (but fell short of advocating outright separation) with advocacy of

René Lévesque (1922–1987)

lower taxes and a smaller government presence in society. While in the 2007 provincial election the ADQ narrowly missed victory and became the official opposition, pushing the PQ into third place, its support quickly dropped and it won only seven seats in the 2008 election. This may indicate some weakening of nationalist sentiment in Quebec when taken with growing dissension within the PQ about the timing of any future referendum on separation from Canada.

The persistence of nationalism in Quebec is also reflected in the way the rest of Canada deals with Quebec. Because appeals to Canadian civic nationalism or pan-Canadian nationalism do not resonate in Quebec, federal politicians are forced to rely on pragmatic arguments that the core values and interest of Quebeckers are best protected within a wider Canadian federation. This leads to apparently endless discussions about how much autonomy for Quebec is attainable, or how little federal power is needed, to achieve this goal. What appears to Canadians outside Quebec to be unprincipled manoeuvring and bargaining is, in fact, driven by the underlying ideological imperative of nationalism.

In the nineteenth and early twentieth centuries, nationalism outside Quebec also focused on independence and autonomy for Canada as a whole, although tinged with ethnic nationalism, because Canada often viewed itself as an English-speaking and ethnically British nation. The demand for greater autonomy was expressed in two quite different ways: in the negative sense of reducing imperial ties and imperial influence, and in the positive sense of viewing Canada as a nation projecting itself on the world and playing a greater role in world affairs (albeit within the confines of the British Empire). The conservative nationalists who took this latter position were largely associated with the imperial federation movement. Its members wanted to maintain close ties within the British Empire. Some wanted to create a free trade zone; others wanted to create a common military force. Its most visionary member, George Parkin, saw the British Empire as an interconnected transportation and communication network that tied together the British nation—a people bound by sentiment, language, and culture. Nationalists saw this as a rejection of colonial status in favour of a co-imperial role for Canada on the world stage. As famed humourist Stephen Leacock said, "I am an imperialist because I will not be a colonial."[12] As well as equating Canadian withdrawal from the Empire as isolationism, which they vigorously rejected, they saw the Empire as a counterweight to the United States. As poet Wilfrid Campbell pointed out, Canada was faced with a choice of two "different imperialisms, that of Britain and that of the Imperial Commonwealth to the south."[13]

The psychological effects of the First World War (in which Canada suffered far more combat deaths proportionate to its population than the United States), the decline of British power, and the persistence of the French fact in Canada led English-speaking Canadians to move away from imperial federation, though the conservative inclination to reject isolationism in favour of a greater role in world affairs is still evident—for example, in the Harper government's more aggressive policy toward participation in the Afghan mission.

Liberals, on the other hand, tended to view the imperial connection as a restriction on liberty—as control exercised by one nation on another—and they sought greater Canadian autonomy and embraced isolationism as protection from imperial influence. They also were

---

[12]Stephen Leacock, "Greater Canada: An Appeal," in *University Magazine,* 2:2 (April 1907), quoted in Carl Berger, *The Sense of Power* (Toronto: U of Toronto P, 1969).
[13]Quoted in Berger 170.

more ideologically sympathetic to the United States, the quintessential liberal society, and at times had difficulty articulating a sense of national identity. For an ideology that placed supreme reliance on individual rationality, the less rational appeal of history and tradition, on which nationalism or patriotism were based, were of limited value. However, from the 1970s onward, some Canadian liberals began to see American influence—political, economic, or cultural—as a perpetuation of the colonial status with Britain they had fought to end; this idea contributed to a nationalist revival in English-speaking Canada. This revival was also supported by Canadian socialists. Socialists were used to assuming the legitimacy of collective action and tended to view the United States as a bastion of the capitalist business liberal ideas they opposed in Canada. They viewed American influence in Canada as a barrier to social democratic policies and an internationalist foreign policy.

All of these factors combined to support the continued existence of civic nationalism outside Quebec. For the civic nationalists (which also included some French-speaking Canadians), Canadian identity as a nation was defined by its history, geography, and, increasingly, its bilingual and multicultural nature rather than by any ethnic or linguistic uniformity. Indeed, the absence of such ethnic or linguistic uniformity has come to be seen as a major distinguishing and, to some extent, unique characteristic of the Canadian state. What in ethnic nationalist terms would be a nonidentity has therefore become an identity in the view of civic nationalists.

Contemporary civic nationalism in Canada has focused on preserving this identity both from French-speaking ethnic nationalists who would disrupt it and from outside influences that would threaten it, principally the United States. The nature of civic nationalist responses to these threats has been determined in part by the kind of ideological alliances they have made. For those whose general political orientation is liberal in nature, nationalism is viewed as a means of protecting individual autonomy from outside influence and safeguarding individual, cultural, and national identity. For civic nationalists who are socialists or welfare liberals, nationalism is viewed as a means of protecting welfare liberal or socialist policies from external (principally American) influences that might be hostile to those policies.

Contemporary Canadian nationalist policies and concerns have focused primarily on economic and cultural matters (although they have been increasingly concerned with Canadian foreign policy in opposition to Canadian participation in the war in Iraq and in the counter-insurgency operations in Afghanistan). Economic nationalism in Canada has focused on restricting foreign ownership and control in the Canadian economy and, conversely, fostering Canadian ownership and control. The debate over the "hollowing-out" of corporate Canada—the sale of major businesses such as Falconbridge, Inco, and Alcan to non-Canadian owners and the consequent loss of head offices—is the most recent example. Cultural nationalism has focused on the protection and fostering of Canadian culture, including the provision of subsidies for the production of books, music, plays, films, and television shows. Other measures protect Canadian cultural products and create opportunities for them to compete in Canada, including minimum play time for Canadian music on Canadian radio stations and quotas for Canadian productions on Canadian television. Nationalist concerns about bulk water exports, security of energy supplies (in the face of NAFTA provisions that require Canada to maintain proportional energy exports to the United States regardless of possible Canadian shortages) and environmental degradation resulting from exploitation of resources such as the Alberta oil sands for the benefit of foreign owners combine elements of both economic and cultural nationalism.

Nationalism as an Ideology

Like liberalism, conservatism, and socialism, there are many types of nationalism. However, certain core assumptions are evident in the way in which nationalism performs the four functions that all ideologies perform.

Explanatory Function. Nationalists do not offer a comprehensive explanation of why social conditions are the way they are, because of the limited nature of nationalism. Instead, they identify the nation as a natural grouping of people that, if endowed with the requisite powers and independence, can put into effect the desires of the nation. Their actions will rectify the disadvantages or injustices suffered by a people if their nation is not independent and will protect the ongoing interests of the people as a nation, including its identity and distinctiveness. According to nationalists, the welfare of the nation-state contributes significantly to the welfare of its citizens.

Evaluative Function. For nationalists, social conditions depend on the welfare of the nation. If the nation is not recognized and does not have political form and political powers, its people will be worse off, whether psychologically or materially. In addition, the nation will be better off if it is an independent political entity.

Orientative Function. Nationalists view people in terms of their status as members of the nation rather than as isolated individuals or members of a social or economic class. Nationality and citizenship therefore play a critical role in one's identity, and when people recognize the importance of that identity, they will act to strengthen and protect it. Whether a policy or action is good or bad is determined in part by its effect on the independence and well-being of the nation-state and the protection of the national identity.

Programmatic Function. The goal of nationalists is to realize the independence and well-being of the nation-state. But nationalists have widely varying views on how important that goal is compared with other competing goals. They also have widely varying views on the types of policies that should be pursued to reach that goal. Nevertheless, all nationalist policies share a common focus on the powers and independence of the nation-state and the protection of the national identity.

Nationalism and the Democratic Ideal

In a sense, nationalism is indifferent to democracy, in that nationalist policies can be pursued outside a specifically democratic political system. It is perhaps more accurate to say that nationalism is capable of making alliances with both democratic (liberalism or socialism) or nondemocratic (fascism) ideologies. For example, in Canada, the United Kingdom, and the United States, the dominant form of civic nationalism has been closely identified with democratic ideologies and has generally been viewed as a way in which the majority in the nation can achieve important political goals.

To say that fascism is in some ways a reactionary ideology is not to say that fascists are simply reactionaries or extreme conservatives. In many ways they are quite different from reactionaries and conservatives. Unlike Joseph de Maistre and the other reactionaries discussed in Chapter 5, fascists do not reject democracy, liberalism, and socialism in order to turn the clock back to a time when society was rooted in ascribed status, with church, king, and aristocracy firmly in power; on the contrary, many fascists have been openly hostile to religion, and few of them have had any respect for hereditary monarchs and aristocrats. Nor have they sought to return to the old, established ways of life; rather, fascism in its most distinctive forms has been openly revolutionary, eager not only to change society but to change it dramatically. This revolutionary fervour sets fascists apart from conservatives, who cannot abide rapid and radical change. So, too, does the fascist plan to concentrate power in the hands of a totalitarian state led by a single party and a supreme leader. Nothing could be further from the conservatives' desire to disperse power among various levels of government and the other "little platoons" that make up what they take to be a healthy society than the fascist vision of a unified state under a single, all-powerful leader.

Fascism, then, is neither conservative nor simply reactionary but a new and distinctive ideology. Although fascism did not emerge as an ideology until the 1920s, its roots reach back over a century to the reaction against the intellectual and cultural movement that dominated European thought in the eighteenth century—the rationalism of the Enlightenment. Taking the scientific discoveries of the seventeenth and eighteenth centuries as their model and inspiration, the Enlightenment philosophers claimed that the application of reason could remove all the social and political evils that stood in the way of happiness and progress. Reason can light the minds of men and women, they proclaimed, freeing them from ignorance, error, and superstition.[14] The two great political currents that flow from the Enlightenment are liberalism and socialism. Different as they are in other respects, these two ideologies are alike in sharing the premises of the Enlightenment—including the following:

1. *Humanism:* The idea that human beings are the source and measure of value, with human life valuable in and of itself. As Immanuel Kant put it, human beings belong to the "kingdom of ends." Each person is an "end in himself," not something that others may use, like a tool, as a means of accomplishing their own selfish ends.

2. *Rationalism:* The idea that human beings are rational creatures and that human reason, epitomized in scientific inquiry, can solve all mysteries and reveal solutions to all the problems that men and women face.

3. *Secularism:* The idea that religion may be a source of comfort and insight but not of absolute and unquestionable truths for guiding public life. The Enlightenment thinkers differed from one another in their religious views. Some, such as John Locke and Kant, remained Christians. Others, such as Voltaire (1694–1778), rejected Christianity but believed in a God who had created a world as well ordered as a watch, which the "divine watchmaker" had wound and left to run. Still others were atheists. But even those who took their religion seriously regarded it as something to be confined largely to private life that was therefore out of place in politics.

---

[14]For a clear statement of this view, see Immanuel Kant, "What Is Enlightenment?" in *Ideals and Ideologies: A Reader,* ed. Terence Ball and Richard Dagger, 8th ed. (New York: Longman, 2011) selection 3.16.

4. *Progressivism:* The idea that human history is the story of progress or improvement—perhaps even inevitable improvement—in the human condition. Once the shackles of ignorance and superstition have been broken, human reason will be free to order society in a rational way and life will steadily and rapidly become better for all.

5. *Universalism:* The idea that there is a single, universal human nature that binds all human beings together, despite differences of gender, race, language, culture, creed, religion, and nationality. Human beings are all equal members of Kant's "kingdom of ends," who share the same essential nature, including pre-eminently the capacity for reason.

These premises of the Enlightenment are often linked to liberalism, but they provided much of the inspiration for socialism as well. Indeed, modern socialism arose in part from the complaint that liberalism was not going far enough in its attempt to remake society in the image of Enlightenment ideals. Fascism, however, grows out of the very different conviction that the ideals of the Enlightenment are not worth pursuing—a claim first put forward in the late eighteenth and early nineteenth centuries.

THE COUNTER-ENLIGHTENMENT

A diverse group of thinkers some call the Counter-Enlightenment mounted an attack on the Enlightenment.[15] Among them were the ethnologist Johan Gottfried von Herder; the French royalists and reactionaries Joseph de Maistre and Louis-Gabriel-Ambroise de Bonald (1754–1840); the Marquis de Sade (1740–1814), notorious as a libertine and pornographer; and racial theorists such as Joseph-Arthur de Gobineau (1816–1882). None of them rejected every premise of the Enlightenment, since each had particular concerns and complaints that the others did not share, but they were alike in dismissing the major premises of the Enlightenment as fanciful, false, and politically dangerous.

These Counter-Enlightenment thinkers were united in denouncing universalism as a myth. Human beings are not all alike, they said, and the differences that distinguish groups of people from one another run very deep. Indeed, these differences—of gender, race, language, culture, creed, religion, and nationality—actually *define* who and what people are, shaping how they think of themselves and other people. Some of the Counter-Enlightenment thinkers stressed differences of one kind, while others focused on other kinds. For Herder, linguistic and cultural differences mattered most; for Gobineau, it was race; and for de Sade, it was gender. Men, de Sade observed, do not admit women to the "kingdom of ends." They treat them as means—as objects to be used, abused, and humiliated—and this is as it should be. Fittingly, the words *sadism* and *sadistic* come from the name de Sade.

Counter-Enlightenment thinkers also brought similar complaints against the Enlightenment's faith in reason. They believed that the problem with rationalism is that it flies in the face of all human experience. The prevalence of *un*reason, of superstition and prejudice, shows that reason itself is too weak to be relied on. Most people, most of the time, use reason not to examine matters critically and dispassionately but to rationalize and excuse their desires and deepen their prejudices. With this in mind, the Counter-Enlightenment writers often deplored the Enlightenment's assault on religion. Some of

---

[15]We take the term *Counter-Enlightenment* from Isaiah Berlin's essay "The Counter-Enlightenment," *Against the Current: Essays in the History of Ideas,* ed. Isaiah Berlin (Harmondsworth, UK: Penguin, 1982) 1–24.

them wrote from sincere religious conviction, but others simply held that religious beliefs are socially necessary fictions. They maintained that the belief in heaven and hell may be all that keeps most people behaving as well as they do. To lose that belief may be to lose all hope of a civilized and orderly society.

In different ways, each of these thinkers challenged the fundamental premises of the Enlightenment. Out of their challenge a different picture of human beings emerged. According to this picture, humans are fundamentally nonrational, even irrational, beings. They are defined by their *differences*—of gender, race, language, culture, creed, religion, and nationality—and they are usually locked in conflict with one another, a conflict sparked by their deep-seated and probably permanent differences. Sometimes this rejection of reason found its expression in art. Richard Wagner (1813–1883) was one of the greatest opera composers of his time. He based his operas on German myths and legends in an effort to create a new German heroic consciousness and a new German spirit. His greatest work, the four-opera *Der Ring des Nibelungen,* portrays an epic struggle between gods and men for control over the earth. Hitler was deeply attracted to Wagner and his music and regularly attended performances at Wagner's festival theatre in the small town of Bayreuth, well into the war.

This emphasis on differences also led fascism to draw heavily on ethnic nationalist sentiment and theories, which we considered in the previous chapter. Fascism also drew on two other intellectual currents of the late nineteenth century: **elitism** and **irrationalism**.

ELITISM

The assumption by liberals and socialists that a more egalitarian society was both desirable and achievable came under sharp attack in the late nineteenth and early twentieth centuries by thinkers who emphasized the importance of elites in society. These *elite theorists* included Gaetano Mosca (1858–1941), Vilfredo Pareto (1848–1923), and Roberto Michels (1876–1936). In one way or another, each contributed to the idea of elitism by concluding that a classless society was impossible. For instance, on the basis of historical studies, Mosca concluded that societies always have been and always will be ruled by a small group of leaders, even when it appears that the majority is ruling. Pareto, an Italian economist and sociologist, reached a similar conclusion. Perhaps most strikingly, so did Michels, a Swiss sociologist who undertook a study of the socialist parties and trade unions of Europe, which professed to be working to achieve a classless society. Yet Michels's study revealed that even these parties and unions, despite their proclaimed faith in democracy and equality, were controlled not by the majority of members but by a relatively small group of leaders.

Michels's discovery led him to formulate the *Iron Law of Oligarchy*. In all large organizations, he said, and certainly in whole societies, power cannot be shared equally among all the people. For the organization or society to be effective, true power must be concentrated in the hands of a small group—an elite, or oligarchy. This is simply the nature of large organizations, and there is nothing that can change it. According to Michels, this "iron law" is destined to defeat the well-meaning designs of democrats and egalitarians. Like Mosca and Pareto, he concluded that elites rule the world; they always have and they always will.

The views of the elite theorists reinforced arguments advanced earlier by German philosopher Friedrich Nietzsche (1844–1900) and others. According to Nietzsche, outstanding accomplishments were the work of a great man—the kind of person he called the *übermensch* ("overman" or "superman"). And yet, he complained, all the tendencies of the age were toward a mass society in which such outstanding individuals would find it ever harder to act in bold and creative ways. Nietzsche suggested elitism *should* be the rule; Mosca, Pareto, and Michels concluded that it *was* the rule. The elite theorists' view of the elite may have been different from Nietzsche's, but the two views in combination helped prepare the way for the explicitly elitist ideology of fascism.

IRRATIONALISM

Irrationalism describes the conclusions of a variety of very different thinkers who all came to agree that emotion and desire play a larger part in the actions of people than reason. Among these thinkers was Sigmund Freud (1856–1939), the founder of psycho-analysis, whose observations of his patients—and even of himself—led him to detect the power of instinctive drives and "the unconscious" in human conduct. In a similar vein, American philosopher and psychologist William James (1842–1910) held that most people have a "will to believe." Exactly what they believe is less important to them, James said, than that they believe in *something*. Psychologically speaking, people need something—almost anything, in fact—in which to believe, for the one thing that human beings cannot endure is a life devoid of some larger purpose or meaning.

French social psychologist Gustav Le Bon (1841–1931) argued in his classic work *The Crowd* (1895) that human behaviour in crowds is different from their behaviour as individuals. Acting collectively and therefore anonymously, people will participate in acts of barbarism that they would never engage in as lone individuals. The psychology of lynch mobs, for example, is quite different from the psychology of the individuals who compose that mob. People acting *en masse* and in mobs are not restrained by individual conscience or moral scruple. A mob psychology, or *herd instinct*, takes over and shuts down individual judgment or reasoning regarding right and wrong.

In a similar spirit, Pareto examined the social factors influencing individual judgment and behaviour and concluded that emotions, symbols, and what he called "sentiments" are more important than material or economic factors. Mosca suggested that people are moved more by slogans and symbols, flags and anthems—by "political formulae," as he called them—than by reasoned argument and rational debate.

All of these thinkers—Freud, James, Le Bon, Pareto, and Mosca—were more imme-diately concerned with explaining how people acted than with leading people to action. Not so for Georges Sorel (1847–1922), a French engineer turned social theorist and political activist. Sorel insisted that people are more often moved to action by political myths than by appeals to reason. To bring about major social changes, it is necessary to find a powerful myth that can inspire people to act. For Sorel, the idea of a nationwide general strike could prove to be such a myth. In other words, the general strike was a myth in that there was no guarantee that it would really lead to the revolutionary over-throw of the bourgeoisie and capitalism. However, if enough people could be brought to *believe* in the myth of the general strike, their efforts inspired by this belief would indeed lead to a successful revolution. What matters most, Sorel concluded, is not the reason-ableness of a myth but its emotional power, for it is not reason but emotion that leads most people to act. And when people act *en masse,* they can smash almost any obstacle in their path.

Mussolini, Hitler, and other fascist leaders quite obviously took Sorel's ideas to heart. The slogans, the mass demonstrations, the torchlight parades—all were designed to stir the people at their most basic emotional and instinctive levels. But stir them to do what? To create powerful nation-states, then mighty empires, all under the leadership of the fascist elite. So it was not only ethnic nationalism, but also the attitudes of the Counter-Enlightenment, elitism, and irrationalism that came together in the early twentieth century in the totalitarian ideology of fascism.

FASCISM IN ITALY

As a young man, Benito Mussolini (1883–1945) took up political journalism and became a revolutionary socialist, proclaiming that capitalism would fall only after a violent proletarian uprising. Even at this point, however, Mussolini placed more emphasis on the *will* to engage in revolutionary struggle than on economic factors and the internal contradictions of capitalism.

Mussolini broke with socialism when, at the beginning of the First World War, European socialists gave up their internationalist and pacifist beliefs and turned to nationalism. Before the war, socialists across Europe had agreed that they would take no part in any capitalist war. If the bourgeoisie of France, England, and Germany wanted to slaughter one another, so be it; the socialists would urge the working classes of all countries to stay out of the war and wait for the opportunity to create socialist societies once the capitalist powers had destroyed one another. When the First World War erupted in August 1914, almost all of the socialist representatives in the legislatures of the warring countries voted to support the war efforts of their countries. For some, such as Mussolini, this was a sign that nationalism was a far stronger force in human life than loyalty to social class, and Mussolini began urging Italy to join the war.

Benito Mussolini (1883–1945)

For Mussolini, the First World War proved once and for all that Marx was wrong: Workers *do* have a fatherland—at least they want to *believe* that they do. Any political party or movement that denies this is doomed to failure. Socialists, he said, "have never examined the problems of *nations* [but only of classes. Contrary to Marx], the nation represents a stage in human [history] that has not yet been transcended. . . . The 'sentiment' of nationality exists; it cannot be denied."[16]

Mussolini took political advantage of the widely shared sentiment of nationalism by forming first the *Fasci di Combattimento,* or combat groups, that consisted largely of First World War veterans, and then the National Fascist Party itself. The party espoused a program that sometimes seemed revolutionary, sometimes conservative, but always nationalistic. Italy had been united for less than fifty years when the First World War ended, and many Italians felt that their country, unlike France and England, did not receive its fair share of the spoils when Germany and Austria surrendered. Playing upon this resentment, the fascists promised action to end the bickering between the various Italian political parties. There had been too much talk, too much debate, they declared; the time had come for forceful action, even violence, if Italy was to take her rightful place among the major powers of Europe.

This emphasis on national unity was apparent in the word *fascism* itself, which derives from the Italian *fasciare,* "to fasten or bind." The aim of the Fascist Party was to bind the Italian people together, to overcome the divisions that weakened their country. Fascism also appealed to the glories of the ancient Roman Empire by invoking one of the old Roman symbols of authority, the *fasces*—an axe in the centre of a bundle of rods, all fastened together as a symbol of the strength that comes from unity. To achieve this unity, the fascists said, it is necessary to overcome certain obstacles. One of these obstacles is liberalism, with its emphasis on individual rights and interests. According to the fascists, no nation can be strong if its members think of themselves first and foremost as individuals who are concerned with protecting their own rights and interests. Another obstacle is socialism, with its emphasis on social classes. Mussolini, the former Marxist, particularly attacked Marxist beliefs about class divisions and class struggle, which he regarded as enemies of national unity. Italians must not think of themselves either as individuals or as members of social classes, he said; they must think of themselves as Italians first, foremost, and forever.

Once in office, Mussolini moved to entrench himself and his Fascist Party in power. He ignored the Italian Parliament, outlawed all parties except the Fascist Party, struck a compromise with the Roman Catholic Church, gained control of the mass media, and stifled freedom of speech. He also set out to make Italy a military and industrial power so that it would again be the centre of a great empire. Indeed, Mussolini made no secret of his ambitions for Italy—ambitions that included war and conquest. In his speeches and writings, Mussolini often spoke of war as the true test of manly virtue, and he had warlike slogans stenciled on the walls of buildings throughout Italy, such as "War is to the male what childbearing is to the female!" and "A minute on the battlefield is worth a lifetime of peace!"[17]

---

[16]Quoted in A. James Gregor, *Contemporary Radical Ideologies* (New York: Random, 1968) 131.
[17]Quoted in William S. Halperin, *Mussolini and Italian Fascism* (Princeton, NJ: Van Norstrand, 1964) 47.

In addition, Mussolini encouraged people to believe that fascism rested on a philosophical or ideological basis. The fascists had a plan for transforming Italy—a plan that grew out of a coherent view of the world. Included in that view were distinctively fascist conceptions of human nature and freedom.

For example, for the fascist, an individual human life has meaning only insofar as it is rooted in and realized through the life of the society or the nation as a whole. In other words, fascists reject both the atomistic view of society and individualism and subscribe to an organic view of society. The individual on his or her own can accomplish nothing of great significance, they say. It is only when the individual dedicates his or her life to the nation-state, sacrificing everything to its glory, that the individual finds true fulfillment.

The Italian fascists also stressed the value of the state, which they saw as the legal and institutional embodiment of the power, the unity, and the majesty of the nation. To be dedicated to the service of the nation was thus to be dedicated to the state—and to its great and glorious leader, *Il Duce.* The state was to control everything, and everyone was to serve the state. As the Italian people were reminded over and over, "everything in the state, nothing outside the state, nothing against the state."

Thus, freedom for the fascists was not and is not individual liberty, but rather the freedom of the *nation,* the integrated and organic whole that unites all individuals, groups, and classes behind the iron shield of the all-powerful state. In fact, individual liberty is an obstacle to freedom because it distracts people from their true mission to "believe, obey, fight." Freedom of speech, freedom of assembly, freedom to live as one chooses—these are all useless liberties, according to the fascists. The only freedom that truly matters is the freedom to serve the state. In terms of our triadic definition of freedom, the Italian fascists conceived of freedom as shown in Figure 9.2.

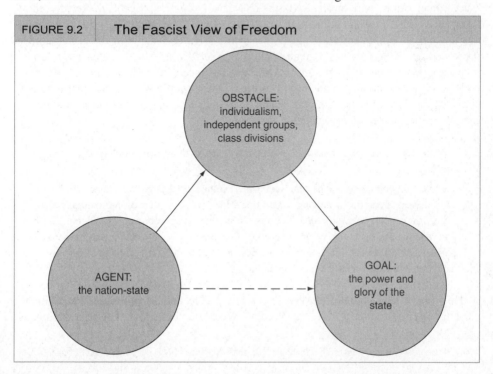

FIGURE 9.2   The Fascist View of Freedom

OBSTACLE:
individualism,
independent groups,
class divisions

AGENT:
the nation-state

GOAL:
the power and
glory of the
state

True freedom, in the fascist view, is found in serving the state, and there is nothing more fulfilling than doing one's part, however small, to promote its glory through military conquest, which required the discipline and loyalty of the Italian people. Mussolini and the fascists attempted to win this discipline and loyalty through massive propaganda efforts, always designed to appeal to the emotions and instincts of the people. The people were a mass, a "herd" incapable of leading themselves. They needed an elite to guide them, and they especially needed a dictator with an almost mystical ability to know where their true interests lay.

However, indoctrination and propaganda are not enough to convert a people into a modern military machine; they also need weapons, fuel, and food. To this end, Mussolini tried to encourage industrial production in Italy. He did this through the policy of corporatism, according to which property was to remain in private hands even as it was put to public use. To prevent disputes between owners and workers from disrupting business and production, the Ministry of Corporations was supposed to supervise economic affairs. The Italian economy was divided into twenty-two sectors, or corporations, each of which was administered by representatives of ownership, labour, and the Ministry of Corporations. The representatives of the ministry were supposed to look after the interests of the public as a whole, and the three groups were supposed to work together in harmony for the good of all Italians. In practice, however, the fascist representatives of the ministry could do pretty much as they pleased. They were often willing to accept bribes and to do as those who paid the bribes—usually the owners—suggested.

FASCISM IN GERMANY: NAZISM

The German counterpart of Italian fascism, Nazism, was inextricably linked to Adolf Hitler (1889–1945). In his autobiography *Mein Kampf* ("My Battle"), written in prison after an unsuccessful attempt to seize power in 1923, Hitler made clear the basic outlines of his ideology. Germany has a great destiny, he wrote, if only the German *Volk* ("folk" or "people") can join forces and throw off those enemies who divide and betray them—particularly the communists and Jews. But the German people will not be able to do this without a single party and supreme leader to forge them into a united and invincible force. As Hitler said in *Mein Kampf*,

> The psyche of the great masses is not receptive to anything that is half-hearted and weak . . .
>
> Like the woman, whose psychic state is determined less by abstract reason than by an indefinable emotional longing for a force which will complement her nature, and who, consequently, would rather bow to a strong man than dominate a weakling, so likewise the masses love a commander more than a petitioner and feel inwardly more satisfied by a doctrine tolerating no other beside itself, than by the granting of liberalistic freedom with which . . . they can do little. . . .[18]

This was Hitler's notion of the *Führerprinzip,* the "leadership principle," according to which the masses and the *Führer,* or "leader," were bound together. The relationship, as

---

[18]Adolf Hitler, *Mein Kampf,* trans. Ralph Manheim (Boston: Houghton, 1943) 42; see Ball and Dagger, selection 7.48.

Adolf Hitler (1889–1945)

Hitler's words indicate, is erotic and even sadistic in the original Sadean sense. Like the Italian fascists' slogan, "war is to the male what childbearing is to the female," Hitler's words also reveal the fascist preoccupation with masculinity, which the Nazis and fascists associated with strength, action, and dominance.

In some respects, Nazism in Germany resembled fascism in Italy. There was the same hatred of liberalism and communism; the same attitude toward the masses, who were to be moulded to the will of the great leader through propaganda and indoctrination; the same reliance on an organic view of society; the same appeal to military might and the need for discipline and sacrifice; the same emphasis on nationalism; and the same totalitarian spirit. Moreover, neither Hitler nor Mussolini had much interest in economic matters, at least not as long as they thought that their countries were producing enough weapons and other war *matériel*. The inclusion of the word "socialist" in the full name of the Nazi Party has led to some confusion on this point, but Hitler certainly was not a socialist in any ordinary sense of the term. As he explained in a speech,

> Every truly national idea is in the last resort social, i.e., he who is prepared so completely to adopt the cause of his people that he really knows no higher ideal than the prosperity of this— his own—people, he who has so taken to heart the meaning of our great song "*Deutschland, Deutschland über alles,*" that nothing in this world stands for him higher than this Germany, people and land, land and people, he is a socialist. . . . [He] is not merely a socialist but he is also national in the highest sense of that word.[19]

---

[19]Quoted in Gregor 197.

For Hitler, *socialism* was merely another name for nationalism; the German economy under Hitler can best be described as state-assisted capitalism. The *nation* did not include everyone born within the borders of Germany but only those born into the racial group to which the German *Volk* belonged.

From the beginning, Nazism relied, and continues to rely, on the idea that *race* is the fundamental characteristic of human beings. Race was not important for the Italian fascists—that is, not until pressure from Hitler led Mussolini to take some steps against Jews in Italy. In other words, fascism was not, and need not be, a racist ideology; Nazism was and is. Indeed, racism is at the core of Nazism—so much so that we can define Nazism in terms of the simple formula *fascism + racism = Nazism.* This belief is especially clear in the Nazi views of human nature and freedom.

For Hitler and his followers, the fundamental fact of human life is that human beings belong to different races. There is no such thing as universal human nature in their view because the differences that distinguish one race from another mark each race for a different role or destiny in the world. There was nothing really new in this, for Hitler was not an original thinker; he used ideas drawn from earlier racial theorists such as Joseph-Arthur de Gobineau and Ludwig Woltmann (1871–1907). According to Gobineau, race was the key to the rise and fall of great civilizations. Like many other people over the centuries, Gobineau wondered why once-mighty empires such as Rome lost their power and collapsed. The answer he hit upon was *miscegenation*, the mixture of races. A people rose to power when its racial composition was pure and vigorous, Gobineau concluded. As it expanded its control over conquered peoples—as it became an empire—the original racial stock was weakened by interbreeding with other races. The result was an inferior people incapable of maintaining its identity and power. And the result was the loss of the empire. Furthermore, the races were not created equal. The white race is superior to the yellow, Gobineau said, and the yellow is superior to the black. As he saw it, this is the pattern of nature, and it ought to be observed in society as well.

Ideas like Gobineau's were much in the air in the late nineteenth century, as were the ideas of the Social Darwinists. As advanced by Herbert Spencer, social Darwinism was not a racist doctrine. But its emphasis on the struggle for survival lent itself to a racist interpretation. All one had to do was to say that the struggle for survival was not a struggle between individuals, but a broader struggle between entire *races* of people.

This was, in fact, the position that Ludwig Woltmann took in two books—*Historical Materialism: A Critique of the Marxist World View* (1900) and *Political Anthropology* (1903).[20] Woltmann argued that what is missing from Marxist theory is the most central concept of all: race. Why, Woltmann asks, have the greatest achievements in art, music, literature, philosophy, and industry been concentrated in Western Europe? It is because the superior Germanic or Aryan race resides there. This race has evolved further and faster than "lesser" races because the European climate is neither as harsh and unyielding as the Arctic nor as lush as the tropics. The Inuit cannot create philosophy or great music because they must spend most of their time and energy in wresting a livelihood from a frigid and infertile environment. Polynesians and Africans, by contrast, live in a climate in which fish are plentiful and fruit falls from the trees. Only in Western Europe is the climate neither excessively harsh nor extraordinarily fecund. This climate has produced a

---

[20]Ludwig Woltmann, *Der historiche Materialismus* (Duffeldorf: Michels, 1900); and *Politische Anthropologie,* 2nd ed. (Leipzig: Doerner, 1936).

race that, over millennia, has transformed nature, created culture, and exhibited its superiority to the rest of the world.

Hitler was also influenced by English and American anti-Semites, including Houston Stewart Chamberlain (1855–1927), Madison Grant (1865–1937), and Henry Ford (1863–1947). Chamberlain, an English aristocrat married to the daughter of German composer Richard Wagner, wrote *The Foundations of the Nineteenth Century* (1911), which praised "Germanism" and criticized Jews as an alien force that had debased European culture. Grant, an American racial theorist, was the author of *The Passing of the Great Race; or, The Racial Basis of European History* (1916), which Hitler read in translation in the early 1920s. Ford, the American automobile manufacturer, wrote *The International Jew: The World's Foremost Problem* (1922), which greatly impressed Hitler. Visitors were often startled to see that the largest picture in Hitler's office was of Ford; and in 1938, Hitler awarded Ford the Grand Cross of the Order of the German Eagle, the highest honour Germany could bestow on a foreigner, for "meritorious service" to the *Volk* and the Fatherland.[21]

Chamberlain, Grant, and Ford sounded similar warnings: The rising tide of "coloured races" threatened to swamp the morally and intellectually superior white race; whites must therefore take protective measures by restricting immigration, outlawing miscegenation, and sterilizing "subhumans." (This last was the goal of the eugenics movement of the late nineteenth and early twentieth centuries.) Hitler's first foray into Nazi social engineering was the mass sterilization of mentally retarded and physically handicapped children. From there, it was a short step to the Final Solution—the systematic extermination of Jews, Gypsies, and other "inferior" peoples. In Hitler's view, Jews were especially dangerous as they were responsible not only for encouraging racial mixing but also for the spread of communism, which divided the white race along class lines and joined together white and coloured peoples in a worldwide struggle. By these and other means the Jews supposedly aimed at world domination. This assertion—that Jews were set on conquering the world—was advanced in *The Protocols of the Elders of Zion* (1905) a document that purported to be minutes of a secret meeting of chief rabbis in the 1880s. Although the *Protocols* was in fact a forgery produced by the Russian secret police to justify pogroms (the state-sponsored attacks on Jews in Russia), many people, including Ford and Hitler, believed it to be authentic.[22]

Woltmann warned that the superior white race faced several threats. Chief among these was the population crisis. Woltmann believed that Malthus's law—that populations grow at an ever-increasing geometric rate while resources grow only at a steady arithmetical rate—portends a racial war for increasingly scarce resources and *Lebensraum,* or "living space." The world is rapidly reaching the point at which population will outstrip the resources available to support human life (as illustrated in Figure 9.3). The competition for scarce resources will pit not one individual against another but one race, or *Volk*—the Aryans—against all others. The Darwinian struggle for survival will be along racial lines, and Aryans had better brace themselves for the coming competition. They must toughen themselves by repudiating "soft" or "sentimental" ideas of racial equality,

---

[21]See Neil Baldwin, *Henry Ford and the Jews* (New York: Public Affairs, 2001), and, more generally, Charles Higham, *American Swastika* (Garden City, NY: Doubleday, 1985).

[22]For a history of the *Protocols* and its influence, see Stephen Eric Bronner, *A Rumour About the Jews: Antisemitism and the Protocols of the Learned Elders of Zion* (New York: St. Martin's P, 2000).

FIGURE 9.3	Malthus's Law

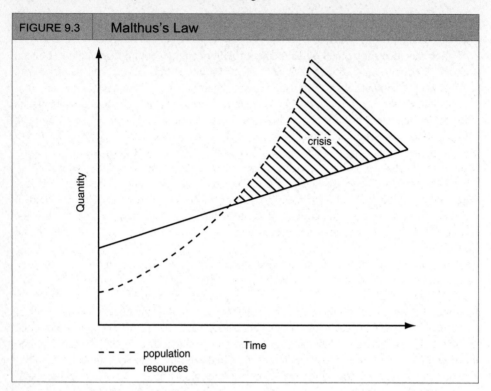

interracial harmony, the "brotherhood of man," and other liberal and socialist sentiments. These "Jewish" ideas weaken the resolve and sap the strength of Aryans, and those who hold and teach them must be censored—or silenced forever.

These ideas reappear in Hitler's *Mein Kampf,* in Alfred Rosenberg's *Der Mythus des XX Jahrhunderts* (*Myth of the Twentieth Century*), and in Nazi military and political practice. They supply the rationale for the German invasion of Poland and the Soviet Union, which extended Aryan *Lebensraum* into the oil and wheat fields of Russia and Ukraine. These ideas justify censorship and book burnings, the banning of Jewish ideas from German classrooms and libraries, and the silencing of critics. Most notoriously of all, these ideas rationalize the systematic enslavement and murder of millions of Jews and other "inferior" peoples, including Slavs, Gypsies, homosexuals, the handicapped, and other "*lebens unwertes Leben*" ("lives unworthy of life").

Hitler claimed that the Germanic or Aryan race was the source—the "culture-creating" source—of European civilization. And the Germanic people were the highest or purest remnant of the Aryan race. Thus the destiny of the German *Volk* was clear: to dominate or even exterminate "lesser" peoples and thus establish a glorious Thousand-Year *Reich* or Empire.

The Nazis also drew upon this racial view of human nature in developing their conception of freedom. Like the Italian fascists, they opposed the liberal view that freedom is a matter of individual liberty, favouring instead the idea that freedom, properly understood, is the freedom of the nation or *Volk*. But the Nazis gave this idea their characteristic racial twist. The only freedom that counts, they said, is the freedom of the *Volk* who belong to the "master race." Freedom should be the freedom of Aryans because that is nature's plan. But there are obstacles in the way of the Aryan race's realizing its destiny. First, there is the obstacle of the members of "inferior" races who are doing what they can to drag the Aryans down to their own level. And there is also the obstacle presented by certain ideas and ideals—specifically, the humanist ideas of the Enlightenment. These were Jewish ideas, according to Hitler, ideas that made even Aryans soft and squeamish. Because these ideas of universal brotherhood and equality are embedded in both liberalism and Marxism, it followed for Hitler that these ideologies are not merely obstacles but enemies to be rooted out and destroyed. This was the rationale for censorship, for book burnings, and for toughening the minds of the young to make them into willing servants of the *Führer* and the *Volk*.

In the Nazi view, every individual is merely a cell in the larger *völkisch* organism. The destiny of the organism is also the individual's destiny. Gottfried Neese, a Nazi party ideologist, illustrated this reliance on organic metaphors when he said that the *Volk*

> form a true organism—a being which leads its own life and follows its own laws, which possesses powers peculiar to itself, and which develops its own nature. . . . This living unity of the people has its cells in its individual members, and just as in every body there are certain cells to perform certain tasks, this is likewise the case in the body of the people. The individual is bound to his people not only physically but mentally and spiritually. . . .[23]

Outside the *Volksgemeinschaft*—the racially pure "folk community"—nothing worthwhile exists. Therefore, to create and sustain such a community, one must not be distracted by softness, compassion, or pity. "Inferior" peoples must be regarded as subhuman animals or "vermin" to be destroyed without a moment's thought or hesitation. Only in that way can the Aryan people be free to achieve their great destiny.

FASCISM ELSEWHERE IN EUROPE

Although fascism has been most closely identified with Italy and Germany in the period from the First World War to the Second World War, it was not confined to those two countries. Fascist parties and movements spread throughout Europe in the 1920s and 1930s, from Romania to France and Britain, and they made a brief appearance in the United States in the 1930s. Aside from Italy and Germany, however, the only European country that arguably had a fascist government was Spain, under the regime of General Francisco Franco. Franco's forces won the Spanish Civil War (1936–1939) with the aid of both Italy and Germany. Once the Civil War was over, and especially when the Second World War began to go against the fascist powers, Franco ousted the more ardent fascists from his government and moved in the direction of a conservative, even reactionary, dictatorship. In addition, the Franco regime showed little tendency toward the anti-Semitism and racist theories that were an integral part of fascism elsewhere. Franco was more concerned with maintaining firm authority in a quiet Spain than in mobilizing mass support in order to win glory and a new empire for his country or in imposing the sort of totalitarian regime that is one of the hallmarks of fascism. The regime of Juan Peron in post-World War II in Argentina was quite similar.

---

[23]Quoted in Raymond E. Murphy et al., "National Socialism," *Readings on Fascism and National Socialism,* ed. Department of Philosophy, University of Colorado (Chicago: Swallow, 1952) 65.

FASCISM AND NAZISM IN CANADA

In the 1920s and 1930s, fascism found some support in Canada, particularly in Quebec, and within Quebec particularly in the large Italian community in Montreal. Mussolini's vision of a new Roman Empire appealed to Italian national pride; his 1929 agreement with the Vatican suggested it was acceptable for Italian Roman Catholics to support fascism. Fascism also attracted support from French-Canadian ethnic nationalists who were sympathetic to the extreme nationalist views that were incorporated in fascism. In addition, even before Hitler's explicitly racist views were fused with fascism, fascism exhibited latent anti-Semitism because Jews were viewed as quintessentially foreign outsiders. For example, a campaign in Quebec in the 1930s to encourage consumers to patronize French-speaking retailers was in part a boycott of Jewish merchants.

Outside Quebec, fascism drew its principal inspiration from the British Union of Fascists led by Oswald Mosley. Its Canadian counterpart, the Canadian Union of Fascists, enjoyed relatively little support and concentrated its attention primarily on fascist economic and social policy and on corporatism. Corporatism has been described by Canadian labour arbitrator and historian Lita-Rose Betcherman as a form of government based on occupation, where "real power rested . . . with the state, which controlled both [labour and business] through its function of compulsory arbitration. Indeed, in every aspect of life, the state, and the person *Il Duce,* was the supreme arbiter."[24]

A more prominent admirer of fascism drew less on the corporatist theories that fascists supported and more on the elitist and irrationalist tendencies in fascism. W. D. Herridge (1888–1961) was the brother-in-law of Prime Minister R. B. Bennett (PM 1930–1935). Herridge was the Canadian ambassador in Washington when Franklin D. Roosevelt proposed his New Deal, and he was impressed by Roosevelt's success in marshalling the support of the American public. In 1934 he advised Bennett that Roosevelt's success was a triumph of irrationalism: Roosevelt had mystified the American people and created the illusion that he was their saviour. It was this illusion, rather than any actual affect of the New Deal policies, that was of real importance. Herridge urged Bennett to adopt a similar program or slogan to persuade the Canadian people that a "new order of prosperity" could be achieved through strong leadership. He urged Bennett to imitate Mussolini, Hitler, and Stalin by putting a dramatic program before the Canadian people to lead them out of the Depression. Herridge's influence probably played a significant role in the so-called Bennett New Deal proposals of 1935, but it disappeared with Bennett's defeat in the 1935 election.[25]

After Hitler came to power in Germany in 1933, Canadian fascism became much more explicitly anti-Semitic and racist. In Quebec, journalist Adrien Arcand founded the National Social Christian Party, which viewed the Canadian government as a facade controlled by Jewish interests and advocated a more authoritarian government dedicated "to preserving the sacred spiritual and traditional values of nationality, Christianity, order, equality, private property and the family."[26] Arcand followed Hitler in forming a paramilitary organization of blue shirts who engaged in street violence and intimidation.

---

[24]See Lita-Rose Betcherman, *The Swastika and the Maple Leaf: Fascist Movements in Canada in the Thirties* (Toronto: Fitzhenry, 1975) 56–60; and Robin 187–195.

[25]See J. H. R. Wilbur, ed., *The Bennett New Deal: Fraud or Portent?* (Toronto: Copp, 1968) 67–71.

[26]See Martin Robin, *Shades of Right: Nativist and Fascist Politics in Canada, 1920–1940* (Toronto: U of Toronto P, 1992) 145.

At that time, similar paramilitary groups or gangs also existed in English Canada, most notably the Swastika Clubs (which triggered the notorious Christie Pits riots in Toronto in August 1933). Other Nazi-related groups in Canada included the Balmy Beaches Protective Association, dedicated to preventing Jews from using Toronto beaches, and the Deutscher Bund Canada, which appealed to ethnic Germans in Canada.[27] The leader of the Bund, Otto Becker, tried to organize boycotts of Jewish stores and was supported by German diplomats in Canada but enjoyed little general support. The closest thing to a Canadian Nazi party was the Nationalist Party of Canada, based in Winnipeg and led by William Whittaker, which, like most similar groups, attracted considerable attention but little support.

Although fascist and Nazi groups disappeared in the aftermath of the Second World War, there was some growth of primarily racist groups, including the Canadian Nazi Party (in the 1960s), the white supremacist Western Guard Party (in the 1970s), and the Ku Klux Klan (in the 1970s). In the early 1990s, members of the Western Guard Party resurfaced in the form of the Heritage Front, which not only spread racist literature, but also turned to recruiting young members by sponsoring racist rock concerts with bands like RaHoWa (Racist Holy War). Some Nazi sympathizers such as Ernst Zundel attempt to minimize the evil committed by the Nazis during the Second World War, denying or minimizing the Holocaust. Although these groups have frequently attracted considerable media attention, none has had any significant membership or following and, as discussed below, it is difficult to say if they are genuinely fascist, even if often so described.

FASCISM TODAY

Two factors make any discussion of contemporary fascism difficult.

First, as Gregor has persuasively argued[28], fascism has only enjoyed real success in Italy and Germany and in both cases was formed and influenced by particular historical circumstances. Each country was reacting to a sense of powerlessness and undeservedly low international status after World War I. In this particular crisis, a charismatic leader was able to exploit the collective psychology with uniforms, ceremony, ritual, and the management of information (that is, propaganda) to take power. Gregor questions whether genuine fascism can arise without these particular and perhaps unique historical circumstances.

Second, because of the crimes and excesses of the German and Italian fascist regimes, the terms "fascism" and "fascist" have become pejorative insult words used to describe any political viewpoint opposed to the prevailing liberal or democratic socialist ortho-doxy. Thus, many right-wing or conservative movements are labelled fascist in addition to, in some eyes, Stalinist or Maoist versions of socialism. Elements such as racism, xen-ophobia, hostility to immigration, an inclination to violence (for example, skinheads and soccer hooligans), or pronounced anticommunism attract the fascist label or its variants—crypto-fascist or neofascist.

Consequently, it is not easy to identify contemporary fascism merely by looking for persons or movements labelled as such. However, it is possible to argue that fascism is not altogether dead and gone—not even in the two countries in which it seemed so

---

[27]See S. R. Barrett, *Is God a Racist? The Right Wing in Canada* (Toronto: U of Toronto P, 1987) 357–385.

[28]A. James Gregor. *The Search for Neofascism* (New York: CUP, 2006) chapters 1 and 2.

thoroughly defeated. The Fascist Party is outlawed in Italy, as is the Nazi Party in Germany. In 1946, former fascists founded the Italian Social Movement (MSI) which had neofascist tendencies, though it was constrained by Italian laws proscribing fascism. By the 1990s, the MSI had clearly abandoned the antidemocratic and totalitarian features of fascism, as well as racism and anti-Semitism, and in 1994 changed its name to the National Alliance. While in 1992, Alessandra Mussolini, granddaughter of Benito Mussolini, was elected to a seat in the Italian Parliament as a member of the MSI, raising concerns about a neofascist revival, the MSI/National Alliance is best classified as a democratic conservative party. In Germany, neo-Nazi organizations have claimed responsibility for firebombing attacks and other assaults on nonwhite immigrants. Similar racist and anti-immigrant agitation and violence has occurred in other European states, including the recent mass killing in Norway of political supporters of liberal immigration policies. These attacks seem to be the result of a renewed racism, which is widely labelled as neofascist. In France, the National Front, led successively by Jean-Marie Le Pen and his daughter, has won control of some municipal governments with campaigns that blame immigrants for high rates of unemployment, crime, and welfare expenses. Le Pen himself finished second in the first round of the French presidential election of 2002 but lost by an overwhelming margin in the runoff election. His daughter succeeded him as a potential presidential candidate. While the relative success of the National Front suggests that a sizable portion of the French electorate is prepared to blame immigrants for various social ills, these attitudes, whether called racist or nativist or xenophobic, fall far short of fascism.

Similar electoral results have occurred elsewhere in Europe. Capitalizing on anti-immigrant (and especially anti-Islamic) sentiments, parties labelled as neofascist have received significant electoral support in Austria, Switzerland, and Denmark. Even in the Netherlands, long a bastion of tolerance, Pim Fortuyn's List, an anti-immigrant party led by the late Pim Fortuyn, came close to electoral victory in 2002. Had Fortuyn not been assassinated in May 2002 shortly before parliamentary elections, his party almost certainly would have won control of the Dutch Parliament, making Fortuyn the prime minister. In Belgium, the Vlaams Blok (Flemish Bloc) made a strong showing in a number of regional and municipal elections before the Belgian Supreme Court banned it in 2004 for advocating racial and ethnic discrimination. The party has since reconstituted itself as Vlaams Belang (Flemish Interest).[29]

As we have noted, it is easy to label such movements as fascist, particularly because they are repellent, and "fascist" is a powerful term of abuse to use in political dialogue. It is important to distinguish regimes and movements that are merely authoritarian from those that are genuinely fascist. As Robert Paxton has observed, "Although authoritarian regimes often trample civil liberties and are capable of murderous brutality, they do not share fascism's urge to reduce the private sphere to nothing."[30] In addition, because fascism stresses leadership and action above any formal program, it is sometimes paradoxically difficult to recognize whether a movement that is out of power and therefore taking neither action nor exercising leadership is truly fascist.[31]

---

[29]See Elisabeth Carter, *The Extreme Right in Western Europe. Success or Failure?* (Manchester: UP, 2005).

[30]Robert O. Paxton, *The Anatomy of Fascism* (New York: Alfred A. Knopf, 2004) 217.

[31]See Paxton, op. cit., pp. 15–20.

Conclusion

Nationalism as an Ideology

Like liberalism, conservatism, and socialism, there are many types of nationalism. However, certain core assumptions are evident in the way in which nationalism performs the four functions that all ideologies perform.

Explanatory Function. Nationalists do not offer a comprehensive explanation of why social conditions are the way they are because of the limited nature of nationalism. Instead, they identify the nation as a natural grouping of people that, if endowed with the requisite powers and independence, can put into effect the desires of the nation. Their actions will rectify the disadvantages or injustices suffered by a people if their nation is not independent and will protect the ongoing interests of the people as a nation, including its identity and distinctiveness. According to nationalists, the welfare of the nation-state contributes significantly to the welfare of its citizens.

Evaluative Function. For nationalists, social conditions depend on the welfare of the nation. If the nation is not recognized and does not have political form and political powers, its people will be worse off, whether psychologically or materially. In addition, the nation will be better off if it is an independent political entity.

Orientative Function. Nationalists view people in terms of their status as members of the nation rather than as isolated individuals or members of a social or economic class. Nationality and citizenship therefore play a critical role in one's identity; and when people recognize the importance of that identity, they will act to strengthen and protect it. Whether a policy or action is good or bad is determined in part by its effect on the independence and well-being of the nation-state and the protection of the national identity.

Programmatic Function. The goal of nationalists is to realize the independence and well-being of the nation-state. But nationalists have widely varying views on how important that goal is compared with other competing goals. They also have widely varying views on the types of policies that should be pursued to reach that goal. Nevertheless, all nationalist policies share a common focus on the powers and independence of the nation-state and the protection of the national identity.

Nationalism and the Democratic Ideal

In a sense, nationalism is indifferent to democracy, in that nationalist policies can be pursued outside a specifically democratic political system. It is perhaps more accurate to say that nationalism is capable of making alliances with both democratic (liberalism or socialism) or nondemocratic (fascism) ideologies. For example, in Canada, the United Kingdom, and the United States, the dominant form of civic nationalism has been closely identified with democratic ideologies and has generally been viewed as a way in which the majority in the nation can achieve important political goals.

Fascism as an Ideology

One feature of fascism is clear. No matter what the form, fascists have always tried to win mass support by appealing to people in the simplest, most emotional terms. This becomes evident as we look at how fascism and Nazism perform the four functions that all ideologies perform.

Explanatory Function. Why are social conditions the way they are? Fascists typically answer this question with some account of heroes and villains. Usually they concentrate on the scoundrels or traitors who conspire to keep the nation or *Volk* weak in order to serve their own personal interests. In other words, they look for scapegoats and blame all problems on them. This is what the Nazis did to the Jews, for instance, and what neo-Nazis or white supremacists do to blacks or Hispanics or other "inferior" and "foreign" groups.

Evaluative Function. Fascists believe that whether a situation is good or bad usually depends on some evaluation of a nation's or *Volk*'s unity and strength. If the people are fragmented or at odds with one another, then it is time to attack the villains who are the enemy of the *Volk* or nation. If the people are united behind their party and their leader, on the other hand, then all will be well.

Orientative Function. What is one's place in the world, one's primary source of belonging or identification? According to the Italian fascists, it is the nation; to the Nazis, the nation defined in racial terms. In either case, the individual should recognize that he or she is of no significance as an individual but only as a member of the organic whole—the nation-state or the race—that gives meaning and purpose to his or her life.

Programmatic Function. What is to be done? Again, the answer is simple—believe, obey, fight! Follow one's leaders in the struggle against the enemies of the nation or race, and do whatever is necessary to bring glory to one's people by helping to establish it as a leading power in the world. Give everything to the state, keep nothing from the state, and do nothing against the state.

Fascism and the Democratic Ideal

In its strongest forms, whether in Italian fascism or German Nazism, fascism is a totalitarian ideology. Of all the ideologies, it is the only one to reject democracy altogether. It does respond to the democratic ideal, to be sure, but it responds with contempt. For the fascist, democracy is merely another name for division and weakness in a world where unity and strength are what truly matter.

For Further Reading

Aho, James. *The Politics of Righteousness: Idaho Christian Patriotism.* Seattle: U of Washington P, 1990.

Arendt, Hannah. *The Origins of Totalitarianism.* Cleveland and New York: Meridian, 1958.

Barkun, Michael. *Religion and the Racist Right: The Origins of the Christian Identity Movement*. Chapel Hill, NC: U of North Carolina P, 1994.

Bosworth, R. J. B. *Mussolini*. Oxford: Oxford UP, 2002.

Bullock, Alan. *Hitler: A Study in Tyranny*, rev. ed. New York: Harper & Row, 1964.

Campbell, Colin, and William Christian. *Parties, Leaders and Ideologies in Canada*. Toronto: McGraw-Hill, 1996 (Chapter 5).

Clarkson, Stephen. *Uncle Sam and Us: Globalization, Neoconservatism, and the Canadian State*. Toronto: U of Toronto P, 2002.

Eatwell, Roger. *Fascism: A History*. NY: Viking, 1997.

Fraser, Graham. *René Lévesque and the Parti Québécois in Power*. Montreal: McGill-Queen's UP, 2001.

Grant, George. *Lament for a Nation*. Toronto: McClelland, 1965.

Gregor, A. James. *The Search for Neofascism. The Use and Abuse of Social Science*. Cambridge: CUP, 2006.

Kershaw, Ian. *Hitler*. 2 vols. New York: Norton, 1999, 2000.

Kohn, Hans. *The Idea of Nationalism: A Study in Its Origin and Background*. New York: Collier, 1967.

Laqueur, Walter. *Fascism: Past, Present, Future*. New York: Oxford UP, 1996.

Mack Smith, Denis. *Mussolini*. New York: Knopf, 1982.

Mosse, George. *The Crisis of German Ideology: Intellectual Origins of the Third Reich*. New York: Grosset, 1964.

Nolte, Ernst. *Three Faces of Fascism: Action Française, Italian Fascism, National Socialism*. Trans. Leila Vennewitz. New York: Holt, 1965.

Orchard, David. *The Fight for Canada: Four Centuries of Resistance to American Expansionism*. Montreal: Robert Davies Multimedia, 1998.

Parizeau, Jacques. *Pour un Québec souverain*. Montreal: VLB, 1997.

Payne, Stanley G. *A History of Fascism, 1914–1945*. Madison, WI: U of Wisconsin P, 1996.

———. "Fascism and Racism," in Terence Ball and Richard Bellamy, eds., *The Cambridge History of Twentieth-Century Political Thought*. Cambridge: Cambridge UP, 2003.

———. *Fascism. Comparison and Definition*. Madison: U. of Wisconsin Press, 1980.

Pfaff, William. *The Wrath of Nations: Civilization and the Furies of Nationalism*. New York: Simon, 1993.

Southern Poverty Law Center. *False Patriots: The Threat of Anti-Government Extremists*. Montgomery, AL: Southern Poverty Law Center, 1996.

Sternhell, Zeev, et al. *The Birth of Fascist Ideology: From Cultural Rebellion to Political Revolution*. Trans. David Maisel. Princeton, NJ: Princeton UP, 1993.

Thompson, Leonard. *The Political Mythology of Apartheid*. New Haven, CT: Yale UP, 1985.

Campbell, Colin, and William Christian. *Parties, Leaders and Ideologies in Canada.* Toronto: McGraw-Hill, 1996 (Chapter 5).

Clarkson, Stephen. *Uncle Sam and Us: Globalization, Neoconservatism, and the Canadian State.* Toronto: U of Toronto P, 2002.

Fraser, Graham. *René Lévesque and the Parti Québécois in Power.* Montreal: McGill-Queen's UP, 2001.

Grant, George. *Lament for a Nation.* Toronto: McClelland, 1965.

Kohn, Hans. *The Idea of Nationalism: A Study in Its Origin and Background.* New York: Collier, 1967.

Orchard, David. *The Fight for Canada: Four Centuries of Resistance to American Expansionism.* Montreal: Robert Davies Multimedia, 1998.

Parizeau, Jacques. *Pour un Québec souverain.* Montreal: VLB, 1997.

Useful Websites and Social Media

www.kkk.com Ku Klux Klan

http://www.alleanzanazionale.it National Alliance (Italy)

http://www.natvan.com National Alliance (United States)

www.frontnational.com National Front (France)

www.nsm88.com National Socialist Movement

www.natfront.com National Front (UK)

www.stormfront.org Stormfront

www.natparty.com Nationalist Party of Canada

www.zundelsite.org Official website of Ernst Zundel

http://actionparty.ca/ Canadian Action Party

Twitter:

@partiquebecois Parti Quebecois

@M_Ignatieff Michael Ignatieff

From the Ball and Dagger Reader *Ideals and Ideologies*, US Eighth Edition

Part Seven: Fascism

7.45. Joseph-Arthur de Gobineau—Civilization and Race, page 288
7.46. Benito Mussolini—The Doctrine of Fascism, page 295
7.47. Alfredo Rocco—The Political Theory of Fascism, page 303
7.48. Adolf Hitler—Nation and Race, page 309

Discussion Questions

1. Are contemporary European movements that are anti-immigrant and hostile to Islam fascist? Why or why not?
2. What is the future of Quebec nationalism?
3. What are the principal differences between fascism and nationalism?
4. Does nationalism play a significant role in Canadian politics today?

MySearchLab   MySearchLab with eText offers you access to an online interactive version of the text, additional quizzes and assessment, extensive help with your writing and research projects, and provides round-the-clock access to credible and reliable source material. Go to **www.mysearchlab.com** to access these resources.

CHAPTER 10

Populism

You shall not crucify humanity on a cross of gold.

William Jennings Bryan, *Speech to the Democratic National Convention***, July 9, 1896**

LEARNING OBJECTIVES

After completing this chapter you should be able to

1. Define the term *populism* and show how it differs from other ideologies.

2. Show how populism fits into the triadic model.

3. Describe the different American and Canadian groups or interests with which populism has allied itself.

4. Illustrate how populism performs the four functions of an ideology: explanatory, evaluative, orientative, and programmatic.

INTRODUCTION

Populism is an ideology based on a belief in "the ability of ordinary people to act together politically."[1] Indeed, the word *populism* is derived from the Latin word *populus,* which means "the people." As we saw in Chapter 9, fascism views the people as a whole that is united by ties of ethnicity and nationality and ruled by an often charismatic elite that either attains or maintains its predominance by nondemocratic means. Nationalism defines a people in relation to a common language, culture, or shared ethnicity. By contrast, populism views the people as a whole that possesses political wisdom and virtue greater than that of any individual and, without the interference of any interest group or faction, as the source of the truest expression of democracy. As we noted in Chapter 2, people acting together in a unity of will and purpose not only express the general will of the community but also can direct it to the common good, transcending the special interests of individuals or groups. Unlike fascism, however, populism believes that ordinary people can act together in this way, without the need for authoritarian or charismatic leaders.

Populism received its chief intellectual inspiration from eighteenth-century French political philosopher Jean-Jacques Rousseau (1712–1778). Rousseau sought to revive the direct democracy practised in classical Greek city-states such as Athens, where the direct vote of the citizens expressed the general will. He believed that the general will of the people was virtuous, transcending the weaknesses and failings of the individual. Acting together, the common people could overcome the greed and corruption of individuals who frustrated the realization of the greater good of the people. Populism also draws upon John Locke's idea of a peaceful and harmonious state of nature and the Renaissance republican tradition, which denounced corruption and division based on special interests—a point echoed strongly in the United States in the late eighteenth century. The notion that the original harmonious and uncorrupted state of the people has

---

[1]"Populism," *Canadian Encyclopedia,* 2nd ed.1150.

been corrupted by special interests—an idea central to populism—flows out of this historic tradition.

The populist view of society is essentially liberal: Society is composed of equal and independent individuals who for the most part are honest, self-determining, and hard working. However, society is corrupted by the greed and power of certain self-interested groups and individuals. Such groups and individuals represent special or limited interests that are at odds with the common good of society, as expressed through the will of the majority of ordinary citizens in the democratic process. These special interests frustrate the popular will either by interfering with the electoral process (excessive or improper spending), or by seducing the elected representatives of the people in far-off (both spatially and culturally) capital cities with promises of position or other rewards, or by lodging power in self-interested groups like bureaucracies, corporations, and unions. Populism has been aptly described by intellectual historian Trevor Harrison as "a movement that . . . stresses the worth of the common people and advocates their political supremacy, rejects intermediate associations between the mass and leaders, and directs its protest against some groups that lie outside the local society."[2]

Often, populism has been defined by what it opposes rather than by what it is for, despite its belief in the common man, the ordinary people, or the average citizen. Sometimes, the enemies of the common good have been business groups such as banks, large railway and mining companies, and monopolies. This perspective sometimes gives populism a left-wing character. Other times, the enemies of the common good have been seemingly corrupt trade unions, insensitive and distant bureaucracies, people perceived to be abusing the welfare system, and minority groups seeking recognition of rights (such as gay or Aboriginal groups). This perspective sometimes gives populism a right-wing character. Because of these variations, some theorists argue that populism is not really a separate ideology, but merely a different form of liberalism. In our view, populism is sufficiently distinctive and has played such an important role in the politics of Canada and, to a lesser degree, the United States that it deserves to be treated as an ideology unto itself.

Populism tends to be cyclical. It strengthens and erupts when social and political circumstances or a sufficiently charismatic leader provoke a populist response. For that reason, we will look at periods when populism has been on the upswing, because it is at these times that the nature of populist thinking is easiest to see. It should not be forgotten, however, that populist tendencies endure even when populism's fortunes ebb, and that they may still influence, albeit more subtly, political parties and the general climate of political opinion.

One of populism's most notable features is its rejection of intermediate associations between the mass of ordinary people and its leaders. This rejection flows from the populists' suspicion of factions, self-seeking individuals, and interest groups (or in some cases, traditional political parties) who put self-interest above the common good. As a result, populist movements have typically established entirely new local organizations led by charismatic leaders to bypass existing political parties. Political parties themselves have become the target of populist attack for distorting or blocking the views of the people, and populists have at times sought to replace political parties with representatives under the more direct control of the people. The theories of group government developed

---

[2]Trevor Harrison, *Of Passionate Intensity* (Toronto: U of Toronto P, 1995) 5.

in Alberta in the 1920s (discussed below) are a good example of this tendency. In rebelling against and rejecting the elites in traditional political parties, populists tend to become dependent on charismatic leaders who lead protest movements. Populists on both the left and right also often seek reform of political institutions to reduce the influence of special interest groups or the corrupting power of money and traditional elites, whether in political parties or in society in general. Measures such as the recall, the initiative, and the referendum, widely promoted by populists, seek to increase direct popular control of elected representatives and direct expression of the general will.

Populism appealed to and idealized independent and self-determining individuals whose judgment was not corrupted on the one hand by lack of education, poverty, or extreme economic dependence, or on the other hand by extreme wealth and power such as that possessed by bankers, aristocrats, and industrialists. In Marxist terms, populism was particularly attractive to the petite bourgeoisie, those people who were neither employed by others and thus not dependent on employers, nor employing of others and thus unable to direct or influence their judgment. In many ways, the ideal populist was the independent Canadian or American farmer or small-business person; it was not by accident that populism in Canada and the United States found its strongest support where groups of these people have been most prominent: in the Prairie provinces in Canada, and the Great Plains states in the United States.

According to the triadic model, used in this book to illustrate the nature of ideologies, in populism, the agent is the people, uncorrupted and acting as a unity; the obstacle is the influence of special or vested interests acting against the interests of the people; and the goal is the implementation of the general will—the will of the people—to defeat the corruption of special interest. (See Figure 10.1.)

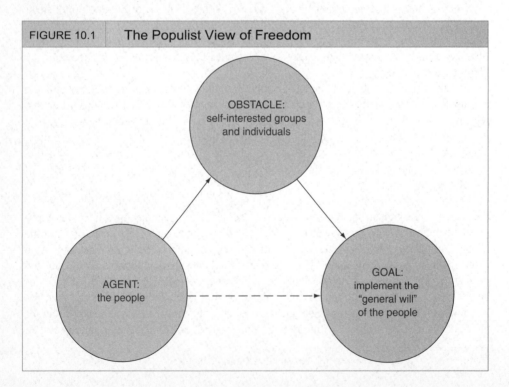

FIGURE 10.1	The Populist View of Freedom

OBSTACLE:
self-interested groups
and individuals

AGENT:
the people

GOAL:
implement the
"general will"
of the people

POPULISM IN THE UNITED STATES

Left-wing populism first became a significant political force in the United States. Its high point was the 1890s. During that time, farmers in the newly settled Great Plains states and in some southern cotton-growing areas were dependent on large monopolistic railway companies to send their crops to market and on banks for credit in times of need. In addition, railway companies, other corporations, and wealthy individuals often held large blocks of land for speculative purposes and hindered development in some communities. As well, the 1890s witnessed a prolonged economic depression that many believed was caused or worsened by a shortage in the money supply. The United States used the gold standard—United States bank notes were redeemable in gold, and the amount of money in circulation and credit available was restricted by the amount of gold available. The shortage in the money supply had a deflationary effect; that is, it caused prices to drop (the opposite of inflation), which was disastrous for farmers, whose income was directly affected by price level. This hard money policy also restricted the credit available to farmers.

Although these conditions existed prior to the 1890s, they were worsened by the economic depression and its accompanying drop in agricultural prices, as well as by the rise in railway rates resulting from the consolidation of railways into large monopolistic companies. In 1892 a number of regional farmers' organizations, generally referred to as the Farmers' Alliance, came together in Omaha, Nebraska, to found the People's Party. The Omaha platform, adopted at that convention, encapsulated populist demands:

- reform of the monetary system, including an increase in the money supply, the use of silver-backed currency rather than gold (the quotation at the beginning of this chapter is from Bryan's famous attack on the gold standard), the issuance of bank notes by the government rather than by banks, and stricter government regulation of banks

- reduction in protective tariffs

- public ownership of railroad, telegraph, and telephone systems

- release of large landholdings for settlement

- political reform, including the introduction of the secret ballot[3]

Other populist demands included the direct election of senators and the imposition of an income tax. The People's Party enjoyed its highest level of support under William Jennings Bryan in the U.S. presidential election of 1896.

The demands of the People's Party were consistent with the main features of left-wing populism: that the collective judgment of ordinary people is particularly virtuous, and that special interest groups, factions, and elites (self-seeking individuals) are the enemies of the common good. Historian Michael Kazin describes the populist view this way:

> Populist speakers in the United States voiced a profound outrage with elites who ignored, corrupted and/or betrayed the core ideal of American democracy: ruled by the common people who expected their fellow citizens to advance by diligence, practical intelligence, and a faith in God alone.[4]

---

[3]See Robert C. McMath, Jr., *American Populism: A Social History, 1877–1898* (New York: Noonday, 1993) 167.
[4]Michael Kazin, *The Populist Persuasion: An American History* (New York: Basic, 1995) 2.

Kazin argues that the moral outrage expressed in the great populist uprising in the 1890s split left-wing populism into two divergent streams. The small independent farmers who had been the backbone of the People's Party began to diminish in number and power. Meanwhile, a new first stream of left-wing populism was growing in the labour movement, which viewed the worker as the average man and trade unions as the champion of the worker. This stream (in the absence of any strong socialist movement or tradition in the United States) inspired a long struggle in the first half of the twentieth century by the labour movement against corporate employers. At the same time, another new stream of left-wing populism developed within the evangelical Protestant movement, which initially shared the populist struggle for temperance and prohibition of the liquor trusts in the early twentieth century. But the middle-class (and often female) temperance movement often lacked sympathy with the workers and immigrants who championed trade unions (and often frequented bars). Kazin concludes that the resulting division in American left-wing populism remained:

> The gap between those who see ordinary Americans primarily in economic terms and those who view the people as belonging to God has never really closed. And it continues to divide populist persuaders today. Activists who blame an immoral, agnostic media for America's problems have little in common with those who indict corporations for moving jobs overseas.[5]

In the latter part of the twentieth century, American populism shifted gradually to the right. The enemies of the common good were no longer corporations and business interests, but government and media elites perceived as amoral and irreligious, if not atheistic. Government and media elites were viewed as threatening the traditional values of America because they supported minority groups seeking special assistance and status (for example, in affirmative action policies, abortion rights, and gay rights). They were also viewed as betraying American values by unpatriotic attacks on American military and foreign policy. The candidacy of Sarah Palin for the Republican nomination for the 2008 American presidential election and the subsequent eruption of the Tea Party movement in the Republican Party illustrate the persistence of right-wing populism in U.S. political culture.

On the other hand, the populist backlash against the financial crisis that began in 2008 is directed against traditional targets of left-wing populism in the United States—the banks and other financial institutions and wealthy individuals who were perceived to have profited on the backs of ordinary people. The Occupy movement, which appeared in New York in 2011 and spread rapidly to other U.S. and Canadian cities, is one very visible expression of this.

POPULISM IN CANADA

Populism in Canada, as in the United States, originated with and enjoyed its strongest support from farmers in the Prairies and in the traditionally Clear Grit rural areas of southwestern Ontario. It was strongly influenced by developments in the United States and, in particular, by an American farm organization called the National Grange, which began to organize in Canada in the 1870s.

The three main features of early Canadian populism were quite predictable: "faith in democracy, hatred of corporate wealth, and distrust of the political system."[6] The Canadian

---

[5]Kazin 4.

[6]D. L. Morton, *The Progressive Party in Canada* (Toronto: U of Toronto P, 1950) 26.

populist faith in democracy reflected the fundamental populist trust in the virtue of the expressed popular will. In the early twentieth century, populists sought to bring about institutional reform to enable the popular will to be more clearly and forcefully expressed through techniques such as the initiative, the referendum, and the recall. Western populists were also among the first in Canada to define *the people* in a political sense to include women and to support the extension of the franchise to women. In fact, the vote was first extended to women in provincial elections in Manitoba, Saskatchewan, and Alberta during the second decade of the twentieth century.

Populists considered that the existing political system was corrupted by the influence of central Canadian corporate interests, which seduced the elective representatives of the people sent to distant Ottawa. R. C. Henders, the president of the Manitoba Grain Growers Association, stated in 1912, "We are governed by an elective aristocracy, which in its turn is largely governed by an aristocracy of wealth. Behind the government and the legislators are the corporations and trusts and behind the political monopolists are the industrial monopolists."[7] Reforms to the electoral system would allow the people to express their view without distortion or corruption and to "break the hold of the 'bosses.'"[8]

The United Farmers and the Progressive Party

Until the beginning of the First World War in 1914, populist pressures in western Canada had been largely contained within the Liberal Party. However, during the First World War, farm organizations felt that the Liberal Party did not adequately represent their interests. They ran candidates in provincial elections and formed governments under the United Farmers banner in Alberta and Manitoba, and, in 1919, in Ontario. Members of the United Farmers organizations banded together to form the **Progressive** Party at the federal level, which succeeded in becoming the second largest party in the 1921 election. The Progressive Party identified the now-familiar enemies of the people as eastern corporate interests that controlled the railways and the grain trade to the detriment of farmers. The party called for regulation or public ownership of railways and the grain-handling industry. It enjoyed some success, with the establishment of large farmer-owned cooperative grain companies.

Perhaps the biggest grievance of Canadian populists was the customs tariff that forced western farmers to buy expensive manufactured products from central Canada rather than cheaper imported goods from the United States. The United Farmers' platform of 1919 argued that the protective tariff

> fostered combines, trusts and gentlemen's agreements in almost every line of Canadian industrial enterprise . . . [making] . . . "the rich richer and the poor poorer" and "has been and is a chief corrupting influence in our national life because the protected interest, in order to maintain their unjust privileges, have contributed lavishly to political and campaign funds, thus encouraging both political parties to look to them for support, thereby lowering the standard of public morality."[9]

In 1921, the Progressive Party sought immediate free trade with the United States for food and agricultural equipment and a substantial reduction in all other tariffs.

---

[7]Morton 25.
[8]Morton 16.
[9]"United Farmers' Platform, 1919," reprinted in D. O. Carrigan, *Canadian Party Platforms 1867–1968* (Toronto: Copp, 1968) 91.

Falling prices in the United States in the 1890s had caused many American farmers to lose their farms and had led to a left-wing populist call for monetary reform. Prices were more stable in Canada, so, while the banks were not beloved by the populists, monetary and banking policy did not become a major issue until the Depression of the 1930s.

The Theory of Group Government

When peace and prosperity returned to Canada in the early 1920s, the Progressive Party's popularity declined. The party was divided between those who rejected party politics and the parliamentary system, and those who wished to make the Progressive movement into a reformist political party. Many members left and rejoined the Liberal Party, while others gradually drifted toward socialism. More radical Progressives, mostly from Alberta, remained with the party and turned their attention to a political theory they called *group government* (discussed below). In his book *The Farmers and Politics* (1920), William Irvine, a leading Progressive radical, argued that social and economic circumstances in Canada had changed as a result of the pressures of the First World War in a way that the traditional political parties did not satisfactorily explain or deal with. The farmers, on the other hand, had a clearer vision. According to Irvine, it was

> the privilege and duty of organized farmers to show the better way in politics and industry. All parties are like them. . . . In their economic oppression and political wandering, the farmers have discovered the new law and the new hope. They do not seek to destroy, but to fulfill government; they do not want to compete with exploiters for the lion's share of the plunder, but seek true cooperation in all things of the highest common good.[10]

Farmers were the appropriate heralds of the better way because they transcended divisions in society between capital and labour: "The farmer, in reality, combines in his own profession the two antagonists. He is both capitalist and labourer."[11] Farmers were the true representatives of the people, and Irvine believed that unity of capital and labour in the farmer would allow the farmers to replace the destructive individualism that allowed the few rich and powerful to exploit the many. With a philosophy that treated group organization as the first democratic union, farmers could lead the people to "cohesion, concentration, solidarity, united action and co-operation."

However, Irvine did not view farmers as a class defined by socio-economic position, as Marxist analysts would have. For Irvine, classes were the rich and privileged or the exploited, dependent, and manipulated poor, neither of whose views represented the common good. Irvine stated that "the history of Canada is the record of the rise, development and supremacy of class rule." The farmers' movement would end this class privilege: "The group policy, logically followed, will prevent any class from dominating. Group organization does not imply class legislation. It is the negation of class legislation."[12] These views and the policy prescriptions that followed from them were quite compatible with the views of more moderate Canadian socialists. As a result, in the 1930s, some former Progressives joined forces with the Co-operative Commonwealth Federation (CCF). The fact that the CCF formed the first democratically elected social democratic government in North America in Saskatchewan in 1944 in an overwhelmingly rural

---

[10]William Irvine, *The Farmer and Politics* (Toronto: McClelland, 1920) 98–99.
[11]Irvine 158.
[12]Irvine 98–99, 101, 157, 158, 168, 198, 193, 202–208.

nonindustrial environment (representing what has been described as agrarian socialism) was in part due to the absorption of populist ideas and attitudes by the CCF. Conversely, socialism in western Canada has always had populist undertones.

Social Credit and Populism

If the Depression drove some former populists to socialism, it drove others to the older American populist preoccupation with the perceived evils of the banking system. In Canada, this preoccupation was expressed most strongly in the Social Credit movement, particularly in Alberta. The Social Credit Party was founded in Alberta in 1935 when William ("Bible Bill") Aberhart (1878–1943), a former school teacher and popular Calgary radio preacher, discovered the teachings of British economist Major Clifford Douglas. The social credit theory put forth by Douglas appealed to western Canadian populists for two reasons. First, Douglas argued that the solutions to the economic dislocation and hardship of the Depression were not to be found in the discredited party system but in technical economic arguments—a reason that appealed to the nonpartisan strain of populist thought. Second, Douglas argued that capitalist societies produced chronic underconsumption, which should be remedied by increasing the money supply. This "soft money" thinking was closely aligned with that of American populists in the 1890s, such as William Jennings Bryan. Douglas's theory, set out in the famous $A + B = C$ formula, was that the cost of manufactured goods (C) was only partially returned to individuals in the form of wages and rent (A), and that the remainder (B) disappeared in depreciation and interest paid to banks. The solution to this shortfall was to create social credit by printing more money equivalent to B in the equation and giving it to the people to spend.

The Social Credit movement demonized bankers and the banking system further than most previous populists by adding a distinctly anti-Semitic element to its arguments. In 1937 the Social Credit Party of Alberta accepted the anti-Semitic forgery called the

William Aberhart (1878–1943)

Protocols of the Elders of Zion (see Chapter 9), which purported to describe a plan for world domination by an international conspiracy of Jews, communists, and bankers. The Social Credit movement never fully escaped association with this anti-Semitic element, an unfortunate byproduct of the populist tendency to view groups outside the local society as suspicious and as potential enemies of the common good.

POPULISM IN CANADA TODAY

With the return of prosperity during and after the Second World War, populist feeling subsided but did not disappear in western Canada. There were, for example, echoes of populist rebellion in the election campaigns of 1957 and 1958, when Saskatchewan-based John Diefenbaker championed Main Street against Bay Street, the symbol of Canada's financial interests.

Populism did not become a serious force again until the 1980s, by which time its focus had significantly shifted. In the 1980s, the enemies of the common good were central Canadian bureaucrats and politicians pressing for French-language rights and Aboriginal groups pressing land and other treaty claims; welfare recipients perceived to be living parasitically off the hard-working majority; and judges, intellectuals, and media elites who championed the rights of minority groups. Like the populist movement in the early part of the twentieth century, this movement was also centred in western Canada and parts of rural Ontario and was driven powerfully by the same sense of distance and alienation from the centres of power in eastern Canada.

The issue that first ignited populist feeling was the question of the position and status of Quebec in Confederation and the related bilingualism policies of the federal government. French-speaking Canadians and Quebec as a province had always enjoyed certain constitutional guarantees, including the right to use French in certain federal institutions and to have a minimum number of Supreme Court justices drawn from the Quebec Bar. During the 1960s, Quebec nationalism grew, which led the federal government to treat Quebec somewhat differently from other provinces with respect to certain federal programs and taxing policies. The federal government also substantially increased the protection of and support for the use of the French language outside Quebec. For English-Canadian populists, particularly in the west, this appeared to be a denial of the fundamental equality of all Canadians. Populists viewed francophones as they had viewed wealthy business interests in the past—as a special interest group acting contrary to the overall common good.

In its most extreme form, this feeling was represented by groups such as the Confederation of Regions Party, which existed in New Brunswick in the 1980s and advocated ending the official status of the French language in Canada and extending English common law to Quebec to replace its distinctive civil code. Only a small minority in New Brunswick supported this position, which verged on being racist. However, opposition to special status for Quebec received much broader support during the controversies over the attempts of Progressive Conservative Prime Minister Brian Mulroney's government to accommodate Quebec nationalism in the Constitution through the Meech Lake Accord of 1987 and the Charlottetown Accord of 1992. Both of these accords eventually failed in the face of strong opposition in parts of English-speaking Canada. The apparent special status these agreements gave to Quebecois and First Nations people, combined with the circumstances of their making—in far-off Ottawa behind closed doors—triggered the worst fears of populists.

The Reform Party Movement

It was this strong opposition that was a major factor in the rise of the Reform Party, which was founded in 1987 under the leadership of Preston Manning. In response to the demands for special status for Quebec, Manning and the Reform Party insisted that all provinces be treated in an identical manner. The party's most prominent expression of that policy was its Triple E proposal for the Senate—that it be equal (the same number of senators from each province), elected, and effective.

Although the initial focus of the Reform Party were the issues surrounding Quebec and bilingualism, other groups that asserted their distinct identity or sought particular support or protection from governments also drew the ire of populists. Thus, the Reform Party opposed special treatment or status for First Nations or for multicultural groups and related multiculturalism policies. Similarly, the Reform Party criticized what it believed was preferential treatment given to immigrants and refugees who, implicitly, were treated as being foreign to Canada and seeking special privileges or assistance unavailable to ordinary Canadians. Hostility also extended to groups whose behaviours or values diverged from the populist ideal of the independent and self-determining individual—the poor and the unemployed, for example. Reformers therefore often criticized welfare policies as being overly generous and unfair to the working people whose taxes supported them. The new populists in the Reform Party connected these illegitimate claims to the system of government. Preston Manning advocated the following reforms in his book *The New Canada* (1991): ending special status for groups, altering bilingualism and multiculturalism policies, treating Quebec as a province like any other, and reforming the Senate so that all provinces were equally represented. Because the Reformers identified the federal government and bureaucracy as the champions of these groups, they championed decentralization of power to the provinces (which were seen as closer to the people and easier to prevent from straying from the path the people wanted) and reducing taxes (particularly at the federal level) as a means of reducing the ability of government to follow these elitist policies.[13]

While the focus of the Reform Party was in many respects very different from populists earlier in the century, in one important respect it remained the same. Populists in the Reform Party blamed many of the problems they identified on a defective political system that either frustrated the will of the people or corrupted their elected representatives in far-off Ottawa. Therefore, the Reform Party resurrected the familiar demand for institutional reforms raised by earlier populists: the initiative, the recall, and the referendum, as well as tight control of Members of Parliament by their local party constituency associations. Preston Manning wrote, "The Reform Party's principles call for us to recognize the duty of members of caucus to represent the will of their constituents in cases where there is a clear consensus within the constituency."[14]

As we noted earlier in this chapter, populism has allied itself with or sympathized with different groups or interests at different points in time. In the 1980s, the perceived enemies of the people were, generally speaking, not business interests. The Reform Party was sympathetic to business liberalism, and its economic policy was closely aligned with

---

[13]Preston Manning, *The New Canada* (Toronto: McClelland, 1991) 21. Manning wrote, "The tradition road is . . . marked by constitutional signposts that say Founding Peoples, Official Bilingualism, Government-Supported Multiculturalism and Special Status."

[14]Manning 322.

business liberal thinking. Manning's position was that "reducing federal spending to the point at which it results in a lower tax burden on Canada and reduces both the cost of living and the cost of doing business in this country is the single most important step towards getting Canada's economic house in order."[15] Canadian right-wing populism has also allied itself with the Religious Right, which objects to the extension of abortion rights and gay marriage. Right-wing populists see these trends as creating special classes of people and therefore even more vested interests.

The Reform Party–Progressive Conservative Merger

The Reform Party's sympathy with business liberal views of late twentieth century populism was a significant factor in the eventual decision of the Reform Party (by late 2003 named the Canadian Reform Conservative Alliance) to merge with the Progressive Conservative Party to form the Conservative Party of Canada in December 2003. In March 2004, former Canadian Alliance leader (and early Reform Party member) Stephen Harper became party leader and, following the January 2006 election, prime minister. The merged Conservative Party platform in subsequent elections (2004, 2006, 2008, and 2011) placed progressively less emphasis on populist policies such as the recall, the referendum, and constitutional reforms, which may indicate that populist ideas are once again subsiding in Canada. In office, the Harper government arguably paid only lip service to populist principles in forcing a free vote on reviewing gay marriage but has moved forward cautiously with proposals for an elected Senate. In its quest for electoral gains in Quebec, the Harper government flirted with proposals that would once have been anathema to western populism, including acceptance of the proposition that Quebec is a nation within a united Canada. However, it is possible to discern populist influence in its fiscal and taxation policy, which has relied heavily on reductions in the Goods and Services Tax (GST). The decision to reduce the GST rather than personal income taxes was unpopular with business liberals, big business groups generally, and academic free market economists but attractive to many of the small business, working class, or rural voters attracted by right-wing populism. The Harper government's strong support for the Canadian military and for traditional national symbols such as the monarchy may also reflect right-wing populist distrust of various dissenting minority groups perceived to be critical of or hostile to those institutions.

The melding of populist and business liberal ideas in the new Conservative Party is evident in a 2005 publication by Mike Harris, the former Progressive Conservative premier of Ontario (1995–2002), and Preston Manning, the intellectual father of the Reform movement and the first leader of the Reform Party, entitled *A Canada Strong and Free*. It identifies a "democratic deficit" in Canada characterized by popular apathy, indifference, and even hostility to democratic institutions and processes attributable to familiar populist targets:

- elected representatives prevented by political parties or a too-powerful executive from pressing the views of their constituents
- activist judges who usurp the proper function of legislators

---

[15]Manning 337.

- the inability of voters to directly influence government decisions or to control their elected representatives

- inadequate representation of regional or provincial interests in the federal government

- excessive influence of unelected bureaucrats in framing government policy

- administration of government programs and policies by distant bureaucracies

While allowing for institutional reforms (presumably including Reform policies such as an elected Senate), the principal objective of the Harris/Manning proposals is to reduce the size of government, and particularly the federal government, by reducing taxes and thereby the degree of government intervention in the economy. "Big bureaucratic government is by its very nature less amenable to democratic control than limited government . . . commands too large a proportion of the nation's resources . . . makes too many decisions . . . assumes too many responsibilities, thereby restricting the resources, decisions and responsibilities left in the hands of free and responsible citizens."[16]

Coupled with this is the prescription that resources and responsibilities for policy making and delivery of services be decentralized and localized as much as possible. These proposals dovetail closely with the business liberal preference for lower taxes and deregulation. They also illustrate how business interests have gone from being one of the objects of left-wing populist attack to either an ally or an emanation of the people in the right-wing populism that is dominant in Canada today (and that has captured the votes of many erstwhile supporters of the CCF/NDP, which inherited the mantle of left-wing populism in the twentieth century).

POPULISM ELSEWHERE

Although populism had its intellectual origins in continental Europe, it has enjoyed the most success in former British colonial societies. In part, this occurred because liberal individualism, a fundamental feature of populism, is strong in colonial societies. As well, this success probably results from the fact that these societies are ethnically heterogeneous and are not receptive to full-blown ethnic nationalism. Accordingly, in English-speaking countries, the definition of *the people* is broad (although it may well exclude some minority or immigrant groups) rather than narrowly restricted to a specific group; as a result of the combination of liberal individualism and resistance to ethnic nationalism, colonial populism did not degenerate into extreme nationalist or xenophobic movements. In contrast, some European populist groups explicitly attacked immigrants and racial minorities and emphasized strong, if not authoritarian, leadership. Examples of such groups are the Italian Social Movement, France's National Front, and the Austrian Freedom Party. Other European groups have not taken as extreme a position and are arguably representative of the more right-wing, anti-bureaucratic variety of populism that has predominated in Canada and the United States in recent years. Examples of such groups include the Northern League and Forza Italia in Italy. The left-wing populism of the PASOK party in Greece is the one exception to this position. There were strong populist tendencies in the British Conservative Party led by Margaret Thatcher in the

---

[16]Harris, Mike, and Manning, Preston, *A Canada Strong and Free* (Vancouver: The Fraser Institute, 2005).

1980s, who mobilized public support against special interest groups such as unions. However, populism remains strongest in Canada and the United States for the reasons discussed above.

Conclusion

Populism as an Ideology

Like other ideologies we have discussed, populist ideas and the objects of populist concern have changed significantly over time. Nevertheless, common core assumptions or attitudes are evident from an examination of the way in which populism performs the four functions that all ideologies perform.

Explanatory Function. Like nationalism, populism does not present a comprehensive explanation of why social conditions are the way they are. Populists identify certain special interest groups, elites, and institutional structures and practices that frustrate the general will of the people and corrupt the virtue of the people acting together. Populists believe that fighting these interests, institutions, and structures ensures that the true general will of the people will govern. According to populists, it is the expression of this general will that benefits the state and its citizens.

Evaluative Function. Populists evaluate social conditions by identifying the special interests that frustrate, or corrupt, the general will of the people. If these special interests and their selfish purposes are identified and opposed, the people will be better off and the greater good of the people will be furthered.

Orientative Function. Populists view the people as common or ordinary citizens rather than members of a social or economic class, or a linguistic or ethnic group. While at times populists may identify *the people* with the particular dominant linguistic or ethnic group in a society, that identification is not central to the populist outlook. What is important is a person's identity as one of the people whose collective will, when expressed and put into effect, will further the well-being both of the individual and of society as a whole.

Programmatic Function. The populist goal is to defeat special interests and ensure that the general will prevails. As we have seen, the content of the general will is unspecified and changes depending on which interests are perceived to be acting against it. Populism's consistent focus over time, however, is the defeat of special interests and the triumph of the general will.

Populism and the Democratic Ideal

Populism began as an attempt to recreate the ideal direct democracy of classic times. Because it stresses the importance and virtue of the will of the majority of the people acting together, populism is difficult to conceive of outside a democratic political system. At the same time, the rejection of intermediate associations and frequent dependence on charismatic leaders may sometimes give populism an authoritarian tinge. In addition, populism tends to be less sympathetic to minority interests (which were often perceived as special or selfish interests) and sometimes diverges from the liberal values that are often associated with democracy.

For Further Reading

Clanton, Gene. *Congressional Populism and the Crisis of the 1890s.* Kansas: UP of Kansas, 1998.

Dobbin, Murray. *Preston Manning and the Reform Party.* Toronto: Lorimer, 1991.

Flanagan, Tom. *Waiting for the Wave: the Reform Party and the Conservative Movement.* Toronto: Stoddart, 1995.

Harrison, Trevor. *Of Passionate Intensity: Right Wing Populism and the Reform Party of Canada.* Toronto: U of Toronto P, 1995.

Hayward, Jack, ed. *Elitism, Populism and European Politics.* Oxford: Clarendon, 1996.

Kazin, Michael. *The Populist Persuasion: An American History.* New York: Basic, 1995.

Laycock, David. *Populism and Democratic Thought in the Canadian Prairies, 1910–1945.* Toronto: U of Toronto P, 1990.

———. *The New Right and Democracy in Canada: Understanding Reform and the Canadian Alliance.* Don Mills: Oxford UP, 2002.

Manning, Preston. *The New Canada.* Toronto: McClelland, 1991.

McMath, Robert C., Jr. *American Populism: A Social History, 1877–1898.* New York: Noonday, 1993.

Morton, D.L. *The Progressive Party in Canada.* Toronto: U of Toronto P, 1950.

Palin, Sarah. *America by Heart: Reflections on family, faith, and flag.* New York: Harper, 2010.

Useful Websites and Social Media

www.thecanadianencyclopedia.com/articles/populism The Canadian Encyclopedia "Populism"

www.teapartypatriots.org American Tea Party Movement

http://faculty.marianopolis.edu/c.belanger/quebechistory/encyclopedia/ProgressivePartyofCanada.htm Marianopolis College "Progressive Party of Canada"

www.politicalpapers.ucalgary.ca/reform University of Calgary "Reform Party of Canada"

www.ontariopc.com Ontario PC Party

www.ndp.ca Canada's New Democrats

Twitter:

@ontariopcparty

Discussion Questions

1. Is it correct to describe Rousseau as the father of populism?

2. What factors contributed to the growth of populism in the late nineteenth and early twentieth centuries in Canada and the United States?

3. Is it surprising that many people in Western Canada who supported the CCF/NDP in the 1950s and 1960s turned to the Reform Party and the Conservatives after 1990?

4. Is there any basis for classifying some European right-wing groups, such as the French National Front, as populist?

MySearchLab   MySearchLab with eText offers you access to an online interactive version of the text, additional quizzes and assessment, extensive help with your writing and research projects, and provides round-the-clock access to credible and reliable source material. Go to **www.mysearchlab.com** to access these resources.

CHAPTER 11

The Politics of Entitlement and Identity

Man is born free, yet everywhere he is in chains. . . . The one who thinks himself the master of others is as much a slave as they.

Jean-Jacques Rousseau, *The Social Contract*

LEARNING OBJECTIVES

After completing this chapter you should be able to

1. Explain the four features of the movements associated with the politics of identity.

2. Describe Aboriginal rights movements in Canada, the United States, Australia, and New Zealand.

3. Analyze how the politics of identity runs counter to liberalism.

4. Discuss the twentieth-century social movements of identity.

5. Identify the ways that the politics of identity perform the four functions of an ideology.

As we saw in Chapter 4, classical liberalism views people in highly individualistic terms. According to this ideology, all people are equal: Each person possesses an identical bundle of rights and is entitled to have those rights respected as part of the implied contract between each person in society. The type of equality referred to in this context is equality of status and opportunity—an equal right to compete in the race of life—not equality of condition, as sought by socialism—an equal right to compete *and* finish the race at the same place. The idea that individuals have an identical bundle of rights reflects the political and economic values of the largely English-speaking societies out of which liberalism arose—what John Locke called the right to life, liberty, and the enjoyment of property or, in the words of Thomas Jefferson in the American Declaration of Independence, the right to "life, liberty and the pursuit of happiness."

Although liberal theorists such as Locke and Jefferson may have thought they were expressing universal, and universally valued, propositions, in fact, they and other liberals reflected the particular values and prejudices of their societies. American liberals, for example, claimed liberty for all, but denied it to African Americans in the extreme through slavery. Until the beginning of the twentieth century, women were denied political rights and were subject to societal restraints related to their work opportunities, their reproductive freedom, and their freedom from the ties of family. As well, Aboriginal peoples were often denied political or economic rights, and their culture was not valued; they were expected to and were often coerced to assimilate to the dominant white society in Canada, the United States, Australia, and New Zealand. Also, lesbian, gay, bisexual, and transgendered and/or queer peoples (LGBTQs) were denied rights with respect to sexual identity and practice, gender expression, and the family (e.g., adoption, parenting, marriage).

THE PURSUIT OF EQUALITY AND IDENTITY

At various points in the twentieth century, certain groups began to assert their rights to be free from restrictions, whether these were legal, economic, political, or cultural. These groups organized their efforts and became movements, with members fighting against injustices and for shared goals, drawing from and expanding upon the traditional language of liberalism—including *entitlement* and *rights*—as well as the socialist insistence on equality of condition. The underlying strength of liberalism in most Western societies has contributed significantly to this development. Indeed, some might suggest that the movements we discuss in this chapter are only variants of liberalism, but we believe they are significantly distinctive to be treated as distinct ideologies.

Movements have several common features. First, each movement addresses a particular *audience*—for example, women, LGBTQ peoples, Aboriginal peoples, and blacks or other racial minorities. Members of these groups have not chosen to be part of the audience, as people attending a concert have. Instead, group members are people who share certain characteristics, such as race or gender or sexual orientation, by birth or by belonging to a particular ethnic or cultural group that has a distinct history, produces a sense of identity, and gives a sense of meaning to its members. These characteristics form a major part of the *identity* of the people who share them. In other words, how others think of a person—and how that person thinks of himself or herself—depends largely upon characteristics such as skin colour, gender, sexual orientation, and the group into which he or she was born, and over which that person has little or no control. Therefore, it is not enough to follow the liberal program of working to promote individual liberty because people are not simply individuals. People identify with certain groups—and are identified by others as members of those groups—and they must be free as members of those groups, as Aboriginal peoples or blacks or women or LGBTQ peoples. Hence, these movements are associated with what has come to be called the politics of identity; what they seek is entitlement to redress perceived mistreatment or oppression.

Second, each movement claims mistreatment or oppression by some dominant group. The term *oppression* refers to the many means—institutional, intellectual, legal, even linguistic—that some people use to "press down," "crush," or otherwise "deform" others.[1] It is in this sense that blacks were oppressed by whites; women by men; LGBTQ peoples by heterosexuals; or Aboriginal minorities by non-Aboriginal majorities.

Third, each movement seeks to liberate an oppressed group not only from external restraints or restrictions, such as unjust or discriminatory laws and barriers to education, housing, and employment, but also from internal restrictions. Internal restrictions are those beliefs and attitudes that oppressed people have come to accept—uncritically and unconsciously—and which then serve to inhibit their quest for freedom or liberation. These groups have in a sense acquiesced or participated in their own oppression or victimization. For example, some blacks have internalized racist attitudes toward blacks; some women have accepted men's diagnoses and explanations of their discontent; some LGBTQ peoples have felt guilty because they are not straight; and some Aboriginal peoples have felt ashamed of their ancestry and customs. The dominance of the ruling race, gender, sexual

---

[1]See Marilyn Frye, "Oppression," in *The Politics of Reality* (Trumansburg, NY: Crossing, 1983) 1–16; see Terence Ball and Richard Dagger, eds., *Ideals and Ideologies: A Reader,* 8th ed. (New York: Longman, 2011) selection 8.56.

orientation, or culture depends on the oppressed group's continuing acceptance of its condition as natural, normal, or inevitable. To break the grip and the legitimacy of the dominant group requires a change of outlook and attitude on the part of the oppressed.

From this third common feature there follows a fourth: Each movement aims to raise the consciousness and change the outlooks of people who have somehow participated—however unwillingly, unwittingly, or unconsciously—in their oppression or victimization. Such participation may take many forms. For example, an Aboriginal person might feel socially or intellectually inferior to members of the dominant racial group; women might think themselves to be helpless, or at least less powerful than men; and LGBTQ peoples might feel ashamed of same-sex attraction. The goal of the politics of identity is to confront and criticize the sources of these feelings of inadequacy, inferiority, or shame—and in so doing to liberate or emancipate members of oppressed groups by helping them to help themselves. A major part of this effort consists of promoting the identification of the individual with the group. For example, a woman who thinks of herself primarily as a wife or mother will be less likely to think of herself as a woman whose opportunities and position in life are largely determined by her gender and will be more likely to identify with other women.

Fifth, each movement seeks to liberate the oppressors as well—to free them from the illusion of their own superiority and to help them recognize their former victims as fellow human beings, to break those "mind-forged manacles," as William Blake put it almost two centuries ago.[2]

Finally, each movement also desires public recognition of the worth of the group's values, practices, or way of life. This desire goes beyond the demand for tolerance or removal of restrictions or discrimination. It is a desire for public recognition of the positive value of the distinctive features of the group—for example, LGBTQ peoples' contributions to culture, gender and identity theory, and sport; feminist approaches to leadership or conflict resolution; and cultural practices such as the consensual decision-making process of First Nations and the distinct dialect, called *Ebonics,* of African Americans. Lack of public regard for these values is viewed as itself a form of discrimination or oppression. Thus, the desire for public recognition has led movements to seek education and public relations programs that promote a positive view of the group and its values. Such pursuits are often linked to an appeal to redress past wrongs, whether through apologies, payment, review of land claims, and the like.

Movements differ from one another in one very important respect, however: their focus on group rights or individual rights. Some movements—those that are defined by ethnicity and culture and are frequently connected with a particular territory—typically search for greater independence and autonomy for the group. They are often referred to, or refer to themselves, as *nations.* Other movements—those that are defined by personal individual characteristics—typically seek redress for specific discriminations in the form of individual rights or affirmative action. For example, Aboriginal peoples fall into the first category, while LGBTQ peoples fall into the second. Some groups, such as blacks in the United States, share elements of both types and are divided internally about the solutions to their grievances. Each movement represents a distinct ideological position characterized by the assertion of a particular identity, a specific view of freedom, and the demand for entitlement to redress historic wrongs. Whether their focus is on individual

---

[2]Quoted in William Barret, *The Illusion of Technique* (Garden City, NY: Doubleday, 1978) xv.

rights or group rights, movements view recognition of identity and the redress of injustice as pathways to greater freedom for the group and its members.

LAW AND IDENTITY: CHARTER POLITICS IN CANADA

In Canada, groups have increasingly sought the assistance of the courts to enforce their rights. This has been the case especially since the constitutional amendments of 1982, which added the Charter of Rights and Freedoms (with its protection of equality rights) and recognition of Aboriginal rights. Therefore, the politics of identity in Canada is sometimes described as Charter politics.

However, this is a misnomer with respect to Aboriginal rights, which are in fact recognized in section 35 of the *Constitution Act, 1982*, which is outside the Charter.[3] Section 35(1) states that "the existing aboriginal and treaty rights of the aboriginal people of Canada are hereby recognized and affirmed," and section 35(3) extends this constitutional recognition to rights acquired under subsequent land claim agreements. Aboriginal rights flow from the original status of Aboriginal peoples as self-governing independent entities prior to European settlement and the assertion of sovereignty by the Crown. These rights have come to be the defining or integral characteristics of Aboriginal society; rights include, for example, Aboriginal hunting and fishing practices.[4]

The most important Aboriginal right is Aboriginal title to land, created by their use and occupation of the land before the assertion of sovereignty by the Crown. Aboriginal title includes the right to exclusive use and occupation of land, but differs from ordinary title to land in that it does not include use of land for any purpose other than that compatible with its traditional use.[5] In addition, land can be transferred only to the Crown and, most importantly, it is held communally by an Aboriginal community, not by individuals. Consequently, it is managed by the community.

Treaty rights have also proven to be important in protecting the rights of Aboriginal peoples. Treaty rights are rights that flow from treaties made from time to time between Aboriginal peoples and the Crown. The Supreme Court of Canada has found that section 35 of the *Constitution Act, 1982*, requires treaties with Aboriginal peoples to be interpreted generously and in their favour and to nullify laws that may take away or reduce those rights.[6] Legislation can infringe on treaty rights only if it recognizes the priority of those rights (for example, to a fishery), gives compensation where appropriate, considers the wishes of the Aboriginal peoples involved, and has a compelling and substantial objective.

The legal recognition and constitutional protection given to Aboriginal rights has produced a flood of claims and litigation asserting these rights. Typically, these cases have been in relation to traditional rights to use land or to claim title to land that was not the subject of a treaty (which is generally the case, for example, in British Columbia). The legal recognition and constitutional protection of Aboriginal rights have also been strongly criticized on ideological grounds. These rights are in large part group or communal rights based on racial and ethnic identity and are at odds with the liberal individualism that is the

---

[3]This is the British statute that patriated the Canadian Constitution in 1982 and added the Charter and amending formula and other provisions to the existing provisions of the British North America Act.
[4]See the decision of the Supreme Court of Canada in *R. v. Van der Peet*, 2 S.C.R. 507 (1996).
[5]See Peter Hogg, *Constitutional Law* (Toronto: Carswell, 1997) looseleaf 26, 26.1 and 26.2, who suggests that land used for hunting could not, for example, be used for strip mining.
[6]See the decision in *R. v. Sparrow*, S.C.R. 1075 (1991).

dominant ideology in Canada. This clash is recognized in section 25 of the Charter, which states that Charter "rights and freedoms shall not be construed to abrogate or derogate from any aboriginal treaty or other rights or practices that pertain to the aboriginal peoples of Canada." Aboriginal rights cannot be attacked on the basis that they are inconsistent with the equality rights guaranteed in section 15 of the Charter:

> 15(1) Every individual is equal before and under the law and has the right to the equal protection and equal benefit of the law without discrimination and, in particular, without discrimination based on race, national or ethnic origin, colour, religion, sex, age or mental or physical disability.
>
> (2) Subsection (1) does not preclude any law, program or activity that has as its object the amelioration of conditions of disadvantaged individuals or groups including those that are disadvantaged because of race, national or ethnic origin, colour, religion, sex, age or mental or physical disability.

Therefore, the Canadian Constitution both recognizes and protects Aboriginal identity and legitimizes Aboriginal identity politics.

Equality rights are conceptually very different from Aboriginal rights in that they are individual, not group, rights. The courts have found that the right to freedom from discrimination guaranteed by section 15 is based on the grounds set out in section 15(1)—race, national or ethnic origin, etc.—and that the listing is not all-inclusive. There can be additional, prohibited grounds of discrimination that are analogous to those listed, providing that they are, like the listed grounds, based on inherent and immutable personal characteristics. Both citizenship and sexual orientation, for example, have been added to the list by the courts.[7] Charter rights, then, can be viewed as the logical extension of the liberal demand for individual equality of status. They also reflect the eighteenth and nineteenth century call for an end to discrimination and unequal treatment based on religious belief, yet extended to a much wider range of discriminatory practices.

Groups that benefit from these individual rights are not organic groups, such as Aboriginal peoples who are linked by ancestry, race, and a common language, culture, and history, but rather aggregations of individuals bearing common characteristics, such as gender or sexual orientation. Some, such as women disadvantaged by gender discrimination, are not even a minority. In some cases, the rights asserted may even create a clash within a group—for example, Aboriginal women who attempt to obtain equal status in matters such as band membership may be opposed by those who invoke the group or collective rights of the band to define group membership.

The availability of Charter protection and remedies since 1985 (the year the Charter came into effect) has led Aboriginal and other groups to seek to preserve and assert their rights through the courts, which have often been more sympathetic to minorities than have politicians, who answer to electoral majorities. Thus, the debate presented in Chapter 2 highlights the importance of the courts in contemporary identity politics in Canada. It is worth repeating here: Are the courts improperly frustrating the democratic will of the majority, or are they protecting individual or minority rights that are more important than democratic majority rights?

---

[7]See *Andrews v. Law Society of British Columbia*, 1 S.C.R. 143 [citizenship] (1988); *Egan v. Canada*, 2 S.C.R. 513 [sexual orientation] (1995).

ABORIGINAL RIGHTS

Over the past forty years or so, various Aboriginal peoples' movements have become more vocal and increasingly militant, including the First Nations, Inuit, and Métis peoples in Canada; Aborigines in Australia; Maori in New Zealand; and Native Americans in the United States. Despite the great geographic distance between them, Aboriginal peoples, as they see it, share several striking similarities. First and most obviously, they live on lands of which their ancestors were the first known inhabitants. Second, their ancestral lands were subsequently taken from them and occupied by European colonizers. Third, they became aliens and outsiders in their own lands, their religious and cultural practices and their traditional way of living undermined by the religious and cultural practice and encroachment of white Europeans. Fourth, with their land taken from them, their people deprived of pride and denied political power, their cultures demeaned or destroyed, they lost a sense of their identity—of who and what they are as a people. Fifth, the destruction of their culture and identity has brought Aboriginal peoples a host of social ills: high rates of unemployment, alcoholism, suicide, and other social problems unknown to their ancestors. The aim of various Aboriginal groups is to break this vicious cycle of poverty, social and economic subordination, and political powerlessness by reclaiming and restoring lost or long-eclipsed group rights and identities.

In the nineteenth and early twentieth centuries especially, white immigration into the territories of Aboriginal peoples in Canada, the United States, Australia, New Zealand, and elsewhere created competition for ever scarcer resources—land, game, timber, and minerals. The ever greater numbers of European settlers and their sophisticated technology—guns, railroads, steamships, and so on—gave them an advantage over the Aboriginal peoples they encountered. The result was their political, economic, and cultural conquest and, in the Indian wars in the United States, military defeat. Aboriginal peoples were forbidden to follow many of the customs and practices of their ancestors; their children were forced to attend schools where they were forbidden to speak the language of their parents and grandparents; they were made, by a variety of means, to feel inferior to "civilized" white settlers and to be ashamed of their ancestors' "savage" ways. Many Aboriginal children were put up for adoption into white families, who often used them as a source of cheap labour. Taken together, these policies were tantamount to cultural genocide—the cultural, if not the physical, eradication of entire peoples.

Consider, for example, what happened to the Aborigines in Australia. Between 1910 and the early 1970s, some 100 000 mixed-blood or "half-caste" Aboriginal children—fully one-third of the present Aboriginal population—were forcibly taken from their families on the ground that theirs was a "doomed race." The lighter-skinned children were handed over to white Australian families for adoption. The darker-skinned children were placed in orphanages but not made available for adoption. Children in both groups were forbidden to speak their native language or to follow the religious and other customs of their birth parents. This policy of "saving" Aboriginal children from their parents resulted in a "stolen generation."

The phrase "stolen generation" was used by Australian Premier John Howard in a personal apology to the Aborigines in May 1997. Speaking before the Australian Reconciliation Convention, Howard said, "I feel deep sorrow for those of my fellow Australians who suffered injustices under the practices of past generations toward indigenous people." Aboriginal leaders say that a personal apology, although a good beginning, is not nearly enough. They want an official apology from the Australian government and monetary compensation for their individual and collective trauma. Australia's Federal Human Rights Commission agrees and recommends that a fund be established to compensate victims of earlier government policy. The Australian government has so far rejected the proposal on the grounds that the present generation of white Australians should not be held accountable for what their parents' and grandparents' generations did to the Aborigines.[8] The controversy was further fuelled by the 2003 film *Rabbit-Proof Fence,* the true story of three Aboriginal girls who were forcibly taken from their mother in 1931.

Similar criticism has been made of the Canadian residential school system, which forcibly removed Aboriginal children from their homes and communities and took them to live in residential schools, where they were sometimes abused and where their culture was ignored or demeaned. Although this system was abandoned in Canada in the late 1960s, many former students continue to suffer its effects and have sought compensation either from the Canadian government or from the churches or other agencies that operated the schools on behalf of the government.

The longstanding Canadian policy of trying to assimilate Aboriginal peoples into white society coexisted with a system of reserves and treaty rights, which in principle treated most Aboriginal peoples (Inuit and Métis were outside the system) as distinct groups. Pierre Elliott Trudeau's government briefly considered abolishing all special status for Aboriginal peoples in the early 1970s, but quickly abandoned the policy in the face of the demand by Aboriginal peoples for self-government rather than assimilation. In 1996, the Report of the Royal Commission on Aboriginal Peoples stated:

> Aboriginal nations have accepted the need for power sharing with Canada. In return, they ask Canada to accept that Aboriginal self-government is not, and can never be, a "gift" from an "enlightened" Canada. The right is inherent in Aboriginal people and their nationhood and was exercised for centuries before the arrival of European explorers and settlers. It is a right they never surrendered and now want to exercise once more.[9]

This view has been reflected to varying degrees in land claim settlements and other agreements reached with Aboriginal groups. Some of these outcomes have given bands powers analogous to municipalities; other outcomes have been more extensive. The agreement that established Nunavut as a separate territory in the eastern Arctic in 1999 created a government with quasi-provincial powers governed by the Inuit people, who form an overwhelming majority of its population.

The extent and nature of Aboriginal self-government have also been the cause of disputes, such as the impasse over the Chrétien government's First Nations Governance Initiative in 2001, which sought to reform Indian band government, and similar more recent initiatives by the Harper government. In a more extreme form, such disputes have led to violent confrontations between militant First Nations peoples and the civil authorities, most notably at Oka in Quebec in 1990.

As a result of the legitimacy and protection of Aboriginal claims provided by the *Constitution Act, 1982*, greater weight has been given to Aboriginal pressure groups such as the Assembly of First Nations, whose national chief has become the main voice of Aboriginal peoples in dealing with the federal government.

---

[8]"Unofficial Apology Offered to Aborigines," *Minneapolis Star-Tribune,* 27 May 1997.
[9]Canada. Indian and Northern Affairs Canada. *Report of the Royal Commission on Aboriginal Peoples*, vol. 2 (Ottawa: Canada Communications, 1996).

Although there has been an upsurge in support and assertion of Aboriginal rights in the courts, the recognition of distinctive Aboriginal rights continues to be a topic of debate on the basis of liberal individualism. Some critics consider support for distinctive Aboriginal practices or favourable treatment of Aboriginal rights (for example, fishing rights) as racist or at least race-based. The majority of Canadians, however, have some sympathy for Aboriginal rights arguments, perhaps reflecting the communal collectivist element in Canadian political culture.

Aboriginal groups in Canada have also sought to restore the sense of identity, power, pride, and dignity that has been stripped, they say, from their people. They do so in a variety of ways. One strategy is broadly cultural: It aims at instilling a sense of identity and pride through the revival of traditional ceremonies and practices, including previously banned or repressed religious practices; the development of Aboriginal-owned and -operated print and electronic media (such as the Aboriginal Peoples Television Network); and the teaching of Aboriginal languages and cultural traditions in schools. Other strategies include the pursuit of land claims, greater powers of self-government, and Aboriginal economic development. The Aboriginal view of freedom held by the Aboriginal rights movement is illustrated in Figure 11.1.

Native Americans have also fought legal battles to assert their rights with federal, state, and local governments. In Wisconsin and Minnesota, for example, Native Americans have recently reclaimed the spearfishing rights guaranteed to them by nineteenth-century treaties. This outcome has angered white fishermen, leading to clashes in court and sometimes to physical confrontation at contested sites. So far federal and state courts in the United States have ruled that the treaties are still valid.

Even so, some Native Americans contend that they can receive justice only in their own tribal courts. Native Americans who break the law, they say, should not be tried in

FIGURE 11.1	The Aboriginal View of Freedom

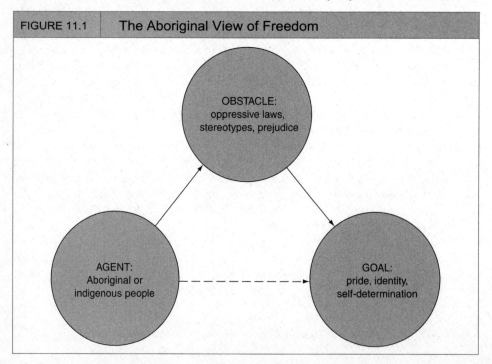

OBSTACLE:
oppressive laws,
stereotypes, prejudice

AGENT:
Aboriginal or
indigenous people

GOAL:
pride, identity,
self-determination

white courts. Instead, Native offenders should be tried by courts of tribal elders and sentenced to traditional punishments—for example, being sent to live by themselves in the forest for a prescribed period so that they can reflect on their wrongdoings and their duties to society. Use of *sentencing circles* and alternative punishment is becoming relatively common in Canada. Only on rare occasions, however, have American courts permitted such alternative punishments to be imposed, and only on first-time juvenile offenders.

As we have noted, such special treatment runs counter to liberalism, with its emphasis on individualism, colour-blind justice, and equality before the law. Critics contend that allowing Aboriginal peoples to be tried in tribal courts or to have special or preferred fishing or hunting rights, or reserves where land is held and managed communally, gives them special treatment as a group. And groups, unlike individuals, should not have rights. But Aboriginal peoples insist that their rights and dignity as individuals require respect for their rights and dignity as a nation or collectively because their individual identity is bound up with the identity of their nation. For the individual to be free, it is first necessary that his or her identity be free as a group from the obstacles imposed on them by the people who have colonized their land.

FEMINISM

Contrary to the widely held view that the women's movement originated in the 1960s, feminism has a long history. Yet this history has until recently remained half-hidden, and women's voices have been submerged or ignored. Some of these voices have, however, come down to us.

Often regarded as the "mother of feminism," English writer Mary Wollstonecraft (1759–1797) chided the French revolutionaries for championing "the rights of man" while neglecting the rights of women—rights she defended in *A Vindication of the Rights of Woman* (1792).[10] Abigail Adams (1744–1818), wife of future U.S. President John Adams, asked him to

> remember the ladies and be more generous and favourable to them than your ancestors. Do not put such unlimited power into the hands of the husbands. Remember, all men would be tyrants if they could. If particular care and attention is not paid to the ladies, we are determined to foment a rebellion, and will not hold ourselves bound by any laws in which we have no voice or representation.[11]

But during the nineteenth century, the demands of women increased in militancy. Suffragettes in England, Canada, and the United States demanded that women be allowed to vote, while others lobbied for changes in the laws regulating marriage and divorce. These women were often also active in the temperance movement, because many wives and children were sexually abused, beaten, neglected, and abandoned by alcoholic husbands and fathers, and they were involved in other activities directed at social reform. Canadian women such as Nellie McClung (1873–1951), a suffragist and politician, and Agnes McPhail (1890–1954), the first woman Member of Parliament in Canada, were prominent in the populist movement in the early twentieth century. Many women of this

---

[10]See Ball and Dagger, selection 8.52.
[11]Quoted in Miriam Schneir, ed., *Feminism: The Essential Historical Writings* (New York: Vintage, 1972) 3.

Mary Wollstonecraft, later Mary Wollstonecraft Godwin
(1759–1797)

time period went on to be active in the Co-operative Commonwealth Federation (CCF) and the New Democratic Party (NDP).

In the early nineteenth century, many in the American women's movement were also active in the antislavery movement. As they pointed out, the conditions of women and of slaves were similar in many ways: Both were without the right to vote, to run for public office, to own property in their own names, or to leave an abusive master or husband.[12] Thus, the women's movement began to further the cause not only of women but of other oppressed people, as well as to reform and improve society as a whole.

The response of many, perhaps most, men of the time was either to ignore or to ridicule women who dared to make such outlandish and radical demands. John Adams, for example, replying to Abigail's letter, wrote, "I cannot but laugh." As it gained strength in the nineteenth century, the women's movement became the butt of jokes and cartoons; newspaper editorials predicted that if these women had their way, husbands would look after the children while their wives worked and went to the saloon to drink whisky and smoke cigars. Not all men laughed, however; some risked ridicule by siding with the women. In England, William Thompson issued *An Appeal of One-Half of the Human Race* (1825), and John Stuart Mill decried *The Subjection of Women* (1869), as did Friedrich Engels in *Origins of the Family, Private Property and the State* (1884). In the United States, ex-slave Frederick Douglass spoke and wrote on behalf of the fledgling

---

[12]For Sarah Grimké's observations on the connection between slavery and the condition of women, see her *Letters on the Equality of the Sexes* (Boston: Knapp, 1838), Letter VIII; see Ball and Dagger, selection 8.54.

women's movement, and antislavery advocate William Lloyd Garrison editorialized in defence of women's rights.[13]

In the twentieth century, variations developed within the women's movement, often in combination with other ideologies, such as socialism and anarchism. Socialist feminists, for example, argued that women could not be free until capitalism was replaced by socialism.[14] Anarchist feminists claimed that women would be oppressed as long as the state existed.[15] More recently, lesbian separatist feminists claim that women will be oppressed as long as they associate with and are dependent upon men.[16]

The history of feminism is often described as having occurred in three waves. The **first wave of feminism** began in the nineteenth century and continued until the early twentieth century. First-wave feminism held a liberal view and sought to overcome overt forms of individual discrimination—in marriage, educational opportunities, legal rights, and the right to vote. In Canada, this stage began in the nineteenth century and the right to vote was won federally and in most provinces by 1919; in the United Kingdom partially by 1918 and fully by 1930; and in the United States in 1920. The removal of these and other legal and institutional barriers has been the primary aim of liberal feminists. Their goal has been to give women the same rights and opportunities that men enjoy. The liberal feminist view of freedom for women is illustrated in Figure 11.2. The most important symbol for

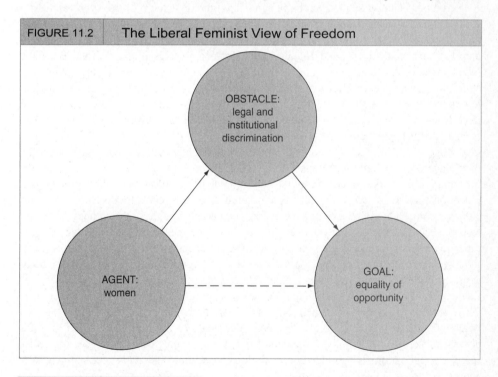

FIGURE 11.2   **The Liberal Feminist View of Freedom**

OBSTACLE:
legal and
institutional
discrimination

AGENT:
women

GOAL:
equality of
opportunity

[13]See Schneir, Part IV: "Men as Feminists."

[14]See, for example, Sheila Rowbotham, *Women's Consciousness, Man's World* (Harmondsworth, UK: Pelican, 1973).

[15]See, for example, Emma Goldman, *Anarchism and Other Essays* (New York: Mother Earth, 1910); two of her essays—"The Traffic in Women" and "Marriage and Love"—are included in Schneir 308–24.

[16]See, for example, Shulamith Firestone, *The Dialectic of Sex: The Case for Feminist Revolution* (New York: Morrow, 1970).

first-wave feminism in Canada was the *Persons' Case* (1930), which ruled that women were "persons" and therefore eligible to sit in the Senate of Canada. This case had been pursued by the "Famous Five": Emily Murphy, the British Empire's first female judge; Louise McKinney, the first woman elected to a legislature in Canada; Irene Parlby, the first female cabinet minister in Alberta; Nellie McClung; and Henrietta Edwards.

The **second wave of feminism** began in the late 1960s. It has been concerned not only with overt sexual discrimination but also with exposing and overcoming more subtle forms of discrimination that go under the heading of sexism. Sexism is a set of beliefs and attitudes about women's supposedly innate inferiority and various inadequacies—intellectual, physical, emotional, spiritual, and otherwise—that prevent them from being men's equals. Second-wave feminists—often called *radical feminists*—worked to expose, criticize, and overcome these sexist attitudes and beliefs, which were widely held by men and—more importantly—by many women as well. To the degree that women shared these sexist views, they were afflicted with self-loathing and lack of respect for themselves and for other women. Until women recognized that their chains were in part "mind-forged manacles," they could not hope to break them. In other words, second-wave feminists believed that women needed to recognize and overcome their own internalized sexist attitudes and beliefs about their gender's supposed limitations and liabilities.

Feminists have pursued several strategies for fighting sexism. In the 1960s and early 1970s, consciousness-raising groups—small groups of women who met to talk about their experiences with and feelings about men, women, sex, love, marriage, children, parents, husbands, lovers, and friends—were formed for this purpose. Take Back the Night marches and demonstrations were held to publicize the crime of rape. Women's counselling centres and battered women's shelters were opened, and women were invited to talk and to do something about their troubles. Women's studies programs were started in colleges and universities to enable women to study women's history and other subjects from a feminist perspective.

Unlike liberal feminists, who tend to stress the essential equality and sameness of the two genders—especially with regard to equal rights, equal opportunities, and equal pay for comparable work—radical feminists tend to emphasize differences. Men and women not only have different biological makeups, but also different attitudes, outlooks, and values. Women should be free to be different, they argue, and these differences should be respected and protected. Nowhere are these differences more pronounced than in attitudes toward sex. Because many men tend to separate sex from love, trust, and respect, they therefore do not see sexual relations as an integral feature of love and mutual respect. Radical feminists believe that this attitude promotes the *objectification* of women, such as the view of women displayed in pornographic pictures and literature. There women are depicted as mere bodies or body parts—as *sex objects,* rather than as whole people; they are shown to enjoy pain, degradation, and humiliation; and they are always subservient to men, who are depicted as proud, cruel, and uncaring. Not surprisingly, radical feminists—unlike liberal feminists—often wage legal and political war against pornography and pornographers.[17]

---

[17]For one radical feminist's case against pornography, see Catherine MacKinnon, *Only Words* (Cambridge, MA: Harvard UP, 1993). For a liberal feminist's rejoinder, see Nadine Strossen, *Defending Pornography: Free Speech, Sex, and the Fight for Women's Rights* (New York: Scribner, 1995).

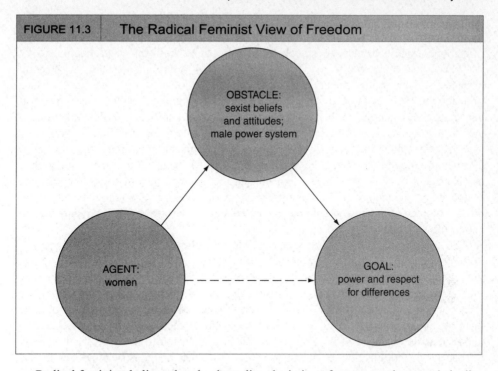

FIGURE 11.3   The Radical Feminist View of Freedom

Radical feminists believe that the degrading depiction of women and women's bodies in the mass media is symptomatic of a systematic and pervasive masculine *system* of power that is not confined to legal and political institutions but suffuses the culture and outlook of modern Western society. For example, pictures of naked or nearly naked women are used to sell everything from soap to automobiles. Older men divorce their wives to marry much younger women who are referred to as *trophy* wives and are regarded as symbols of masculine status and power. Hollywood movies seldom depict older women as attractive, desirable, or wise. In these and other ways, women are systematically exploited and oppressed through cultural representations and images. Therefore, radical feminists say it is not enough to confront legal or institutional discrimination against women; feminists must wage a broadly *cultural* struggle as well. The radical feminist view of freedom for women is illustrated in Figure 11.3.

The most important second-wave feminism group in Canada was the National Action Committee for the Status of Women (NAC). It was founded in 1971 to lobby for the implementation of the recommendations of the 1970 Royal Commission on the Status of Women. Under the leadership of Lorna Marsden, Kay Macpherson, and Lynn McDonald, it had a considerable impact on Canadian political discourse in the 1970s and early 1980s. Its lobbying activities resulted in substantial changes in the equality rights provisions of the Charter of Rights and Freedoms.

The election of Thunera Sobani as head of NAC in 1993 caused a serious split in the organization. A black woman, Sobani was a proponent of the third wave of feminism, which caused serious conflict with second-wave feminists in the NAC such as June Caldwell and Doris Anderson.

Third-wave feminism is a movement that began in the mid-1980s. Intellectually it was influenced by postmodernist and poststructuralist ideas. It thought that first- and second-wave feminism had uncritically accepted society's norms and had sought to fit women into a white, middle-class mould. Third-wave feminism treated feminism, class, colour and sexuality as mere social constructs in the first step toward liberation.

Where first- and second-wave feminism focused on discrimination, third-wave feminism focuses on empowerment of women, typified by the Riot Grrl movement, which started in the 1990s and quickly became a complete subculture of fashion, music, art, writing, and activism centred on themes of self-reliance and self-sufficiency. Most importantly, the Riot Grrl movement introduced much younger women to feminist values.

Third-wave feminism conflicts with second-wave feminism in its approach to sexuality. Second-wave feminists tend to be sex-negative, emphasizing the role that pornography has played in treating women as mere objects, for example. Third-wave feminists are sex-positive, challenging the idea that pornography is necessarily exploitative and believing that women's sexuality should be celebrated and encouraged as a healthy and natural part of life and identity.

Late eighteenth-century political theorist Mary Wollstonecraft is often acknowledged as the founder of feminist thought because of writings such as *Rights of Woman*, though in fact her work was largely without influence. She is primarily a symbolic figure. The first important feminist theorist was probably Simone de Beauvoir (1908–1986), a French writer and author of *The Second Sex* (1949), an existentialist work that argues that there are no essential differences between men and women, and that women need to realize that they choose to be women in order to be free. In the United States, Betty Friedan (1921–2006) critiqued the social role of women in industrial societies in *The Feminine Mystique* (1963). In *The Female Eunuch* (1970), Australian-born Germaine Greer (1939–) argued that women's sexuality has been demeaned by the nuclear family, that women have been taught to be ashamed of their bodies, and the result is political powerlessness. More recently, Catherine MacKinnon (1946–), an American law professor, has argued influentially that the courts need to take positive action to protect women from the impact of sexual harassment and pornography, even at the expense of free speech.

LESBIAN, GAY, BISEXUAL, TRANSGENDER, AND QUEER SOCIAL MOVEMENTS

Lesbian, gay, bisexual, transgender, and queer (LGBTQ) social movements represent groups of peoples who are by no means uniform, and the individual terms used can overlap. The LGBTQ acronym has been extended variously in an attempt to encompass intersex (people born with both female and male sexual characteristics), asexual, polyamorous, genderqueer (people who do not conform to traditional gender roles), two-spirits (Aboriginal conception of queer), and people who support LGBTQ peoples. Due to the heterogeneous nature of the LGBTQ label, the LGBTQ community has had to manage internal dissension in order to advance a coherent political agenda. Some in the LGBTQ movement have reclaimed the term *queer*, which is often used in place of the cumbersome acronym. This usage has generated a discipline of academic scholarship called queer studies or sexual diversity studies, which offers a program of study focussing on sexual or gender identity. Many bookstores have sections devoted to queer writings, and there is an increasing recognition in academia of a distinct queer literature.

The LGBTQ movement is a relatively recent arrival on the political scene. This might at first seem surprising, since homosexuality is as old as heterosexuality. In the ancient Athens of Socrates, Plato, and Aristotle, for example, thinkers acknowledged that heterosexual relations were necessary in order to produce children and continue the species, but they also pointed out that necessary activities, like eating and sleeping, are not necessarily noble or beautiful. As they saw it, homosexual love might be superior to heterosexual love under certain restricted circumstances because it represents an intimate relationship between equals (man to man or woman to woman) rather than between unequals (man to woman).[18] Similar attitudes sometimes prevailed in ancient Rome.

If philosophers and poets in the classical world were hospitable to homosexuality, however, the religions that emerged from the Middle East took a decidedly different view of the matter. Jewish, Christian, and Islamic doctrines all condemned homosexuality as perverted, unnatural, and sinful.[19] LGBTQ peoples would call these religious doctrines **homophobic**—fearful of non-heterosexuals. From these doctrines followed centuries of persecution of LGBTQ peoples. In medieval Europe, "sodomites" were sometimes burned at the stake. Until very recently, in most Western countries, homosexuality was a crime punishable by imprisonment; in some countries of the Near and Middle East, it still is. Even where legal penalties have been repealed or unenforced, other forms of discrimination persist. In many communities LGBTQ peoples face difficulties securing employment, housing, and medical care—difficulties aggravated by the fear of HIV/AIDS. LGBTQ parents may be denied legal custody of their children or may be barred from adopting. Until very recently, same-sex couples in Canada did not possess the same rights in respect of their partners, including the right to marry and ancillary rights, afforded to opposite-sex couples.

The same sexual revolution that inspired feminism in the 1960s encouraged LGBTQ peoples to demand an end to their social and legal discrimination. Toward the end of the 1960s, men began to use the word *gay* in opposition to the word *straight* to describe their identity; women proudly described themselves as *butch* or *dyke*. In Canada, formal equality started with the now-famous changes to the Criminal Code made on Trudeau's initiative in the late 1960s on the basis of his belief that the state had "no place in the bedrooms of the nation." These changes included the decriminalization of homosexual acts between consenting adults. A major turning point for the LGBTQ movement was "Operation Soap," a police raid on four gay bathhouses in Toronto on February 18, 1981, resulting in the mass arrest of over 300 men under the bawdy house provisions of the Criminal Code. Thousands of people demonstrated in response, bringing national attention to the LGBT movement. A gay freedom rally held during the protests became the Toronto Pride Parade, which now attracts an audience of over 1 million people each year. The bathhouse demonstrations marked the end of the use of the bawdy house provisions in the Criminal Code to prosecute homosexuality.

In retrospect, another major legal milestone for the gay rights movement was the adoption of the Charter in 1982 because subsequent decisions of the courts added sexual

---

[18]For Greek attitudes toward sexuality and same-sex love (the term *homosexuality* was not coined until the late nineteenth century), see Plato, *The Symposium*; K. J. Dover, *Greek Homosexuality* (Cambridge, MA: Harvard UP, 1978); Michel Foucault, *The History of Sexuality,* vol. 1, trans. Robert Hurley (New York: Pantheon, 1986).

[19]Elaine Pagels, *Adam, Eve, and the Serpent* (New York: Random, 1988) 10–11; but note the statement of the National Conference of Catholic Bishops, *Always Our Children: A Pastoral Message to Parents of Homosexual Children and Suggestions for Pastoral Ministers* (Washington, DC: Office of Communications, National Conference of Catholic Bishops, U.S. Catholic Conference, 1997).

orientation as one of the grounds of discrimination prohibited in the equality rights provisions of section 15. These changes have reflected, and likely to some extent encouraged, shifts in public opinion in Canada (and in other Western countries) toward homosexuality in general. In the United States, for example, advocacy groups succeeded in persuading the American Psychiatric Association that there was no scientific basis to classify homosexuality as a mental disorder and to remove homosexuality from its list of mental disorders in 1973. In Canada, because freedom of religion is also protected by section 15 of the Charter, as well as by other sections of the Constitution (particularly relating to Catholic education), the rights of LGBTQ peoples within religious organizations has created a conflict that must be balanced. Religious organizations and clergy are not required to marry same-sex couples if it would conflict with their religious beliefs. Recently, the right of Catholic elementary or secondary schools to prohibit LGBTQ-interest student associations, often called gay–straight alliances, has caused much controversy. In Ontario, legislation has recently been introduced to specifically allow student groups to form for the purpose of combating bullying.

While sexual orientation and gender are protected grounds under the Charter, transgendered people do not fit neatly under either of these spheres because gender identity is a distinct concept. Many provinces have enacted human rights codes or other legislation that specifically includes transgendered people.

LGBTQ peoples form a distinct group on the basis that an individual in the group expresses his or her identity in some way that deviates from society's traditional notions concerning gender and sexuality. Consequently, the members of the group have a common interest in combating any form of discrimination that is rooted in antipathy toward sexual nonconformance. As a result, and because most political questions do not involve issues of sexual nonconformity, LGBTQ peoples can be supporters of different political ideologies or political parties and they may only share common views of issues directly related to LGBTQ rights. It is also important to note that there is considerable difference of opinion within interest groups and associations concerning LGBTQ issues. For example, even the appropriateness of gays and lesbians making common cause with the transgendered community has faced resistance.

In general, the LGBTQ rights movement has been integrationist—that is, seeking acceptance of its members into the wider straight society on the basis of individual acceptance and equality. Perhaps the best example of this in Canada is the recent legal battle to allow same-sex marriage, which was successfully fought in several provincial appeal courts and in the Supreme Court of Canada. The aim of this struggle was not to be separate or different from the larger society but to be able to participate fully in it—and, in particular, in the institution of marriage.

Like other groups that have been discriminated against, the LGBTQ rights movement has sought to provide support and encouragement for LGBTQ peoples who wish to publicly acknowledge and practise their gender or sexual identity and to counter negative internalized attitudes of guilt or self-criticism in LGBTQ peoples themselves. The movement does this through LGBTQ media, education and counselling, support groups, pride marches, and other events and activities. The tactics employed and the public image of LGBTQ groups may vary greatly. However, these differences are mostly in the details, not in fundamental principles and ideas, including the fundamental principle of liberal individualism that is at the core of LGBTQ identity politics. The LGBTQ view of freedom held by the LGBTQ rights movement is illustrated in Figure 11.4.

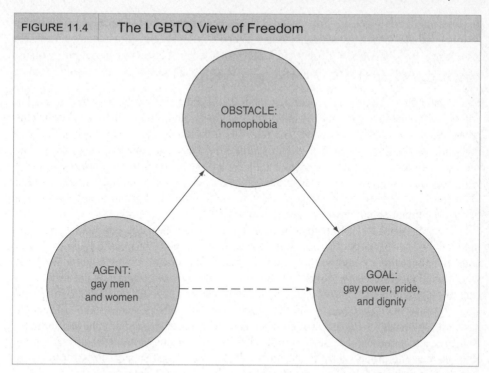

FIGURE 11.4   The LGBTQ View of Freedom

OBSTACLE:
homophobia

AGENT:
gay men
and women

GOAL:
gay power, pride,
and dignity

Toronto police face demonstrators following the bathhouse raids of February 5, 1981.

In general, the LGBTQ rights movement has been integrationist, as seen in the struggle for the legal recognition of same-sex marriage.

RACIAL AND ETHNIC MINORITY RIGHTS

Racial and ethnic minorities in Western countries have generally followed two alternative approaches to achieve equality of condition. The first is an individualistic approach. This approach views members of minority groups as individuals who have individual rights that they need to assert so that they can become full and equal members of society. The second is a group or communal approach. This approach views the minority group as a whole that has group rights to be obtained and protected by fostering linguistic or cultural identity and, in some circumstances, by dealing with individual group members through group or communal representatives or institutions.

In our discussion of nationalism in Chapter 8, we saw how the conflict between the individualistic and group approaches has played out in Canada between English-speaking and French-speaking communities. Should French Canadians be viewed as individuals who have certain language rights, as Trudeau asserted, or as a *nation* or group that has certain collective or communal rights that should be recognized (for example, in special status or powers to Quebec), as the Parti Québécois and other Quebec nationalists have asserted? A milder form of this conflict can be seen in Canadian multiculturalism policies, which recognize the cultural identity of various non–French-speaking or English-speaking groups but provide limited legal or financial support for the protection or encouragement of those cultural identities.

Minority groups that work to end **racism**—discrimination based on race, skin colour, or other external features that suggest a place of origin—face these same conflicts. In the United States, systemic racism directed against black Americans has produced a division between black rights groups that take an *integrationist* or *assimilationist* approach to achieve equality of condition and those who call for a more radical *separatist* or *nationalist* orientation. But this division is not sharp or rigid. Some people who have taken a generally integrationist position, such as Martin Luther King, Jr. (1929–1968), also agree with some aspects of black separatism; and some who have been separatists, such as Malcolm X (1925–1965), later modified their views in a more integrationist direction. As the name indicates, the principal aim of the integrationist approach is the full integration or assimilation of black people into society. This is mostly a matter of removing the barriers to blacks' full and free participation in the social, economic, and political life of their countries—barriers such as laws that deny them equal rights or equal opportunities for housing, employment, and education. Their point is that blacks ought to be treated first and foremost as individuals, with the same rights and liberties as the other individual members of society. After all, if justice is blind, it must also be colour-blind. In this respect, the integrationist approach is essentially liberal in outlook. When white-dominated society has excluded blacks from full membership, the integrationist response has been to take legal and political action to overturn the laws and break down the prejudices that have enforced racial segregation and discrimination. The goal, as Martin Luther King, Jr., said in his "I Have a Dream" speech (1963), is a society in which people "will not be judged by the colour of their skin but by the content of their character."

In contrast, black separatists insist that integration is not the solution to the problems that confront black people in white-dominated societies. The first and most important task is to build racial pride and economic self-sufficiency—something that can be done only if blacks recognize that they are not merely individuals but members of a distinct community, nation, or people. Some black nationalists have campaigned for a separate territory or homeland for blacks. One of these was Marcus Garvey (1887–1940), a Jamaican immigrant to the United States who condemned racial integration and intermarriage and founded the Universal Negro Improvement Association, with the eventual aim of establishing an independent, black-governed nation in Africa. Other black nationalists have called for a "nation within a nation." This would mean, for example, converting part of the United States into a black-governed territory, as in one organization's plan for turning five southern states into a Republic of New Africa.[20] Like other nationalists, some black separatists, or nationalists, hold that separate nations (or peoples) should each be united in its own self-governing nation-state.

However, most black separatists have not taken the idea of nationalism that far. Instead, they have devoted themselves to promoting a stronger sense of identity, community, and pride among blacks. In the 1960s, while Martin Luther King, Jr., was leading marches and boycotts and the National Association for the Advancement of Colored People (NAACP) was filing lawsuits to bring an end to racial segregation, the Black Panthers and other black nationalists were calling for "Black Pride" and "Black Power." In apartheid South Africa, Steve Biko (1946–1977) led a movement for "Black Consciousness."[21] The message of all these groups was that black people must take charge of their own lives, and they cannot do this as long as they are under the illusion that they can become free and equal members of societies that are in fact racist to the core. The first step toward liberation is liberation from the racist thinking that infects not only whites, but also, all too often, black people themselves.

From the separatist or nationalist point of view, the most pernicious form of racism may well be that which lodges inside the individual and warps the psyche of blacks themselves. Visible minorities, and perhaps black people in particular, have long felt the sting of prejudice and racial discrimination, and to avoid it some may try, if not actually to pass as white, then at least to be accepted by whites by, for example, adopting "white" tastes in music, food, clothes, and friends, and taking care not to use "black" expressions or turns of phrase. Since such attempts are almost always unsuccessful, one might then turn one's anger inward, toward oneself, hating one's own blackness even more than one hates white racists.

This double rage—hatred of one's oppressors and of oneself and one's race—has often been noted by black writers, including James Baldwin (1927–1987) and Malcolm X, the assassinated Black Muslim leader. Suppressed and turned inward, this anger sometimes comes to the surface in self-destructive ways. Psychoanalysts call this process sublimation and the return of the repressed. It may take a skilled psychoanalyst to help someone delve deep inside his or her psyche to bring such long-suppressed anger to light. So perhaps it is not surprising that some of the most far-reaching analyses of black self-loathing have been made by psychoanalysts. Two of them, Dr. William Grier and Dr. Price Cobbs, call the

---

[20]According to Michael Dawson, these are the ideologies of radical egalitarianism, disillusioned liberalism, black Marxism, black nationalism, black feminism, and black conservatism. See Michael Dawson, *Black Visions: The Roots of Contemporary African-American Political Ideologies* (Chicago: U of Chicago P, 2001) 94.

[21]See, for example, Steve Biko, "Black Consciousness and the Quest for a True Humanity," *I Write What I Like,* ed. Malusi and Thoko Mpumlwana (London: Bowerdean, 1996); see Ball and Dagger, selection 8.51.

syndrome *black rage*—an anger against whites that blacks vent on themselves and each other.[22] This rage, in conjunction with poverty, despair, lack of educational opportunities, and other social and economic inequalities, helps explain the disturbingly high homicide and drug addiction rates among inner-city blacks in the United States.

Nor are these pathologies confined to the United States. In *Black Skins, White Masks,* Algerian psychoanalyst Frantz Fanon (1925–1961) describes the despair of black Africans who tried to adopt white European attitudes and values and, in the attempt, lost their identity and sense of self-worth. Their French might be exquisite and more eloquent than that of their colonial masters, their European suits of impeccable cut and quality, and their manners charming; but, try as they may, they never will be white Europeans. The result, as Fanon recounts it, is an unrequited love for white Europeans and all things European, on the one hand, and an abiding hatred of all things black and African on the other. Such self-loathing gives rise to self-destructive behaviour.[23] The only way out of this impasse, says Fanon, is for black people to break out of their mental prisons, not to be freed by others but to free themselves from the false beliefs and illusions in which they have for too long been ensnared. The process of healing, of recovering from the massive psychic injury that whites have visited upon blacks (and blacks upon themselves), begins by calling white culture into question, and by showing that "white" standards are not necessarily the true or the only standards of intelligence, beauty, and achievement. Blacks need to recognize that feelings of ugliness and inferiority are "mind-forged manacles"—or, to change the metaphor, an illusory bubble that bursts as soon as it is seen for what it is.

Black separatists try to burst this bubble by several means. One is to recover black history—the story of how blacks have retained their dignity despite the indignities heaped upon them by slaveholders and other oppressors; and how they have developed an affirmative culture, including art, music, poetry, and literature, that has infused and influenced the dominant culture of today. Another means of bursting the bubble is to repudiate white views of blacks (and of some blacks' internalized views of themselves) by reclaiming and proclaiming "black" values and standards. This is done, for example, by affirming that "black is beautiful," that curly or nappy hair is attractive, and that "black" English (or Ebonics) and dress should be displayed proudly as badges of black identity and solidarity. In these and other ways, black nationalists have attempted to instil a sense of racial pride and black identity. Public assertion of pride in black- or black-related heritage, in such events as Toronto's annual Caribana parade and festival, is another way of building group pride and identity.

Conclusion

Identity and Ideology

Each of the ideologies of identity reflects the concerns of a particular group that sees itself as oppressed or discriminated against. The concerns of groups sometimes overlap or even clash—for example, Aboriginal women and Aboriginal LGBTQ peoples (or "two-spirits") have sometimes come into conflict with the traditional values and customs that Aboriginal

---

[22]William Grier and Price Cobbs, *Black Rage* (New York: Bantam, 1969).
[23]Frantz Fanon, *Black Skins, White Masks* (New York: Grove, 1982).

identity politics seek to protect. Nevertheless, it is useful to consider the common ways the politics of identity perform the four functions that all ideologies perform.

Explanatory Function. Ideologies of identity do not try to explain all social conditions and circumstances. They begin, instead, with the condition of the specific group with which they are concerned—for example, Aboriginal peoples, blacks, women, LGBTQ peoples. This condition they then explain in terms of certain beliefs—racist, sexist, homophobic, and so on—held by oppressors and internalized by the oppressed. To this they add the fact of domination and oppression. They begin with the conviction that the plight of their group is not simply a natural fact of life that must be accepted, but the result of oppression—of Aboriginals by whites, of women by men, and so on.

Evaluative Function. Oppression is also the key word in these ideologies' evaluation of the condition of their group. Oppression prevents people from living full and free lives. And every ideology of identity teaches that things are not yet as they should be, since each of the groups they address continues to suffer (or sometimes to cause) oppression. Rather than saying that conditions are good or bad, they tend to evaluate them in terms of better or worse. In societies and times in which women are relatively free to speak and think for themselves, for instance, conditions are better—less oppressive—than they are in societies and times in which women are treated simply as the property of men. To say that conditions are better is not to say that they are already as good as they can and should be, however.

Orientative Function. One of the central features of ideologies of identity is the attempt to make members of oppressed groups conscious or aware of their oppression—to see themselves as the victims of some dominant or powerful group. This is a matter of orientation and identity—of who or what one is. Far from being isolated atoms, people are apt to identify themselves—and be identified by others—according to race, gender, sexual orientation, or other group affiliation. People must understand their location in the social world before they can do anything to change their circumstances. The victim of injustice must be brought to see that he or she is not responsible for the suffering he or she endures, nor is this suffering simply his or her inevitable fate. So, too, must the oppressor be brought to see the injustice that he or she is doing, wittingly or unwittingly, to other human beings. Sometimes these two imperatives clash. For example, some Aboriginal women are concerned that a return to traditional ways of life will mean abandoning the gains of the liberal Charter of Rights and Freedoms and a return to a society of patriarchal subjection.

Programmatic Function. Orientation or understanding by itself, of course, is not enough to overcome oppression. It must be joined to action. The identity ideologies take many different courses, depending upon the challenges they confront in different circumstances. Here the differences between the national or communal demands of Aboriginal peoples and the individualist demands of LGBTQ peoples or the liberal variants of feminism or black rights become more pronounced. The liberal or integrationist variants typically try to bring about change by action, such as the court cases to legalize gay and lesbian marriage. The radical or separatist variants tend to favour activities that challenge the established social and legal framework, such as attempts to achieve Aboriginal self-government and assert a greater degree of national independence from the dominant white society. Identity movements of all sorts often resort to boycotts, demonstrations, and civil disobedience—public and peaceful acts of lawbreaking—to call attention to their views. Some advocate violence in some circumstances as a form of self-defence against the oppressors who are doing violence to them.[24] But whatever their tactics, in general terms they all share the same program: to bring an end to the oppression of a group of people so that they may live full and free lives.

Ideologies of Identity and the Democratic Ideal

One final question remains: How do ideologies of identity construe the democratic ideal? They typically think of democracy as self-rule, which is consistent with the conception of democracy found in other ideologies. But identity ideologies also point out that self-rule is impossible unless people have a more or less well-developed sense of self-worth and self-respect; for this reason, they aim to reinforce that sense of dignity, self-worth, and identity in their respective audiences. This they do in the ways that we listed at the beginning of this chapter. Each addresses a particular audience whose experiences are historically unique, although all have experienced oppression of some sort. Each recognizes these experiences as real and valid and leads those whom it addresses to examine the origins, memory, and effects of such oppression. Typically, these include internalized inhibitions and barriers—feelings of inferiority or inadequacy, for example—that stand in the way of their being actively self-ruling agents who seek to achieve the goals they have set for themselves. Since these effects are not only physical but also psychological, an ideology of identity helps people recognize and overcome the damage oppression has done to their psyches by affirming their identities and raising their consciousness—that is, by making conscious and articulate what had previously remained unconscious and inarticulate. Finally, these ideologies intend to inform and educate not only victims but also their oppressors. Oppressors suffer (usually without knowing it) from the stifling and stunting of their moral, intellectual, and civic capacities.

At first glance, the ideologies of identity, which are based on personal characteristics such as gender or sexual orientation (rather than identity with a national group), fit well with liberal democracy. Indeed, those ideologies are arguably merely variants of liberalism, or perhaps the logical extension of liberalism, which tends to view people as independent and isolated units with equal status regardless of personal characteristics. Thus, the theoretical equality of status inherent in classical liberalism can be realized fully only when different groups have successfully pursued their politics of identity and eliminated the differential treatment to which their group was subject. Liberal democracy is a compromise between the concept of democracy as self-rule by the majority and the liberal defence of individuals and minorities; and, as noted in Chapter 4, it stresses the right of the individual to do what he or she pleases, free of outside interference. In Canada, which has a constitutionally entrenched set of human rights in the Charter, the tension between group and individual rights is very clear when the courts are asked to uphold the rights of individuals and minorities against laws and policies democratically approved by a majority.

The politics of identity practised by national groups such as Aboriginal peoples are often difficult to reconcile with liberal democracy because of their focus on the group and its rights rather than on the individual. The result may be conflict between group and

---

[24]See, for example, Malcolm X, *Malcolm X Speaks* (New York: Grove, 1966).

individual rights, such as those of Aboriginal peoples as a whole and Aboriginal women as individuals who have objected to traditional but discriminatory rules or practices. More generally, these ideologies of identity also clash with the democratic principle of majority rule against which they assert group rights. The politics of identity rejects elements of both liberalism and democracy. For this reason, critics have viewed politics of identity practised by national groups as both race-based (and therefore unliberal) and inconsistent with democratic rule, because such groups consider themselves to be separate and immune from rule by the majority of the larger society in which they exist. These critics hold that all individuals should be equal before the law and that courts should be blind to race, ethnicity, or other forms of group identification. They also point to the possibility of racial or ethnic strife and the fragmentation of national political systems resulting from the politics of identity.

The politics of identity of national groups is perhaps easier to reconcile with theories of social democracy for two reasons. First, social democracy, with some roots in socialism, is more comfortable with viewing society as composed of groups as well as individuals. Consequently, the suggestion that individual rights should to some extent be subordinated to group rights is not one that social democrats find unacceptable in theory. As well, social democracy has given high value to achieving equality of condition, and national groups that practise the politics of identity tend to be poor and economically powerless. Therefore, to the extent that the politics of identity promises to combat poverty and underdevelopment, those groups find a sympathetic ear in social democracy. Whether drawing inspiration and support from social democratic ideas or from liberal ideas, however, the politics of identity has become a well-entrenched feature of the democratic landscape in Western countries.

For Further Reading

Aboriginal Rights

Andrews v. Law Society of British Columbia. 1 S.C.R. 143 [citizenship] (1988); *Egan v. Canada.* 2 S.C.R. 513 [sexual orientation] (1995).

Brown, Dee. *Bury My Heart at Wounded Knee: An Indian History of the American West.* New York: Holt, 1970.

Cairns, Alan. *Citizens Plus: Aboriginal Peoples and the Canadian State.* Vancouver: UBC P, 2001.

Deloria, Vine, Jr., and Clifford Little. *The Nations Within: The Past and Future of American Indian Sovereignty.* New York: Pantheon, 1984.

Flanagan, Thomas. *First Nations, Second Thoughts.* Montreal: McGill-Queen's UP, 2000.

Hedican, Edward J. *Understanding Aboriginal Issues.* Toronto: U of Toronto P, 1995.

Little Bear, Leroy, Menno Boldt, and J. Anthony Long, eds. *Pathways to Self-Determination.* Toronto: U of Toronto P, 1984.

Monture-Angus, Patricia. *Thunder in My Soul: A Mohawk Woman Speaks.* Halifax: Fernwood, 1995.

Richardson, Boyce, ed. *Drumbeat: Anger and Renewal in Indian Country.* Assembly of First Nations: Summerhill; distributed by U of Toronto P, 1989.

Wub-E-Ke-Niew. *We Have the Right to Exist.* New York: Black Thistle, 1995.

Feminism

Beauvoir, Simone de. *The Second Sex.* New York: Bantam, 1968.

Elshtain, Jean Bethke. *Public Man, Private Woman: Women in Social and Political Thought.* Princeton, NJ: Princeton UP, 1981.

Friedan, Betty. *The Feminine Mystique.* New York: Norton, 1963.

Grimké, Sarah. *Letters on the Equality of the Sexes.* Ed. Elizabeth Ann Bartlett. New Haven, CT: Yale UP, 1988.

hooks, bell. *Feminist Theory: Margin to Center.* Boston: South End, 1984.

Jaggar, Allison. *Feminist Politics and Human Nature.* Lanham, MD: Rowman, 1988.

James, Susan, "Feminisms." *The Cambridge History of Twentieth-Century Political Thought.* Ed. Terence Ball and Richard Bellamy. Cambridge: Cambridge UP, 2003.

Mill, John Stuart. *The Subjection of Women* [1869] in *John Stuart Mill: Three Essays.* Ed. Richard Wollheim. Oxford: Oxford UP, 1975.

Mitchell, Juliet. *Woman's Estate.* New York: Vintage, 1973.

Schneir, Miriam, ed. *Feminism: The Essential Historical Writings.* New York: Vintage, 1972.

Tong, Rosemarie. *Feminist Thought.* 2d ed. Boulder, CO: Westview, 1998.

LGBTQ Rights

Adam, Barry. *The Rise of the Gay and Lesbian Movement.* New York: Twayne Publishers, 1995.

Bawer, Bruce. *A Place at the Table: The Gay Individual in American Society.* New York: Poseidon, 1993.

Cain, P. *Lesbian and Gay Rights.* Toronto: HarperCollins, 2004.

Corvino, John, ed. *Same Sex: Debating the Ethics, Science, and Culture of Homosexuality.* Lanham, MD: Rowman, 1997.

Cruikshank, Margaret. *The Gay and Lesbian Movement.* London: Routledge, 1992.

Goldie, Terry. *In a Queer Country: Gay and Lesbian Studies in the Canadian Context.* Vancouver: Arsenal, 2001.

Knegt, Peter. *Queer Rights.* Halifax: Fernwood Pub., 2011.

Marcus, Eric. *Making History: The Struggle for Gay and Lesbian Equal Rights, 1945–1990.* New York: HarperCollins, 1992.

Mohr, Richard. *Gays/Justice.* New York: Columbia UP, 1988.

Sullivan, Andrew. *Virtually Normal: An Argument about Homosexuality.* New York: Knopf, 1995.

Racial and Ethnic Minority Rights

Biko, Steve. *I Write What I Like.* Ed. Malusi and Thoko Mpumlwana. London: Bowerdean, 1996.

Branch, Taylor. *Parting the Waters: America in the King Years, 1954–1963.* New York: Simon, 1988.

————. *Pillar of Fire: America in the King Years, 1963–1965.* New York: Simon, 1998.

Carmichael, Stokely, and Charles Hamilton. *Black Power.* New York: Vintage, 1967.

Clairmont, D., and D. Magill. *Africville: The Life and Death of a Canadian Black Community.* Toronto: Canadian Scholars', 1987.

Fanon, Frantz. *Black Skin, White Masks.* New York: Grove, 1982.

Grier, William H., and Price N. Cobbs. *Black Rage.* New York: Bantam, 1969.

Gutman, Amy, ed. *Multiculturalism: Examining the Politics of Recognition.* Princeton, NJ: Princeton UP, 1994.

King, Martin Luther, Jr. *Why We Can't Wait.* New York: Harper, 1964.

West, Cornel. *Race Matters.* New York: Vintage, 1994.

X, Malcolm. *The Autobiography of Malcolm X.* New York: Grove, 1965.

————. *Malcolm X Speaks.* New York: Grove, 1966.

From the Ball and Dagger Reader *Ideals and Ideologies*, US Eighth Edition

Part Eight: Liberation Ideologies and the Politics of Identity

Useful Websites and Social Media

www.chrc-ccdp.ca Canadian Human Rights Commission

Aboriginal Rights

www.bctreaty.net BC Treaty Commission

www.afn.ca Assembly of First Nations

www.nwac.ca Native Women's Association of Canada

Racial and Minority Rights

www.naacp.org National Association for the Advancement of Colored People

http://blackhistorycanada.ca Black History Canada

Women's Rights

www.law-lib.utoronto.ca/diana University of Toronto Women's Human Rights Resources Programme

www.leaf.ca Women's Legal Education and Action Fund

http://www.amnesty.ca/blog/index.php?TopicID=132 Amnesty International Canada and Women's Human Rights

www.dawncanada.net DisAbled Women's Network of Canada

www.swc-cfc.gc.ca Status of Women Canada

www.elizabethfry.ca Canadian Association of Elizabeth Fry Societies

LGBTQ Rights

www.pflagcanada.ca Parents and Friends of Lesbians and Gays Canada

www.lambdalegal.org Lambda Legal

www.egale.ca Egale Canada

www.uwo.ca/pridelib The University of Western Ontario Pride Library

Twitter:

@pridelibrary

Discussion Questions

1. Are feminists and LGBTQ supporters properly viewed as proponents of liberalism, albeit applied in a very specific context, rather than espousing a distinct ideology?

2. Some commentators, particularly on the right wing of the political spectrum, advocate abolishing the system of Indian reserves and allowing individual ownership of First Nations lands. Consider the extent to which these proposals are ideologically-driven.

3. Contrast the provisions of the Charter of Rights and Freedoms that focus on individual rights with those that protect group or collective rights.

4. Do the politics of identity put such emphasis on the needs or demands of particular groups that they threaten the cohesion of the wider society or impair the ability of government to act in the wider public interest?

MySearchLab   MySearchLab with eText offers you access to an online interactive version of the text, additional quizzes and assessment, extensive help with your writing and research projects, and provides round-the-clock access to credible and reliable source material. Go to **www.mysearchlab.com** to access these resources.

CHAPTER 12

Green Politics: Ecology as Ideology

I hold a vision of this blue green planet, safe and in balance. At the end of the Fossil Fuel Era, we are emerging to a new reality. We are ready to make the next leap—as momentous as abolishing slavery or giving women the vote. We are ready to make the fundamental shifts that allow us to live in balance with our life support systems, respecting each other, achieving social and economic justice, peace and democracy.

—Elizabeth May (Green Party leader)

LEARNING OBJECTIVES

After completing this chapter you should be able to

1. Describe the diversity of ideas that make up the Green movement, and explain the goals of the animal rights movement.

2. Explain the concept of stewardship and its implications.

3. Effectively evaluate the unresolved differences in Green ideology.

4. State the importance of speciesism to the animal rights movement.

5. Outline the concerns Greens have regarding globalization.

6. Contrast the Green view of democracy with the liberal view.

Although many of its ideas are old, this ideology is quite new. For some, environmentalism as an ideology was born on September 27, 1962, when Rachel Carson published *Silent Spring;* others say that an even more important event was April 22, 1970, the first Earth Day. Because many within this movement call their perspective **Green politics** and themselves Greens, we will refer to them and their ideology in this way.[1]

The crisis out of which a broadly based Green movement emerged is the environmental crisis. Actually, this is not a single crisis but a series of crises arising in connection with the ecological and environmental damage wrought by population growth, pollution of air and water, the destruction of the tropical rain forests, the rapid extinction of entire species of plants and animals, the greenhouse effect (the warming of the earth's atmosphere), the destruction of old-growth forests, the killing of lakes by acid rain, the depletion of the earth's protective ozone layer, and the melting of the polar ice cap, which threatens the way of life of Canada's Aboriginal peoples.

These crises are interconnected. Moreover, all are the result of human actions and practices over the past two centuries. Many are byproducts of technological innovations such as the internal combustion engine. Yet the causes of these environmental crises, according to many environmentalists, are as much ideological as they are technological. That is, they stem from ideas and ideologies that place human beings above or apart from nature.

---

[1]For two very different exemplars, see Fritjof Capra and Charlene Spritnak, *Green Politics* (New York: Dutton, 1984), and Robert E. Goodin, *Green Political Theory* (Cambridge: Polity, 1992). For an historical overview, see Terence Ball, "Green Political Theory," *The Cambridge History of Twentieth-Century Political Thought,* ed. Terence Ball and Richard Bellamy (Cambridge: Cambridge UP, 2003).

The Green movement proposes its own *counter-ideology,* which has two main aspects. First, this counter-ideology critiques some of the key assumptions underlying the ideologies that have long dominated modern politics. Second, it attempts to offer a more positive and hopeful vision of human beings' relation with the natural environment and with one another. This second aspect does not mean that we should think of advocates of a Green or environmental ideology as exclusively liberal or left-leaning. Some call themselves conservative environmentalists in the tradition of Edmund Burke, who wrote that each generation has a duty to leave to posterity "a habitation," not a "ruin."[2] Others call themselves free-market or libertarian environmentalists because they believe that free-market competition and private ownership of property are the best means of protecting the natural environment.[3] Still others proceed from the religious premise that the earth is God's creation and that human beings may not exploit or despoil it for momentary pleasure or profit. These people contend that nature is to be treated with reverence, which is to say that humans have an obligation to care for and be good stewards of God's creation.[4] There are differences among Greens, then, just as there are differences among liberals, conservatives, socialists, and the adherents of other ideologies. But there is little disagreement about the urgency of the need to rethink our attitudes toward and actions within the natural environment.

THE GREEN CRITIQUE OF OTHER IDEOLOGIES

According to Greens, devising and implementing an alternative environmental ideology is not merely one option among many; it may be the only remaining chance that human beings have to save the planet and its myriad of species—including the human species. This is because the human species is linked to and deeply dependent upon other species of plants and animals. All are, in a word, interdependent. To see this interdependence in action, consider the tale of the tree. Trees are a source not only of shade and lumber but also of oxygen, which they exchange for the carbon dioxide (CO_2) that is a byproduct of burning and other processes of oxidation, including breathing: Approximately twenty times per minute we breathe in a mixture of oxygen, nitrogen, and other gases, and we exhale CO_2 with every breath. Clearing tropical rain forests or destroying northern forests with acid rain therefore reduces the amount of oxygen available for us and other creatures to breathe. Less oxygen in turn increases the amount of carbon dioxide in the atmosphere, which results in the further warming of the earth's atmosphere known as the **greenhouse effect**. This global warming in turn brings drought, transforms formerly fertile land into deserts and dustbowls, and thereby reduces plant life and crop production, which means that humans and animals go hungry or perhaps even starve. It also brings in its wake the gradual melting of the polar ice caps, thereby raising sea levels and

---

[2]Gordon K. Durnil, *The Making of a Conservative Environmentalist* (Bloomington: Indiana UP, 1995); James R. Dunn and John E. Kinney, *Conservative Environmentalism* (Westport, CT: Quorum, 1996); John R. E. Bliese, *The Greening of Conservative America* (Boulder, CO: Westview, 2001); John Gray, *Beyond the New Right: Markets, Government, and the Common Environment* (London: Routledge, 1993) chapter 4; Edmund Burke, *Reflections on the Revolution in France,* ed. C. C. O'Brien (Harmondsworth, UK: Penguin, 1969) 192.

[3]Terry L. Anderson and Donald T. Leal, *Free Market Environmentalism* (Boulder, CO: Westview, 1991); William C. Mitchell and Randy T. Simmons, *Beyond Politics* (Boulder, CO: Westview, 1994).

[4]Max Oelschlaeger, *Caring for Creation: An Ecumenical Approach to the Environmental Crisis* (New Haven, CT: Yale UP, 1994); Robert Booth Fowler, *The Greening of Protestant Thought* (Chapel Hill: U of North Carolina P, 1995).

potentially flooding many low-lying coastal areas, including most of coastal British Columbia and much of countries like Holland.

The moral of the tale of the tree is simply this: All things are connected. To put the point another way: What goes around comes around. In one sense, this is not an entirely new message. All of the world's great religions have said much the same thing in one way or another. According to Christianity: "Whatsoever a man soweth, that shall he also reap" (New Testament, Galatians 6:7). According to Buddhism: "Just as the nature of earth is one / While beings each live separately / And the earth has no thought of oneness or difference / So is the truth of the Buddha" (Avatamsaka Sutra). And according to Hinduism: "Everything within this world is possessed by God. He pervades both the animate and the inanimate. Therefore one should only take one's fair share, and leave the rest to the Supreme" (Isa Upanishad).

This is true not only of individuals but also of human beings from one generation to another. In other words, what human beings do in one time and place will affect other human beings and other species in other times and places. All actions, however small, can have large and long-lasting consequences.

While the world's major religions have taught that all things are interconnected, most of the major modern ideologies have not. It is for this reason that Greens tend to be quite critical of other ideologies, **right** and **left** alike. They criticize not only the specific beliefs and doctrines of those other ideologies but, no less important, their *unexamined assumptions* as well.

APPROACHES TO NATURE IN THE WESTERN PHILOSOPHICAL TRADITION

Consider, for example, the assumptions about nature and human beings' relationship to nature shared by several modern ideologies. Liberals, socialists, and individualist conservatives share a similar attitude toward nature, one that celebrates the ever-increasing human conquest or mastery of nature. They see nature as either a hostile force to be conquered or a resource base to be harnessed for such human purposes as growth and economic development. Therefore, they measure technological, scientific, and economic progress in terms of the human species' power over nature. In the view of Canadian philosopher George Grant, the roots of the problem are very deep. The technological stance toward nature began in the seventeenth century in the writings of British philosopher Francis Bacon (1561–1626). Bacon is often thought of as the inventor of experimental science, but his motive for doing so was deeply rooted in Christianity. Christianity had taught its followers to feed the hungry and heal the sick, and Bacon took that responsibility very seriously. He wanted to do it as efficiently and as productively as possible and his new scientific method was his means to achieve the dream that had eluded Christians for centuries. However, the discourse used early on by seventeenth-century European thinkers tended to exhibit an adversarial attitude. Indeed, Bacon speaks of nature much as the Marquis de Sade was later to speak of women. Nature (always "her") is haughty and proud but must be dominated, humbled, and humiliated by "man," whose sense of power increases with his "conquest" of nature. Nature must be "interrogated," "subdued," and made to "yield up her secrets" to man, Bacon declared, so that man can then turn nature's secrets against her, "shaping nature as on an anvil." Through their technology, men do not "merely exert a gentle guidance over nature's course; they have the power to conquer and subdue her, to shake her to her foundations." Finally, "by art and the hand of man she is forced out of her natural state, and squeezed and moulded" for human purposes.[5]

Similarly, though less sadistically, British philosopher John Locke (1632–1704) believed that nature in itself was without value. It is only when people put "waste" land and resources to human use that they acquire whatever "value" they have: "land that is left wholly to nature, that hath no improvement of pasturage, tillage, or planting, is called, as indeed it is, waste; and we shall find the benefit of it amount to little more than nothing."[6] (By "benefit" Locke meant direct *human* benefit; "waste land" is of enormous benefit to the nonhuman creatures and plants that inhabit it.) British physicist and mathematician Isaac Newton (1642–1727), who discovered the laws of planetary motion and gravity, was also a deeply religious thinker, for whom the laws of nature were the laws of God. The greater understanding scientists had over nature, the closer they were coming to understanding God, in the opinion of Bacon and Newton. So the impulse to understand was very powerful. The impulse to control was just as strong. In the first book of the English translation of the Bible, these scientists in the Western tradition had read: "Be fruitful and increase, fill the earth and subdue it, rule over the fish in the sea, the birds of heaven, and every living thing that moves upon the earth."[7] They interpreted this to mean that human beings were supposed to dominate and control nature according to their will.

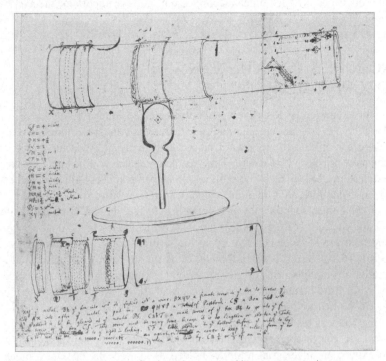

Rough sketch showing a reflecting telescope and its components, Isaac Newton (1642–1727)

---

[5]Quoted in William Leiss, *The Domination of Nature* (New York: George Braziller, 1972) 58–59.
[6]John Locke, *Second Treatise of Government,* paragraph 42; see Terence Ball and Richard Dagger, eds., *Ideals and Ideologies: A Reader,* 8th ed. (New York: Longman, 2011) selection 3.11.
[7]*New English Bible,* Genesis 1, 28–29 (Cambridge: Oxford UP and Cambridge UP, 1970).

Even Karl Marx (1818–1883), critical as he was of capitalism and the liberal ideology that justified it, nevertheless waxed enthusiastic about the increased power over nature that capitalism had brought about:

> The bourgeoisie, during its rule of scarce one hundred years, has created more massive and more colossal productive forces than have all preceding generations together. Subjection of nature's forces to man, machinery, application of chemistry to industry and agriculture, steam-navigation, railways, electric telegraphs, clearing of whole continents for cultivation, canalization of rivers, whole populations conjured up out of the ground—what earlier century had even a presentiment that such productive forces slumbered in the lap of social labour?[8]

As Western science became more sophisticated, the test it gave itself was: Will this work? Can we use this machine to pump water out of mines? Can this machine weave cotton cloth faster than individual weavers? Can a steam-driven engine on steel rails pull people and goods faster from city to city than horse-drawn carriages? The perception was that if the answer to any such questions was yes, then the science was good, and those who objected stood in the way of God and progress.

Technology also spread throughout the world because of military demands. New advances in warfare rendered existing military equipment obsolete, placing a nation lacking the new technology potentially at risk from a hostile neighbour. The atomic bomb is a case in point. Even Albert Einstein, who abhorred the idea of an atomic weapon, encouraged President Roosevelt to build one because he knew the Nazi scientists were capable of creating such a weapon and feared they would create one first. As well, after the Second World War, some left-leaning Americans gave nuclear secrets to the Soviet Union because they wanted the communist state to be able to protect itself from aggressive American capitalism. More recently, India developed nuclear devices because its potential enemy China had them; then Pakistan, India's uneasy neighbour, created its own nuclear weapons with China's help and sold the technology to countries such as North Korea and Libya, which felt they had defensive needs of their own. Although the Nuclear Non-proliferation Treaty was signed in 1968, the danger that nuclear weapons will be used between states has increased over the years.

There are two other problems with nuclear weapons. One is that the knowledge to build nuclear weapons is no longer difficult to come by. It is unlikely, but not impossible, that terrorists could come into possession of a nuclear device, or could create one themselves, and use it to terrible effect in a great city. Another problem is the fleet of the former Soviet Union, many of whose ships and submarines are nuclear powered. Now that the Russian government is not prepared to spend such a high proportion of its national income on its armed forces, many of these ships are left to decay untended in their dockyards with the possibility of causing serious damage from their nuclear cores. When nuclear weapons and other nuclear facilities were created, few people reckoned the real cost of decommissioning them.

In light of these problems, Greens say that it is scarcely surprising that liberal capitalist and communist societies are alike in sharing the bias called **anthropocentrism**.[9] Both prefer economic growth and productivity at the expense of the natural environment. Nor

---

[8]Karl Marx and Friedrich Engels, *The Manifesto of the Communist Party* in *Marx and Engels: Basic Writings on Politics and Philosophy*, ed. Lewis S. Feuer (Garden City, NY: Doubleday, 1959) 12; see Ball and Dagger, selection 35.

[9]David Ehrenfeld, *The Arrogance of Humanism* (New York: Oxford UP, 1978).

is it surprising, they say, that rivers like the Volga and the Mississippi are little more than open sewers and that the lakes and fish and pine trees of Siberia, New England, and eastern Canada are being poisoned by acid rain. Although Ukraine was the scene of the world's worst nuclear accident to date—at Chernobyl in 1986—the United States came quite close to disaster at Three Mile Island in Pennsylvania in 1979. Past and possible future accidents aside, Canada, the United States, Russia, China, and other countries are producing deadly nuclear and chemical wastes without any means of storing them safely for the thousands of years that they will remain highly dangerous to the health of humans and other beings. Countries with unstable governments such as North Korea and Iran are also developing a nuclear capability.

Greens see little difference between socialism and capitalism. Before the fall of the Soviet Union, it seemed as if socialism and communism, as capitalism's enemies, were the natural allies of Greens. Since the early 1990s that alliance has dissolved, and Greens increasingly seek power in their own right. Even social democracy and regulated capitalism are too deeply in league with modern industrialism to make the changes necessary for a healthy and sustainable environment.

TOWARD AN ECOLOGICAL ETHIC

Many Greens prefer not to call their perspective an ideology but an "ethic." Early twentieth-century ecological thinkers, such as Aldo Leopold (1887–1948), spoke of a **land ethic**.[10] More recently, others have spoken of an ethic with earth itself at the centre,[11] while others, in a similar spirit, have spoken of an emerging "planetary ethic."[12] More often, however, Greens embrace an ethic they call **ecocentrism** (ecosystem-centred) or **biocentrism** (life-centred).

Greens say that an ecocentric or biocentric ethic emphasizes the web of interconnectivity and mutual dependence within which we and other species live. People are connected not only with one another but also with other species of animals and plants. The latter include not only those that human beings eat—fish, cows, and corn, for example—but also the tiny plankton on which whales and ocean fish feed, the insects and minnows on which lake and river fish feed, and the worms that loosen and aerate the soil in which the corn grows. The corn feeds the cows that fertilize the fields, and the humans eat the fish, the corn, and the cows. All are interdependent participants in the cycle of birth, life, death, decay, and rebirth. And all the participants in this cycle depend upon the air and water, the sunlight and soil, without which life is impossible. Greens also argue that it is important to be aware of the conditions under which what we consume is produced. For example, the Fair Trade Coffee movement insists on a minimum payment for workers, a ban on child labour, on sanitary working conditions, and organic farming methods with the coffee trees grown under shade canopies. The fair trade movement has raised awareness of industrial farming practices in poor countries and now extends to other products such as cut flowers.

Greens believe that interconnection and interdependence are elemental truths that humans forget at their peril. Yet we separate ourselves from nature and divide our lives and experiences into separate compartments. For instance, we think of vegetables and

---

[10]Aldo Leopold, *A Sand County Almanac* (New York: Oxford UP, 1968); see Ball and Dagger, selection 9.61.

[11]See, for example, Christopher Stone, *Earth and Other Ethics* (New York: Harper, 1987).

[12]Hans Jonas, *The Imperative of Responsibility* (Chicago: U of Chicago P, 1984).

meats as commodities that come from the grocery store wrapped in plastic and Styrofoam, and water as it comes from the faucet or bottle. We rarely pause to reflect upon what makes these things possible and available to us, or how much we depend on them—and they on us. But this sense of disconnectedness, Greens charge, is an illusion that, unless dispelled, will doom our species and many others to extinction.

But where do we go to learn about interconnection and interdependence? There are many available avenues. There is science, particularly the disciplines of biology, **ecology**, and geology, and also literature, music, and art. Philosophy and various religions also have much to contribute. One neglected source, Greens remind us, is the folk wisdom of Native peoples, such as Canada's Aboriginal peoples. According to the Assembly of First Nations, "First Nations traditional philosophy holds that everything is interconnected. Humanity is part of the ecosystem not separate and apart from it. First Nations peoples hold an inexorable connection to the land they have traditionally occupied. Our Elders are deeply concerned about the state of the environment."[13]

Several other features of an ecological, or Green, ethic follow from the recognition of interconnectedness and interdependence. The first of these is a respect for life—not only human life but all life, from the tiniest micro-organism to the largest whale. The fate of our species is tied to theirs and theirs to ours. Since life requires certain conditions to sustain it, a second feature follows: We have an obligation to respect and care for the conditions that nurture and sustain life in its many forms. From the aquifers below to the soil and water and air above, nature nourishes its creatures within a complex web of interconnected conditions. To damage one is to damage the others, and to endanger the existence of any creature that dwells within and depends upon the integrity of this delicate, life-sustaining web is to endanger all. That leads many Greens to be vegans or vegetarians or, if they eat meat, to insist on extremely high and humane standards in the treatment of animals.

A Green ethic does not deny the enormous power that humans have over nature. On the contrary, it requires that people recognize the extent of their power—and take full responsibility for restraining it and using it wisely and well. Greens point out that the fate of the earth and all its creatures now depends, for better or for worse, on human decisions and actions. Not only do we depend on nature, they say, but also nature depends on us— on our care and restraint and forbearance. It is within our power to destroy the earth many times over. This we can do very quickly in the case of nuclear war (or rather, since the word *war* implies victors and vanquished, and nuclear war will have no winners, *nuclear omnicide*—that is, the destruction of everything and everyone). Every local conflict, however small at first, could turn into a nuclear confrontation, with predictably deadly results. In the words of His Holiness the Dalai Lama:

> We know that to wage a nuclear war today, for example, would be a form of suicide; that to pollute the air or the oceans, in order to achieve some short-term benefit, would be to destroy the very basis for our survival. As individuals and nations are becoming increasingly interdependent we have no other choice than to develop what I call a sense of universal responsibility.[14]

---

[13]*Assembly of First Nations,* 26 May 2004. www.afn.ca/Assembly_of_First_Nations.htm.
[14]HH The Dalai Lama. *Buddhism as Ecology.* ed. M. Batchelor and K. Brown (Delhi: Motilal Banarsidass, 1994) 10.

CIVIL DISOBEDIENCE

From this point emerges another feature of a Green ethic: employing the tactics of direct confrontation and nonviolent protest and resistance in the manner of Mohandas (Mahatma) Gandhi, Martin Luther King, Jr., and others. Many activist Greens have used these tactics to protest the clear-cutting of old-growth forests, the construction of nuclear power plants, and other activities they deem to be destructive of the natural environment. They will sit across logging roads to prevent equipment from reaching a forest, or block railway lines or highways to stop a shipment of toxic waste.

According to Greens, taking a stand to protect the environment is now necessary because the earth and all its inhabitants can be destroyed not only by nuclear omnicide but also by slower, though no less destructive, methods of environmental degradation, including the cumulative effects of small-scale, everyday acts. All actions, however small or seemingly insignificant, produce consequences or effects, sometimes out of proportion to the actions that bring them about. Thus, a Green ethic also includes a duty of **stewardship** toward the environment.

To be a steward is to be responsible for the care of something, and Greens contend that we all must be stewards of the earth. This stewardship includes an obligation to take into account the health and well-being of distant future generations. Humans now have the power to alter the natural environment permanently in ways that will affect the health, happiness, and well-being of people who will not be born until long after we are all dead. The radioactive wastes generated by nuclear power plants, for example, will be intensely "hot" and highly toxic far into the future. No one yet knows how to store such material safely for hundreds, much less the necessary tens of thousands, of years. Obviously, it would be unjust for the present generation to enjoy the benefits of nuclear power while passing on to distant posterity the burdens and dangers brought about by our actions.

There are many other less dramatic but no less serious examples of intergenerational harms and hazards: global warming, loss of topsoil, disappearing rain forests, the emptying and/or polluting of underground aquifers, and the depletion of nonrenewable energy sources such as fossil fuels. Reserves of oil, coal, and natural gas are finite and irreplaceable. Once burned as gasoline—or turned into plastic or some other petroleum-based product—a gallon of oil is gone forever. Every drop or barrel used now is therefore unavailable for future people to use. As poet and essayist Wendell Berry observed, the oft-heard claim that fossil-fuel energy is cheap rests on a simplistic and morally doubtful assumption about the rights of the present generation:

> We were able to consider [fossil fuel] "cheap" only by a kind of moral simplicity: the assumption that we had a "right" to as much of it as we could use. This was a "right" made solely by might. Since fossil fuels, however abundant they once were, were nevertheless limited in quantity and not renewable, they obviously did not "belong" to one generation more than another. We ignored the claims of posterity simply because we could, the living being stronger than the unborn, and so worked the "miracle" of industrial progress by the theft of energy from (among others) our children.

And that, Berry adds, "is the real foundation of our progress and our affluence. The reason that we [in the United States] are a rich nation is not that we have earned so much wealth—you cannot, by any honest means, earn or deserve so much. The reason is simply that we have learned, and become willing, to market and use up in our own time the birthright and livelihood of posterity."[15] These and other considerations lead Greens to advocate limits on present-day consumption so as to save a fair share of scarce resources for future generations. Obviously, it would be unjust for the present generation to enjoy the benefits of fossil fuels, nuclear power, and disposable products while passing on to distant posterity the shortages, dangers, and pollution brought about by our actions.

PROBLEMS THE GREEN ETHIC FACES

Time Horizons. Why, skeptics ask, should we do anything for posterity? After all, what has posterity ever done for us?[16] What motivation might we have to act now for the sake and safety of future people? These questions raise the so-called **time horizon** problem.

Time horizon refers to how far ahead people think when they are deciding what to do. Horizons mark the limits of our vision—of how far we can see—so a *time* horizon marks the limit of how far into the future people can or will see. Those people who always seem to be planning years and even decades in advance have long time horizons; those who have trouble thinking beyond today have very short ones. Everyone faces the question of how to weigh the value of something near at hand against the value of something in the future. If someone offers to give you $20 today or $20 tomorrow, for instance, you would almost certainly take the money today. If you were offered a choice between $20 today or $22 tomorrow, you would have to decide whether the extra $2 is worth the wait. And if you had to choose between $20 now and $200 a year from now, what would you do? In general, the more distant the benefit, the greater the benefit must be to compensate for the delay in receiving it.

This time-horizon problem is especially troublesome for Greens. First, they have to persuade people that it is worthwhile to make a sacrifice now in the expectation that it will benefit someone else in the future. Second, they have to convince people to care about future generations. Third, they have to find a way to assure each individual that other people won't take advantage of his or her sacrifices. In other words, if I drive an environmentally friendly car, what's the point of my sacrifice if both of my neighbours are driving SUVs?

Faith in Technology. Greens often face strong critics and counterarguments. For example, Pierre Elliott Trudeau (1919–2000) was convinced that environmentalists who worried that the world would exhaust its supply of fossil fuels were merely timid. In the past, he observed, technology had always replaced one form of energy with another. Why expect the future to be different? If we left our resources in the ground, we would just be wasting them. Trudeau felt that people should actively embrace the *cybernetic revolution*. The state should guide technological change using tools "made up of advanced technology and scientific investigation . . . [T]he political tools of the future will be designed and appraised by more rational standards than anything we are currently using in Canada today."[17]

---

[15]Wendell Berry, *The Gift of Good Land* (San Francisco: North Point, 1981) 127.

[16]Although this is not the position he takes, this is how Robert Heilbroner poses the challenge facing those who want to curtail present-day consumption. See Robert Heilbroner, "What Has Posterity Ever Done for Me?" *New York Times Magazine*, Jan. 19, 1975.

[17]Pierre Trudeau, "Federalism, Nationalism and Reason," *The Future of Canadian Federalism,* ed. P. A. Crepeau and C. B. Macpherson (Toronto: U of Toronto P, 1965) 26.

Cybernetics works at a grand political level. At the other extreme is **nanotechnology**, science that works at the level of the infinitesimally small. Its proponents, who include politicians such as former Republican Speaker of the U.S. House of Representatives Newt Gingrich, expect that scientists will eventually be able to extract the harmful elements from a technology while preserving that which is good. For example, scientists might be able to make ethanol so efficient that it would replace gasoline and thereby dramatically reduce the problem of global warming. Both of these arguments are based on **ecotechnology**, the belief that technology can resolve the problems that it created in the first place.

Collective Action and the Tragedy of the Commons. Greens also face the problem of *collective action*—when they urge people to consume less and conserve more for the benefit of future generations. The problem applies to sacrifices made for the good of people who are now living as well as of those who may or will live in the future. To understand this collective action problem, we must grasp the difference between *private* and *public* goods. A **private good** is anything that can be divided and distributed, such as money or food. If Ann and Bob buy a cake, they can divide it between themselves as they see fit. They can also refuse to give any of it to anyone who did not help to pay for the cake. But a **public good** cannot be divided or distributed in this way. In technical terms, public goods are indivisible and nonrival. In other words, a public good cannot be divided into portions, nor is there any competition or rivalry to possess it. Clean air is a standard example: It cannot be divided, and no one's enjoyment or use of it prevents anyone else from enjoying or using it equally.

Problems arise when a public good requires the cooperation of many people, as in efforts to reduce pollution or conserve resources. In such cases individuals have little reason to cooperate by joining the effort, especially when cooperation is unpleasant. One person's contribution—using less gasoline or electricity, for example—will make no real difference to the success or failure of the effort, but it will be a hardship for that person. So a rational, self-interested person will try to be a free rider—that is, try to withhold cooperation while hoping that enough people will participate to make the effort a success. If that happens, then the free rider will eventually enjoy the public good of cleaner air even though he or she did nothing to help reduce air pollution. If too many people try to be free riders, the attempt to produce the public good will fail for lack of cooperation (see Figure 12.1). But every person who tries to be a free rider can always say, "My actions didn't make the difference. The effort would have failed whether I joined in or not."

This collective action problem leads to many social and political difficulties, not the least of which are environmental. For example, it may explain why voluntary efforts to reduce automobile traffic and cut energy or water use so often fail. As formulated in the "tragedy of the commons," moreover, collective action theory accounts for the tendency to overuse and exhaust common resources, such as grazing land, fishing banks, and perhaps the earth itself. American ecologist Garrett Hardin (1915–2003) developed this idea in an essay, "The Tragedy of the Commons," by using the history of the village commons in England to illustrate the relationship between modern society and the natural environment.[18] As Hardin explained, English villagers once had the right to graze their livestock on common land that belonged to the whole village. If they grazed too many animals

---

[18]Garrett Hardin, "The Tragedy of the Commons," *Science* 162 (December 13, 1968): 1243–1248.

FIGURE 12.1	The Collective-Action Problem Illustrated: Is It Rational for the Individual to Try to Conserve Resources When He or She Does Not Know Whether Others Will Conserve?

CHOICE FOR OTHERS:

		conserve	don't conserve
	conserve	2(M), 2(O)	4(M), 1(O)
CHOICE FOR ME:	don't conserve	1(M), 4(O)	3(M), 3(O)

Best outcome = 1; Worst outcome = 4
M = Me; O = Others

there, the grass would be depleted and no more grazing would be possible. Yet every villager had an incentive to add more and more animals to the common land, for from the individual's point of view, the gain from raising another sheep or cow always outweighed the damage to the commons that one more animal would cause. One more sheep or cow would not ruin the commons by itself, so why not add it to the land? The commons was thus a public good, and every villager had an incentive to try to be a free rider—in this case, to put more animals on the land while hoping that others would reduce their herds or flocks. As long as the villagers thought and acted in this way, the result, sooner or later, would be the overgrazing of the commons and a disaster for the entire village.

Hardin's conclusion—and the conclusion reached by most Greens—is that society cannot rely on voluntary efforts or appeals to individual consciences to solve such environmental problems as overfishing, overgrazing, and pollution of the air and water. The earth itself may be in danger of exhaustion, but no individual's action will be sufficient to prevent its collapse. Instead, Hardin's solution is "mutual coercion, mutually agreed upon by the majority of the people affected." Just as the villagers need to arrive at a collective solution to the problem of overgrazing by setting a limit to the number of animals anyone may put out to graze on the commons—and by punishing those who exceed the limit—so people in modern industrial societies need to find ways to force themselves, through taxes and penalties, to limit their use of fossil fuels and other natural resources. Otherwise, the destruction of the environment will proceed apace. However, it is sometimes possible to find modern solutions. For example, in London, England, the municipal government introduced a sophisticated technological response to the problem of severe traffic congestion in its city centre in the late 1990s. It installed devices that track and charge cars that entered certain areas at peak periods. Traffic volume declined substantially.

Together, the problems of collective action and time horizons explain why Greens engage in politics. If they are to meet and overcome environmental crises, Greens must be able to persuade people to change how they think about the world and their place in it. But that is not enough. Greens must also bring about changes in laws and policies so that people have an incentive, as individuals, to think about the effects of their actions on future generations and to cooperate in the preservation of clean air, fresh water, and other natural resources.

Green Ideology in Canada

The Canadian government assumed responsibility for the wilderness as the railways began to open up vast tracts of the country to travel in the late nineteenth century. It established Banff National Park in 1887 and Algonquin Provincial Park in 1893. Concern for the land was reflected in Canada's first major school of painters, the Group of Seven, who tried to capture the uniqueness of the Canadian landscape in their paintings. At a popular level, many Canadians showed their love for the landscape when they spent parts of their summers at camps or cottages where they felt that they were part of nature—being in picturesque surroundings that contrasted with the urban setting they lived in the rest of the year.[19]

Canadians differ from Americans in their attitude toward the environment and environmental policies. Americans incline more toward personal activism. Like Arnold Schwarzenegger, former governor of California, many think that it is possible to fix the planet while still driving a Hummer. They believe in the efficacy of personal action. By contrast, Canadians are concerned with Canada's reputation abroad. They approach the environment in a more collective spirit, with more points of leverage on Canadian consciences. Although branches of Greenpeace and the Sierra Club operate in Canada, possibly the two most important Canadian foundations are the David Suzuki Foundation and the Pembina Foundation. The Suzuki Foundation does not have a large annual budget compared to its American counterparts, but it enjoys considerable influence because of the celebrity and popularity of its founder. The Pembina Foundation gets its influence from the high-quality and reliable research it provides to decision makers.

David Suzuki (1936–)

[19]McKenzie 59.

Environmental Foundations and Coalitions in the United States. In the United States, the most effective work in the environmental area is carried out by a number of relatively large foundations, the biggest of which is the **Nature Conservancy**, with its total annual revenue of about $1 billion. With more than a million members, it works worldwide to protect ecologically important lands and waters. The **Natural Resources Defence Council**, with half a million members and an annual revenue of about $60 million, lobbies government directly on environmental issues and uses cyberactivism among its membership base.

Perhaps the most interesting coalition is the Climate Action Partnership—a consortium of large companies, such as Alcan, Dow Chemical, General Electric, and Shell, with some major environmental groups, including the Nature Conservancy, the Natural Resources Defence Council, the National Wildlife Federation, and the Pew Foundation on Climate Change. Al Gore (1948–), former vice-president of the United States, Nobel Peace Prize laureate, and winner of an Academy Award for his documentary film on global warming, *An Inconvenient Truth*, is chairman of the alliance. Such a partnership is known as a **Baptist-bootlegger alliance**. (Historically, Baptists didn't want alcohol sold on Sundays. Bootleggers backed them in their drive to make Sunday a "dry" day because they knew people would drink anyway, and the only place they could get liquor would be from the bootleggers.)

In this case, not only do the companies get good publicity, but each can also lobby for special benefits. For example, Westinghouse makes very little profit on its tungsten light bulbs, but it makes significantly greater profit on its energy-efficient bulbs, so it's happy to lobby for regulations that require energy-saving bulbs.

UNRESOLVED DIFFERENCES AMONG GREEN IDEOLOGIES

Environmentalists come in several shades of green, so to speak. "Light Green" reform-minded environmentalists favour laws and public policies that serve human needs and wants while minimizing damage to the natural environment. "Dark Green" environmentalists favour more radical measures to roll back development and to protect and even extend wilderness areas.[20] Another way of describing this difference was suggested by the Norwegian "ecosopher" (eco-philosopher) Arne Naess (1927–2004). Naess drew a distinction between "shallow environmentalism" and **deep ecology**. The former perspective puts human beings at the centre of concern and views environmental problems in anthropocentric and instrumental terms. Thus a shallow environmentalist might favour saving the spotted owl or some species of whale so that human owl- or whale-watchers might derive satisfaction from seeing such animals. The deep ecologist, by contrast, contends that owls and whales—indeed, all living creatures and the ecosystems that support them—have **intrinsic value**, not **instrumental value**. That is, they have value in and of themselves, quite apart from the value that human beings may place on them. Deep ecology is thus a *biocentric* (or life-centred) perspective that places other species and ecosystems on a par with human beings.[21]

---

[20]See Andrew Dobson, *Green Political Thought* (London: Unwin, 1990), 206–213.
[21]Arne Naess, "The Shallow and the Deep Long-Range Ecology Movement: A Summary," *Inquiry* 16 (1973): 95–100. See also Naess, *Ecology, Community, and Lifestyle*, trans. and ed. David Rothenberg (Cambridge: Cambridge UP, 1989).

The Garden and the Wilderness. Still another way of describing these differences among environmentalists is to say that some subscribe to a "garden" and others to a "wilderness" view.[22] Defenders of the garden view, such as René Dubos (1901–1982) and Wendell Berry, hold that human beings are part of nature and that part of *their* nature and their need is to cultivate the earth.[23] This they must do if they are to feed, clothe, and shelter themselves. Such cultivation should be done carefully and reverently, but it must be done if human well-being is to be advanced. Defenders of the garden view tend to be critical of the wilderness perspective that puts the interests of nonhuman animals and their habitats ahead of legitimate human interests. Humans are animals too, with their own species-specific needs and their own ways of living in and transforming nature. As Berry puts it,

> People cannot live apart from nature; that is the first principle of the conservationists. And yet, people cannot live in nature without changing it. But this is true of *all* creatures; they depend upon nature, and they change it. What we call nature is, in a sense, the sum of the changes made by all the various creatures and natural forces in their intricate actions upon each other and upon their places.[24]

Defenders of the wilderness view, such as Edward Abbey (1927–1989) and Dave Foreman (co-founder of Earth First!), see matters differently. Humans have taken over—and despoiled—too much of the earth, all in the name of progress or development. They have clear-cut old-growth forests, destroyed animal habitats and entire ecosystems, dammed rivers, turned forested mountainsides into ski slopes—all the while heedless of the effects of their actions on animals and the long-term health of the ecosystems that sustain them. Bears and other wild animals have as much right as humans to live satisfying lives. We humans are not, and should not regard ourselves as, masters of nature. On the contrary, as Aldo Leopold put it in *A Sand County Almanac*—which Foreman calls "the most important, the loveliest, the wisest book ever penned"[25]—an alternative "land ethic" requires that humans see themselves in a more humble role: "In short, a land ethic changes the role of *Homo sapiens* from conqueror of the land-community to plain member and citizen of it. It implies respect for his fellow-members, and also respect for the community as such."[26] Leopold began to appreciate the need for this land ethic when, as an employee of the U.S. Forest Service, he shot a she-wolf. Leopold had accepted the Forest Service's policy of exterminating predators, but he had an epiphany when he approached the wolf he had shot and saw "a fierce green fire dying in her eyes." Wolves and other predators, he came to realize, have their rightful place in the order of nature. Like their prey, they are indispensable parts of complexly interdependent ecosystems. Remove them, and the entire ecosystem is endangered. For Leopold, the central precept of an environmental or land ethic is that "[a] thing is right when it tends to preserve the integrity, stability, and beauty of the biotic community. It is wrong when it tends otherwise."[27]

---

[22]See Roderick Nash, *Wilderness and the American Mind,* 3rd ed. (New Haven, CT: Yale UP, 1982) 379–388.

[23]René Dubos, *The Wooing of Earth* (New York: Scribner's, 1980); Wendell Berry, *The Gift of Good Land* (San Francisco: North Point, 1981).

[24]Wendell Berry, "Getting Along with Nature," in Wendell Berry, *Home Economics: Fourteen Essays* (San Francisco: North Point, 1987) 7; see Ball and Dagger, selection 9.62.

[25]Dave Foreman and Murray Bookchin, *Defending the Earth: A Dialogue,* ed. Steve Chase (Boston: South End, 1991) 116.

[26]Leopold 240; see Ball and Dagger, selection 9.61.

[27]Leopold 262.

But what, exactly, are the bases of these moral and philosophical precepts? How are they to be translated into political action? And can the differences between the different "shades" of Greens be resolved? These are among the questions that the relatively new Green or environmental movement has raised but has yet to answer in a clear and comprehensive manner.

Spiritual and Humanist Ethics. Consider the character and source of the emerging ecological land ethic itself: Is it sacred, as some Greens suggest, or is it secular and scientific, as others insist?

According to some Greens, an ecological ethic is really religious or spiritual, resting as it does on the virtues of humility, respect, and reverence. An ecological ethic entails humility in the face of our individual mortality and our collective status not as solitary dwellers on or masters of our planet, but as one species and generation among many. An ecological ethic also requires that we respect life in all its forms and the conditions, both animate and inanimate, that sustain and nurture it. And finally, such an ethic entails an attitude of reverence and awe. It requires that we revere, cherish, and care for other people and other species not only in our own time but also in the generations and ages to come. To paraphrase Edmund Burke, we have a sacred obligation to leave to future generations a habitation instead of a ruin.

On this much, at least, most Greens agree. But beyond this point agreement ends and differences begin to appear, as some Greens take a spiritual or religious turn that other Greens find odd, or worse. Those who conceive of an ecological ethic grounded in spiritual or religious values say that we should look upon the earth as a benevolent and kindly deity—the goddess Gaia (from the Greek word for "the earth")—to be worshipped in reverence and awe. A number of Greens, including some (but not all) of those who call themselves deep ecologists, suggest this approach as a way of liberating ourselves from the confines of a purely materialistic or scientific perspective into another state of mind, one more attuned to listening to and learning from nature than to talking to and dictating for it.[28] However, others seem to speak of the goddess Gaia in a less metaphorical and more literal fashion.[29]

Some deep ecologists, particularly those affiliated with the Earth First! movement, are inclined to speak neither in humanistic nor in religious terms but in a more Malthusian idiom. Thomas Malthus was the nineteenth-century English cleric and economist who claimed that human population increases geometrically (that is, at an ever-increasing rate) while the resources available to sustain that population increase arithmetically (that is, at a steady rate). Thus, according to **Malthus's law**, the ever-growing human population increasingly outstrips available resources, with widespread hunger and starvation as the inevitable result. From widespread starvation comes a further result: a new equilibrium between population and resources. Unfortunately, this short-lived equilibrium ends as population increases and the cycle begins all over again. Taking their cue from Malthus, the leading thinkers of Earth First! claim that nature is not without its own resources for countering human hubris and error. Widespread starvation, famine, floods, the AIDS epidemic—by these and other means, nature chastises the heedless human species and punishes at least some of its members for their species' pride, ignorance, and/or

---

[28]See John Seed et al., *Thinking Like a Mountain* (Philadelphia: New Society, 1988).
[29]See Judith Plant, ed., *Healing the Wounds: The Promise of Ecofeminism* (Philadelphia: New Society, 1989).

indifference. Although the language of Earth First! is not religious, its vision of dire punishments sometimes seems to come straight from the vengeful God of the ancient adage.

By contrast, ecologists of a more social and secular stripe are apt to regard any talk of religion and goddesses and deep ecology with deep suspicion, if not downright hostility. These critics come from several Green perspectives, including **social ecology** and **ecofeminism**. Social ecologist Murray Bookchin and ecofeminists Val Plumwood and Ynestra King, among others, contend that talk about goddesses is mystical mumbo jumbo to be avoided at all costs. And they view Earth First! as an antihuman and inhumane organization that seeks to remove human beings from the ecological equation entirely. By contrast, social ecologists acknowledge humanity's dependency on and responsibility for the environment, but hold that human life has special status and importance. Social ecologists also contend that it is not human beings per se who are responsible for the systematic and continuing destruction of the earth's ecosystems; rather, it is *some* wealthy industrialists and international corporations who bear the greatest responsibility for environmental plunder and pillage. Ecofeminists add that such systematic destruction is due to a mindset they call *androcentrism*—that is, a male-centred perspective that celebrates the "masculine" triumph over "feminine" nature even as it devalues the life-giving and nurturing characteristics of women.

Political Action. Other differences within the broadly based Green movement are beginning to emerge. What strategies and tactics should the environmental movement use? Although all agree about the importance of informing and educating the public, they are divided over how this might best be done. Some say that Greens should take an active part in electoral politics. However, mindful of the difficulties facing minority third parties, Greens have generally opted for other strategies. Social ecologists, for example, tend to favour local grassroots campaigns to involve neighbours and friends in efforts to protect the environment. Some, though not all, social ecologists are anarchists who see the state and its pro-growth policies as the problem rather than the solution and seek its eventual replacement by a decentralized system of communes and cooperatives.[30]

Other Greens have chosen to pursue quite different strategies. Some groups favour dramatic direct action calculated to make headlines and capture public attention. When Greenpeace was founded in Canada in 1971, its first mission was to set out in an old fishing boat for Amchitka, Alaska, the home of endangered sea otters, bald eagles, and falcons, where the United States was planning to hold a nuclear test. The boat was intercepted and the test went ahead but, as a result of the publicity Greenpeace received, nuclear testing at Amchitka ended within a year, and the island became a bird sanctuary. In 1982, Greenpeace's actions led to a European Union (EU) ban on the importation of seal pelts. In 1989 its exposé on fishing practices led to a ban on the use of driftnets. And in 2006 its ship, *Arctic Sunrise*, forced Estonia to take action against a ship that had dumped toxic waste off the Ivory Coast, killing eight people and poisoning thousands more. Greenpeace is now an international institute with a $10 million annual budget. In addition to direct action, it encourages **cyberactivism**, the active use of the Internet for networking and for bringing pressure on governments and businesses.

Militant groups, such as the Earth Liberation Front (ELF), the Sea Shepherd Conservation Society, and Earth First!, have advocated **ecotage** (ecological sabotage) and **monkey**

---

[30]See Murray Bookchin, *The Modern Crisis* (Montreal: Black Rose, 1986).

wrenching (a form of sabotage that creates serious economic damage as a means of putting an end to economically undesirable activities) as morally justifiable means of protesting, if not always preventing, injuries and insults to the natural environment. ELF was founded in the United Kingdom, and the movement has been active in the United States and Canada. The FBI declared ELF the top domestic terror threat in the United States in 2001. Some members of Earth First! have allegedly "spiked"—that is, driven long metal spikes into—thousand-year-old redwood trees to prevent their being cut down by logging companies seeking short-term profits. The spike does no harm to the tree, although it poses a serious danger to any chainsaw or sawmill operator whose blade might strike it. These and other tactics are described, and even celebrated, in Edward Abbey's novel *The Monkey-Wrench Gang* (1975), and described in detail in Dave Foreman's *Ecodefense: A Field Guide to Monkey Wrenching* (1985). These tactics are controversial within the environmental movement. Some believe that it is never justifiable to harm other living creatures, including human beings. Others worry that violent actions will create hostile public opinion.

Strategies and Tactics

There are disputes within the Green movement over strategies and tactics. Anarchists are opposed to the strategies and tactics favoured by environmental lobbyists; social ecologists are appalled by the political pronouncements of Earth First!; and the moderate and conservative members of The Nature Conservancy and Sierra Club are embarrassed by all the adverse publicity. And yet, as Greens are quick to note, the important point is not that environmentalists disagree about means but that they agree about fundamental assumptions and ends. They are alike in assuming that all things are connected—*ecology* is, after all, the study of interconnections—and they agree that the maintenance of complex ecosystems is not only a worthy goal but also a necessary one if the human race and other species are to survive.

A recent movement has tried to make these concerns very personal. Although the **locavore** movement was created only in 2005, it can trace its roots to American chef Alice Waters. Her San Francisco restaurant Chez Panisse, which opened in 1971, sourced as much food as possible from local organic farmers and served only produce that was in season. Locavorism encourages people to eat locally and "celebrate their foodshed." Locavores argue that the globalization of the food supply leads to environmental deterioration because food travels on average 1500 miles before it reaches the consumer. Some of the implications of this supply system are air pollution and global warming, the ecological costs of large-scale monoculture, and the loss of family farms and local community dollars. The locavore movement urges consumers to seek fresh, organically produced food within a hundred-mile radius of their homes.

Closely related are **omnivores**. Michael Pollan adapted the term in *The Omnivore's Dilemma* (2006). As omnivores, human beings have been given by evolution an enormous range of sensory and mental tools that allow them to screen food for value and safety. These tools served in the past to help decide whether to eat one mushroom and not another. Equally now we need it to decide what kind of food we will eat today, from McDonald's at one extreme to the opposite extreme of eating only food that we have hunted, grown, and gathered ourselves. Pollan argues that the important thing is that we need to think about our choices and to remember that we eat by the grace of nature, not industry; "What we're eating is never anything more or less than the body of the world."[31] Some of the suggestions he makes are

1.　Don't eat anything your grandmother wouldn't recognize as food.

2.　Don't eat food containing ingredients you can't pronounce.

3.　Don't eat anything that won't eventually rot.

4.　Eat food from animals that eat grass.

Animals too are interconnected with nature. It is only recently, though, that human beings have come to consider that animals might actually have rights like human beings do.

Animal Rights and Animal Welfare

The forerunner of the ideology of animal liberation can be found in nineteenth-century England, particularly in the increasingly widespread revulsion against the wanton use and abuse of animals for spectator sports.[32] Such suffering, said Jeremy Bentham (1748–1832), offends—or rather should offend—the moral sensibilities of any reasonably sensitive human being. At a time when growing numbers of people were attempting to abolish slavery in the British Empire, Bentham wrote:

> The day may come when the rest of the animal creation may acquire those rights which never could have been with[held] from them but by the hand of tyranny. [Some] have already discovered that the blackness of the skin is no reason why a human being should be abandoned without redress to the caprice of a tormentor.[33]

But why, Bentham asked, are animals different? Is it because they have four legs? Or do animals deserve different treatment because they lack the use of reason? Or is it because animals cannot speak? Bentham goes on to say that to argue in this way is self-subverting. For surely, he says,

> A full-grown horse or dog is beyond comparison a more rational, as well as a more conversable animal, than an infant of a day, or a week, or even a month, old. But suppose they were otherwise, what would it avail? The question is not, Can they reason? Or can they talk? But, Can they suffer?[34]

This increasing awareness of and sensitivity to the suffering of animals led to the formation of the Society for the Prevention of Cruelty to Animals in 1824 in the United Kingdom, in 1866 in the United States, and in 1869 in Canada.

The animal liberation movement of the late twentieth and early twenty-first centuries traces its origins to such nineteenth-century thinkers as Bentham and Henry Salt (whose *Animal Rights*, first published in 1892, made the moral case for vegetarianism).[35] But to its moral argument, the movement adds a certain militancy and a willingness to take personal

---

[31]Michael Pollan, *The Omnivore's Dilemma* (New York: Penguin, 2006).

[32]Peter Singer and Tom Regan trace some of the sentiments and ideas of "animal liberation" back as far as Plutarch (c. 49–119 CE) and St. Thomas Aquinas (1224–1274): Tom Regan and Peter Singer, eds., *Animal Rights and Human Obligations* (Englewood Cliffs, NJ: Prentice-Hall, 1976) 111–121.

[33]Quoted in Peter Singer, *Practical Ethics* (Cambridge: Cambridge UP, 1979) 49.

[34]Singer, *Practical Ethics* 50.

[35]See the selections from Salt's works in Regan and Singer 173–178, 185–189. For a more substantial selection, see George Hendrick and Willene Hendrick, eds., *The Savour of Salt* (London: Centaur, 1989).

and political risks to protect the rights of animals. Members of such groups as the Society for Animal Rights (SAR) and People for the Ethical Treatment of Animals (PETA) have not only lobbied their legislative representatives but also picketed furriers' shops and animal laboratories. Some have freed caged laboratory animals, including mice, monkeys, and dolphins. In the United Kingdom, the Animal Liberation Front (ALF) has poured blood on expensive fur coats and set fire to furriers' warehouses. In 1988 animal liberationists in Sweden succeeded in their campaign to outlaw certain kinds of beef- and poultry-raising practices. In the 1990s several supermodels and other celebrities protested against the manufacture, sale, and wearing of fur coats, while The Body Shop developed a highly successful retail business on the basis of selling perfumes and cosmetics that were manufactured without testing on animals. Under pressure from PETA and other groups, some manufacturers have followed suit. Other activists have gone further. They designate April 17 World Day for Lab Animals, and have taken active steps to intimidate scientists who work for companies that engage in animal testing by shoving excrement through their post boxes or pouring paint stripper on their cars. Another tactic is to blockade such companies with constant phone calls, faxes and e-mails. A British group, Stop Huntingdon Animal Cruelty (SHAC), claims that it has forced suppliers to stop providing services to Huntingdon Life Science, a leading British company.[36]

PETA protestors demonstrate outside the Republican National Convention, September 1–4, 2008, Minnesota.

---

[36]*Economist*, Apr. 17, 2004: 54.

In Canada, there are over 300 animal protection groups.[37] The International Fund for Animal Welfare lobbies actively to draw public attention to the Canadian seal hunt. It wants to limit the size of the cull and insists that there should be a sufficient number of inspectors to ensure that the hunt meets Canada's standards for cruelty to animals. In 2008 a radical animal rights groups, the Sea Shepherd Conservation Society, used its boat, the *Farley Mowat*, to monitor closely the 2008 hunt. Its activities gave further impetus to European animal rights activists who want to ban to import of seal pelts. If this prohibition were adopted by the EU, if would effectively put an end to the seal hunt. Other Canadian groups have been concerned with the cruelty of leghold traps, the use of animals in research, and the growth of factory farming.

Human beings are both audience and oppressor to cruelty to animals. The ideology of animal liberation therefore directs its appeals to humans who (1) oppress or abuse animals, (2) derive some supposed benefit from such oppression, or (3) do not benefit but stand by and do nothing to prevent the further abuse and oppression of animals. An example of the first might be a hunter who clubs baby seals to death; an example of the second might be a woman who wears a sealskin coat; and an example of the third might be those who take no action—such as writing letters of protest and making financial contributions—to protect baby seals.

The ideology of animal liberation is addressed primarily to human beings whose beliefs and attitudes have a bearing upon their approach to the treatment of animals. Many, perhaps most, people subscribe to **speciesism**—the belief or unexamined prejudice that human beings are superior to animals; that we have rights where they have none; that we may treat them in any way that will benefit us, either as individuals (the steak on my plate) or as a species (monkeys in medical experiments). The German Nazis, as animal liberationists remind us, also subscribed to their own version of speciesism: Before murdering or performing medical experiments on Jews, they first took great pains to reclassify them as subhumans, as "animals" without rights and thus undeserving of humane treatment.

If Nazis could blur the line between Jews and animals, say the animal liberationists, we should at least reflect on our attitudes toward the "lower" animals whose flesh we eat and on whom we perform experiments of various and often vicious kinds. These experiments range from surgical removal of limbs and organs to testing the toxicity of detergents, bleaches, cosmetics, and other products by injecting them into the eyes of rabbits and other laboratory animals. In *Animal Liberation,* Peter Singer, an Australian philosopher, examines each of the arguments advanced in favour of speciesism and finds them unwarranted, untenable, or incoherent.[38] Consider, for example, the claim that humans are entitled to eat the flesh of "lower" animals such as cows. On what, Singer asks, is this claim based? It rests on the belief that humans are a "higher" species. On what, then, is this claim to superiority based? It is based on the unique qualities of human beings— qualities that they do not share with lower and lesser creatures. These qualities include, pre-eminently, the fact that human beings have the use of speech and reason. But Singer says this claim is singularly self-subverting. For by this logic we should be prepared to eat

---

[37]McKenzie 51.

[38]Peter Singer, *Animal Liberation,* 2d ed. (New York: Random, 1990); and Peter Singer, "All Animals Are Equal," Ball and Dagger, selection 59. As a Utilitarian, Singer is skeptical of the idea of the intrinsic worth of life and the language of rights. He rests his case on the claim that animals, like humans, are capable of experiencing pain and pleasure.

the flesh of severely retarded human beings, who lack the power of reason, and of humans who are unable to speak. That we are unwilling to do so only shows that the standard arguments in defence of human superiority are without rational and moral foundation.

Animal liberationists hope to raise awareness of human abuse of animals. Once humans come to see their relationship with animals in a new and different light, they will no longer exploit or oppress them. Humans will at last be freed from their false and self-demeaning sense of their own innate superiority. The aim of animal liberation is not only to deliver animals from human oppression but also to deliver human beings from the self-destroying confines of speciesism.[39] Marcel Wissenburg, a Dutch political theorist, suggests three variants of anthropocentrism that are relevant to our relationship to animals: *sentientism* (also known as *pathocentrism*), the view that all sentient creatures have moral worth; *zoocentrism,* the view that all animals have value whether they are sentient or not; and *biocentrism,* the view that gives value to all nature.[40]

The animal liberation movement is the militant part of a broader concern to ensure the humane treatment of animals. Respect for the rights of animals is important because animals too are part of the ecosystem. It is worth noting that the rise of the animal rights movement coincided with the growth, in the latter half of the twentieth century, of large, industrial-scale "factory farming." Cattle, hogs, and other animals that once grazed in open pastures are now typically kept in confined spaces so that they will not move around and become tough and muscular rather than tender and meaty. Veal calves are kept in cages and fed an all-milk diet so that their meat will be pink and tender. Chickens and turkeys are confined to small cages with wire floors through which their manure can drop.

These and other creatures have become "nutrient units" whose diet and movement are carefully calculated and measured to ensure their profitability. In the United States, cows are injected with Bovine Growth Hormone (BGH) to increase the yield of milk. In Canada and the United States, cattle and poultry are injected with large quantities of antibiotics, which remain in their flesh to be ingested by humans and create antibiotic-resistant bacteria. Until recently, cattle were fed processed residue of other livestock, which led to continuing outbreaks of BSE ("mad cow disease").

Although supporters of animal rights believe that the lives of both human beings and animals would be enhanced if animals were treated with greater respect, there is disagreement as to how far that respect needs to extend. At a minimum, all agree that animals have rights, including legal rights to bodily safety and security.[41] Under Canadian law, certainly, animals do have rights; they are protected against cruel treatment, and universities with veterinary colleges and agricultural schools have strict protocols for the humane treatment of animals. In addition, most people would agree that animals have interests that are worthy of moral consideration and deserving of respect and protection by human beings.[42] Some animal liberationists go further. They argue that no medical experiments of any kind should

---

[39]The most systematic philosophical defence of the ideas of intrinsic worth and the rights of animals is found in Tom Regan, *The Case for Animal Rights* (Berkeley and Los Angeles: U of California P, 1983). Like Singer, Regan also argues that animal liberation entails the liberation of humans, freeing them from previously unexamined speciesist prejudices and practices.

[40]McKenzie 14.

[41]In addition to Regan, *The Case for Animal Rights* (see note 39), see Steven M. Wise, *Rattling the Cage: Toward Legal Rights for Animals* (Cambridge, MA: Perseus, 2000), and Wise, *Drawing the Line: The Case for Animal Rights* (Cambridge, MA: Merloyd Lawrence, 2002).

[42]Lawrence E. Johnson, *A Morally Deep World* (Cambridge: Cambridge UP, 1991) Chapter 6.

FIGURE 12.2	The Animal Liberationist View of Freedom

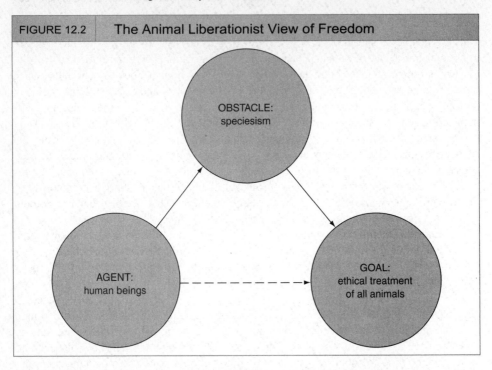

be performed on or with the aid of animals, no matter how great the potential benefit to humans. Overwhelmingly, though, Canadians would agree that such experiments may be justified if the suffering of a relatively small number of animals is outweighed by the benefit to a large number of other creatures, human or nonhuman. Many animal liberationists hold that the hunting of any and all animals is immoral and should be illegal; but a radical minority dissent, saying that the killing of (for example) a deer that has had a good "deer life" until the moment it is shot is much more humane than keeping a cow confined and condemned to live a short and unhappy "cow life" until it is taken to a slaughterhouse. Hunters, they say, take responsibility for their actions, whereas most people rely on others to do the killing and butchering for them. These and other issues remain the subject of debate between animal rights activists, animal rights supporters, and the general public. The animal liberationist view of freedom is illustrated in Figure 12.2.

Many of Canada's Aboriginal peoples also show a profound affinity for other life forms, or **biophilia**. Their motivation is different from that of animal liberationists. "Adequate land and wildlife were fundamental to Indian cultures. More than other cultures, theirs were founded on a practical and spiritual relationship to the land and wildlife."[43] Although they needed to hunt for food, they tried to do so within the context of the spiritual values and practices of their culture.

In an important sense, both animal liberationists and environmentalists function in a similar way to Hegel's master-slave dialectic. Until people respect sentient beings other than humans, say animal liberationists, or until they respect the earth and its ecology, say environmentalists, people will not respect themselves, and without self-respect they cannot be truly free.

---

[43]Menno Boldt, *Surviving as Indians* (Toronto: U of Toronto P, 1993) 170.

GLOBALIZATION

Despite their disagreements, liberals, socialists, and some conservatives, especially individualists, share a faith in material progress. They believe that human life can and will become easier—less subject to starvation, disease, and unremitting labour—through the mastery of nature. That is why they have usually encouraged industrial and technological development. In the course of the twentieth century, however, material progress came to be seen as a mixed blessing. Although life is better for many people in many ways, it is now clear that much of this improvement has come at the expense of the natural environment. Nature has not proved so easy to master or harness as earlier champions of progress had thought. In short, ecological problems have become political problems as well. All ideologies will have to respond in some fashion to the challenge of these new circumstances.

The ecological crisis could conceivably provoke a resurgence of fascism. According to Robert Heilbroner, it may prove impossible to persuade people to make the sacrifices necessary to meet the ecological crisis.[44] Those of us who have grown used to the benefits of material progress—gas-guzzling SUVs and air conditioners, for example—will not want to downsize or surrender them, and those who do not now enjoy those benefits will want them as much as we do. Few people will voluntarily give up what they have; indeed, most people will continue to want more and more. But if these demands continue, the ecological crisis will result in outright ecological disaster. To prevent this from happening, coercion may be necessary. That is, governments may have to force people to lower their expectations and live more modestly. In a democracy, Heilbroner says, this will be all but impossible, for the people are unlikely to elect leaders who promise them hardship. On the contrary, they may turn to leaders who promise to protect them and their economic well-being from foreigners who want what they have. Militant nationalism may thus increase, bringing with it a tendency to silence dissenting opinion, to concentrate power in the hands of a few leaders, and to foster hostile relations among the nation-states of the world—a highly unsettling prospect in the age of nuclear, biological, and chemical weapons. Heilbroner does not predict that all this will happen, but he does see it as a distinctly possible outcome of the environmental difficulties we now face. Even if there is no broad revival of fascism, moreover, many observers believe that ecological pressures pose a serious challenge to those ideologies that embrace democracy.

So too do those pressures that fall under the broad heading of globalization. *Globalization* refers to the cultural and technological changes that seem to draw the peoples of the world more closely together. Advances in transportation and communication, and a corresponding reduction of their costs, have dramatically increased mobility and the opportunity to engage in commercial and social interactions with people in distant places. CNN and the Internet seem to be everywhere, as do the images of various pop stars and athletes. The distances between peoples seem to be shrinking, as do the differences that have made them distinctive. Globalization also has a narrow or specific meaning: the spread of free trade around the world. From the early 1960s to the present, there has been an international movement to lower or eliminate barriers to international trade, culminating recently in the Central American Free Trade Agreement (CAFTA) and a free trade deal signed between Canada and Colombia. Such barriers have included

---

[44]Robert Heilbroner, "What Has Posterity Ever Done for Me?" *New York Times Magazine*, Jan. 19, 1975.

tariffs on imported goods, subsidies to domestic producers, and other measures that aim to protect businesses in one's own country against foreign competition. The General Agreement on Tariffs and Trade (GATT), the North American Free Trade Agreement (NAFTA), and other free-trade treaties have committed the United States and other countries to reducing or eliminating all (or almost all) restrictions to the free movement of goods across national boundaries. Countries that do not cooperate may find themselves under pressure from the World Bank and the International Monetary Fund (IMF), two institutions created near the end of the Second World War to promote a stable, depression-free global economy. Following Adam Smith and the early liberals, advocates of globalization argue that free trade promotes efficiency, rewards producers who manufacture and sell goods at the lowest possible price, and benefits consumers, who can afford to buy more and better goods as competition drives prices down and quality up. Individualist conservatives and neoclassical liberals are thus among the leading proponents of globalization, which they believe to be the reason for significant gains in health and prosperity in many parts of the world.

Critics—members of labour unions and environmental groups foremost among them—contend that global free trade means that workers in developing countries, including young children, will be overworked and underpaid, that workers in the United States and other industrial countries will lose jobs as manufacturing moves overseas to take advantage of cheap labour, and that laws protecting the environment and the safety of workers will be repealed or weakened in the name of higher productivity and reduced costs. These critics complain that the World Trade Organization (WTO), which oversees the international terms of trade, is an unelected and undemocratic body that systematically favours the interests of international corporations to the detriment of workers and the natural environment. According to its critics, the WTO interprets barriers to trade to include democratically enacted laws and public policies that promote worker safety and environmental protection. Critics also complain that free-trade agreements override these same concerns. NAFTA, for example, has touched off a lengthy legal and political battle over trucking safety. According to the agreement, Mexican and American trucks were to be free to travel on the highways of both countries; but the Teamsters Union, the Sierra Club, Public Citizen, and other groups objected that American standards for exhaust emissions and road worthiness were being lowered to accommodate Mexican trucks. After thirteen years of delays, the U.S. government won a court case in 2007 that allowed it to proceed with a one-year experiment in which the trucks of pre-inspected Mexican firms would be permitted to operate throughout the United States. If the experiment proves successful—that is, if American roads are as safe as they were before the introduction of Mexican trucks—then the trucking provision of NAFTA will finally take effect. Moreover, Greens oppose global trade because it consumes vast amounts of fossil fuels and contributes to global warming.

In 1997 thirty-seven industrialized countries and the European Union agreed at a conference in Kyoto, Japan, to reduce greenhouse gas emissions (GGE) by 5 percent, taking the year 1990 as a baseline. The Kyoto Convention only encouraged states to adhere to the guidelines, but the Kyoto Protocol create a regime that was binding under international law, though there were no effective enforcement provisions. Although the main responsibility was for each country to reduce its own GGE, there were additional ways they could achieve their targets. Countries that were below their designated carbon use levels were entitled to sell carbon credits, in effect giving a reward to the good country and a financial penalty to the bad. Countries were also entitled to create removal units (RMU) if they altered their farming practices or created an environmental resource, such as a forest. The Protocol came into force in 2005 and bound states from 2008 to 2012.

Taxes based on the amount of GGEs are normally called carbon taxes. Large companies prefer a cap-and-trade system. Under this regime, there is no initial cost. They pay only when they exceed their quota for admissions. A major benefit for companies in a cap-and-trade regime is that it is harder for new companies to enter the industry because they would have to buy the carbon credits that existing companies got for free.

Almost all environmentalists prefer a carbon tax because it has the capacity to reduce carbon emissions, whereas cap-and-trade generally aims to prevent GGEs from getting worse. Canadians took great pride in the fact that the Chrétien government signed the Kyoto protocol even though the United States didn't. However, neither the Chrétien nor the Martin governments did anything to implement the provisions of that agreement.

When Stephen Harper's Conservative government came to power in 2006, it was actively hostile to the provisions of the Kyoto Protocol. Harper argued that GGEs did not cause smog and that poor air quality was an important issue his government wanted to address. Harper contended that carbon taxes are, as their name implies, taxes, mostly on business. This tax was therefore ill-advised in Canada since it would hamper the country's competitive position in relation to the United States, one of the very few industrial countries that had not signed the Protocol. Harper was also aware of the negative impact on the Alberta oil industry.

The Kyoto Protocol expired in 2012. The Durban Conference of 2011 was held to decide how to replace it. Its members agreed to create a new legal framework by 2015, the provisions of which would be implemented by 2020. It also imposed the same requirements on developing as on developed countries, a move strongly opposed by India, a leading source of GGEs. On December 12, 2011, the Canadian government announced that it was pulling out of the Kyoto Protocol, the first country to do so. It gave the high penalties Canada would face if it stayed a member as the reason for withdrawal. Green Party leader Elizabeth May vigorously protested the withdrawal, calling it illegal and regressive.

Opposition to globalization brings together ideologically diverse allies, including anarchists, Marxists, traditional conservatives, and welfare liberals. These groups are concerned about the effects of globalization on people. In contrast, environmentalists are concerned about the effects of globalization on people, animals, natural resources, the environment, and the future of life. They contend that free trade endangers the natural environment by rolling back gains made with the passage and enforcement of environmental laws.

Freedom and the Democratic Ideal

As we noted in Chapter 1, every ideology subscribes to its own particular view of freedom. The Green ideology is no exception. Greens believe that human beings and other species can be truly free to flourish and survive only if they overcome the arrogance of humanism—the humanist outlook that ignores the worth of other species and their environment. The Green view of freedom can therefore be encapsulated in our triadic model. (See Figure 12.3.)

FIGURE 12.3	The Green View of Freedom

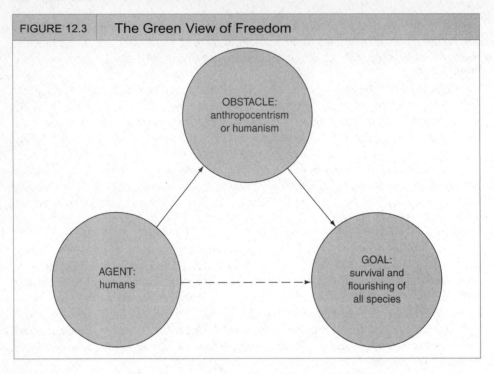

IS THERE A UNIQUELY GREEN FORM OF DEMOCRACY?

Rise of the Green Parties

The Green movement is so ideologically diverse that it would have been surprising if it had formed stable and ideologically coherent political parties. Probably the most successful has been the German Green Party. Founded in 1980, it formed a so-called Red–Green power-sharing alliance with the Social Democrats, in government from 1998 to 2005. In 2001, the Green Party in Germany was instrumental in forging the historic agreement that would see its country close down all of its nuclear power stations by 2021. In the United States in 2000, Ralph Nader attracted media attention as a Green Party presidential candidate, and Greens have achieved modest success in jurisdictions such as Australia and New Zealand, where various forms of proportional representation have allowed them to elect members.

The Green Party in Canada

Greens in British Columbia established the first Green Party in North America in 1983, and the Green Party of Canada became a registered Canadian party in 1984. However, it took almost twenty years for the Green parties to make any sort of electoral impact. There were two reasons for this delay. First, in the 1980s, many environmentalists were concerned with single issues such as old-growth forests or acid rain or the destruction of the rain forest. They saw the New Democratic Party (NDP) as the best vehicle for protest at the federal level. At the provincial level, especially in British Columbia, they hoped that an NDP government would come to power and would act in an environmentally

Elizabeth May, Canada's first Green Party M.P. (1954 –)

sensitive way. But NDP provincial governments proved a disappointment to many environmentalists. Many of British Columbia's forestry workers supported the NDP, and they and their unions were often at odds with environmentalists regarding proper forest management practices. When environmentalists came to the conclusion that the NDP had betrayed them, many joined the Green Party of British Columbia, and the Green vote rose as high as 12 percent of the total vote in the 2001 provincial election.

The electoral system in Canada may inhibit the Green Party's political influence. Greens have achieved political success where the electoral system is based on some form of proportional representation. But Canadian voters and politicians prefer to retain a simple plurality system, in which candidates with the most votes win seats and the party with the most seats forms the government. In the 2007 election in Ontario, although the Green Party won 8 percent of the total vote, none of its candidates was elected to the 103-seat legislature. Had the Green Party won the same proportion of seats as votes, eight of its candidates would have been elected as MPPs. It is possible that even more Ontarians might have voted for the Green Party if they had not felt that their vote would have been "wasted." So the Green Party favours the introduction of a form of proportional representation to "empower Canadians in a truly representative and fair democracy."[45] In the

---

[45] *Green Party of Canada,* May 24, 2004 www.greenparty.ca/platform2004/en/policies.php?p=41.

2008 federal election, the leader of the Green Party was accepted as one of the major party leaders for the purposes of participating in the national leaders' debate.

However, many Greens see democracy as more than simply voting. From the Green perspective, each citizen is an actor—whether as producer, consumer, or in some other role—so each bears full responsibility for his or her actions and, in a democracy, partial responsibility for others' actions as well. Each of us has, or can have, a hand in making the laws and policies under which we live. For this reason Greens give equal emphasis to collective and individual responsibility for protecting the environment that protects us. Greens are, in short, "small d" democrats whose ethic emphasizes the importance of informed and active democratic citizenship. But as to what that ethic consists of, and with regards to the best way of informing oneself and others and of being an active citizen, Greens differ among themselves.

When Elizabeth May succeeded Jim Harris as leader of the Green Party in 2006, many people believed that her election would mark a sharp break in policy. Harris favoured market solutions to many environmental problems, as does the New Democratic Party. But May affirmed her belief in the "invisible green hand of the market." Although she believes that social justice, nonviolence, sustainability, participatory democracy, respect for diversity, and ecological wisdom are integral to Green politics, she rejects the various forms of deep Green ideologies as extremely anticapitalist and anachronistic. Although they continue to form part of the Green movement and the Green party, in her view, they are part of its history rather than its policy-oriented future. In 2011, May became the first Green Party MP, though the party's share of the popular vote dropped below 4 percent, down 3 percent from the prior election.

The End of Environmentalism?

Beginning nearly two decades ago, critics such as Anna Bramwell predicted "the fading of the Greens" and "the decline of environmental politics in the West." More recently, others, such as Ted Nordhaus and Michael Shellenberger, have predicted not merely the decline but "the death of environmentalism." Critics claimed either that the environmental movement was a passing fad and unable to gain political traction as actual public policy (Bramwell) or was predicated on a false picture of nature as an idyllic and harmonious whole that had been despoiled by heedless human beings. The ensuing predictions of gloom and doom (especially concerning global warming) were more likely to produce pessimism and resignation than to promote environmental activism (Nordhaus and Shellenberger). The former view is more negative and dismissive than the latter, which holds that everyone—even environmentalists—benefits by self-criticism and a rethinking of means if not necessarily of ends.

Environmentalists reply that what both of these viewpoints fail to note is that the environmental movement, far from dying or being already dead, is continuing to evolve and is adapting its ideology to changing conditions and circumstances. Instead of shouting insults from the sidelines they are involved in various political and lobbying organizations and are forging alliances with seemingly unlikely allies. One of these is the "black-green" alliance of people of colour and (mostly) white environmentalists. The Black Liberation theologian James H. Cone, for one, reminds us that poor African Americans, Hispanics, and white people (in Appalachia and elsewhere) are much more likely than affluent whites to bear the brunt of environmental degradation. Most toxic waste dumps are located far from homes and businesses owned by affluent Americans and much closer to or even inside neighbourhoods occupied by the poor, who are disproportionately people of colour. In Appalachia large mining companies strip the tops off mountains to take the coal and dump the tops into the valleys, which greatly degrades the environment in which poor white people live and work. These and other forms of exploitation of the poor are unfair and unjust, and call for remedies that recognize the rights of all God's creatures, whatever their colour or creed. Environmentalists have also made common cause with labour unions to promote fair trade (instead of unregulated free trade) in manufactured goods, the end of unfair labour practices in the United States and abroad, and the promotion of sustainable practices in manufacturing and agriculture. These and other alliances suggest that, far from fading or dying, the environmental movement continues to add a vibrant, vital, and distinctive voice to the oft-times off-key chorus of contemporary politics.

Conclusion

We have seen how and for what reasons Greens criticize many modern mainstream ideologies. We have also noted their reluctance to view their perspective as an ideology. Is their ethic an ideology? We believe it is, according to the criteria that we have proposed for identifying and explaining ideologies. First, both an ecological ethic and animal liberation fulfill the four functions of an ideology. Second, they propose and defend a specifically Green view of liberty or freedom.

The emerging Green ideology performs the four functions that all ideologies perform.

Explanatory Function. The Green ideology explains how the environmental crisis grew out of the human hubris, or pride, that some Greens call *anthropocentrism* and others call *humanism*—the mistaken belief that human beings are self-sufficient masters of nature. Damage to the earth is a result of human disregard for the delicate and interconnected web of life. It is this disregard that leads human beings to destroy the ecosystem and to oppress other sentient beings.

Evaluative Function. The Green ideology supplies a standard for evaluating actions, practices, and policies. It applauds actions that preserve and protect the natural environment—rain forests, wildlife habitats, wetlands, and other ecosystems—and condemns those that damage and destroy the natural environment. It tells us that sentient beings are worthy of respect because they are sentient.

Orientative Function. Greens think of themselves as members of a species whose health and very existence are deeply dependent upon other species and upon the conditions that nourish and nurture them all.

Programmatic Function. The Green ideology gives Greens a program of political and social action. Greens assume a responsibility for promoting practices or policies that protect the natural environment and for educating people about the environment. As they see it, only a massive and worldwide change of consciousness can save the planet and its species from careless human depredation.

For Further Reading

Amory, Cleveland. *Man Kind?* New York: Harper, 1974.

Berry, Wendell. *The Gift of Good Land.* San Francisco: North Point, 1981.

Bramwell, Anna. *Ecology in the Twentieth Century: A History.* New Haven, CT: Yale UP, 1989.

Carson, Rachel. *Silent Spring.* Boston: Houghton, 1962.

The PETA Practical Guide to Animal Rights: Simple Acts of Kindness to Help Animals in Trouble
Coats, C. David. *Old MacDonald's (Factory) Farm.* New York: Continuum, 1989.

Dobson, Andrew, ed. *Fairness and Futurity: Essays on Environmental Sustainability and Social Justice.* New York: Oxford UP, 1999.

Donaldson, Sue, and Will Kymlicka. *Zoopolis: A Political Theory of Animal Rights.* Oxford: OUP, 2011.

Dryzek, John S. *The Politics of the Earth: Environmental Discourses.* Oxford: Oxford UP, 1997.

Dryzek, John S., and David Schlosberg, eds. *Debating the Earth: The Environmental Politics Reader.* Oxford: Oxford UP, 1998.

Dwivedi, O. P. *Governmental Response to Environmental Challenges in Global Perspective.* Amsterdam: IOS, 1998.

———. *Sustainable Development and Canada: National and International Perspectives.* Peterborough, ON: Broadview, 2001.

Ehrenfeld, David. *The Arrogance of Humanism.* New York: Oxford UP, 1978.

Francione, Gary L., and Alan Watson. *Introduction to Animal Rights.* Philadelphia: Temple UP, 2000.

Goodin, Robert E. *Green Political Theory.* Cambridge: Polity, 1992.

Hardin, Garrett. *Filters Against Folly.* New York: Viking, 1985.

Heilbroner, Robert L. *An Inquiry into the Human Prospect.* 3d ed. New York: Norton, 1991.

Humphrey, Matthew, ed. *Political Theory and the Environment: A Reassessment.* London: Frank, 2001.

Kay, Jane Holz. *Asphalt Nation: How the Automobile Took Over America and How We Can Take It Back.* Berkeley and Los Angeles: U of California P, 1998.

Kelly, Petra. *Thinking Green! Essays on Environmentalism, Feminism, and Nonviolence.* Berkeley, CA: Parallax, 1994.

Leopold, Aldo. *A Sand County Almanac.* New York: Oxford UP, 1968.

Nash, Roderick Frazier. *The Rights of Nature: A History of Environmental Ethics.* Madison, WI: U of Wisconsin P, 1989.

Newkirk. Ingrid. *The PETA Practical Guide to Animal Rights: Simple Acts of Kindness to Help Animals in Trouble.* London: St Martin's Press, 2009.

Partridge, Ernest, ed. *Responsibilities to Future Generations: Environmental Ethics.* Buffalo, NY: Prometheus, 1981.

Pollan, Michael. *The Botany of Desire.* NY: Random House, 2002.

Pollan, Michael. *The Omnivore's Dilemma: A Natural History of Four Meals.* NY: Penguin Group, 2007.

Porritt, Jonathon. *Seeing Green: The Politics of Ecology Explained.* Oxford: Blackwell, 1984.

Regan, Tom. *All That Dwell Therein.* Berkeley and Los Angeles: U of California P, 1982.

———. *The Case for Animal Rights.* Berkeley and Los Angeles: U of California P, 1983.

———, ed. *Earthbound: New Introductory Essays in Environmental Ethics.* New York: Random, 1984.

Roszak, Theodore. *Person/Planet.* Garden City, NY: Doubleday, 1978.

Sagoff, Mark. *The Economy of the Earth: Philosophy, Law, and the Environment.* Cambridge: Cambridge UP, 1988.

Schumacher, E. F. *Small Is Beautiful: Economics as if People Mattered.* Garden City, NY: Doubleday, 1973.

Seed, John, et al. *Thinking Like a Mountain.* Philadelphia: New Society, 1988.

Sessions, George, ed. *Deep Ecology for the Twenty-First Century.* Boston: Shambhala, 1995.

Singer, Peter. *Animal Liberation.* 2d ed. New York: Random, 1990.

Worster, Donald. *Nature's Economy: A History of Ecological Ideas.* 2d ed. Cambridge: Cambridge UP, 1994.

Useful Websites and Social Media

www.davidsuzuki.org David Suzuki Foundation

www.earthfirst.org Earth First!

www.earthliberationfront.com Earth Liberation Front

www.ecofem.org Ecofeminism

www.environmentaldefence.ca Environmental Defence

www.greenparty.ca Green Party of Canada

www.greenpeace.org/canada Greenpeace

www.nature.org The Nature Conservancy

www.pembinafoundation.org Pembina Foundation

www.seashepherd.org Sea Shepherd Conservation Society

www.sierraclub.ca Sierra Club Canada

Twitter:

@ElizabethMay Elizabeth May

@algore Al Gore

@GreenpeaceCA Greenpeace Canada

@Globalexchange Global Exchange

@DavidSuzuki David Suzuki

Discussion Questions

1. "A smart economy is efficient. It relies on non-polluting systems and energy sources. It ends waste. It reuses and recycles. Through closed-loop systems it is massively more efficient. That efficiency will bring greater competitiveness and prosperity to the entire Canadian economy." Is the Green Party economic platform socialist, capitalist, or, as it claims, neither?

2. Do you think it's acceptable to harm human beings through ecotage or monkey wrenching in order to protect the environment?

3. Do animals have rights? Are their rights very similar to the rights of human beings, or are they fundamentally different?

4. Does globalization harm the environment? If it does, how can we counteract the harm?

MySearchLab   MySearchLab with eText offers you access to an online interactive version of the text, additional quizzes and assessment, extensive help with your writing and research projects, and provides round-the-clock access to credible and reliable source material. Go to **www.mysearchlab.com** to access these resources.

CHAPTER 13

Radical Islamicism

As Muslims we believe in a progressive, liberal, pluralistic, democratic, and secular society where everyone has the freedom of religion. We want our communities to be equal and active contributors and participants in the development of a just, democratic, and equitable society in Canada.

Muslim Canadian Congress

LEARNING OBJECTIVES

After completing this chapter you should be able to

1. Explain the major features of the Islamic religion.
2. Discuss the differing interpretations of the term *jihad* in the Muslim world.
3. Understand radical Islamicism's view of human nature and freedom.
4. Demonstrate how radical Islamicism fulfils the four features of an ideology.

In recent years a number of horrific events—the airplane hijackings of September 11, 2001, and terrorist bombings in Kenya and Tanzania in 1998, Indonesia in 2002, Spain in 2004, and England in 2005 among them—have awakened people in the Western world to a new threat to their peace and security. This threat takes the form of an ideology that is variously called political Islam, radical Islamicism, Islamic fundamentalism, or simply Islamicism. Whatever we call it, it is clear that we must understand the main elements of this new ideology if we are to understand the world in which we now live and respond properly to the threat it poses to Muslims and non-Muslims alike. As all of its various names indicate, this new ideology is an outgrowth and an extreme form of the Islamic religion. To understand this ideology, we must begin with a brief exploration of the major features of Islam. Before beginning, however, we must emphasize that Islam is a religion, and no more an ideology than Buddhism, Christianity, Hinduism, or Judaism. But one minority variant of Islam—radical or fundamentalist Islamicism—does qualify as an ideology, for reasons we set out in this chapter.

Muslims—people of the Islamic faith—are of many different nationalities and inhabit almost every part of the globe. However, their numbers are concentrated in North Africa, the Middle and Near East, and Indonesia, India and Pakistan. Islam has dominated most of this territory virtually since the religion began around 620 CE, when the Prophet Muhammad announced in Arabia that he had received a revelation from the Angel Gabriel. The report of this and subsequent revelations make up the Qur'an, the holy book of Islam that Muslims take to be the divine word of Allah, or God. Together with Muhammad's own words and deeds (or Sunna), which Muslims are supposed to emulate, the Qur'an forms the basis of the Islamic faith—a monotheistic faith, like Judaism and Christianity, that worships one all-knowing, all-powerful, and merciful God, the God of Abraham and Isaac that the Jews and Christians worship.

Ground Zero under construction, New York.

Within a century of Mohammed's death in 632 CE, Islam had spread from Arabia throughout the Middle East, across North Africa, and through most of Spain. The Muslim rulers of Spain were generally tolerant of other religions, allowing both Christians and Jews to practice their faiths. Spain soon became the chief point of contact between Christian Europe and the Islamic world—a contact that enabled Europeans to enjoy such fruits of Islamic culture as Arabic numerals (which the Arabs themselves had imported from India) and algebra. Islamic universities also preserved many of the works of classical philosophy that had been lost to Europe for centuries before being rediscovered through contact with Islamic Spain.

Even before Muslims invaded Spain, however, a split developed within Islam that continues today. This is the split between the Sunni and the Shi'ite Muslims. The division initially began with a controversy over the question of who was to follow in Mohammed's footsteps as *caliph,* or leader of the Islamic community, but it also raised the further question of what the nature of this leadership should be. Sunnis conceived of the *caliph* as a kind of elected chief executive, while Shi'ites insisted that the *caliph* is an infallible *imam,* a divinely gifted leader who must be a member of the house of Ali (Mohammed's son-in-law). Today, among Muslims in general, Sunnis are by far the larger of the two groups, but Shi'ites outnumber Sunnis in some countries, such as Iraq, and in Iran they are easily the dominant faction.

For Sunnis and Shi'ites alike, the practice of Islam requires ***jihad***, the struggle against evil. Many Muslims, perhaps even most of them, think of *jihad* primarily as the individual's inner struggle to overcome the temptation to be selfish and evil. Others, however, take *jihad* to be first and foremost an outward struggle against the enemies of Islam. This latter notion of *jihad* is central to *radical* **Islamicism**.

Whether Sunni or Shi'ite, mainstream or radical, most Muslims have believed that religion is not simply a personal matter. Islam is a way of life with profound political and social implications. It draws no distinction, as Christians and secular Westerners do, between church and state or religion and politics.[1] The law of the land and the precepts of the faith should be one and the same. Thus the *Shari'a*—Islamic law derived from the *Qur'an* and the *Sunna*—prohibits usury, calls for a tax on the wealthy to aid the poor and needy, and prescribes severe punishment for premarital sex and adultery. These and other injunctions are to be enforced by the rulers. In other words, Islam calls for **theocracy**, a form of rule in which the law of the land is supposed to follow directly from God's commands. In the case of radical Islam, the law of the land is to be *Shari'a,* narrowly interpreted and strictly enforced.

In the twentieth century many predominantly Muslim countries began to move away from theocracy as they began to separate government and politics from matters of faith, with Turkey probably going the furthest. In this respect, they followed the example of Western liberals and socialists. In making these liberalizing and modernizing moves, however, they provoked a strong reaction from radical Islamists, who see **secularism** as a betrayal of their faith. Muslims in the Middle East and North Africa have long felt themselves and their faith threatened by external enemies. Radical Islamicism differs from mainstream Islam largely because the radicals see the threat as greater and the danger more imminent.

To put the point simply, these threats have come in four waves. The first wave comprised the Christian Crusades (roughly 1100–1300 CE)—military expeditions to retake the Holy Land for Christendom, to convert or kill infidels (that is, non-Christians), and, not least, to gain territory and wealth for Europeans. Untold thousands of Muslim men, women, and children were butchered in the name of Christianity; others converted to Christianity under threat of death. A second threatening wave came with European imperial expansion into North Africa and the Middle East in the nineteenth and early twentieth centuries. France governed much of North Africa, and Britain controlled most of the territory from Egypt through India, including Palestine, Arabia, and Persia (now Iran). The British were also instrumental in paving the way for what many Muslims saw as a third threat: the establishment of the state of Israel in Palestine after the Second World War. To them, a Jewish state in a predominantly Muslim region was both injury and insult. More recently, a fourth wave of threat has appeared in the form of influential Western ideas—liberalism, secularism, materialism, religious toleration, and sexual equality among them—that fall under the general heading of modernity or modernism. These ideas are communicated through satellite television, the Internet, home videos, and other media. Reruns of *Baywatch* and other (mainly American) programs depict a world in which scantily clad and sexually available women are on socially equal terms with men, and women and men alike live lives in which God and religion play no part whatsoever. These Western cultural imports are deeply shocking to conservative Muslim sensibilities. Moreover, conservative Muslims fear that such immorality (or amorality) is infectious, with young Muslims being particularly susceptible to the temptations represented by American movies and other cultural media.

---

[1]As Bernard Lewis and other scholars have observed, the distinction between church and state is largely a Christian invention, with no clear counterpart in Islam. See Lewis, *What Went Wrong? Western Impact and Middle Eastern Response* (New York: Oxford UP, 2002) 97–99.

Many Muslims also complain that the United States has added military insult to moral injury by using covert operations and military force to topple regimes believed to be unfriendly to American political and business interests. The United States has also supported pro-Western but undemocratic governments headed by hereditary monarchs in Saudi Arabia, Kuwait, and elsewhere. The monarchs have returned the favour by keeping the oil flowing to the United States and other nations. Moreover, following the Gulf War of 1991, Saudi rulers allowed the United States to station troops inside Saudi Arabia, the home of Mecca and Medina, the two most sacred sites in Islam. To many Muslims, including a Saudi named Osama bin Laden (1957–2011), these military bases were tantamount to an American invasion and occupation of Muslim holy lands and thus a grave threat to Islam itself. Many Muslims have also been alarmed by the United States' strong and long-standing support of Israel, which in their view illegally occupies the land of Palestine and threatens its Arab neighbours.

For these reasons, among others, many Muslims are wary of Western—and particularly American—influence in the Middle East, North Africa, and other parts of the world where Islam is prevalent. What distinguishes moderate or mainstream Muslims from radicals such as bin Laden and the other members of al Qaeda ("The Base"), or the Taliban of Afghanistan, turns on the question of what is to be done, and how, and by whom. To see how they answer these questions, we must understand the origin and development of radical Islamicism.

RADICAL ISLAMICISM

Radical or fundamentalist Islamicism is an amalgam of various strands within Islamic thought and culture. Taken together, these strands form an ideology that may be said to represent the Muslim **Counter-Enlightenment**. Just as the European Counter-Enlightenment of the late eighteenth and early nineteenth centuries (discussed in Chapter 9) rejected the scientific and secular ideas of the Enlightenment, so the Muslim Counter-Enlightenment is a reaction against attempts to make Islam and Islamic societies more modern or enlightened. In other words, like Joseph de Maistre and other leaders of the European Counter-Enlightenment, radical Islamists adhere to a **reactionary** ideology that aims to restore Islam to its "pure" state, untouched by the secularism that marks so many of the intellectual, political, and scientific developments of the past several centuries—including those contributed by Muslim scholars and scientists. Thus radical Islamicism is directed not only against the West but also against Muslims who subscribe to Western ideas and aspirations that would make Islam into a more open and tolerant religion.

There is no single theorist to whom one can point as the source or fountainhead of radical Islamic thought—certainly not Osama bin Laden, who was primarily a practitioner rather than a theorist of radical Islamicism. But if there is one especially influential thinker in this movement, it is Sayyid Qutb (1906–1966), the Egyptian author of numerous books, including *Islam and Social Justice* (1949), *The Battle Between Islam and Capitalism* (1950), *In the Shade of the Qur'an* (eight volumes, 1952–1982), and, most notably, *Milestones along the Road* (1964). Qutb began his career as a novelist, journalist, literary critic, teacher, and high-ranking member of Egypt's Ministry of Education. He was also an outspoken critic of the corruption that characterized the regime of King Faruq, who ruled Egypt from 1936 to 1952. The king sent Qutb into exile in the United States, hoping that exposure to "Western ways" would lead him to cease his criticism.

Fluent in Arabic, English, and several other languages, Qutb studied at Colorado State College of Education, earning a master's degree in 1949. Contrary to the king's hopes, however, Qutb's American experience led him in an even more radical direction. Appalled by America's racism, social and economic inequality, sexual promiscuity, alcohol consumption, secularism and materialism, and uncritical support of the then-new state of Israel, Qutb reconnected with his early religious upbringing. Upon his return to Egypt in 1951, Qutb joined the radical Muslim Brotherhood, which had been founded by Hasan al-Banna in 1929 while Egypt was under British imperial domination. Qutb agreed with al-Banna that Western influence could be resisted only by Muslims who are resolute in their faith and prepared to practise *jihad*. After al-Banna's assassination in 1949, Qutb became the Muslim Brotherhood's leading thinker. In 1952 Qutb was fired from the Ministry of Education for his outspoken criticisms of King Faruq's regime. Shortly thereafter Faruq was overthrown by an Egyptian nationalist, Colonel Gamel Abdul Nasser. Nasser attempted to curry favour with Qutb and the Muslim Brotherhood, but he rejected Qutb's proposal to turn Egypt into an Islamic state—that is, a state governed in strict accordance with *Shari'a*. Qutb, in turn, was critical of Nasser's program of modernization and reform. In 1954 Qutb was arrested, imprisoned, and tortured. In 1965 he was again arrested and tortured for plotting the overthrow of Nasser's secular regime. In 1966 he was executed, and he has ever since been regarded as hero, theorist, and martyr of the radical Islamist cause.

Qutb's massive eight-volume commentary on the Qur'an, much of which he wrote while imprisoned in Egypt, is titled *In the Shade of the Qur'an*. The title is intentionally suggestive. For desert dwellers in the Middle East and elsewhere, shade is rare and all the more valued for that. Qutb views the modern world as a spiritual desert—a vast and arid wasteland of secularism, materialism, consumerism, hedonism, egoism, self-centredness, and selfishness—from which the message of the Qur'an comes as a welcome relief. All good Muslims must accordingly seek the shade of the Qur'an. But Qutb and his radical Islamist disciples advocate and adhere to an austere interpretation of the Qur'an that many, indeed most, Muslims find offensive and objectionable.

In Islam, as we have seen, there are not separate spheres labelled "religion" and "politics" but a single seamless interweaving of all aspects of individual and collective life. Qutb shared this view, and he was highly critical of Muslims who seek to modernize and reform Muslim societies—and even Islam itself—by introducing Western and secular ideas of religious toleration, freedom, sexual equality, and justice.[2] He believed that the fact that many Muslims found reform attractive indicates only the pervasive influence of the West, which is mired in *jahiliyya* ("darkness" or "ignorance") and threatens to drag Muslim societies into that darkness. *Jahiliyya* referred originally to the ignorance that

---

[2]Because most of Qutb's books have not been translated into English, and we do not read Arabic, we have relied on several scholarly sources in developing this account of Qutb's political views, especially the excellent study by Roxanne L. Euben, *Enemy in the Mirror: Islamic Fundamentalism and the Limits of Modern Rationalism* (Princeton, NJ: Princeton UP, 1999). Other helpful sources are Salwa Ismail, "Islamic Political Thought," in *The Cambridge History of Twentieth-Century Political Thought*, ed. Terence Ball and Richard Bellamy (Cambridge: Cambridge UP, 2003); Shahrough Akhavi, "Qutb, Sayyid," *The Oxford Encyclopedia of the Modern Islamic World*, vol. 3 (Oxford: Oxford UP, 1995), and "The Dialectic in Contemporary Egyptian Social Thought: The Scripturalist and Modernist Discourses of Sayyid Qutb and Hasan Hanafi," *International Journal of Middle East Studies* 29 (1997): 377–401; and William Shepherd, "Islam as a 'System' in the Later Writings of Sayyid Qutb," *Middle Eastern Studies* 25 (1989): 31–50.

enveloped the world before the teachings of the Qur'an were revealed to the Prophet Mohammed. The "new *jahiliyya*" to which Qutb refers comes from Western ideas and influences. It is a kind of wilful rejection of divinely revealed truth that is brought about by misplaced pride in the successes of science and technology. This rejection in turn has spawned a mindset that is a mixture of philosophical skepticism, secularism, and even atheism. People afflicted with this mindset mistakenly think that human reason can penetrate all mysteries and that they can replace God's will with their own and substitute their judgment for His and human justice for divine justice. In particular, the ideologies of liberalism and communism embody this modern Western outlook, which is deeply opposed to the spirit and teachings of Islam. Liberalism emphasizes the sovereignty of the individual, and communism the sovereignty of the proletariat; neither recognizes the true sovereignty of God.

It follows, said Qutb, that modernizers and reformers in the Middle East are attempting nothing less than the importation of the "new *jahiliyya*" into Muslim societies, thereby subverting and corrupting Islam itself. Qutb's critique of such subversion was not new. What was new was the thoroughness and subtlety of his critique, which in several respects resembles Marx's critique of capitalism and Lenin's vision of a vanguard party. Qutb believed that non-Muslims—and many Muslims—suffer from a kind of false consciousness that leads them to see the world and their place in it in an inverted or distorted way. Thus they welcome Western ways and ideas, and call them "progressive." If the Muslim world is to be saved from these progressives, a small band of exceptionally devout Muslims (*jama'a*) will have to lead the way. That is, they must wage a holy war or *jihad* against everything that the West stands for—modernity, capitalism, religious toleration, sexual equality, and so on—and be prepared to give their lives in this sacred cause. In short, Muslims must go on the offensive against the aggressors who import these ideas into Muslim society. This is the ideological basis of radical Islamicism.

Since Qutb's death in 1966, other Islamists have continued to press for *jihad* against the West and its corrupting ways. How would they conduct this struggle? One way is to attack those Muslims who have supposedly betrayed the faith by adopting secular or Western ideas and institutions. This was their justification, for example, for the assassination of Egyptian President Anwar Sadat in 1981;[3] it also explains the opposition to the secularist and socialist Saddam Hussein when he ruled Iraq. Another way to wage *jihad* is to launch terrorist attacks directly on Western countries and their troops. Thus American military barracks in Saudi Arabia were blown up (1996), the naval ship USS *Cole* was attacked and almost sunk (1998), and U.S. embassies in Kenya and Tanzania were destroyed by suicide bombers (2000), with grave loss of life, mostly African (and many Muslim). Most infamous of all were the terrorist attacks of September 11, 2001, on Washington, DC, and New York—attacks that killed nearly 3000 people, most of them Americans—and the subsequent bombings in Madrid (2004), Indonesia (2005), London (2005), and elsewhere that killed hundreds more people. The murderers and suicide bombers who are called terrorists in the West are often praised as "martyrs" or "blessed martyrs" in the Middle East, where some regard them as people who have undertaken the sacred but too often neglected duty of *jihad*.[4] From the perspective of radical Islamicism,

---

[3]As explained in Johannes J. G. Jansen, *The Neglected Duty: The Creed of Sadat's Assassins and the Emergence of Islamic Militance in the Middle East* (New York: Macmillan, 1986).
[4]Jansen 159–234.

terrorism is permissible when it promotes the greater good of ridding the Islamic world of Western infidels and their pernicious ideas about free speech, sexual equality, and religious toleration. By contrast, from the perspective of moderate or mainstream Islam, suicide and the murder of innocents are strictly forbidden by the Qur'an and the Haddith (sayings of the Prophet).

A third way in which radical Islamists wage *jihad* is through the education—or perhaps more precisely, the indoctrination—of young people, and boys in particular. In *madrassas,* or religious schools, in most Middle Eastern countries, students study only one book, the *Qur'an,* which is said to teach everything they need to know. In many of these *madrassas* students are taught a radical interpretation of the *Qur'an.* To take but one example: The *Qur'an* states that women must cover their hair and dress modestly. But what counts as modest? Short shorts and bikinis are obviously impermissible, but interpretations differ beyond that point. Moderate or mainstream Muslims are apt to interpret modest to mean that women may or may not wear head scarves and expose their faces. By contrast, militant or radical Muslims, such as the Taliban of Afghanistan, insist that modest means that women must be completely covered from head to toe; they must wear the *burka,* which conceals even their faces and feet; and any woman who reveals any part of her body in public should be beaten. Here, as elsewhere, a great deal hangs on how the *Qur'an* is interpreted.

HUMAN NATURE AND FREEDOM

As with any ideology, radical Islamicism has its own views of human nature and freedom. These are derived not only from its particular way of reading and interpreting the *Qur'an* but also from a particular understanding of the long history of encounters between the Muslim and Christian (or Western) worlds.

Human Nature. Radical Islamicism's view of human nature is rooted in religious belief. Together with the other great monotheistic religions, Judaism and Christianity, Islam shares the view that there is one God who created the heavens, the earth, and all its creatures, including human beings. Humans are by nature weak and prone to sin. To overcome temptation, faithful Muslims must engage in *jihad*, the struggle against evil. As we have noted, this struggle takes place at both an individual and a collective level.

As individuals, Muslims must adhere to a strict regimen that involves praying five times a day, fasting from dawn to dusk during the holy month of Ramadan, giving generously to charities to help the poor, making a *haj* or pilgrimage to the holy shrine at Mecca if possible, and, more generally, living a pious and upright life. Muslims call the struggle to live this way the "greater *jihad*." Such a life cannot be lived in isolation from others, but only as part of a wider community of believers. If it is to serve its members well, this community must be tightly knit and strict in its enforcement of Islamic law (*Shari'a*). This community engages collectively in *jihad* by helping its members to resist the evil within each individual and the evil without—that is, external enemies who threaten the community by undermining the faith upon which it is based. Muslims call the struggle against external enemies the "lesser *jihad*." Radical Islamicism reverses this order, placing greater emphasis on *jihad* against all enemies of Islam, including (in its view) moderate or reform-minded Muslims as well as infidels from the West.

Radical Islamicism is antiliberal in that it is anti-individualist and has no room at all for the liberal-individualist idea of the individual as isolated or distinct from the larger society or community of which he or she is a small and very dependent part. This antiliberal tendency is especially marked in radical Islamists, who reject individual rights or rights against the larger society (as in the U.S. Bill of Rights) as perverted ideas utterly foreign or alien to their vision of Islam. To have rights against that which gives you moral guidance and sustenance amounts to having rights against morality, which is absurd. The Canadian Charter of Rights, because of its commitment to multiculturalism, does not evoke the same level of hostility, but many issues relating to race, religion, and ethnicity in a multicultural society remain unresolved. The Bouchard-Taylor Commission established in 2007 by the Quebec government demonstrated just how difficult reconciling competing visions can prove.

It is important to remember that Islam is not a unified monolith, any more than is Christianity or Judaism. It is a religion deeply divided within itself—between Sunnis and Shi'ites, liberal modernizers and conservative traditionalists, tolerant moderates and radical extremists. A number of Muslim sects, such as Sufi Islam and the populist Islam practised in Indonesia and Egypt, favour the toleration of all faiths, a fairly flexible interpretation of the Qur'an, and taking full advantage of science and modernity. Other sects, such as the Salafi sect, the Taliban of Afghanistan, and the Wahhabis of Saudi Arabia, reject modernity and seek a return to the rigid and austere Islam preached and practised in the era of the Prophet Mohammed. The Salafis, for example, hold that the Islam introduced by the Prophet was perfect and needed no further development; hence all later variants of Islam, such as the mystical, love-preaching Sufism, are degenerate, imperfect, and illegitimate. Most radical jihadists follow the Salafist teachings of the thirteenth-century scholar Ibn Tamiyyah. They resolutely reject the teachings of Hirith al-Muhaasibi, the founder of Sufism, and Mohammed Abdu, who founded the forward-looking rationalist sect within Islam.[5]

Thus, unlike moderate variants of Islam, radical Islamicism is, as previously noted, a *reactionary* ideology that seeks to return its adherents—and the wider world—to a culturally and theologically "purer" time. As the Ayatollah Khomeini thundered in a sermon shortly before taking power in Iran in 1979 (paraphrased): Yes, we [radical Islamists] are reactionaries, and you [Western secularists and Muslims who favour "modernizing" Islam] are "enlightened intellectuals." You intellectuals do not want us to go back 1400 years.[6] But such a reversal is required if the lessons of the Prophet are to be learned and applied to everyday life. Foremost among these is a repudiation of liberal and Western ideas of "freedom."

Freedom. It might seem that radical Islamicism has no conception of, or room for, freedom. Radical Islamicism certainly has no room for or sympathy with a *liberal* view of freedom, but that does not mean that it has no view of freedom at all. On the contrary, it has its own distinctive conception of freedom, as Khomeini and Qutb both argued.

Khomeini held that devout Muslims must reject the modern, liberal conception of freedom: "You, who want freedom, freedom for everything, the freedom of parties, you who want all the freedoms, you intellectuals: freedom that will corrupt our youth, freedom that will pave the way for the oppressor, freedom that will drag our nation to the

[5]Lawrence Wright, *The Looming Tower: Al-Qaeda and the Road to 9/11* (New York: Knopf, 2007).
[6]Wright 47.

bottom."[7] Muslims must reject this false freedom, Khomeini declared, replacing it with the true freedom that comes only when one surrenders and submits one's will to the Supreme Will of Allah. This view of freedom-as-submission is a staple feature of Islam generally—again, Islam means "submission"—and of radical Islamicism in particular, where it assumes a violent and specifically *political* form. "Islam is not merely 'belief,'" wrote Sayyid Qutb in *Milestones along the Road*. "Islam is a declaration of the freedom of man from servitude to other men. Thus it strives . . . to abolish all those systems and governments which are based on the rule of man over man."[8]

Qutb goes on to argue that to live without Islam is to live as a slave—a slave to sexual desire, to material wants, and to other masters—while to live as a faithful Muslim is to be free from these earthly temptations. Only by submitting to the divine will of Allah can human beings become truly free.[9] At an individual level, such freedom results from the "greater *jihad*" of internal struggle for spiritual strength and self-control. At a collective level, however, Muslims will become free only if and when they band together in an armed struggle (the "lesser *jihad*") to expel or exterminate infidels—Westerners and Muslim moderates and modernizers foremost among them—from predominantly Muslim lands. The radical Islamist conception of freedom thus can be illustrated by way of our triadic model (see Figure 13.1).

These competing conceptions of *jihad* underlie many of the differences between radical and moderate Muslims. Moderate or mainstream Muslims reject radical Islamicism,

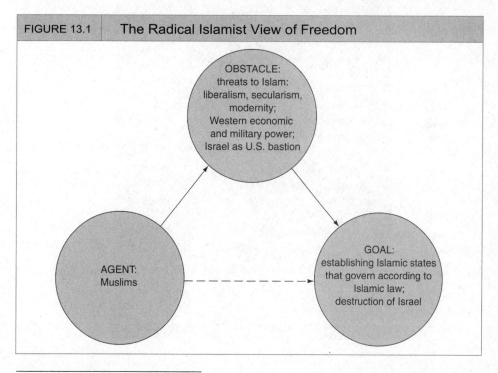

FIGURE 13.1   **The Radical Islamist View of Freedom**

OBSTACLE:
threats to Islam:
liberalism, secularism,
modernity;
Western economic
and military power;
Israel as U.S. bastion

AGENT:
Muslims

GOAL:
establishing Islamic states
that govern according to
Islamic law;
destruction of Israel

---

[7]Quoted in Wright, 47.
[8]Quoted in Wright, 108.
[9]See Roxanne L. Euben, "Comparative Political Theory: An Islamic Fundamentalist Critique of Rationalism," *Journal of Politics* 59 (February 1997): 28–55.

and especially its ready recourse to terrorism, as a perversion of the Prophet's teachings in the Qur'an and *Sunna*. These teachings include a prohibition on the killing of innocent noncombatants. How then, moderate Muslims ask, can radical Islamists justify the killing of other Muslims and of innocent civilians? Radical Islamists respond by claiming that their resort to terror and killing is a form of *takfir*—the excommunication of Muslim "apostates" who have forfeited their status as Muslims and can therefore be justifiably killed. Thus, to cite one of many examples of *takfir,* members of the Muslim Brotherhood declared that Egyptian President Anwar Sadat deserved to be assassinated because he had negotiated with the Jewish prime minister of Israel. As for the killing of innocent civilians, Osama bin Laden had a ready answer: Civilians in Western democracies are not really innocent. In a democracy, he said, the citizens elect leaders and representatives, and the citizens of Western democracies have elected leaders who send soldiers into the Middle East to kill Muslims. "The American people," charged bin Laden, "choose their government by their own free will" and "have the ability and choice to refuse the policies of their government." If they choose a government that pursues anti-Islamic policies in the guise of a "war on terror," they are every bit as responsible as their government and military are, and may therefore be targeted as enemy combatants.[10]

Osama bin Laden (1957–2011)

---

[10]Quoted in Noah Feldman, "Islam, Terror, and the Second Nuclear Age," *New York Times Magazine,* October 29, 2006, 56–57. See also Osama bin Laden et al., "Jihad Against Jews and Crusaders," in *Ideals and Ideologies,* ed. Ball and Dagger, selection 67; and Peter Bergen, *The Osama bin Laden I Know: An Oral History of Al Qaeda's Leader* (New York: Free P, 2006).

Another difference between radical Islamists and mainstream Muslims is their way of reading or interpreting the Qur'an. Like Christians and Jews, Muslims are divided over what constitutes the correct interpretation of scripture. Other religions have their fundamentalist sects—those who believe that their sacred scripture has a definite, unchanging meaning that the faithful can discern by reading it literally rather than figuratively, metaphorically, or historically. From the fundamentalists' perspective, those who read scripture in nonliteral ways are apostates or heretics who disavow or deviate from the fundamental truths of the faith.

Sometimes this division appears even within families of the faithful. Hassan Al-Banna, the Egyptian founder of the radical Muslim Brotherhood, subscribed to a fundamentalist reading of the Qur'an, according to which holy war against infidels, including many Muslims, is a divine duty. By contrast, his younger brother, Gamal Al-Banna, is an eminent Islamic scholar who is highly critical of Islamic fundamentalism. He holds that the Qur'an should be interpreted in a more liberal and less literal way than radical Islamists advocate, saying that "man is the aim of religion, and religion is only a means. What is prevalent today [among radical Islamists] is the opposite."[11] Gamal Al-Banna is the author or translator of more than 100 books, including *A New Democracy* (1946), in which he criticizes Islamic fundamentalists for looking not at the text of the Qur'an itself but at the earliest interpretations of its meaning, which the fundamentalists then accept as authoritative and eternally valid. His own view is that the Qur'an must be interpreted in light of new knowledge and changing conditions and circumstances. He contends that to do otherwise is to be hopelessly stuck in the past. Radical Islamists hope and fight for just such a return to a "purer" past. In that respect radical Islamicism is indeed a reactionary ideology.

Conclusion

Radical Islamicism as an Ideology

Like other ideologies, radical Islamicism guides and inspires its followers by performing the following four functions in its own distinctive way.

Explanation. Radical Islamicism explains the current situation in the parts of the world where Muslims predominate—the Middle and Near East, North Africa, and parts of South and Southeast Asia—in terms of sweeping threats to Islam. The Islamic world and indeed Islam itself are under threat from an enemy that aims to destroy them by all available means: military, economic, intellectual, cultural, and spiritual. The threat of military force, great as it is, pales in comparison to the more insidious ideas with which the West tries to poison the minds of Muslims, especially young Muslims: liberalism, secularism, sexual equality, religious tolerance, materialism, and so forth. There is a concerted, highly organized global conspiracy to inject these ideas into Islamic culture, with the aim of undermining and ultimately destroying Islam as a religion and way of life.

Evaluation. Radical Islamicism supplies its adherents with a view of personal piety, social justice, and communal harmony that provides a perspective from which Western culture

---

[11]Quoted in Michael Slackman, "A Liberal Brother at Odds with the Muslim Brotherhood," *New York Times,* October 21, 2006, A4.

can be criticized and its incursions resisted. From this perspective Western ideas—of individualism, liberalism, secularism, sexual equality, materialism, and so on—are revealed to be transgressive and disrespectful to both body and spirit; they confuse and jumble natural and God-given distinctions between holy and unholy, men and women, rulers and ruled, acceptable and unacceptable behavior. Western liberal individualism dethrones God and attempts to put man or "the individual" in His place as the source of all value—what Immanuel Kant called "the kingdom of ends" and John Stuart Mill called the "sovereign self" ("Over himself, over his own body and mind, the individual is sovereign").[12] What in the West is called religious toleration really amounts to a pervasive indifference to religion, to God, and to everything that matters most. What is called sexual equality represents confusion or confounding of the God-given sexual and biological differences that leads to an easy familiarity between the sexes, encouraging premarital and extramarital sex (i.e., adultery) and sexual promiscuity. Men and women have deeply different abilities and needs. This means, among other things, that they should be educated separately. Some radical Islamists, such as the Taliban, even say that women should not be educated at all.

Orientation. As a theologically based ideology, radical Islamicism supplies its adherents with a sense of individual and collective identity—of who they are and where they belong, who their friends and enemies are, what their purpose in life is. A truly faithful Muslim says, in effect, "I am a Muslim. I belong to and am a small part of a larger community of believers, dependent on that community for my faith, for moral and spiritual guidance. My friends are fellow Muslims who believe and behave as I do. My enemies include any individual, group, or nation that disagrees with or is in any way hostile to the community of which I am a member. My purpose in life is to live an upright life, and my sacred duty is to oppose the enemies of Islam." Radical Islamists differ from moderate or mainstream Muslims in whom they identify as enemies of Islam and how they propose to deal with them. Radical Islamists believe that only they, and people who agree with them, are truly faithful Muslims. Those who disagree with them—Muslims and non-Muslims alike—are enemies of Islam to be denounced and killed.

Program. The radical Islamist political program is, in a word, *jihad*—a faith-based struggle against the enemies of Islam; that is to say, those who espouse any and all ideas that are inimical to or threaten the ideas and beliefs of Islam: liberalism, secularism, and so on. To protect the Islamic religion and way of life is a sacred duty. To that end radical Islamists believe that any means are permissible—including violence. Terrorism is a weapon of the weak against the strong. To those so-called moderate Muslims who say that the Qur'an forbids suicide and the shedding of innocent blood, radical Islamists say that they are following the Qur'an in giving like for like: Israelis have shed the blood of innocent Palestinian women and children; the Palestinian "martyrs" are therefore justified in shedding their own and the blood of so-called "innocent" Israeli women and children in whose names and for whose sake the Israeli government has killed or crippled innocent Palestinians. And, as in Israel, so too elsewhere: Whoever threatens Muslims and their Islamic faith can—and should—be opposed by any means possible. In a sacred struggle to defend the faith, any

---

[12]Mill, *On Liberty,* in Mill, *Utilitarianism, Liberty, and Representative Government,* ed. A. D. Lindsay (New York: E. P. Dutton, 1910), p. 96. This passage is included in the excerpt from *On Liberty* in Ball and Dagger, *Ideals and Ideologies,* selection 3.17.

means are morally permissible. Moreover, *jihad* is not only to be waged against the West—against the United States and its European and Israeli allies—but also against corrupt and secular governments or regimes in purportedly Muslim countries. This belief supposedly justified the assassination of Egypt's President Sadat. It also explains the hostility of al Qaeda and other radical Islamists to the royal family of Saudi Arabia, which in their view rules ruthlessly and corruptly, and which for a time even allowed American bases and troops on the sacred soil of Islam. Before Iraq was invaded by the United States and its allies in 2003, moreover, radical Islamists were at odds with Saddam Hussein, who paid only lip service to Islam while ruling a secular state that allowed a measure of religious toleration, sexual equality, the selling of alcohol, and other abominations.

In short, radical Islamicism lives and flourishes in a world filled with real or imagined threats, of conspiracies and cabals, against Islam and its faithful adherents. It is a response to a real or perceived crisis—the crisis brought about by the clash of West and (Middle) East, of secular modernity and religious tradition. Radical Islam is at war not only with the West but also with would-be modernizers and reformers within Islam itself.[13] Radical Islam is thus a *reactionary* ideology, inasmuch as it represents a reaction against the threats posed by the pressures of modernization and secularization.

Radical Islamicism and the Democratic Ideal

There is nothing in mainstream Islam that precludes the establishment of democracy, and some things seem to point in the direction of democracy. Islamic teaching suggests, for example, that "consultation" (*shura*) be practised between rulers and ruled. What form (democratic or otherwise) such consultation might take is not specified, however, which leaves open the concept to radically different interpretations. Radical Islamicism tends to be suspicious of if not hostile to democracy, and certainly to *liberal* democracy, in which different factions, parties, and interest groups vie for political power with little apparent concern for some shared or greater good. Moreoover, liberal democracy is avowedly secular inasmuch as it draws a sharp distinction between religion and politics, viewing the former as a purely private or personal matter that has no place in the public or political arena. Liberal democracy, in Radical Islamicism's view, does not exist for the purpose of making its citizens better or more moral people.[14] Liberal democracy also places a premium on individual rights at the expense of individual and collective duties. Not least, these rights are to be enjoyed by everyone—believers and atheists, women and men, Muslims and Jews and infidels. All this is anathema to radical Islamists.[15]

---

[13]Michaelle Browers and Charles Kurzman, eds., *An Islamic Reformation?* (Lanham, MD: Lexington Books, 2004).

[14]Whether this is an accurate characterization of liberal democracy is doubtful. No less a liberal than John Stuart Mill proclaimed in his *Considerations on Representative Government* that "the most important point of excellence which any form of government can possess is *to promote the virtue and intelligence of the people themselves*" (Mill, *Utilitarianism, Liberty, and Representative Government* [cited above, n. 5] 259, emphasis added). As we point out in Chapter 4, the question of whether liberal-democratic governments should or should not try to make their citizens better or more virtuous people is now the subject of a vigorous debate among liberal theorists.

[15]For a helpful discussion of Islamic liberalism, see Michaelle Browers, "Modern Islamic Political Thought," in *Handbook of Political Theory,* ed. Gerald Gaus and Chandran Kukathas (London: Sage Publications, 2004), esp. pp. 373–377.

What might an Islamic state look like? Would (or could) it be democratic? Views differ. Sayyid Qutb saw democracy as a Western invention to be viewed with suspicion if not outright hostility. After all, democracy rests on the sovereignty of the people and not (necessarily) on the sovereignty of God. Otherwise Qutb had very little to say about democracy or any other form of government.[16] By contrast, Iran's Ayatollah Khomeni (1900?–1989) had quite a lot to say about the structure of an Islamic state, and today we find at least some features of a *radical* Islamic state in the "Islamic Republic" of Iran.[17] Iran has a parliament whose members are elected, but the only candidates eligible to run for public office are those who have been screened and approved by the Islamic council of religious elders, or *mullahs*. The *mullahs* also have the power to veto any law passed by the parliament. There is virtually no freedom of the press, and journalists and writers who criticize the government are jailed. There is little or no academic freedom, and students and professors who speak their minds are punished harshly. In reality, the Republic of Iran is neither a republic nor a democracy but something approaching a theocracy.

Following in the footsteps of prominent Muslim scholars and theologians such as Abu Zayd (1943–), some feminist scholars are challenging interpretations of the Qur'an that relegate women to second-class status. Applying critical and historical methods of investigation and interpretation, Amina Wadud, Asma Barlas, Kecia Ali, and others are challenging Islamist readings of the Qur'an and the fairly widespread and longstanding male monopoly on interpreting it. They argue that one must separate the patriarchal context in which the Qur'an was written (or, as devout Muslims believe, received) and the universalist and egalitarian principles implicit in the text and in the teachings of the Prophet. All human beings are made in Allah's image, and He loves them all equally, men and women alike. Allah commands humans to respect and love each other without regard to race, to differences of wealth, social status, or gender. To discriminate against women, to make them into servants and second-class citizens, is contrary to the spirit and the principles of Islam. Such a feminist rereading of the Qur'an has not found favour among traditionalist scholars and has encountered strident resistance and threats of death against women who dare to defy the supposed supremacy of men. To be sure, traditional attitudes about women's proper place in life—attitudes that would keep them out of politics—are not confined to Muslim-majority societies. Those attitudes are especially strong in those societies, however, and they are taken most seriously by radical Islamists. If a society that denies political rights to women can no longer be called a democracy, then radical Islamicism cannot be considered a democratic ideology. Indeed, a radical Islamist state would almost certainly deny the vote to women and would probably restrict the political powers and civil rights of men as well. If the examples of Iran and the even more repressive rule of the Taliban in Afghanistan are accurate guides, in sum, it seems safe to say that radical Islamicism is, together with fascism, one of those rare ideologies that reject the democratic ideal.

Some critics believe that hostility to democracy is not the only feature that radical Islamicism and fascism have in common. Former President George W. Bush and some neoconservatives have even gone so far as to describe radical Islamicism as "Islamofascism"

---

[16]Euben, *Enemy in the Mirror* 77–78.

[17]See *Islam and Revolution: Writings and Declarations of Imam Khomeini,* trans. Hamid Algar (Berkeley, CA: Mizan P, 1981). Excerpts from this book are included in *Ideals and Ideologies,* ed. Ball and Dagger, selection 66.

or "Islamic fascism." However, this description has more rhetorical value—"fascism" is, after all, a word with negative connotations—than intellectual merit. Radical Islamicism is an ideology rooted in religion, not nationalism or devotion to the state. That is, radical Islamicism is a transnational movement that neither recognizes nor respects national boundaries, while fascism is nationalist and state-centred, emphasizing the unity and integrity of the nation-state (as in Italy under Mussolini or Spain under Franco). Radical Islamists look forward to the establishment of a transnational Caliphate or international Muslim community—the umma—that encompasses all predominantly Muslim nations in the Near and Middle East and in parts of Asia (most notably Indonesia). The fact that Muslims are people of many different nationalities and ethnic groups is of no real concern to them, as it certainly would be to fascists. Moreover, fascism is a form of state-worship that Muslims, both moderate and radical, find idolatrous, abhorrent, and blasphemous. No radical Islamist could agree with Mussolini, for example, when he declared, "for the fascist, everything is in the State, and nothing human or spiritual exists, much less has value, outside the State." Nor can a radical Islamist happily follow the fascist tendency to glorify one supposedly all-wise, all-powerful leader who must be obeyed without doubt or question. On the contrary, Muslims of every stripe believe that no human should command such blind and unquestioning loyalty; only Allah deserves that. For all of these reasons, it is a mistake to brand radical Islamicism as a kind of fascism.

In 2011, the so-called "Arab Spring" suggested to some the possible development of western liberal democracy in North Africa and the Middle East. Arab Spring began in Tunisia in December 2010 with the death of an antigovernment protester. The protests quickly spread to other states in the Middle East, including Egypt, Saudi Arabia, Libya, Syria, Yemen, Bahrain, and Jordan, and in some led to the overthrow of the old dictatorial powers, but there was no uniformity across the region. In Syria, President Bashar al-Assad launched a bloody crackdown on demonstrations that was so severe that the Arab League suspended Syria's membership, a UN report condemned Syria's human rights violations, and the United States imposed economic sanctions. In Libya a rebellion against Muammar Gaddafi, who had ruled that country since 1969, was assisted by a coalition of NATO and non-NATO countries that enforced a no-fly zone over Libya and provided covert military assistance. After nine months of heavy fighting, the rebels killed Gaddafi and proclaimed a provisional government.

Egypt was an especially interesting case. Eighteen days of conflict between demonstrators and the police led to the resignation of Egypt's president, Hosni Mubarak, who was put on trial. Subsequent elections resulted in the dominance of Islamist rather than Western-style secularist parties. The Muslim Brotherhood's Freedom and Justice Party, no longer the radical force it once was but still Islamist in nature, won 46 percent of the seats. Its main rival, Nour (the "Party of Light") won 21 percent of the seats. Nour is a faction of the Salafist movement; Salafists believe in a violent, political *jihad*. Although the party's economic platform is liberal, it promised if elected to strive for social justice and to be guided by *Shari'a* law in its actions. This outcome is consistent with a poll conducted in 2010 by Pew Research Center for the People and the Press, an American organization. It found that Egyptians favoured traditional Islamic values. For example, over half wanted men and women to be separated at work. This is consistent with the view that the underlying social attitudes in many Islamic countries do not favour the development of liberal-style democracies.

For Further Reading

Benjamin, Daniel, and Steven Simon. *The Age of Sacred Terror*. New York: Random House, 2002.

Beverley, James. *Peace, Order, and Extremism: A Canadian Perspective on Moderate and Militant Islam*. Toronto: John Wiley & Sons, 2010.

Davidson, Lawrence. *Islamic Fundamentalism*. Westport, CT: Greenwood P, 1998.

Esposito, John L. *Islam: The Straight Path*. Oxford: Oxford UP, 2010.

———, ed. *Political Islam: Revolution, Radicalism, or Reform?* Boulder, CO: Lynne Rienner, 1997.

Euben, Roxanne L. *Enemy in the Mirror: Islamic Fundamentalism and the Limits of Modern Rationalism*. Princeton, NJ: Princeton UP, 1999.

Gray, John. *Al Qaeda and What It Means to Be Modern*. London: Faber, 2003.

Khan, Sheema. *Of Hockey and Hijab: Reflections of a Canadian Muslim Woman*. Tsar Publications, 2009.

Ismail, Salwa. "Islamic Political Thought," in *The Cambridge History of Twentieth-Century Political Thought*, ed. Terence Ball and Richard Bellamy. Cambridge: Cambridge UP, 2003.

Lewis, Bernard. *What Went Wrong? Western Impact and Middle Eastern Response*. Oxford: Oxford UP, 2002.

Mawsilili, Ahmad. *Radical Islamic Fundamentalism*. Beirut: American U of Beirut, 1992.

———, ed. *Islamic Fundamentalism: Myths and Realities*. Reading, UK: Ithaca P, 1998.

Sivan, Emmanuel. *Radical Islam: Medieval Theology and Modern Politics*, 2d ed. New Haven, CT: Yale UP, 1990.

Useful Websites and Social Media

www.csis.org U.S. Center for Strategic and International Studies

www.fas.org Federation of American Scientists

www.crisisgroup.org International Crisis Group

www.meforum.org Middle East Forum

pewglobal.org/reports/display.php?ReportID= 253 Pew Global Attitudes Project

www.canadianislamiccongress.com The Canadian Islamic Congress

www.aljazeera.com al Jazeera

www.macnet.ca Muslim Association of Canada

Twitter:

@AJEnglish al Jazeera English

From the Ball and Dagger Reader *Ideals and Ideologies*, US Eighth Edition

Part Ten: Radical Islamicism

Discussion Questions

1. Why is there so much hostility in Western countries to Muslim women who wear the *niqab,* the cloth that covers most of the face? Do you see it as a sign of the oppression of women or the expression of religious freedom?

2. Will militant Islam pose a serious threat to Canada in the foreseeable future?

3. Is Western-style democracy possible in Muslim countries?

4. Are the Muslim Brotherhood or other Islamist groups representative of Islam?

MySearchLab   MySearchLab with eText offers you access to an online interactive version of the text, additional quizzes and assessment, extensive help with your writing and research projects, and provides round-the-clock access to credible and reliable source material. Go to **www.mysearchlab.com** to access these resources.

CHAPTER 14

Postscript: The Future of Ideology

In no society is it possible for many men to live outside the dominant assumptions of their world for very long.

George Grant, *Lament for a Nation*

LEARNING OBJECTIVES

After completing this chapter you should be able to

1. Discuss the differences between the two surviving forms of the democratic ideal in contemporary society.

2. Compare four arguments about why we will not see the end of ideologies or ideological conflicts.

Ideology became an important factor in politics during the French Revolution. From that point on, politics was no longer a matter reserved exclusively for the aristocracy, the educated middle class, and intellectuals. The masses became involved, and their leaders needed to explain political issues to them and persuade them that one course of action was better than another.

By the late nineteenth century, in Canada and the United Kingdom, voters' choice of ideology was simple—Liberal or Conservative. Americans had a similarly simple choice between Republican and Democrat. Other ideologies later challenged the dominance of liberalism and conservatism. Many socialists—including Karl Marx—were active in Europe. Bomb-throwing anarchists and peace-loving anarchists were also operating, as were the various nationalists, elitists, and racial theorists who were sowing the seeds of fascism and Nazism. Anyone seeking an alternative to liberalism and conservatism did not have far to look.

Even within the ranks of liberals and conservatives, moreover, there was disagreement. This was especially true of the liberals, who argued among themselves almost as much as they quarrelled with their ideological rivals. Liberals were divided into the groups we have calledwelfare liberals and neoclassical liberals. Both groups agreed on the value of individual liberty, but they disagreed strenuously on whether a strong government was needed to promote liberty—as T. H. Green and the welfare liberals maintained—or, conversely, whether the only safe government was a weak government—as Herbert Spencer and the neoclassical liberals insisted.

Over the course of the twentieth century many of these ideologies were tested in practice, with varying results. The brutality of the totalitarian Nazi and fascist regimes proved so hideous that only a tiny handful of racist- and nationalist-oriented adherents want to restore them. Communism had greater staying power, and it formed the government in the Soviet Union for over seventy years. Eventually, the combination of a totalitarian political system and a severely inefficient, centrally planned economy discredited communism, and it quickly fell out of favour, except in a few rogue states such as Cuba and North Korea.

During the 1980s, it looked as if British Prime Minister Margaret Thatcher's and U.S. President Ronald Reagan's conservatism had discredited democratic socialism and welfare liberalism both intellectually and in practice. Neither democratic socialism nor welfare liberalism had been able to respond to the economic crises of the 1970s, and they both seemed intellectually bereft after dominating the policy agenda for the previous half century. In Canada, Prime Minister Brian Mulroney was confidently restructuring the economy with the North American Free Trade Agreement (NAFTA) and the Goods and Services Tax (GST), and all the Liberal Party and the New Democrat Party (NDP) could do was complain that these actions would hurt existing social programs.[1]

However, by the 1990s, the pendulum swung in a decidedly welfare-liberal direction. Democrat Bill Clinton became U.S. president, New Labour's Tony Blair was in power in the UK based on his party's Third Way, and Liberal Jean Chrétien was elected prime minister based on his party's Red Book (which promised, though did not deliver, significant social change).

Then, a decade later, Republican George W. Bush became U.S. president. He called himself a "compassionate conservative." Stephen Harper became leader of the Conservative Party in Canada in 2003, and he promised tax cuts, a balanced budget, decentralized government, more spending on the military, and closer ties with the United States as part of his party's platform.

Over the years, almost all ideologies have shifted in content. That is why we have taken a historical approach to understanding ideologies in this book. Ideologies are dynamic; they do not stand still but change and respond to changing circumstances. Trying to define a particular ideology is thus a little like trying to hit a moving target. But if we look back in history to see how a particular ideology emerged as a political force and how it has responded to changing circumstances and new ideological challenges, we are at least able to use our grasp of what *has happened* to understand what *is happening* now. The past is usually the best guide to the present. Furthermore, it is only in this way that we can hope to understand what is likely to happen to ideologies in the future. With that in mind, our purpose in this final chapter is to take stock of the state of ideologies today and to try to foresee their future, at least in dim outline.

THE FUTURE OF THE DEMOCRATIC IDEAL

What is the future of democracy? Early in the twenty-first century, two things seem clear. The first is that democracy—or at least lip service to the democratic ideal—is more popular than ever. Except for some critics—neo-Nazis, some conservatives, and some socialists—hardly anyone these days flatly rejects democracy. Indeed, the ideal of democracy is inspiring challenges to established leaders and regimes around the world. Many who helped to dismantle the Marxist-Leninist state in Eastern Europe and the Soviet Union, for instance, acted in the name of democracy, as have those who have rebelled against right-wing governments in Latin America.

---

[1]Among these people were J. S. Woodsworth and Tommy Douglas. For an excellent account of the religious and moral dimensions of Woodsworth's life, see Kenneth Mcnaught, *A Prophet in Politics* (Toronto: U of Toronto P, 1960), and George Mills, *Fool for Christ: The Political Thought of J. S. Woodsworth* (Toronto: U of Toronto P, 1991). For a broader account of the role of religious inspiration in political struggles, see Michael Walzer, *Exodus and Revolution* (New York: Basic, 1985).

The second thing that seems clear about the future of democracy is that it has no place for one of the three versions of the democratic ideal dominant in this past century. This version, people's democracy, has fallen victim to the general demise of Marxism-Leninism. As we saw in Chapter 2, a people's democracy is supposed to consist of rule by the communist party in the interests of the people. In this way, the party could both speak for the people and use its powers to defeat their counter-revolutionary enemies. As long as the party itself was a democratic institution, with room for debate and disagreement among the friends of the people, the country would be a people's democracy even though no other party was allowed to compete for power. It became increasingly obvious that the party was *not* a democratic institution, however, but a rigid bureaucratic apparatus in which party members clung to power and privilege, exploiting rather than liberating the people. George Orwell developed this theme in the form of a fable, *Animal Farm*, in 1945.[2] Yugoslav Marxist Milovan Djilas also made this argument in the early 1950s in his book *The New Class*—and was promptly thrown in prison.[3] The student radicals of the 1960s New Left in the United States and Europe advanced a similar argument. Indirectly, so too did Alexander Dubcek, the communist leader of Czechoslovakia who took steps to loosen the party's control over his country in 1968—only to be removed from office when the Soviet Union sent tanks and troops into Czechoslovakia to put an end to the reforms of the Prague Spring.

The situation began to change in the 1980s, first with the emergence of the Solidarity trade union in Poland—a noncommunist trade union in a country where the Communist Party controlled all unions. Then came Mikhail Gorbachev and **perestroika** in the Soviet Union itself. Gorbachev's restructuring of the Soviet Union amounted to an admission that Marxism-Leninism had failed to achieve its promises economically or politically. Some dissidents inside the party dared to say that the people's democracy was no democracy at all. Once it became clear that Gorbachev would not use the military might of the Soviet Union to intervene in Eastern Europe, various opposition elements began to make claims upon the state. Communist dominance in Eastern Europe was never homogeneous. Each country had its national characteristics. The transition in Poland and Czechoslovakia enjoyed the greatest popular support. The most dramatic event of 1989 was the literal dismantling of the Berlin Wall, long a symbol of oppressive communist rule. In the same year, the People's Republic of Hungary dropped "People's" from its name. Hard-line Communist Party leaders in the Soviet Union tried to reverse the direction of change when they attempted to seize power in August 1991, but the popular reaction, led by Boris Yeltsin, defeated their *putsch* and spelled the end of the Soviet Union, which itself unravelled into a collection of independent states.

During the same period, in the People's Republic of China, communism appeared less like an ideological movement and more like severe authoritarian rule. There, in the country Mao Zedong once called a "people's democratic dictatorship," student protesters who occupied Tiananmen Square in the spring of 1989 called upon Communist Party leaders to relinquish some of their power so that China could become a democracy. What they wanted was not people's democracy but something resembling liberal democracy. The party responded by sending troops, which opened fire on the demonstrators. In this massacre, hundreds, perhaps thousands, died in a single night. Other demonstrators were

---

[2]George Orwell, *Animal Farm* (New York: Harcourt, 1945).
[3]Milovan Djilas, *The New Class: An Analysis of the Communist System* (New York: Praeger, 1957).

arrested and imprisoned and some were executed. Party leaders condemned the protestors' plea for democracy as an attempt at "bourgeois liberalization" and reaffirmed their commitment to people's democracy.[4] To observers throughout the world, the events of Tiananmen Square confirm the view that people's democracy is not democracy at all but a front behind which an entrenched elite protects its power and privilege. In both China and Russia, it has become clear that the regimes have become simply authoritarian and have provided little justification for staying in power other than that the economy is generally prosperous and that they command the loyalty of the police and armed forces.

Thus, the democratic ideal survives in just two principal forms—liberal democracy and social democracy. There is some chance that these two views will converge, since both are committed to freedom of speech, competition for political office, and other civil and political rights. There are also signs that some socialists are adopting some aspects of a capitalist, market-oriented economy. But the differences between the two forms are still quite significant. Those who favour liberal democracy continue to stress the importance of privacy, including private property, so that individuals may be free to choose how to live. In contrast, the proponents of social democracy continue to stress the necessity of equality, claiming that people will not be able to rule themselves unless they have an equal voice in the decisions that affect their lives. And the people will not have an equal voice as long as some have far more wealth and property—and therefore more power—than others. In the near future, the primary ideological contest will probably continue to pit liberalism and conservatism against each other, and both against socialism, with all proclaiming their devotion to democracy. Almost all socialists have now abandoned Marxism. It is possible that more welfare liberals will renew the alliance they have historically held in Canada with the social democrats in the NDP. For their part, neoclassical liberals and conservatives may conclude that they should make a common cause against those who favour an active government and a more egalitarian society, and favour the Conservative Party. The first group would then speak for social democracy, the second for liberal democracy.

But what of the politics of identity and the Greens, who will almost certainly play a part in the politics of the near future? The main question is whether liberalism or socialism or perhaps conservatism will manage to absorb them, or whether these new ideologies will develop sufficient strength and scope to challenge the older, mainstream ideologies. The politics of identity, for instance, shares a sense of frustration with liberalism and socialism, but it also owes much of its desire for respect to these two ideologies. If either liberalism or socialism can give women, LGBTQs, Aboriginal peoples, and blacks or other racial minorities reason to believe that they will receive the recognition and respect they deserve, then their concerns are likely to assimilate with those of other Canadians. Members of Canada's Aboriginal peoples are those most likely to continue to assert a separate identity, and they will probably continue to follow an independent course as challengers to liberalism, socialism, and conservatism, all of which they see as forces of assimilation. But if the aforementioned realignment takes place, it is probable that the politics of identity would become part of the social democratic alliance of welfare liberals and socialists. Conservatives who favour traditional forms of society and individualists who prefer an individualistic, competitive society would then form the opposition, perhaps in the name of liberal democracy. Or perhaps we shall simply see ideologies splinter into many small

---

[4]See "Tiananmen Square," *BBC News Online*, Nov. 22, 2004.

fragments, with no ideology popular enough to overwhelm the others. There are a great many possibilities, and the political world is always capable of surprising us. The dismantling of the Berlin Wall, the collapse of the Soviet Union, and the demise of apartheid in South Africa are all dramatic examples of events that almost no one predicted. Political predictions are always precarious. Why have some analysts confidently predicted that ideology itself will soon end?

THE END OF IDEOLOGY?

At the end of the twentieth century, amid talk about the end of communism, some commentators predicted the end of ideology itself. With the downfall of communism, they declared, not only were the great ideological conflicts of the twentieth century coming to an end, but also all significant ideological conflict would evaporate into a widespread consensus on the desirability of liberal democracy. From this time forward, virtually everyone would agree on the general forms and purposes of political life; the only disagreements would be over how best to achieve the goals—especially the goal of individual liberty, including the liberty to own property—that nearly everyone accepted. Since this would leave ideology with no useful function to perform, it would simply disappear.

This outcome is unlikely. We believe there are four reasons that ideologies cannot and will not end. The first is that the "end of ideology" argument has appeared—and failed—before. In the late 1950s and early 1960s, other scholars predicted that a growing consensus on the desirable ends of politics was leading to the end of ideology, at least in the West. As Daniel Bell put it in 1960,

> Few serious minds believe any longer that one can set down "blueprints" and through "social engineering" bring about a new utopia of social harmony. At the same time, the older "counter-beliefs" have lost their intellectual force as well. Few "classic" liberals insist that the State should play no role in the economy, and few serious conservatives, at least in England and on the Continent, believe that the Welfare State is "the road to serfdom." In the Western world, therefore, there is today a rough consensus among intellectuals on political issues: the acceptance of a Welfare State; the desirability of decentralized power; a system of mixed economy and of political pluralism. In that sense, too, the ideological age has ended.[5]

This "consensus," however, was either short-lived or remarkably superficial. The turmoil of the 1960s—and with it the emergence of various liberation movements—suggested that the end of ideology was nowhere in sight. Moreover, rather than continue the welfare state, conservative governments in the 1980s and 1990s tried to replace it with a regime of lower taxes and streamlined government that they thought would make citizens simultaneously freer and more prosperous. It is possible that the earlier prediction was premature and that now the end of ideology has truly come.[6] But the fact that the prediction failed before suggests to us that it is likely to fail again.

A second reason to question the prediction is that enough differences remain, even after the demise of Marxism-Leninism, to keep ideological conflict alive for quite some time. Socialism, as we suggested in Chapters 7 and 8, has presented a serious alternative

---

[5]Daniel Bell, *The End of Ideology: On the Exhaustion of Political Ideas in the Fifties*, rev. ed. (New York: Collier Books, 1961) 397.
[6]Bell defends his end-of-ideology thesis in "The End of Ideology Revisited (Parts I and II)," *Government and Opposition* 23 (Spring/Summer, 1988): 131–150, 321–328.

to liberalism and conservatism since the late nineteenth century. Enough differences remain between socialists, liberals, and conservatives to fuel many an ideological dispute. In addition to disputes *between* ideologies, there will continue to be differences *within* ideologies. The split between welfare and neoclassical liberals, for one, seems deep enough to prevent the emergence of any widespread consensus on the forms and scope of government activity. And a great many unresolved issues and tensions continue to press for resolution. What should be the role of religion in public life? Is nationalism something to be encouraged or discouraged? What about the status of people such as blacks, LGBTQs, women, the poor, and Aboriginal peoples, who have been pushed to the margins of society, prevented from grasping the power they need to liberate themselves and thus to define and celebrate their respective identities? And, as animal rights advocates remind us, what of creatures who cannot speak for themselves? Do they have rights—or at least legitimate interests—that require our protection? These are among the many questions that must be answered before anything like an ideological consensus can be reached. Yet such questions are more likely to provoke conflict than agreement. The ideological diversity of Canada is readily apparent in its registered political parties. The 2010 Canadian federal election saw Quebec nationalists, democratic socialists, welfare and classical liberals, neoconservatives, Red Tories, and Greens vie for seats in Parliament, with fringe parties representing the Christian Right, populism, and libertarianism. There also is an animal rights party, a First Nations party, a party dedicated to the legalization of marijuana, and the Pirate party, which aims to reform the copyright and patent system.

A third reason to question the prediction is that what Bell and others have forecast is not the *end* of ideology but the *triumph* of one particular ideology—liberalism. In 1965 George Grant published *Lament for a Nation*. He argued that Canada's creators had attempted an impossible task: the creation of a conservative alternative to the United States. The United States, he suggested, was the spearhead of technological modernity, a nation that made the conquest of nature central to its existence. Because it had no recorded history before the age of progress (the eighteenth century), it had no tradition to restrain it. The technological modernity that defined the United States was universal and homogeneous. It was also dynamic, driving rapidly beyond the borders of all nations as capitalism later did in the nineteenth century. This force, he believed, was irresistible. It would destroy all uniqueness and particularity, not because it wanted to, but because its very nature was to homogenize everything that stood before it. Canada's fate was to exist beside the dynamo, and therefore Canada was destined to be the first country to be swallowed up. "Fate leads the willing, and drives the unwilling," Grant wrote.[7] It may very well be the case that Canada will disappear as the world progresses toward a universal and homogeneous state. Whether the achievement of such a state—where there are no classes and no nations, and therefore no wars or conflicts—was good or bad was a matter for debate, according to Grant. Therefore, the question of the goodness or badness of the disappearance of Canada was also a matter of debate.[8]

After the collapse of the Soviet Union, Francis Fukuyama, an American social critic, pursued Grant's argument some thirty years later. As Grant had foreseen, liberalism in

---

[7]George Grant, *Lament for a Nation* (Toronto: McClelland, 1965) 86.
[8]Grant 96.

the form of technological modernity was now the dominant ideology.[9] For Fukuyama, liberalism represented the highest achievement possible for human beings. Human beings were not just free, but also conscious of themselves as free. They were free politically and economically and now, as Grant had foreseen, they dominated human and nonhuman nature alike. If freedom is a central fact of human beings, then human beings had become absolutely free. They had become god-like, since they had the ability to create nature and the ability to create human beings. So there was nothing left for humanity to achieve, philosophically speaking. Of course, there were "backward" corners of the world where some skirmishes remain, but the liberal emphasis on individual liberty, private property, equality of opportunity, and tolerance has been rapidly gaining ascendancy throughout the world. This triumph, Fukuyama says, marked "the end of history" in the sense that the major ideological conflicts of the modern world have brought us to a goal or fulfillment. In the sense of a record of events, history will continue. People will continue to act, argue, quarrel, and reach decisions. Yet nothing fundamental will change or be challenged, since there is no advance beyond absolute freedom.

Even if Fukuyama is right, we would not expect the end of ideological conflict immediately. Hegel, a nineteenth-century German philosopher who first theorized the universal and homogeneous state, saw Napoleon as its instigator of this type of state at the beginning of the nineteenth century. It has taken until the beginning of the twenty-first century for the European Union to encompass most of Europe. Meanwhile, countries like China and Russia have actively sought entry into the WTO with its globalizing trade rules, and for the time being, the United States is the only superpower.

Other social critics, such as Benjamin Barber, an American political theorist, envisage the same Americanization of the world but through different dynamics. In *Jihad vs. McWorld* (1995), Barber analyzes religious and tribal fundamentalism in the context of expanding international consumerist internationalism.[10] He contends that these forces seem opposing, but they are in practice connected, and they both undermine democracy and the nation-state on which they initially depended. At the global level, capitalism dissolves the barriers between nations, transforming what were very diverse populations such as the European Union into a uniform market. At the same time, ethnic, religious, and racial hostilities fragment the political landscape into smaller units. For example, many separatists in Quebec were enthusiastic supporters of the creation of the Canada–U.S. Free Trade Agreement in 1988 because they believed that the more trade Quebec was able to divert to the United States, the less dependent it would be on Canada. Political separation would therefore be less of a traumatic event. Some Scottish nationalists believe that British membership in the European Union combined with a devolved Scottish Parliament will eventually lead to an independent Scotland. But Barber maintains that the power of local religion and local nationalism will ultimately be defeated by McWorld:

> If the choice is ultimately to be (as the French writer Debray has argued) "between the local ayatollah and Coca-cola"—if "the satellite [TV dish] is exactly against the honorable Prophet, exactly against the Koran"—the mullahs will lose, because against satellite television and videocassettes they have no long-term defense. Over the long haul, would you bet on Serbian nationalism or Paramount Pictures? Sheik Omar Abdul Rahman or Shaquille

---

[9]Francis Fukuyama, *The End of History and the Last Man* (New York: Free P, 1992).
[10]Benjamin Barber, *Jihad vs. McWorld* (New York: Times, 1995).

O'Neal? Islam or Disneyland? Can religion as a fundamentalist driving force survive its domestication and commodification and trivialization as something akin to a fun fiction? A consumer fairy tale?[11]

In 1996, Samuel Huntington published a widely discussed alternative to Barber's and especially Fukuyama's argument in *The Clash of Civilizations and the Remaking of World Order*.[12] The idea that there was an end of ideology because liberalism had somehow triumphed with the fall of the Soviet Union was a complete misunderstanding of the dynamics of world history. Ideology may have mattered in the short period of the Cold War, but the great theme of history has been the patterns of cohesion, disintegration, and conflict that he called "the clash of civilizations." In the future, instead of the three power blocs of the Cold War—the United States, the Soviet Union, and China—the dynamic of the world would work itself out among its seven major civilizations and, in the long run, power would shift from Western to non-Western civilizations. Huntington identifies the world's major civilizations as follows: Sinic, Japanese, Hindu, Islamic, Western, Latin American, and (debatably) African. For most of the twentieth century the West was expansionist and dominant; but late in the twentieth century some of the other civilizations, such as the Sinic and the Japanese, discovered that they could completely modernize while retaining significant aspects of their traditional civilizations.

Huntington argues that the West has faced a slow process of decline. Asian economic success strengthened confidence in its cultural values. Islam turned to religion as a way of accepting those aspects of technology it thought desirable, while rejecting others that might undermine the basis of Muslim faith and culture. Global politics was becoming reconfigured along cultural lines, and political boundaries were being redrawn to coincide with cultural, rather than ideological, ones. America as the leader of the West must recognize that it is the leader of one culture among many: "In the merging world of ethnic conflict and civilizational clash, Western belief in the universality of Western culture suffers from three problems: it is false; it is immoral; and it is dangerous."[13] If the West persists in basing its foreign policy on beliefs like those expressed by Fukuyama, Western values are destined to dominate the world, Huntington warns, which "could lead to a major intercivilizational war between core states, and it is dangerous to the West because it could lead to the defeat of the West."[14]

Canadian writer Naomi Klein also believes that the universal and homogeneous state will collapse under its own weight. She focuses on the worldwide reach of branding, or "logos" as she calls them: "Global youth marketing is attempting to engineer a third notion of nationality—not American, not local, but one that would unite the two, through shopping."[15] The current phase of globalization is not being led by homogeneous entities, but by huge corporations such as Walmart, Nike, Starbucks, and McDonald's. As these brands become more invasive and more dominant in their own areas, though, with their advertising and their monopolistic business practices, they breed public resentment.

---

[11]Barber 82.

[12]Samuel Huntington, *The Clash of Civilizations and the Remaking of the World Order* (New York: Simon, 1996).

[13]Huntington 308.

[14]Huntington 311.

[15]Naomi Klein, *No Logo: Taking Aim at Brand Bullies* (Toronto: Vintage, 1999) 120.

Public resentment of the dominance of international brands arises on two fronts. On the one side, workers are paid low wages to produce products in unsafe or insecure working conditions. On the other, consumers themselves increasingly feel exploited rather than benefited by the constant pressure of advertising that reaches even into washrooms. However, new means of communication such as the Internet mean that the two groups can now link and communicate their sense of exploitation with one another and form a plan of resistance. "This logo web has the unprecedented power to connect students who face ad bombardment in their university washrooms with sweatshop workers who make the goods in the ads and frustrated McDonald's workers who sell them."[16]

A broad-based movement opposed to globalization now exists, according to Klein, with connections across national lines: "Ethical shareholders, cultural jammers, street reclaimers, McUnion organizers, human-rights hacktivists, school-logo fighters and Internet corporate watchdogs" are building a global and high-tech movement that is just as capable of coordinated action as the multinational corporations they oppose.[17]

The extended financial crisis that has gripped the Western world since 2008 and by late 2011 threatened the continued existence of the European Monetary Union, if not the European Union itself, has galvanized opposition to globalization. Supporters of the "Occupy" movements that emerged across the English-speaking world in late 2011 (and violent protests in Europe against austerity measures) reflect the new impetus given to those dissident groups. The crisis has even prompted orthodox Marxists to dust off Marx's theory that advanced capitalism would eventually collapse as a result of its internal contradictions.

Finally, a fourth reason to question the prediction of the end of ideology is that ideologies are going to be with us for quite some time because new challenges and difficulties continue to arise. The clearest evidence of this is the environmental crisis (or crises) that we discussed in Chapter 12. Barring some miraculous discoveries—such as a cheap, safe, reliable, and nonpolluting source of energy—this crisis will require a political response. And this response will almost certainly take an ideological form. In other words, any adequate response must fulfill the four functions of an ideology. First, people will seek some *explanation* of the nature of the crisis, along with, second, an *evaluation* of the situation they face. Third, they will also need *orientation*—that is, some sense of where they stand with regard to the crisis. Fourth and finally, they will need a *program* for action telling them what they can, and should, do. And they will need all these things to be set out in fairly simple terms. In short, they will need the guidance of an ideology. If more than one ideology offers this guidance, as seems likely, then ideological conflict will certainly persist.[18]

For these reasons, we do not expect to see the end of ideology. Ideologies are too useful and too important to wither away. People need ideologies to join thought to action, to provide some vision of human possibilities that will move people to act. As long as we live in a complicated and confusing world full of challenges and conflicts, we shall need ideologies to explain why social conditions are as they are, to evaluate those conditions,

---

[16]Klein 357.

[17]Klein 445.

[18]For an early twenty-first century reassessment of the major ideologies, see Michael Freeden, ed., *Reassessing Political Ideologies* (New York and London: Routledge, 2002).

to provide a sense of orientation, and to set out a program of action—an attempt to take the world as it is and to remake it as it should be. We shall also need ideologies to give meaning to the democratic ideal and substance to the concept of freedom. With this work still to be done, it is difficult to see how we could do without them. We must conclude, then, that as long as ideologies have these ends to serve, there will be no end of ideology.

For Further Reading

Aslan, Reza. *Beyond Fundamentalism: Confronting Religious Extremism in the Age of Globalization.* New York: Random House, 2010.

Barber, Benjamin. *Jihad vs. McWorld.* New York: Times Books, 1995.

Baylis, John, Steve Smith, and Patricia Owens, eds. *The Globalization of World Politics: An Introduction to International Relations.* Oxford, OUP, 2011.

Breznitz, Dan and Michael Murphree. *Run of the Red Queen: Government, Innovation, Globalization, and Economic Growth in China.* New Haven, CT: Yale UP, 2011.

Cowen, Tyler. *Creative Destruction: How Globalization Is Changing the World's Cultures.* Princeton, NJ: Princeton UP, 2002.

Fukuyama, Francis. *The End of History and the Last Man.* New York: Free Press, 1992.

McNally, David and Alan Campbell. *Global Slump: The Economics and Politics of Crisis and Resistance.* Fernwood Publishing, 2010.

Micklethwait, John, and Adrian Wooldridge. *A Future Perfect: The Challenge and Hidden Promise of Globalization.* London: Heinemann, 2000.

Rodrick, Dani. *The Globalization Paradox.* New York: Norton, 2011

Steger, Manfred B. *Globalism: Market Ideology Meets Terrorism*, 2d ed. Lanham, MD: Rowman and Littlefield, 2005.

Stiglitz, Joseph. *Globalization and Its Discontents.* New York: Norton, 2002.

From the Ball and Dagger Reader *Ideals and Ideologies,* US Eighth Edition

Part Eleven: Globalization and the Future of Ideology

Useful Websites and Social Media

www.elections.ca/home.aspx Elections Canada

Discussion Questions

1. Why do we keep using the same names, like conservative and liberal, to describe different sets of ideas?
2. Do you think that liberal democracy or social democracy is better?
3. What is the difference between a political party and an ideological movement?
4. Can you think of some ideologies that have arisen recently? Can you imagine circumstances in the near future that will demand ideological solutions?

MySearchLab   MySearchLab with eText offers you access to an online interactive version of the text, additional quizzes and assessment, extensive help with your writing and research projects, and provides round-the-clock access to credible and reliable source material. Go to **www.mysearchlab.com** to access these resources.

Glossary

achieved status The condition of earning one's place in society through effort and ability. Contrast with *ascribed status.*

affirmative action The attempt to promote equality of opportunity by providing assistance to members of groups, such as women and racial minorities, that have been the victims of discrimination.

anarchism A term from the Greek *anarchia,* meaning without a government. Anarchism aims to abolish the state, replacing political relations with cooperative or voluntary social ones.

anarcho-communism The version of anarchism that aspires to a cooperative society in which all property is owned or controlled by the whole community.

anthropocentrism The "human-centred" outlook that Greens say sees the world as something to be exploited for human benefit. See also *biocentrism* and *ecocentrism.*

aristocratic privilege A belief that one class of people is superior to others. Certain rights and opportunities—such as access to governing power—are reserved for the exclusive enjoyment of the nobility.

arrogance of humanism Greens charge that a human-centred (or anthropocentric) outlook ignores or devalues the worth of other species of animals and plants and the environment that sustains them.

Aryan The name given to a group of people from whom all Indo-European languages supposedly derive. Nazis believe that the Germanic peoples are the purest descendants of the Aryan race, a "master race" whose destiny was to conquer and rule—or exterminate—"inferior" races.

ascribed status The condition of being born into a particular social status—such as noble or serf—with little opportunity either to raise or lower social standing. Contrast with *achieved status.* See also *feudalism.*

atomistic view of society The view that society consists of individuals who are inherently unconnected to or independent of one another. Contrast with *organic view of society.*

Baptist-bootlegger alliance An alliance of organizations with seemingly contrary objectives that work together toward opposing goals. Historically, Baptists didn't want alcohol sold on Sundays. Bootleggers backed them in their drive to make Sunday a "dry" day because they knew people would drink anyway, and the only place that they could get the liquor would be from them.

base (also called *material-productive base*) Marx's metaphor for the "social relations" of production that constitute the "real basis" or foundation of material production. For example, the relationship of landowner to farm worker is part of the *base* of an agricultural society. See also *ideological superstructure* and *materialist conception of history.*

biocentrism The "life-centred" perspective embraced by Greens because it is broader and more inclusive than the prevailing human-centred (or anthropocentric) outlook. See also *anthropocentrism* and *ecocentrism.*

biophilia An affinity for life forms other than human beings.

Bolsheviks The faction of the Russian Communist Party, created in 1903, that Lenin led to power in 1917.

bourgeoisie A generally derogatory term that refers to the urban middle class—merchants and professional people—in general. In Marx's terms, the bourgeoisie is the ruling class in capitalist society because it owns and controls the *material forces of production.*

business liberalism The form of liberalism that stresses the importance of individual economic or property rights in contrast to individual human rights, such as the right to education or health care. See also *neoclassical liberalism*.

cap-and-trade An administrative approach to control pollution that legislates caps on pollutants and emissions but permits companies and organizations to purchase rights to exceed those caps from other organizations; sometimes called *emissions trading*.

capitalism An economic system in which the major *material forces of production* are privately owned and operated for the profit of the owners, investors, or senior management.

carbon tax An environmental tax on emissions of carbon dioxide and other greenhouse gases.

categorical imperative Kant's notion that moral rules should be universal laws and that human beings should treat other human beings as ends, not as means.

centralized control Control of all resources and decisions concerning production and distribution of goods concentrated in a central planning authority, often the central government. Contrast with *decentralized control*.

centre The moderate or "middle of the road" position of the political spectrum, in contrast to *left* and *right*.

civic nationalism The belief that the nation is defined not in terms of a particular ethnic, racial, or linguistic identity, but on the basis of loyalty to a particular geographic unit with a common history or common political allegiance. See also *ethnic nationalism*.

class In socialist, and particularly Marxian, analysis, class refers to one's socially determined location in the structure of socio-economic relations. If you are part owner of the *material forces* (or *means*) *of production,* you are a member of the *bourgeoisie* or *capitalist* class; if you are yourself a means of production, then you are a member of the working class, or *proletariat*. There are many other views of the nature of social classes, and even Marxist theory admits that there are more than the basic two.

command economy Favoured by the proponents of *centralized control*, the attempt to plan and direct economic production and distribution instead of relying on market forces.

communism A system whereby the major *material forces of production* are state owned. Originally used to describe any scheme of common or social control of resources, this term is now associated with Marxian socialism. For Marx and the Marxists, the communal ownership and control of the *material forces of production* represents the fulfillment of human history. The culmination of a long-term revolutionary sequence, a mature communist society subscribes to the principle, "From each according to ability, to each according to need."

communitarianism In general terms, a philosophy that advocates the idea of binding people together into a strong, mutually supportive society. The term is now used to describe the approach of those who criticize liberalism for putting too much emphasis on the rights and interests of individuals while ignoring the needs of the community as a whole.

constitutional monarchy The form of government in which the head of state is a monarch (either hereditary or elective), but the head of government is an elected politician. The monarch possesses limited powers to advise the prime minister and to resolve constitutional crises.

corporatism A policy instituted by Benito Mussolini in Italy to harmonize owners, workers, and government to promote economic production and social cooperation. Property was to remain in public hands even as it was put to public use.

Counter-Enlightenment A term referring to a diverse group of thinkers in the early and mid-nineteenth century who rejected some of the leading ideas of the *Enlightenment* philosophers.

critical Western Marxism The position taken by a number of twentieth-century scholars, principally European, who accepted most of Marx's critique of capitalism as a repressive social and economic system, but who rejected Marxism-Leninism and concentrated their efforts on analyzing capitalism as a form of cultural domination that prevents people from being free and creative beings.

cultural conservatism Closely connected to *traditional (or classical) conservatism*, a brand of conservatism critical of commerce, industry, and progress because it degrades the social environment in which human beings live and destroys their cultural links with the past.

cunning of reason Hegel's phrase for the process by which intentional actions produce unintended, but nonetheless "rational," consequences that permit history to unfold.

cyberactivism The use of communication technologies (e-mail, websites, podcasts, etc.) by activists to enable faster communications by citizen movements and deliver a message to a large audience.

decentralized control The dispersion of control of resources and production into the hands of people at the lowest possible level, such as the town or workplace. Contrast with *centralized control*.

deep ecology A biocentric (or life-centred) philosophical, ethical, and political view that places the welfare of human beings on a par with other species and the conditions that nurture and sustain them. Contrast with *social ecology*.

democratic centralism Lenin's attempt to combine democracy with central control of the revolutionary *vanguard party*. The party should encourage debate and discussion within its ranks before decisions are made, Lenin said. Once the leadership reaches a decision, however, debate must stop and all members must follow the orders of the central leadership.

dialectic Generally speaking, the process whereby opposite views or forces come into conflict, which eventually leads to the overcoming or reconciliation of the opposition in a new and presumably higher form. Plato used the term to describe a method of reasoning, while Hegel, Marx, and Engels used it to describe a process of historical change.

dialectical materialism The Soviet Marxist-Leninist view that traces all social, economic, and political phenomena to physical matter and its motions. The phrase, although never used by Marx, became standard during Stalin's era.

ecocentrism An ecosystem-centred orientation favoured by Greens over and against a human-centred (or anthropocentric) outlook. See also *anthropocentrism* and *biocentrism*.

ecofeminism A perspective within Green political thought that combines the principles of feminism with those of environmentalism. Its gender-based approach traces environmental plunder to an androcentric (or male-centred) view that devalues nature ("mother nature") and celebrates its "conquest" by men. Ecofeminists hold that this mindset—and the actions that follow from it—must be challenged if the earth's ecosystems are to be saved and protected for posterity.

ecology The scientific study of the interconnections, interdependencies, and energy flows within and between species and ecosystems. In its more recent political sense, however, *ecology* refers to a perspective that values the protection and preservation of the natural environment.

ecotage Short for *ecological sabotage,* a form of direct action practised by Earth First! and other militant environmentalist groups. Such sabotage, or *monkey wrenching*, ranges from "decommissioning" bulldozers to cutting power lines to "spiking" old-growth trees to save them from loggers.

ecotechnology A belief that technology can resolve the environmental problems that technology created in the first place.

elitism A belief that society will always be governed by a small group.

empire A political union of several states governed by a single sovereign power.

empirical A description or explanation of how things are: for example, "In the last election, 61 percent of eligible Canadian voters cast ballots." Contrast with *normative*.

Enlightenment The influential philosophical movement of the seventeenth and eighteenth centuries, especially in France, that fought to achieve the triumph of reason and science over custom and superstition.

equality of condition The situation in which each person has not only *equality of status*, but has approximately the same wealth and power as every other person.

equality of status The situation in which each person has the same rights, privileges and opportunities, but not necessarily the same wealth or power.

essentially contested concept A concept—such as art, religion, or democracy—that generates controversy because it lacks a complete set of clear standards for determining when something falls under the concept. Indeed, this openness or indeterminacy seems to be the nature or essence of this type of concept.

ethnic cleansing A euphemism for genocide, the systematic murder or removal of members of one nationality or ethnic group by another. For example, this term was used by militant Serbian nationalists in the early 1990s to justify the expulsion and murder of Bosnian Muslims and members of other ethnic groups supposedly standing in the way of a united Serbian nation-state.

ethnic nationalism The belief that the nation is defined by a common race, ethnicity, and language, and that each such nation should be an independent state.

Fabian socialism The British brand of socialism emphasizing the nonrevolutionary, peaceful, piecemeal, and gradual transition from a capitalist to a socialist society.

false consciousness A Marxian phrase referring to the false or distorted beliefs of members of a subordinate class who fail to understand their true position in society. These false beliefs are theorized to work to the advantage of the ruling class because they prevent the subordinate class from seeing the cause of its oppression.

fascism An extreme right-wing, totalitarian, nationalist ideology and system of government, imposed in Italy by Benito Mussolini and in Spain by Francisco Franco.

federalism A system of government in which the powers of government and sovereignty are divided between regional and national governments, each of which is pre-eminent in its own sphere of responsibility.

feudalism Specifically, the social and economic system of medieval Europe that centred on the relationship of the lord, who promised protection and the use of land in exchange for service, and the vassal. By analogy, feudalism refers to any similar agricultural society in which a relatively small number of people control the land while most others work it as tenants or serfs. Often associated with *ascribed status.*

first-wave feminism A period of feminist activity during the nineteenth and early twentieth centuries in the United Kingdom and the United States. Originally it focused on the promotion of equal contract, property, and voting rights for women. However, by the end of the nineteenth century, activism focused primarily on gaining political rights, particularly the vote.

fraternity The French Revolution introduced the idea that human beings shared a common social and emotional bond.

free rider A rational, self-interested person who, in the absence of authority, will seek to enjoy the benefits of a communal project without making a fair contribution. If too many people try to be free riders, the project is prone to collapse.

gay The sexual orientation of someone who favours exclusive sexual relations with persons of the same gender. More common is the phrase "lesbian, gay, bisexual, transgendered, and queer," (LGBTQ) which recognizes the diversity of sexual orientation.

gender A central concept within feminist thought referring to the social construction and meaning of the categories "masculine" and "feminine." That is, what makes something masculine or feminine is largely determined by social attitudes and beliefs.

general will Rousseau's belief that once the divisive characteristics of people are removed, such as class, region, and religion, a fundamental humanity remains that can form the basis of just political decisions.

glasnost The Russian word for "openness"; it was used by Mikhail Gorbachev in the 1980s to signal a policy of greater tolerance and freedom in the former Soviet Union.

Green politics The use of various strategies and tactics to put environmental concerns at or near the top of the political agenda.

greenhouse effect The gradual warming of the earth's atmosphere due to the buildup of carbon dioxide (CO_2) that results from the burning of fossil fuels (oil, gas, coal, and so on) and the destruction of forests.

harm principle The principle, defended by Mill and others, that we should be allowed to do whatever we want unless our actions harm or threaten harm to others.

homophobic Having a fear of people who are gay, lesbian, bisexual, queer, or transgendered and/or their real or imagined influence.

ideological superstructure (also called *superstructure*) Marx's metaphor for the set of beliefs, ideas, and ideals that justifies or legitimizes the social arrangements that constitute the foundation or *base* of society. See also *base* and *materialist conception of history.*

ideologue Someone who is strongly committed to a particular ideology and works to promote its triumph.

immiseration of the proletariat The Marxian prediction that the working class or proletariat would become progressively worse off under capitalism.

imperialism According to Lenin, the policy whereby capitalist countries conquer, colonize, and exploit developing countries. It represents, in Lenin's view, the "highest" and last stage of capitalist domination of the world economy. It is also a central concept of Mao Zedong and other Marxist-Leninists.

individualist conservatism A belief that government should promote individual liberty by protecting against foreign threats, but otherwise leave people alone to do as they see fit. Such a belief may be closer to *neoclassical liberalism, business liberalism,* or *libertarianism* than to other forms of conservatism.

initiative An element of direct democracy that would allow voters to propose legislation that Parliament must consider if a majority of voters approve it. In some American states, citizens can draft laws and constitutional amendments and then vote on them directly.

innovation According to Edmund Burke, a radical change for the sake of change or novelty. The desire to innovate, Burke says, leads people to neglect or reject their time-tested customs. Contrast with *reform.*

instrumental value The value that a thing has to achieve certain independently determined ends.

intrinsic value The value a thing has in itself.

irrationalism The belief, associated with thinkers like Sigmund Freud and Gustave Le Bon, that human beings are moved more by instincts, urges, or subconscious forces than by reason.

Islamicism A politicization of the religion of Islam. It is antagonistic to Western values. A minority of Islamists interpret *jihad* as being an armed struggle to wage a holy war against enemies of Islam, usually perceived to be the West or those in the Islamic world who have been corrupted by Western values.

jihad The literal meaning of this Arabic word is "struggle." In Islamic thought, *jihad* refers to an individual's internal struggle to cleanse his or her soul. A minority of Islamists interpret it to justify an armed struggle to wage a holy war against the West or those in the Islamic world who have been corrupted by Western values.

laissez-faire The doctrine that society operates best with the least intrusive government and the minimum amount of government regulation.

land ethic A phrase coined by ecologist Aldo Leopold to refer to an attitude of reverence and respect for the land and the myriad of life forms it sustains.

left (or left-wing) The left-end position of the political spectrum. People who take this position believe that a significant, perhaps even radical, change in a new direction will lead to great improvement in social and economic arrangements. In general, socialists are situated on the left.

levelling The effort, criticized by many conservatives, to diminish or eliminate the gap between the wealthiest and poorest members of a society. Critics maintain that these efforts promote mediocrity and reduce everyone to the same miserable level.

liberal democracy An emphasis on the importance of individual rights and liberty, including the right to own private property. Contrast with *people's democracy* and *social democracy.*

libertarianism Generally, the desire to expand the realm of individual liberty. Specifically, libertarianism is another name for *neoclassical liberalism*, which proposes that the only legitimate power of government is to protect its citizens and their property. Some libertarian anarchists believe that all governments are illegitimate and immoral.

little platoons Burke's name for those traditional local organizations, such as clubs, churches, and neighbourhood organizations, to which individuals feel a strong attachment compared with abstract concepts such as the nation.

locavore A person who eats locally grown/produced food for environmental reasons.

Malthus's law The assertion that human population tends to grow faster than the resources required to sustain it. Specifically, population grows geometrically and resources grow arithmetically.

market socialism The attempt to combine some features of a free market economy with social ownership and control of resources. For example, the people who work in a factory may jointly own it, but they must compete for profits with other worker-owned factories.

mass society According to some critics, a dangerously unstable society in which the common people—and the politicians and advertisers who appeal to their tastes—bring everything and everyone down to their own level by abolishing traditional social hierarchies and the secondary associations that Burke called "*little platoons.*"

master-slave dialectic A philosophical construct of Hegel's. He portrays the confrontation between an all-powerful master and his presumably powerless slave. The conflict between the two reveals that the master is dependent upon his slave; the slave, by winning his struggle for freedom and recognition, liberates both himself and the master. Marx and later "liberation" ideologists also employ this parable of emancipation.

material forces of production (also called *means of production, forces of production*, or simply *productive forces*) Marx's phrase for the material means or resources that human labour transforms into useful goods or commodities. Examples include trees that are transformed into lumber, ores that are transformed into metal, and the machinery and the human labour necessary to accomplish the transformation.

materialism The philosophical doctrine that all reality—social, political, and intellectual—is ultimately reducible to combinations of physical matter. Different versions can be found in Hobbes, in Engels, and in twentieth-century *dialectical materialism.*

materialist conception (or interpretation) of history The Marxian framework for interpreting or explaining social change. The central idea is that changes in the material-productive *base* bring about changes in the *relations of production* and the *ideological superstructure.*

means of production See *material forces of production.*

mercantilism The economic policy of promoting a country's wealth at the expense of others by establishing monopolies and regulating foreign trade to favour domestic industry.

mixed constitution (or government) The *republican* policy of combining or balancing rule by one, by the few, and by the many in a single government, with the aim of preventing the concentration of power in any single individual or social group.

monkey wrenching A form of direct action practised or advocated by Earth First! and other militant environmentalist groups. Such action ranges from "decommissioning" bulldozers to cutting power lines to "spiking" old-growth trees to save them from loggers. See also *ecotage*.

monopoly Exclusive control of a commodity or market by a single firm.

nanotechnology The attempt to manipulate nature at the extremely small, even atomic level to promote technological change.

nationalism The belief each linguistical and cultural group forms a distinct nation, and that each nation has the right to constitute a separate political unit or *nation-state*. See also *civic nationalism* and *ethnic nationalism*.

nation-state In theory, a self-governing political unit that unites the members of a single nation or people. In practice, most existing nation-states are linguistically and culturally diverse.

natural aristocracy According to Burke, a governing class of landed nobility, trained from childhood for the responsibilities of ruling, but one that did not exclude admission to talented members of lower social classes.

natural right A right that everyone has simply by virtue of being human. Such a right can neither be granted nor taken away by any person or political authority.

negative freedom The absence of political, legal, or economic restraint. You are free, in this view, if no one else is preventing you from doing what you want to do. Contrast with *positive freedom*.

neoclassical liberalism The belief that government is a necessary evil that should do nothing but protect its citizens and their property. See also *libertarianism* and *business liberalism*.

neoconservatism Beginning among disenchanted welfare liberals in the 1960s, a movement advocating less reliance on government, an assertive foreign policy, and an emphasis on the value of work, thrift, family, and self-restraint.

normative A statement or proposition prescribing how things should be or judging what is good or bad: for example, "Voting is a civic duty." Contrast with *empirical*.

omnivore A person who rejects nonorganic food sources for environmental and spiritual reasons.

opium of the masses (also called *opium of the people*) Marx's phrase for religion, which he believed dulled the critical capacity of oppressed people by directing their attention and hopes away from this life to eternal and blissful afterlife.

organic view of society The view that individuals within a society are connected and interdependent, like the parts of the body, and that society itself is more than merely the sum of its parts. Contrast with *atomistic view of society*.

original sin The belief, in Christian theology, that the first sin—Adam and Eve's defiance of God in the Garden of Eden—rendered all humanity imperfect and prone to sin.

pan-Canadian nationalism The variety of nationalism that identifies Canada (rather than Quebec) as the proper object of nationalist allegiance for Canadians.

people's democracy Historically favoured by communist countries, the view that democracy is government in the interests of the common people, or the working class. Contrast with *liberal democracy* and *social democracy*.

perestroika The Russian word for "restructuring," used by Mikhail Gorbachev in the 1980s to refer in particular to the restructuring of the Soviet Union's economy.

petite bourgeoisie In Marxism, people who owned small shops or workshops but did not own substantial capital and employed few workers, if any. They had a different class consciousness from either the *bourgeoisie* or the *proletariat*.

Physiocrats French economic theorists of the eighteenth century who believed that land is the basis of wealth and that unrestricted competition promotes prosperity.

political absolutism Any form of government in which the ruler (or rulers) has nearly complete power, unrestrained by law or other governing bodies.

polity Rule by those who are neither wealthy nor poor, in the interests of the whole community. In Aristotle's view, this is generally the best form of government.

populism The belief that the people, as a whole, possess a political wisdom and virtue greater than that of either any individual or any limited interest group or faction.

positive freedom The belief that freedom is not only the absence of restraint but also the power or ability to act and to develop one's capacities. Contrast with *negative freedom.*

private good A commodity that can be divided, distributed, and used for private benefit. Contrast with *public good.*

Progressives The Canadian agrarian reform movement and political party of the early twentieth century, populist in nature and mildly left-wing in orientation.

proletariat Marx's word for wage-labourers, the industrial working class. The proletariat was originally the lowest class in ancient Rome.

Protestant Reformation The religious movement to reform the Roman Catholic Church that led to the establishment of separate Protestant churches.

public good A commodity that is nonexcludable (you can't stop people from using it) and nonrivalrous (everybody can benefit from it); because of its inherent character, a good that must be shared, such as municipal drinking water. Contrast with *private good.*

racism A dislike of races other than one's own, and a belief that these aversions are politically relevant. The belief that one race is innately superior to other races or ethnic groups. Religious adherents sometimes behave similarly.

rationalism A movement that became prominent in eighteenth-century France that believes that the world and society could be understood and reformed by the agency of reason alone.

reactionary Someone who wants to recreate an earlier form of society or government.

recall An element of direct democracy that allows the constituents of an elected representative to force him or her to face a new election for the position.

red A derogatory term for a member of the Communist Party. The term was a reference to the colour of the flag used by early socialist groups and used in the flag of the USSR.

Red Toryism A term introduced by Canadian political scientist Gad Horowitz in the 1960s to mean a Progressive Conservative who preferred the NDP to the Liberals. It now means a Conservative who favours socially progressive policies.

referendum An element of direct democracy that allows major public issues to be decided not by elected representatives but by popular vote.

reform A gradual and cautious change that corrects or repairs defects in society or government and, according to Burke, is safer and wiser than *innovation.*

relations of production (also called *social relations of production*) Marx's phrase describing the social division of labour (for example, managers, supervisors, labourers) required to transform the *material forces of production* into useful goods.

religious conformity The policy of requiring everyone in a society to follow or acknowledge the same religious beliefs publicly.

Religious Right The movement of evangelical fundamentalists, such as the Christian Heritage Party, who seek to restore "traditional family values."

Renaissance The period of the "rebirth" (re-naissance) of classical learning in fourteenth- and fifteenth-century Europe.

representative government A form of government in which power rests with elected representatives of the people, not the populace acting directly to make decisions.

republic A form of government by the people that includes the rule of law, a *mixed constitution (or government)*, and the cultivation of an active and public-spirited citizenry. Sometimes it is used to describe any state that does not have a monarch.

revisionists The name given to later Marxists who attempted to amend or revise Marxian theory in light of developments after Marx's death.

revolution A sweeping or fundamental transformation of a society. Originally used to describe an attempt to restore or revolve back to a previous condition, the word acquired its present meaning from the French Revolution.

revolutionary dictatorship of the proletariat (also called *dictatorship of the proletariat*) The form of government that Marx expected to provide the transition from the revolutionary overthrow of the *bourgeoisie* to the eventual coming of communist society. This interim or transitional state will presumably lead to a *withering away of the state*.

right (or right-wing) The right-end position of the political spectrum. People who take this position are often opposed to change and prefer an established social order with firmly rooted authority. Both conservatives and fascists are usually considered right-wing, though fascist ideology is in fact revolutionary.

scientific socialism Marx's term to distinguish his superior brand of socialism from the utopian socialism of his predecessor. He meant that he could explain how the revolution would necessarily take place.

second-wave feminism A period of feminist activity from the early 1960s to the late 1980s, which linked women's cultural and political inequalities and encouraged women to understand that aspects of their personal lives were deeply politicized and reflected sexist power structures.

secularism The tendency to turn away from religious considerations and to emphasize the value of earthly life as the sole good.

sexism The belief that men are innately superior to women.

social contract An agreement to form political societies and establish governments, thus creating political authority. How do some people acquire authority over others? Some theorists, such as Hobbes and Locke, have answered that individuals in a *state of nature* have in some way entered into a social contract.

Social Credit movement A political movement that holds that most problems in society derive from control of the money supply and monetary policy by the banking industry and the consequent restriction of liquidity in the monetary system.

Social Darwinists A group of neoclassical liberals of the late nineteenth and early twentieth centuries who adapted Darwin's theory of evolution to social and political life, concluding that the struggle for survival between individuals is a natural feature of human life, and government should not intervene.

social democracy A view that democracy requires equality of power or influence for every citizen. This process may require the redistribution of wealth and/or the control of resources and property by the community. Contrast with *liberal democracy* and *people's democracy*.

social ecology A view that attaches special importance to human life, but also holds that humanity is dependent upon—and responsible for—the environment that sustains it and other species. Contrast with *deep ecology*.

socialism A broad set of economic theories of social organization advocating some degree of state or collective ownership and administration of the means of production and distribution of goods, and aiming at the creation of greater economic and social equality.

speciesism The belief that one species (human beings) has different and greater rights than other species.

Stalinism Stalin's main contribution to communist theory was to insist that the revolution should establish itself firmly in the Soviet Union before it sought to expand abroad.

state of nature In the theories of Hobbes and Locke, among others, the hypothetical condition in which people live before they create society and government. Everyone is free and equal in this state, and no one has authority over anyone else.

stewardship An orientation emphasizing human beings' responsibility for protecting, preserving, and sustaining the natural and social environment for the sake of future generations.

syndicalism The belief that direct actions, such as a general strike, will provoke a revolution.

theocracy A form of government in which religious leaders, who see themselves as agents of God (or the gods), try to enforce divine commands by making them the law of the land.

third-wave feminism A branch of feminism beginning in the early 1990s as a response to perceived failures of the second wave of feminism. It attempts to forge alliances between women and other socially oppressed groups, and stresses that gender and sexuality are merely social constructs.

time horizon How far ahead people think when they are deciding what to do.

Tory (party) The conservative political party in Great Britain during the eighteenth and early nineteenth centuries; succeeded by the Conservative Party. Also used to describe the Conservative Party in Canada under its different names.

tory democracy A policy, initiated by British Conservative leader Disraeli, supporting voting rights and other benefits for the working class in order to forge an electoral alliance between the upper and the working class against the predominantly middle-class Liberal Party.

totalitarianism The attempt to control every aspect of a country's life—military, press, schools, religion, economy, and so on—by a single, all-powerful party that systematically smothers all opposition.

traditional conservatism A belief that the first aim of political action must be to preserve the social fabric by pursuing *reform* cautiously, when it is necessary. Burke was a traditional conservative.

tyranny of the majority De Tocqueville and Mill both feared that mass democracy would stifle the small handful of creative individuals who provided the spark that led society to continue to progress.

Ultramontanism A conservative movement in the Roman Catholic Church, which became politically important in Quebec in the nineteenth century, that deferred to the leadership of the pope in matters of politics and morality.

Utilitarianism The view that individuals and governments should always act to promote *utility* or, according to Bentham, the greatest happiness of the greatest number.

utility Anything that has value, or usefulness, for anyone. As used by Bentham and the *Utilitarians,* utility refers to our tendency to pursue pleasure and avoid pain.

utopia A term coined by More from Greek words (*ou* and *topos*) meaning both" no place and good place." Utopia now refers to a perfect society from which greed, crime, and other social ills have been banished.

utopian socialism A phrase Marx and Engels used to denote the moralistic and unrealistic schemes of earlier socialists.

vanguard party Lenin's term for the Communist Party, which is to take a tutelary or "leading role" in the overthrow of capitalism and the transition to communism.

welfare liberalism The form of liberalism that stresses the importance of individual human rights, such as the right to education or health care, and accepts as legitimate the use of government to promote positive liberty, welfare, and *equality of opportunity.* Contrast with *neoclassical liberalism* and *business liberalism.*

Whig A political faction in eighteenth- and early nineteenth-century England, usually in opposition. Many Whigs supported the American and French Revolutions and opposed the slave trade.

withering away of the state Marx's description of the process whereby the interim *revolutionary dictatorship of the proletariat* loses its reason for being and gradually ceases to exist.

Credits

Photo Credits

p. 20: Personalities/GetStock.com; **p. 24:** Prisma Archivo/Alamy/GetStock.com; **pp. 47, 84:** Georgios/Dreamstime/GetStock.com; **p. 49:** Library of Congress Prints and Photographs Division, LC-USZ62-59655; **p. 57:** Classic Image/Alamy/GetStock.com; **p. 60:** Quagga Media/Alamy/GetStock.com; **p. 61:** Library of Congress Prints and Photographs Division, LC-USZ62-2939; **p. 71:** Library and Archives Canada/Hands Studio/William Lyon Mackenzie King fonds/C-009063; **p. 73:** © Government of Canada. Reproduced with the permission of the Minister of Public Works and Government Services Canada (2012). Library and Archives Canada/Credit: Robert Cooper/Canada. Office of The Prime Minister Collection/PA-212560; **p. 110:** Courtesy of William Christian; **p. 111:** Photo of Prime Minister Harper. URL: http://www.pco-bcp.gc.ca/index.asp?lang=eng&page=pm. Privy Council Office. Reproduced with the permission of the Minister of Public Works and Government Services, 2012; **p. 128:** Library of Congress Prints and Photographs Division, LC-USZ62-16530; **p. 148:** Bain Collection, Library of Congress Prints and Photographs Division, LC-DIG-ggbain-30798; **p. 151:** The People's Republic of China Printing Office/Wikimedia Commons: http://commons.wikimedia.org/wiki/File%3AMao_Zedong_sitting.jpg; **p. 162:** Courtesy of the Archives of Manitoba, Woodsworth, James S.-1 (N22204); **p. 163:** © Library and Archives Canada. Reproduced with the permission of Library and Archives Canada. Library and Archives Canada/Credit: Duncan Cameron/Duncan Cameron fonds/C-036222; **p. 177:** Nicku/Dreamstime/GetStock.com; **p. 181:** © Library and Archives Canada. Reproduced with the permission of Library and Archives Canada. Library and Archives Canada/Credit: Duncan Cameron/Duncan Cameron fonds/PA-115039; **p. 189:** Library and Archives Canada/National Film Board of Canada fonds/PA-130046; **p. 193:** Library of Congress Prints and Photographs Division, LC-USZ62-12667; **p. 213:** Library and Archives Canada/Canadian Broadcasting Corporation fonds/C-009339; **p. 230:** Library of Congress Prints and Photographs Division, LC-USZ62-64309; **p. 237:** Don Dutton/GetStock.com; **p. 250:** Library of Congress Prints and Photographs Division, LC-USZ62-110449; **p. 258:** Courtesy of the David Suzuki Foundation; **p. 265:** Carol M. Highsmith Archive, Library of Congress, Prints and Photographs Division, LC-DIG-highsm- 03802; **p. 273:** Aaron Harris/Toronto Star/GetStock.com; **p. 280:** Carol M. Highsmith Archive, Library of Congress, Prints and Photographs Division, LC-DIG-highsm-04963; **p. 288:** The Canadian Press/AP.

Text Credits

p. 15: Reproduced with permission of Curtis Brown, London, on behalf of the Estate of Sir Winston Churchill. Copyright © Winston S. Churchill; **p. 99:** Courtesy of Oliver Letwin; **p. 146:** Communist Party of Canada; **p. 247:** The Green Party of Canada; **p. 279:** Muslim Canadian Congress–http://www.muslimcanadiancongress.org/; **p. 296:** George Grant, *Lament for a Nation*, McGill-Queen's University Press, 40th anniversary edition, 2005, p. 41.

Name Index

Note: Page references followed by "*n*" and "*f*" indicates notes and figures, respectively.

Subject Index

Note: Page references followed by "*n*" and "*f*" indicates notes and figures, respectively.